MW01701395

THE SPARK
THE LOGS
AND THE GASOLINE

The *long* road to the New Zealand Wars

PIERS SEED

ISBN: 978-0-473-73380-3

Publisher: Probitis Publishing

Other books by Piers Seed:

Hoani's Last Stand
- The real story of Rangiaowhia (2022)

Taonga and Contra Proferentem
- Thoughts on the Waitangi Tribunal process (2023)

Cover: The coast-line of Taranaki at the time of the Taranaki War, from New Plymouth (brown block on the left) to Waitara (brown block on the right) – detail of map after p14, British Parliamentary Papers, March 1861.

CONTENTS

Introduction

PART 1 – The Spark

PART 2 – The Logs

PART 3 – The Gasoline

Introduction

Does the world really need yet another book on the New Zealand Wars?

The answer to that is a big, fat, emphatic *no*. The shelves of the book shops and libraries of New Zealand are already groaning under the weight of books on this subject. A century of historians have picked the subject as bare as a Christmas chicken. No, the world needs another book on the New Zealand Wars like it needs another recording of Beethoven's Fifth.

So what is this book about?

This book is not about the war itself but about *the reasons why they happened*. Some may argue that this is a fine distinction but in the current state of the world the "whys" of the wars are now all that really matters to New Zealand while the "whats" of the wars are of little practical relevance other than to academics.

Let me explain.

All over the world countries with a colonial legacy are grappling with their past. Historical chickens are coming home to roost like there is no tomorrow and "decolonisation" is the word of the moment. It is a situation without precedent, the first time in the entire history of mankind that an attempt has been made to selectively atone for the sins of the recent past, let alone the ancient ones. There is no roadmap, no template to guide our way as we bumble our way blindfolded into uncharted territory without a compass.

It is a process fuelled by emotions – anger and resentment on one "side" and back-dated "guilt-by-proxy" on the other – a path littered with seemingly insurmountable obstacles and booby traps: political agendas, historical ignorance, historical reinvention, post-modernism, political correctness, identity politics and unchallengeable moral high-grounds – to name a few. All over the world history wars are being waged and the whole philosophy of what is "truth" – and if it even exists – is in tatters.

So how does the New Zealand "truth and reconciliation" project fit into this worldwide "decolonisation" zeitgeist? We are finding that trying to ram 200 year-old historical genies back into their lamps is a fraught business. Despite having been in progress since at least 1985 the process is still in its early days and the most controversial decisions are still ahead of us. It has no other choice other than to be a deeply divisive business since it can only be a zero sum game – there will be a "winner" and a "loser" – and since no one likes losing it is bound to be contentious.

In a process that involves the exhumation and microscopic post-mortem of thousands of historical skeletons "The New Zealand Wars" emerge not only as one of the most high-profile but also the most conducive to a turbocharged emotional response. The battle for moral superiority turns on a single, very simple question – were the New Zealand Wars – whatever they were – "fair" or "justified". At a distance of 150 years this may well be an unanswerable question and perhaps the most sensible answer is to admit we can never know what anyone thought 150 years ago and it is as stupid as it is arrogant to presume that we ever can.

But if we are must enter the game then what might be helpful is not a book about the wars themselves but one that gives the complete story of *how and why they started,* written not as an academic "history book" but as a "book on history" – a very different animal – written specifically for the "average New Zealander", a book that requires no prior knowledge of anything, a single, convenient volume written in plain language that asks nothing of the reader other than the ability to read.

This is an attempt to provide that book. No doubt it will be found wanting. No doubt some will be angry it may not always affirm their deeply held convictions. So be it. Whatever its flaws it is an honest attempt to provide information that New Zealanders really need to know, information that allows readers to judge for themselves the moral issues associated with the Wars and from which they may judge if anger and resentment are really the appropriate responses, and if so how much.

Surely this has been done before you say. Yes, but no. It is true that the mountain ranges of books whose main focus is the wars themselves inevitably cover their backstory to a greater or lesser extent. A few have even addressed the reasons for the wars as a specific topic. They are all excellent in their way and in an ideal world every New Zealander would read them all.

But it is not an ideal world. First the books I would recommend are long out of print. Second, these are books written by academics for academics and a hard slog for a general audience. Third you would be lucky to entice most readers to read a single history book, let alone multiple books to get a balanced opinion. Fourth – and to me, most crucially– none of these existing books, individually or even collectively, left me with a sense of holistic understanding of the issues behind the wars. While technically all the key elements may have been mentioned and duly ticked off there is no sense of continuity or connection, just the equivalent of a power point presentation in which things are presented one by one to fell off into oblivion and out of the story as each slide is replaced by the next and it is only the last slide that is remembered. They are a series of disconnected episodes rather than a story with an arc.

The road to the New Zealand Wars is indeed a long one – a full 40 year long road in fact – and if you do not step back and look at this road in its entirety as one long panorama you will reach erroneous conclusions. This book attempts to reframe the data given by its predecessors, to reassemble the pieces of a jigsaw puzzle and search down the back of the couch for the missing bits to create the big picture, a narrative. It was written to make sense to me, an ordinary New Zealander, in the hope that it will do the same for other ordinary New Zealanders.

You will find a great many facts in this book but your mission as reader is not to remember any of them in detail, or even at all. Your mission, when you finally close this book, is not to be a walking encyclopaedia capable of appearing on Mastermind. Your mission is simple – to be left with an *impression, a feeling*. Perhaps you will be angry. Perhaps you will be bewildered. Personally, and perhaps paradoxically, I would be happy if you are more confused when you finish than when you started, because that means you have learnt something – that things which perhaps once appeared blackest black and whitest white are now a shade of grey that admits of some understanding of concession and respect, however grudging.

The overall message of this book can be summarised in three words – "life is complicated". It always has been and it always will be. You cannot expect to find history summarised in neat little bullet points. History is not a story of heroes and villains, of black hats and white hats.

The rules of this book are simple. It does not play favourites and there are no sides. Everyone is judged by the same set of rules. We are not setting out to prove anything. We will not be pushing any ideological narratives or identity politics. If it sometimes appears otherwise the intention is simply to offer balance to the received narratives. Readers need to make up their own minds, if and when that is possible. If we sometimes find that is not possible then at least we will understand why.

We will not be looking at history sitting in a plush lazy-boy looking back on the past with 20:20 hindsight, furrowing our brows and making moral judgements based on modern constructs. We will be entering the world of, and thinking like, the people of the time. Maori will be thinking with the mind-sets and customs of the day, intelligently weighing up the pros and cons of European culture, picking out all the good bits while trying to maintain their control and their identity. Europeans will be thinking with the mind-set of someone raised in Regency England, at the height of the technical triumphs and human misery of the Industrial Revolution, the aftermath of the Napoleonic Wars, the peak of evangelistic humanitarianism, the massive unemployment, desperation and famine that forced literally millions of Europeans to seek their fortunes in distant countries. These are the worlds the reader must enter otherwise you may as well not enter at all.

In line with this approach this book is woven around generous quotations from primary sources. Modern authors can reword, summarise, paraphrase, cherry-pick and re-interpret these sources all they like but the best thing we can do for history is to let it speak for itself, warts and all. These quotations tell us, literally, how their writers saw the world of their day and explain why they did the things they did. In the present we can with a few key-presses rummage endlessly through mountains of documents and find alternative views that refute any particular document and/or that support our own personal theories. But that is not history. The people we will meet – the George Greys, the Wiremu Tamihanas, or any of the cast of the past, did not have that luxury – what they wrote was the world as they saw it and that is what they acted on. We cannot blame them for what they could not see then but which we can see now.

The title of this book refers to the three key ingredients required to make a roaring fire. The analogy of war to fire is, of course, commonplace to the point of cliché but there is a reason clichés become clichés – because they have obviously been helpful. If this simple cliché can help clarify the path to the New Zealand Wars then I am happy to use it.

Anyone who has ever tried to light a fire will know that it is very difficult and more often than not ends in failure. There are a great many variables involved but the minimum requirement is at least two ingredients – fuel and something to light it with. If your fuel is tinder-dry then it may not take a lot to light – maybe just a spark. If your fuel is damp and thick like a log you may need a third ingredient to assist the lighting process – an accelerant for instance.

Like most analogies this one is no doubt simplistic and may become forced in some places. But hopefully it will nonetheless clarify that the New Zealand Wars cannot be explained by a pithy sound bite, or even by pages of pithy sound bites, and that to try and dumb history down in such a way is both an absurdity and irresponsible. The wars were the result of a long and complex interaction of both sequential and simultaneous events that were forty years in the stoking, a forty year-long chain of dominoes that relentlessly led to what we will find is a largely predictable conclusion. The absence of *any one* of these many dominoes would have resulted either in the wars not occurring, or more realistically, to their postponement.

Along our forty year path we will meet a whole cast of characters, and events, many of them already well known in generic New Zealand history but not necessarily previously assessed from the angle necessary for this particular story. And for variety, specific chapters will be devoted to generic subjects which provide additional insight to the actual story.

By the end of the book we will not reach a definitive conclusion that enables us to say with 100% authority – Group 1 = BAD, Group 2 = GOOD. That is as impossible as it would be ridiculous. But perhaps we will be a little wiser and more philosophical about the subject and less eager to point fingers. If nothing else it will remind us that life is rarely simple, there are at least two sides to every story, and that in life there are rarely heroes and villains. Usually there are just mere mortals trying to do the best they can in difficult, if not impossible, circumstances.

That said, given that the road to the New Zealand Wars is long and windy, we had better get on our way.

PART 1

THE SPARK

Chapter 1-1

The mother of all dominoes.

Since the New Zealand Wars of the 1860s were a contest between British/Colonial forces and central North Island Maori tribes it would be logical to think our story should commence in, and concentrate on, the post Treaty of Waitangi period. But strangely enough, the reasons why European colonisation was possible, and why issues developed to generate the spark that ignited the New Zealand Wars, have their genesis in purely Maori-Maori interaction. The pivotal event – the first and biggest domino in the long string that leads inexorably and inevitably to the New Zealand Wars – was in fact another "war" – one which had little to do with Europeans – the so-called "Musket Wars"

For this reason our starting point in the long road, where we back the car out of the garage, is 1820, at the height of these Musket Wars.

It has been said that "the past is a foreign country". Those who are old enough will know that the "normal" of 25 years ago may as well be in the dark ages. 1820 – a whole eight generations ago – is these upheavals of the previous generation that we can relate to, raised to the power of eight. 1820 is, then, not so much a foreign country as another planet.

As we sit, comfortably strapped into our time machine, whirring back in time two hundred years, let us do some homework and study what we think we know of the past, try and predict what we will find when we open the door to our capsule and step out into the blazing sun of 1820.

In 1820 New Zealand is a Maori world and has been for 500 years.

Maori traditions tell us how Maori first arrived on these islands and although these traditions do not give us dates the latest analytical data at the time of writing places the earliest Maori arrival at 1300 plus or minus 30 years[1]. Regrettably our knowledge of the 500 years of Maoridom between 1300 and 1800 is minimal, a mixture of inherited traditions augmented by the gleanings of more recent archaeology. It is conjectured that over the next few hundred years more Maori colonists arrived from wherever the origin point known as "Hawaiki" may be[2]. We presume tribal populations grew, sub-tribes split off as required and migrated in different directions around the country. Some tribal traditions speak of major events such as migrations within the country, major battles and heroic deeds but it is a murky area.

Although in 1820 New Zealand may have been a Maori world it is not as if Maori were living in a bubble. Fifty years previously Captain Cook had popped in for a couple of months and from then on visits by foreign vessels were not uncommon. Despite occasional disasters the relationship between Maori and Europeans was generally positive, as is the way of these things when each party has something the other party wants.

In 1820 Maori can be found in shipping crews sailing the world, manning whaling boats, even swanning around in Sydney or London, not in high volume perhaps but the Maori world is very well aware of the European world and is intelligently picking through what that world has to offer. On one hand, in 1820 Maori are in thrall to European technology and can't get enough of it – the benefits are immediately obvious to anyone in a

---

[1] See for instance *Mass Migration and the Polynesian Settlement of New Zealand*, Richard Walter, Hallie Buckley, Chris Jacomb, Elizabeth Matisoo-Smith, p354 (*Journal of World Pre-History*, 2017, pp351-376).

[2] It is, for instance, debated as to whether the "Hawaiki" of at least some traditions is somewhere in Polynesia or actually places within what is now called New Zealand. Ultimately the meaning of "Hawaiki" is usually interpreted as "the last place I came from", rather than a literal geographical location.

heartbeat. On the other hand, and as one might expect, Maori are very happy with their own culture which has served them well for thousands of years, and have elected – at least for the time being – not to embrace the more esoteric, theoretical aspects of European "civilisation". Maori are aware, for instance, of the European God, but have chosen to stick to their own spiritual world for the time being. It is, as we have said a Maori world, and foreigners interact with that world only on Maori sufferance and on Maori terms. The relationship will be whatever Maori say it will be.

In 1820 the number of Europeans resident in New Zealand could be counted on the fingers of a small number of hands and represented the extremes of the European social bell-curve – the insufferably pious missionaries at one end balanced by the equally insufferably dubious and debauched escaped convicts, ship deserters, whalers, sealers, traders and other random ne'er-do-well at the other. At any particular time this European population temporarily fluctuated as vessels from all over the world came and went, particularly to the Bay of Islands where a flourishing trade business was established. What the Europeans got was boring stuff, the stuff of existence – pigs and potatoes, water, timber, and sometimes, girls. What Maori got was exciting stuff – new, life-changing, miraculous technology. Some of this technology simply made life easier and pleasanter – iron axes, fish-hooks, pots, blankets and the like. But the most coveted trade item of all was that which kills – muskets.

If we know little of Maori history between 1300 and 1800 it is generally accepted that the resolution of differences, grievances and insults was generally settled according to the Maori principle of "*utu*", the Maori name for the universal concept of reciprocation on which every action in the history of mankind can ultimately be explained, justified and rationalised.

One contemporary European observer summarised the heady brew of *utu*, the warrior creed typical of tribal society which means that balancing of *utu* is achieved through violence, and the tribal effect that guarantees that individual affronts automatically become tribal affronts, as follows:

"Without the establishment of such an authority by some civilized state, I cannot, after a full consideration of every circumstance connected with the actual condition of this people, see the least prospect of any permanent peace being established amongst them [Maori] whilst there remains a stronger man to murder his weaker neighbour. There are few persons so insignificant as not to have it in their power, at any time, to plunge the country into war.

The crime of an individual involves his most distant connexions, as each of them is a legitimate object of retaliation to the connexions of the injured party. It is in vain to represent to them that the criminal alone should suffer; their answer is ready, and it is perfectly consistent with the dictates of natural justice, namely, that his tribe will not surrender him to suffer for his crime, and by standing up in his defence they have become participators in it; while on the other hand, provided the criminal be not a slave, his connexions are never without a grievance, more or less ancient, which they bring forward as a justification of his crime.

Thus, by every attempt to administer the law of retaliation – the rude justice of nature – the breach is made wider. New deaths involve more distant connexions. Tribe after tribe becomes a party to the contest; and peace, or rather an intermission of murders, can only be procured when one of the parties becomes too weak to continue the contest, or when the loss on both sides happens to be so nearly balanced, that neither party has an advantage over the other. In this way has the depopulation of the country been going on, till district after district has become void of its inhabitants; and the population is, even now, but a remnant of what it was in the memory of some European residents."[3]

---

[3]*Letter from James Busby to Colonial Secretary of New South Wales*, dated 16th June, 1837 (BPP, April 8, 1840, pp12-18). Note that throughout this book quotes are given as recorded at the time, warts and all. No attempt has been made to correct grammar or irregular spelling, or to italicize Maori words.

Given that according to the principle of *utu* the payment for a perceived insult could be the total obliteration of your tribe, or, if that were not possible, someone else's tribe, it is hardly surprising that war/violence was not unusual and that Maori life could – to use the immortal words of Thomas Hobbes – be "nasty, brutal and short". But, to keep things in historical and international perspective, this could be said of most tribal societies throughout history and given that Maori society not only survived but flourished under this regime *utu* was clearly a cornerstone of the Maori "legal framework" which maintained "balance", and "order", albeit a violent form of order, over a period of 500 years.

This cultural cornerstone, however, had a fatal flaw. This system to achieve balance only works if the weaponry of the opposing parties is also in balance. If one party suddenly has access to superior weaponry then that hitherto "healthy" mechanism of balance swings violently to one side and all hell breaks loose.

Enter – in the early 1800s – the technical marvel known as the "musket", first in ones and twos and ultimately in the hundreds. Suddenly the whole concept of balance is blown to the four winds. And if the extraction of *utu* – real or perceived – was not sufficient justification to try out one's new weaponry then the less altruistic temptations of simple plunder – of things and/or people – were hard to resist.

We must not be deluded by the expression "Musket Wars", which is a modern term invented by historians who like to give names to things. "Musket Wars" is as unhelpful and misleading a term for the belonging of our journey as "New Zealand Wars" is for the events at the end of our journey.

First "Musket Wars" is misleading in that it gives the impression that the "Musket Wars" were an unusual event, like "World War 1", a sudden period of warfare after centuries of peace, and brought about by the introduction of the musket. While the introduction of muskets is obviously a necessary prerequisite for something called the "Musket Wars" they did not fire themselves. Muskets did not invent the warrior creed – that was already there. In truth there was nothing "new" in what is now called the "Musket Wars", it was simply traditional Maori "business as usual" in action but with new weaponry. Muskets simply ramped up the slaughter associated with the traditional norms of Maori culture a notch or ten.[4]

"Musket Wars' is also misleading because the events purported to be encapsulated by that phrase have no actual resemblance to "wars" as they are perceived in European terms. Wars have a reason, even if in hind-sight these reasons may appear to us as unimportant if not just plain ridiculous. People fight for freedom, for beliefs, for justice, for causes, or, less altruistically, for land. But there *is* a reason beyond revenge and plunder.

By contrast the Musket "Wars" were more like a decades-long series of opportunistic raids[5], much the same as the Danes raiding Britain and other countries in their long-boats a thousand years earlier. *Utu*, plunder, the warrior creed and the gratification of the cult of war, the law of the strong over the weak, or in this case, of those who had muskets over those who did not. One historian has summed it up in three words – "testosterone fuelled adventurism".[6] It is not that complicated.

This imbalance of musket availability is not difficult to understand. Muskets came from Europeans, Europeans came on ships, and ships only harbour in safe locations. If you are a foreign vessel wanting to resupply with minimum diversion south while plying the Pacific your ideal port of call is the northernmost harbour on the east coast. By this locational stroke of luck the Bay of Islands reigned supreme as the port of choice for foreign vessels, with its fine, sheltered harbour and native inhabitants who had in the space of a microsecond grasped the finer points of capitalism and knew a good thing when they saw one.

---

[4] James Busby's observations quoted earlier sum this up perfectly by mentioning neither muskets nor wars, simply the nature of Maori culture.

[5] Estimated at about 140 raids over a four decade period between about 1807 - 1845.

[6] *Guns and utu, Mathew Wright*, p85.

Thus the Bay of Islands was the best placed location in New Zealand to obtain muskets, in Maori terms something akin to acquiring nuclear weapons when everyone else had pointed sticks. To reduce it to its crudest terms the Musket Wars were simply the boys from the north at play with their new toys. Raids on their musket-less brethren to the south became common, the northerners setting out not in long-boats but in war canoes, or sometimes on foot, making epic, overland road-trips of mayhem.

Consequently the Bay of Islands iwi of Nga Puhi, and in particular its most celebrated chief Hongi Hika, loomed large in the saga of the Musket Wars. Apparently not content with muskets obtained in dribs and drabs organically through trading, Hongi, in an early master-stroke of capitalism, ambition and strategy, famously accelerated the process of musket acquisition by returning from a visit to England with 800 muskets. It is probably 1821, the date of Hongi's return with this precious arsenal, which marks the nominal start date of the "Musket Wars", the point at which the natural background level of inter-tribal warfare ramped by to its catastrophic zenith.

So what was the direct effect of these so-called "Musket Wars" to Maori? We could probably summarise this in a simple sentence:

> "The Musket Wars were a series of Maori inter-tribal raids in which an estimated 50,000 people were killed, and the ownership of a sizeable proportion of land in both islands either changed hands or became disputed"[7].

To put this in perspective, in 1820 50,000 people represented probably a third of the entire Maori population. Entire tribes were essentially wiped

---

[7] Author's own summary. The estimates for deaths range between 20,000 and 80,000, see for instance, *Taua: Musket Wars, Land Wars or Tikanga?,* Angela Ballara, p42-44. If we settle for a middle figure of say 50,000, given that the estimated post-Musket War population was about 90,000 this makes the death rate about 35%. While acknowledging that these figures are wild guesses on top of wild guesses it is clear we are talking about a cataclysmic period in Maori history.

off the face of the earth[8]. If this slaughter had been caused by another nation it would be called genocide. But it wasn't, it was caused by Maori fighting Maori. We could say that the Musket Wars were an example of "self-inflicted genocide".

OK, this is all very interesting but so what? Why have we picked the Musket Wars as the first big, domino in our chain of dominoes leading to the New Zealand Wars of the 1860's to which we are inexorably headed? We are here not because of the Musket War's obvious and immediate *direct* effects – the slaughter – but because of the *indirect* turmoil and uprooting of Maori *tikanga*[9] that these "wars" caused. We will first list these in simple bullet points so there shall be no mistake. The "Musket Wars" caused, or were major contributors to:

- Maori acceptance of European Christianity.
- Maori acceptance of European law and civilisation.
- Maori acceptance of the concept of peace.
- Tribal migration south, which greatly facilitated future land-sales to Europeans.

In short, the Musket Wars created a catastrophic fissure in the landscape of Maoridom which rolled out the red carpet for European colonisation.

As we will see, all of these effects were necessary requirements to continue along the path to war once again in the 1860s. Without the Musket Wars there would be no New Zealand Wars for the simple reason

---

[8] At least Ngati Ira, Ngati Kuia and Ngati Tumatakokiri were actually annihilated. Ngati Apa, Rangitane and the Muaupoko were very much diminished and/or reduced to vassal status.

[9] *Tikanga* refers to "the Maori way of doing things" or the "norm" in Maori society. It is sometimes more formally described as Maori customary law.

that, in all probability, there would be no Europeans to fight[10]. The effect of the Musket Wars is that simple and that catastrophic.

Let us attempt to explain what to some might seem an outlandishly audacious connection between the Musket Wars and these mooted bullet points. No, there is no handy, contemporary Maori document which states "we changed our way of life because of the Musket Wars"– life is rarely that considerate. But in the absence of such concrete evidence the following suppositions have been made:

- The all-pervasive Maori principle of *utu* ensured that wars were absurdly easy to start and almost impossible to stop. When these wars were waged with traditional weapons there were relatively few casualties and in a warrior oriented society in which prowess in battle was the key to acquiring status, war was not only sustainable but necessary – it defines the culture and if you do not have it your culture is dead. This is invariably how tribal or clannish societies have acted historically in any culture.

- The transition to modern weaponry, from greenstone mere to musket, from hand to hand personal contests of strength, bravery and skill to remote, impersonal killing which could be done by a mere slave and which consequently meant and proved nothing, resulted in mass slaughter, tipping the balance of what had been "healthy" to something that was – literally – obliterating the Maori race. The Musket Wars were Maori's first experimental foray into a new world and when you experiment things do not always end well. The Musket Wars are where Maori learnt not to mix and match with other people's cultures.

  The disastrous combination of a race constantly at war and armed with weapons of mass destruction was something for which Maori *tikanga* had no answer. Maori had seized upon European

---

[10] No doubt it is possible, indeed inevitable, that European colonisation would have occurred by other mechanisms which did not require the "Musket Wars", but chasing shadows and "what ifs" is outside the scope of this book.

technology with alacrity not understanding that it came as part of a matched set – European technology only "works" when used in conjunction with the matching European rules and system of living that provide the necessary control.[11] The only face-saving way to escape this descent into self-genocide was to "take the full package", the full European *tikanga*, including Christianity and its close stable-mates European law and the mind-blowing concept of peace – that not only was living in peace a viable alternative world-view but that it was actually advantageous to do so. Essentially it was a wake-up call to the limitations of a warrior culture and the opening of eyes to alternative world-views and ways of living.

The "Musket Wars", then, were a major – if not *the* major – driver for the Maori uptake of European Christianity, European law and living by a new law of peace – in short, a huge embracing not necessarily of "Europeans" as a people but at least of key parts of their culture, along with the myriad benefits and prosperity that came with it. This realisation that a new way of living was required in order to survive would in turn lead to the Treaty of Waitangi and everything that has subsequently happened between the two races.

- When helpless peoples are attacked from the north by an unbeatable opponent a not-unnatural reaction is to flee to the south. Thus the "Musket Wars" caused major displacements of peoples, particularly on the lower-west coast of the North Island and the top of the South Island.

  During this process great swathes of land were depopulated and this migration south in turn displaced other peoples – domino effects within domino effects. The wars created both large areas of abandoned land and whole districts of people "squatting" in non-traditional areas by the simple expedient of the fleeing migrators driving the original inhabitants out. "Ownership" of land, both that

[11] To use a modern analogy, trying to put an Apple motherboard in a Microsoft PC rarely ends well – it is one platform or the other, you cannot pick and mix.

which the migrators abandoned and that which they in turn conquered, thus became extremely complex and contested.

It was this instability and the fact that the migrators had no ancestral or sentimental attachment to their new lands which would in a few years' time make it so easy for European colonising companies to make bulk land purchases around Cook's Strait and Taranaki[12] – the sold land meant nothing to the recent migrators/conquerors other than chips for bargaining. In short, without the Musket Wars and the seismic confusion regarding land ownership and the inter-tribal rifts they created, the various European colonisation schemes simply could never have happened.

These mass colonisation schemes in turn necessitated official British intervention in the form of British control of New Zealand, a process ratified by the Treaty of Waitangi. This in turn led to the gradual formation of two "sides" with conflicting opinions over governance, which in turn encouraged the development of a Maori break-away movement, which in turn led to the New Zealand Wars. This is a very simplified, introductory sneak preview of the very clear set of dominoes which we shall shortly discuss in detail and which link the Musket Wars to the New Zealand Wars.

It is at this point that we turn our attentions from the northern aggressors of the Musket Wars to their hapless southern victims as they flee south to escape the "wild wind from the north".[13] We leave the north, never to return – the northerners have pushed their domino and their work is done. It is time to bid adieu and take a flight in our time capsule to where that domino hits – the south-west coast of the North Island, that part which stretches from Kawhia, round past Mount Taranaki, down past Waikanae right down to modern Wellington. It is here that we find the

---

[12] This process will be described in detail in subsequent chapters.

[13] The title of a book by Don Stafford, referring to its subject of Hongi Hika, the wildest of all winds from the north.

main cast in our story, the tribes we will meet time and again over the next few hundred pages.

If we divide the North Island in half vertically, and in thirds horizontally, the tribes of interest are those in the left-hand middle portion and can be roughly categorised as:

- The Tainui tribes.
- The Taranaki tribes.
- The Ngati Toa tribe.

Map 1 suggests what might be approximate tribal boundaries for our tribes of interest circa 1810. Trying to define tribal boundaries of that time is somewhat of a fool's errand which has traditionally resulted in maps with tribal names plonked on them at odd angles leaving the viewer none the wiser as to the extent and boundaries of each tribe. In truth, unhelpful as this approach is, this is the only "honest" way of tackling the issue since we really do not know in detail and, given the dynamics of the day, "boundaries" must have been changing on a regular basis. We can also be pretty sure that what any tribe thought its boundary was would be hotly contested by its neighbours.

Be that as it may, since the major thrust of this book is to document the movement of tribes over this period it helps to have their start and end points nailed down as accurately as we can and for this reason our key tribes of interest have been delineated on Map 1 with assumed, clear-cut boundaries.[14]

---

[14] This map is based on "Map No.1" shown in *History and Traditions of the Maoris of the West Coast...*, S. P. Smith. The demarcations of the Tainui Tribes are best guesses. No doubt there was also a good deal of "no-man's land" and/or contested territory between the tribes to complicate things further.

The tribes which lined this coast circa 1810, from north to south, were:

	Ngati Koata	
	Ngati Toa	
	Ngati Rarua	
"Taranaki" Tribes	Ngati Tama	"Ngata Awa"
"Taranaki" Tribes	Ngati Mutunga	"Ngata Awa"
"Taranaki" Tribes	**Te Ati Awa**	"Ngata Awa"
"Taranaki" Tribes	Ngati Maru	"Ngata Awa"
"Taranaki" Tribes	Taranaki	
"Taranaki" Tribes	Ngati Ruanui	
"Taranaki" Tribes	Ngati Rauru	
	Ngati Hau	
	Ngati Apa	
	Rangitane	
	Muaupoko	
	Ngati Kahungungu	

A significant portion of this chain of west coast tribes comprised the "Taranaki"[15] tribes. As was usual in Maori society of the time, although each tribe was its own entity they were interconnected to greater or lesser extent through kinship, intermarriage, physical proximity and common borders, trade and a common enemy in the form of the Tainui tribes.

Of these tribes this book will be concentrating almost exclusively on that of the Ati Awa, literally the "tribe of the river" [16]. Their western boundary

---

[15] "Taranaki" at that time referred to the area from the Mokau River in the north to the Wanganui River in the south, a very considerable portion of the west coast of the North Island. Note also that confusingly "Taranaki" also refers to a specific tribe as well as a geographical area.

[16] There is much inconsistency in the early literature regarding the early 1800's use and meaning of the terms "Ngati Awa" and "Te Ati Awa". First there is confusion as to whether "Ngati Awa" refers to the Ngati Awa of Taranaki or the Ngati Awa of Whakatane. Secondly, even if we assume the term applies to the Taranaki Ngati Awa, there is confusion as to what exactly that means. This book will follow the convention outlined by Ballara (*Taua*,

was the set of small islands called Nga Motu, later given the European name of the "Sugar Loaves" and close to the site of future New Plymouth. Their northern boundary was roughly the Urenui River and their inner boundary, like many "Taranaki" tribes, was Mount Taranaki itself.

The second tribe which features heavily in our story, at least for the next few chapters, is the Ngati Toa[17] of Kawhia. While this was a numerically small tribe what it lacked in numbers was more than made up for by the many skills of its leader, the famous Te Rauparaha[18], who while not the actual paramount head of Ngati Toa as defined by lineage[19] assumed practical leadership by virtue of these skills. In addition to his martial prowess Te Rauparaha seems to have had a natural gift for diplomacy and for forming alliances and it was by this mechanism that the fate of the Ati Awa and Ngati Toa tribes would become inextricably entwined for a period of about 25 years, from about 1820 to about 1845.

To the west of this line of coastal tribes was, and is, is the Tasman Sea. To their east at that time was our third main cast member, the Tainui Tribes[20], so called because of their origins in one of the great migration canoes of that name, suggested to have arrived in Kawhia in the 1300s. By

---

Angela Ballara, p322) who defines Ngati Awa as the group of tribes between Cape Taranaki up to Kawhia, as shown above. Each of these four tribes is in turn comprised of a number of *hapu* which we shall introduce as required.

[17] Strictly speaking Ngati Koata and Ngati Rarua were *hapu* of Ngati Toa, but since these tribes eventually found themselves as individual identities in the north of the South Island ("Te Tau Ihu o te Waka") it is helpful to treat them as separate identities rather than bundle them under the umbrella of Ngati Toa.

[18] The name is said to mean "convolvulus leaf".

[19] The official "head" of Ngati Toa as determined by lineage was Te Rauparaha's uncle, Te Pehi Kupe.

[20] Technically Ngati Toa was/is a Tainui tribe but since they seem to have been perennial enemies with the bulk of the Tainui tribes it makes sense to treat them as a separate, unrelated unit.

1820 the descendants of this canoe had multiplied and split into two confederations of tribes – the "Waikatos", the collective name given to a confederation of perhaps twenty or so tribes – and a separate confederation called Ngati Maniapoto which is said to have broken away from the main Tainui group in about 1700.

I am not aware of any map that has attempted to delineate even the rough tribal areas of the Tainui tribes at the time of interest. The best we can do is to say that, as we might guess from their name, the Waikato/Tainui sub-group was centred around the lower part of the Waikato River[21], from about the point at which the river takes a major bend west towards its outflow to the sea in the north to roughly the Waipa delta in the south, while the Ngati Maniapoto sub-group occupied the area south of that to somewhere around the Mokau river. These two Tainui sub-groups were somewhat geographically separated from the coastal chain of Taranaki tribes by the hill ranges that divided them.

The upshot of this is that the coastal tribes – including Ngati Toa – were therefore the meat in a geographical sandwich, living in daily dread of annihilation from the Tainui tribes pushing at their eastern boundary.

Thus the scene is set for a cataclysmic upheaval in the disposition and ownership of all the coastal land running the 500 kilometre stretch from Kawhia in the north to future Wellington in the south, and of the top two thirds of the South Island. We need to hold onto our hats for within a few short paragraphs New Zealand will never be quite the same. Not only will the Maori world be upended in its own right but by one of those strange twists of fate this upending occurs at the precise time it is needed to facilitate European "colonisation".

---

[21] Confusingly, because in river terminology "upper" refers to the source of a river and "lower" to its destination, since the Waikato River flows from South to North "Lower Waikato" refers to the Northern portion as seen on a map.

Chapter 1-2

Te Rauparaha heads south.

Some things in life, and in history, happen by plan. They are like games of chess – you see a goal, you have a strategy, you predict the likely obstacles, you make the right moves in the right order and – *voila* – the King falls, the goal is reached.

The "colonisation" of New Zealand, does not fall into this category. In fact, when and if you think about it, the entire history of this country is just one jaw-dropping chain of alignment of planets and lurching from one crisis to the next. A Bobby Fischer could not plan it, a Nostradamus could not predict it, and a Hercules could not force it to happen artificially, if they tried. The whole manner in which the early history of this country "happened" is a thing of staggering, random providence.

For all that, there is one man who almost singlehandedly set in motion the events that would lead to the mass colonisation of New Zealand, the New Zealand Wars and the way New Zealand is in the present, for better and for worse. Some might say that this is an audacious – possibly ridiculous – claim, but as you read and reflect on the following chapters you can see that it is true. As we have intimated this did not happen according to a meticulous and cunning plan or by some far-seeing vision but by a more or less random and opportunistic sequence of events. But in all of these opportunistic events one man's name looms largest.

This man is Ngati Toa chief Te Rauparaha.

Jerningham Wakefield, whom we shall meet in detail later, described Te Rauparaha, then in his seventies and with his best years behind him, thus:

> "As we leaped from our boat he [Te Rauparaha] advanced to meet us, and, with looks of evident fear and distrust, eagerly sought our hands to exchange the missionary greeting. During the whole of the ensuing conversation he seemed uneasy and insecure in his own opinion; and the whalers present described this behaviour as totally at variance with his usual boastfulness and arrogance. He made us a pious speech about the battle, saying that he had had no part in it, and that he was determined to give no encouragement to fighting. He agreed to come on board the next day; and departed to one of the neighbouring islands.
>
> He is rather under the average height, and very dignified and stately in his manner, although on this occasion it was much affected by the wandering and watchful glances which he frequently threw around him, as though distrustful of every one. Although at least sixty years old, he might have passed for a much younger man, being hale and stout, and his hair but slightly grizzled.
>
> His features are aquiline and striking; but an overhanging upper lip, and a retreating forehead, on which his eyebrows wrinkled back when he lifted his deep-sunken eyelids and penetrating eyes, produced a fatal effect on the good prestige arising from his first appearance. The great chieftain, the man able to lead others, and habituated to wield authority, was clear at first sight; but the savage ferocity of the tiger, who would not scruple to use any means for the attainment of that power, the destructive ambition of a selfish despot, was plainly discernible on a nearer view."[22]

CMS missionary Henry Williams on the other hand gave an alternative view on his first meeting with Te Rauparaha on 19 November 1839:

---

[22] *Adventure in New Zealand – Volume 1*, E. Jerningham Wakefield, p113.

"After dinner the boat arrived from Kapiti to convey us over to Rauparaha, who we found to be more agreeable than I anticipated. He had none of the savage appearance of so celebrated and bloody a warrior and was a very intelligent man. He received us very graciously and entered fully into conversation upon politics and upon the necessity of laying aside his sad evil ways."[23]

On balance it is probably fair to say that at any particular time Te Rauparaha was whoever he needed to be to achieve his desired goal from a particular audience.

Te Rauparaha is sometimes known as "The Napoleon of the South" and the sobriquet is not inappropriate for, like Napoleon, his goal – at least at that phase of his life – seems to have been to create an empire. While that may not be as altruistic and heart-warming a goal as we might like, it was at least a sign of thinking well outside the box in Maori terms. Not only was he the only one of his peers with such an ambitious goal but he succeeded beyond all expectations, ultimately becoming the supreme commander not only of the lower-west quarter of the North Island but also of the top two-thirds of the South Island.

If Te Rauparaha was an undeniable slaughterer – and it would be unusual in his time, place and culture if he were not – then he stands alone as an organiser, diplomat, facilitator, team player, and thinker, someone able to rally together and unite a disparate cast of players to achieve his end. And we have to give him credit for some degree of honour, for when his run came to an end he willingly gave up his homeland of Kawhia and made no attempt to reclaim it, something that cannot be said of his allies, as we shall see in due course.

Jerningham Wakefield summarised in a single paragraph the first of the falling dominoes that would lead directly to the sale of lands in which he was so intimately involved and to which he was a personal witness:

---

[23] *The early Journals of Henry Williams*, Henry Williams, edited Lawrence Rogers, p453.

> "Previous to 1825 he [Te Rauparaha] had lived among his tribe, the Ngatitoa, in the neighbourhood of Kawia [Kawhia]. Hongi returned from his visit to England in 1820, provided with muskets and devoured with restless ambition. His followers became, by their possession of fire-arms, the most powerful tribe in New Zealand. At their head he ravaged the whole northern end of the North Island. In consequence of these devastating wars the Waikato and Kawia tribes pressed upon each other, and the latter were obliged to give way in the struggle.[24]

Wakefield has identified the first three falling dominoes in the path to the New Zealand Wars:

Domino 1 = Hongi Hika pushes south into Waikato territory

Domino 2 = The Waikatos push west into Ngati Toa territory.[25]

Domino 3 = Ngati Toa under Te Rauparaha heads south.

Domino 2 fell in about 1820[26] when a large combined force of Ngati Maniapoto and Waikato *hapu* attacked Ngati Toa in what has been described as a "three way pincer" movement[27], leaving Te Rauparaha no choice but to flee south down the west coast to seek greener pastures.

Opinions differ as the size of this *heke*[28]– one commentator suggests it was a small, highly vulnerable band "including persons of all ages, being

---

[24] *Adventure in New Zealand – Volume 1*, E. Jerningham Wakefield, p113. This is a sweeping, simplistic statement but one that makes things easier to follow.

[25] It is not quite as simple as Wakefield suggests – there was a longish history of antagonism between Ngati Toa/Te Rauparaha and the Tainui tribes quite apart from knock-on effects from the "The Musket Wars".

[26] The actual year is debatable and ranges from 1819 to 1821 depending on the account. For consistency we will use 1820 throughout.

[27] *Guns and utu*, Mathew Wright, p91.

[28] *Heke* = Migration.

about 400, of whom 170 were tried fighting men"[29] while another suggests "perhaps 1500, men woman and children"[30]

As the fleeing Ngati Toa contingent headed south it had to pass through the lands of many of the coastal tribes we have introduced previously. This was possible for a number of reasons. Firstly, because of their close proximity, Ngata Toa was interconnected to some of these tribes by intermarriage. Secondly, Te Rauparaha's ability to bring people together – what today we might call "networking"– had established at least an "understanding" between them, if not complete trust. Thirdly, and perhaps most importantly, the coastal tribes were united by the common fear of, and vulnerability to, the Waikatos. As the saying goes, desperate times call for desperate measures and create strange bed-fellows.

In this way Te Rauparaha and his party passed down the west coast, on occasion fighting rear-guard battles against the Waikato who filled the vacuum left in their wake. If we are to believe the books Te Rauparaha performed many acts of derring-do and strategic brilliance along the way which ultimately tell us more about the gullibility of early European recordists than they do about Te Rauparaha.

On reaching Taranaki Te Rauparaha paused at Urenui for a planting season to make preparations before continuing his migration south. By the time he continued on his way he had managed to persuade a number of the Ati Awa tribe to accompany him and, since the joint contingent that finally continued the journey south comprised 200 of Te Rauparaha's own Ngati Toa people augmented by 400 fighting men of the Ati Awa and accompanied by their families, it might be said that at this point the expedition changed from a Ngati Toa migration to an Ati Awa migration. In this cunning way Te Rauparaha effectively leveraged Ati Awa manpower to achieve his own goals.

This 1820 "semi-migration" of a portion of the Ati Awa is just the first

---

[29] A rewording of *The Stirring Times of Te Rauparaha*, W.T.L. Travers, pp88-89.

[30] *Guns and Utu*, Mathew Wright, p92.

instance of what might be called "The Diaspora of the Ati Awa", the progressive fragmentation of this tribe into four groups who over the next two decades would find themselves scattered from Waikanae in the north to Queen Charlotte Sound in the south. It is this diaspora which is the root cause of the confusion that would within two decades facilitate European buying of land and the subsequent colonisation on which the entire history of New Zealand is predicated.

To make things easier to follow we will assign these four "groups" of Ati Awa numbers and names – this first group heading south with Te Rauparaha in 1820 we will call "Group 1 - The Tourists", for in 1820 there was no other reason for Ati Awa to leave their ancestral lands other than a joyride and a change of scenery.

We note in passing that two of the members of this Group 1 Ati Awa migration were a chief called Reretawhangawhanga and his son Te Rangitake. This seemingly trivial piece of information is, in fact, pivotal in the context of our story. At this time Te Rangitake was a youth in his mid-twenties and played no significant part in events. However in 20 years' time he would be baptised under the name "Wiremu Kingi" and in 40 years' time he would be one of the two key players who banged their heads together to create the spark that started the New Zealand Wars. While we will not encounter him again for some time his is a name to file away and remember.

In the autumn of 1820 this combined Ngai Toa/Ati Awa party set off south and after various tribulations established themselves at Ohau, near present day Levin, where Te Rauparaha resumed his favourite hobby of unleashing Hell on what remained of the *tangata whenua*[31] around that area, the perennially luckless Muaupoko, Rangitane and Ngati Apa tribes, to the point of virtual extinction.

---

[31] *Tangata whenua*, in this context, means the local inhabitants, occupiers and owners of the land.

In perhaps 1822 Ngati Toa invaded the island of Kapiti and in perhaps early 1823 the Ati Awa Group 1 contingent - including the previously introduced Reretawhangawhanga and presumably his son, the future Wiremu Kingi - returned temporarily to their original tribal area in Taranaki.[32]

In 1824 Te Rauparaha demonstrated his complete control over his newly acquired area by soundly defeating an attack on his Kapiti Island stronghold by a confederation of the many and various disgruntled, displaced tribes in what is known as the battle of Waiorua. This definitive trouncing of his many enemies confirmed Te Rauparaha's position as undisputed master of his new domains and after this attempted coup all opposition dried up completely. What little remained of the original *tangata whenua* of the area "were reduced to the merest tributaries".

News of Te Rauparaha's latest and definitive success at Kapiti induced a second "semi-migration" of Taranaki tribes to the area of the Kapiti coast:[33]

> "The news of the battle [Waiorua] having reached Taranaki...Te Puaha...shortly afterwards brought with him from Taranaki, a considerable number of fighting men, with their families, consisting of Ngatiawa proper, partly of Ngatihinetuhi, and partly of Ngatiwhakatere, being members of a hapu of Ngati Raukawa..."[34]

This migration also included components of Ngati Mutunga and Ngati Tama and it is suggested that Ati Awa Group 1 including Reretawhangawhanga and his yet-to-become famous son Te Rangitake were part of this migration, returning south yet again[35]. This detail is

---

[32] *Traditions and history ...*, S. P. Smith, p393.

[33] *The Stirring Times of Te Rauparaha*, W.T.L. Travers, p114. This migration is given the name *heke hikoputa* (pig's tooth migration), see also *Taua*, Angela Ballara, pp338-339, *History and Traditions...*, S. P. Smith, pp399-401.

[34] *The Stirring Times of Te Rauparaha*, W.T.L. Travers, pp115-116.

[35] *Dictionary of New Zealand Biography - Vol 1,* Various, p499.

largely irrelevant but is included to demonstrate the continuous back and forward movement along the coast, and what might appear to us today as a rather cavalier abandonment of their ancestral lands by the Ati Awa people, and indeed by many tribes, at this time.

In addition to these new Ati Awa arrivals Te Rauparaha was in due course also joined by further arrivals from his near-kin tribe, the Ngati Raukawa of Muangatautari. Now that all the fighting had been done for them this tribe, who had hitherto resisted Te Rauparaha's entreaties to join him in his migration, were suddenly very enthusiastic.

With his control of the Kapiti coast thoroughly established, and all opposition soundly trounced, Te Rauparaha turned his attention to the South Island and with the assistance of Ati Awa Group 1 occupied himself over the next few years by exterminating most of the population of the Marlborough Sounds and wreaking his inimitable havoc as far as Canterbury. Just to keep tabs on our friend Te Rangitake it is said that his father Reretawhangawhanga was involved in these forays south which raises the possibility that Te Rangitake himself may also have been involved in some of these massacres. And to further confuse things, during this time a portion of Ati Awa Group 1 elected to settle in Queen Charlotte Sound, with the result that by 1832 Ati Awa was scattered across three disparate areas – the bulk of them still in their original homelands in Taranaki, and portions of Group 1 at Waikanae and in Queen Charlotte Sound. In this way Reretawhangawhanga, his son Te Rangitake, and the remainder of his hapu, ended up domiciled in Waikanae.

Now that Te Rauparaha had complete control of the Kapiti coast he was like the little red hen – with all the hard work done and the danger over suddenly everyone wanted to be his friend and every tribe within earshot was suddenly on their way to share in his success and spoils. In addition to a further migration of Ati Awa escaping the 1832 devastation of the Pukerangiora and Nga Motu pas – of which we shall read in detail in the next chapter – there were sections of, or entire tribes of, Ngati Tama,

Ngati Mutunga, Ngati Ruanui, Ngati Rauru and Taranaki lining up for their slice of the action. These tribes found themselves banked up all the way from present day Levin to present day Wellington.

MAP 2 gives a rough idea of the situation in 1839 and a comparison with MAP 1, which shows the situation circa 1810, demonstrates the absolute upheaval in the geographical, political and land-owning status of the tribes of the south-west of the North Island over this period.

With all these new arrivals things are starting to get messy. The Kapiti coast is starting to look a little like tribal soup and Te Rauparaha like a car-park attendant surveying with horror an endless stream of new arrivals and wondering where to park them. There was tension between many of these tribes which sometimes boiled over into actual violence. Te Rauparaha finds that the only way to control what is turning into a herd of cats is by physically separating them – Ngati Raukawa, for instance, are relegated to Otaki, and fragments of Ati Awa end up scattered over a string of places – Waikanae, Wanganui a Tara and Queen Charlotte Sound. One senses that perhaps Te Rauparaha has not quite thought things through this far and that an unravelling is not far off.

Chapter 1-3

Things go pear shaped in Taranaki

Let us temporarily leave Te Rauparaha pondering his problems dealing with an increasingly volatile rabble of "allies" on the Kapiti Coast and head back to Taranaki, homeland of the Ati Awa, and catch up on what has been happening there in the interim.

It is now 1832 and a whole 12 years since Ati Awa Group 1 chose to join Te Rauparaha on his little jaunt south. Astoundingly during those 12 years the Waikato tribes have not bothered the remaining Ati Awa, despite Waikato being owed a monumental amount of *utu* for their losses at the hands of Ati Awa at the battle of Motunui in 1819.

Evidently the Waikato tribes are adherents of the "revenge is a dish best served cold" philosophy and in 1832 they feel the dish is cold enough. Ati Awa's always fragile peace is about to be shattered in style, as graphically described by Wells in his summary of the early history of Taranaki:[36]

---

[36] *The History of Taranaki*, Benjamin Wells, pp7-11. In this account "Ngati Awa" refers to the specific tribe "Te Ati Awa". Other accounts of these events include: *History and Traditions of the Maori of the West Coast etc*, S.P. Smith, pp459-482, *New Zealand – Vol 2*, Joel Pollack, pp295-321 and *The Old Whaling Days*, Robert McNab, pp38-59.

"PUKERANGIORA is the abrupt termination of a high ridge on the banks of the Waitara River, situate about seven miles from the river's mouth. In the course of ages the waters of the stream have eroded the foot of the hill and caused at this spot a high and steep escarpment, the verge of which forms a strong military position. On this account the spot was selected by a hapu of the Ngatiawa as a fit site for their pa. The spot received its name from the fact of the hill being in old time clad with rangiora, a well known shrub remarkable for its large leaves, green on the upper surface, and covered with a white and papery epidermis beneath...

It was early summer in the year 1831, when a Waikato canoe came to Ngamotu for a cargo of that Maori delicacy, dried shark. The strangers excused themselves by saying that the fish in question were scarce in their district, while here they are abundant. Friendly greetings were exchanged, the fish prepared, the canoe, which was damaged, repaired, and the Waikatos sent back in peace. Little did the Ngatiawas think these men were spies; such, however, was their character, and in a month afterwards - December, 1831 - a taua[37] consisting of nearly 4,000 Waikatos was at the Waitara. The enemy at first scattered himself about in disorderly parties at Tikorangi and its neighborhood. A few Ngatiawas soon fell into his hands; these were sacrificed to Tu, the god of war, and Wiro the evil spirit.

Soon an unsuspecting party of twenty-five persons, returning from a distant village, was taken, slain and devoured. A panic seized the Ngatiawas, who flew to their stronghold with such precipitation that they had not time to procure any quantity of provisions. Next the enemy destroyed all their sacred places, crossed the river and attacked the Pa. He was, however, repulsed, and fell back with the loss of four chiefs and several men of inferior grade. For twelve successive days the enemy made repeated assaults, but was constantly repulsed, and lost in these attacks thirty-six men.

---

[37] *Taua* = Raiding party

Famine and watchfulness now reduced the garrison to a state of despondency. Instead of stealing away under the cover of the night, they made the mistake of attempting an evacuation in the day time. The enemy perceiving this, pursued and captured numbers of the half famished wretches. Then mothers threw their children over the precipice, and leaped themselves into the river below to avoid a more dreadful fate at the hands of their sanguinary foes. The captives were driven into whares and guarded by sentinels armed with sharp tomahawks. On that day the Waikatos glutted themselves with the flesh of the slain.

On the morrow morning, nearly two hundred prisoners were brought out; those who were well tatooed were beheaded on a block for the sake of their heads. Some of the remainder were slain by a blow or cut on the skull; on others every refinement of cruelty was practised, particularly the thrusting of a red hot ramrod up the bowels. Children and youths were cut open, eviscerated, spitted, and roasted over fires made from the defences of the dismantled Pa. In the afternoon, a similar massacre took place, and so greedily did some of these vampires feast that they died from the effects of their gluttony. The feast was graced with the tatooed heads of the slain, which were stuck on short poles, and placed vis-a-vis with the captors, who would at times pause in their feasting to address them with the most insulting expressions.

Having finished the work to their satisfaction, the Waikatos proceeded to the Sugarloaves to attack Ngamotu Pa, the garrison of which consisted of eleven Europeans and three hundred and fifty Maoris. The presence of the Europeans, who were possessed of four carronades, somewhat intimidated the enemy; but he remembered that he was strong in numbers; moreover, he determined, if possible, to affect his object by treachery.

At daybreak on a morning of February, 1832[38], the watchers discovered the enemy advancing in his usually disorderly manner along the beach. Every preparation was immediately made for his reception. All the provisions at hand were taken within the pa, the walls of the whares were defended with earth or sods, and the guns were got into position. The garrison possessed no round or grape shot, accordingly scraps of iron and stone were improvised for the occasion.

Fearful of the kind of reception he should meet with, the enemy halted, deliberated, and then signalled for a parley. Then a Waikato chief advanced along the beach to the front of the pa, and the Ngamotu chief came out alone to meet him. The two sat down on the sand, rubbed noses, and commenced the tangi.

The Ngamotu chief enquired what his people had done to provoke the anger of Waikato, and wished to know whether it were wise for Maoris to destroy each other for the benefit of strangers. The Waikato chief could not reply to this question, and promised to return peacefully; "but first," said he "let us into your pa to embrace our friends." This could not be acceded to. In less than an hour after this parley the Waikatos danced the war dance in front of the pa, fired a volley, and charged, but were repulsed with loss.

The next day, while shots were exchanging, a Ngatiawa chief in a fit of valour rushed from the pa in the direction of the enemy, discharged his piece and retired. Before he could reach the pa he fell shot through the back, and a party from the enemy rushed to take him, while another party of his friends flew to protect him. Then followed a skirmish in which several fell or were taken prisoners. Several Waikato chiefs now advanced to the pa with expressions of the purest affection, and advised the besieged to surrender; some of the Maoris felt inclined to comply, but the English would not hear of it.

---

[38] According to eye-witness Daniel Sheridan the events described took place between January 2 and February 23, 1832 (*The Old Whaling Days*, Robert McNab, p42).

On the fourth day of the siege, a slave came to the pa with a message requesting another parley. The two chiefs met again on the beach in front of the pa. The Waikato chief professed to be ashamed of his former perfidy, and promised to withdraw his people immediately. When this news reached the pa the foolish people wished to invite the Waikatos to a friendly dance, but the English and many of the natives feared treachery. Then followed quarrelling. One man, the son of a chief, threw himself on a fire in a fit of vexation, and burned himself so severely that he died a few days afterwards. Two sisters quarrelled; one who had confidence in the promise of the enemy ran out of the pa to prove his good faith, but she was taken and cut to pieces within sight of her friends, and her flesh washed in the streamlet from which the garrison procured their water, to tapu it, so that they should not be able to drink it. An assault was next made and bravely resisted, after which a sap was commenced under the pa, but this work was frustrated. Firebrands were also thrown into the pa, but by the vigilance of the people no damage was sustained by them.

In the midst of the siege the schooner Currency Lass, of Sydney, came in with supplies for the Europeans. The enemy tried to take her, but was prevented by the vigilance of the master, Mr. Love. One of the besieged managed to board her under the enemy's fire, and to return to the pa unhurt. A message was now sent to the pa, desiring that Mr. Love, who had landed, would return to the schooner and there confer with the Waikato chief. The meeting took place, and ended precisely as the other parleys had done, the wily chief's treacherous intentions being apparent. Strange as it may appear, business was carried on at times between the contending parties. For blankets and tobacco the Englishmen bought muskets and ammunition of the enemy while skirmishes were going on around them.

The enemy now built mounds, from which, under cover, he could fire down into the pa. During a brisk trade a quarrel arose about a musket, during which three Waikatos were killed, and were afterwards roasted, and eaten. The next day one of the carronades burst without seriously hurting any of the besieged. The enemy cheered by this accident, sent a message stating that he should storm the pa at day break on the following morning. The siege had now lasted for three weeks, and the enemy's food was getting short, for he had not a single slave or prisoner left to cut up into rations. That night many of the besieged slept as soundly as though perfect peace reigned around, but others, with the Englishmen, kept an anxious watch.

At the first dawn of the day the assault was made by the whole force of the enemy. Amid terrific yells, the fences were cut, and a party was within the pa before some of the besieged were well awake. A brave and faithful little band of the besieged fought with the energy of despair, cutting off the retreat of those who had entered the pa. British courage now rose to heroism. The three remaining carronades were served with celerity and precision, the missiles which they belched out inflicting horrible wounds in the bodies of the assailants.

The enemy charged again and again, until at last a panic seized him, and he retreated, dragging his dead chiefs but leaving his wounded. Three hundred and fifty mutilated bodies lay around the pa, some dead and some living. Then the Ngamotus rushed out to wreak vengeance on the wounded. Some were burned alive. One prisoner had a tomahawk thrust into his mouth, while an incision was made in his throat, and a wretch drank his warm flowing blood. He was then quartered, and his heart sent as a present to an old chief. A traitor coming to the pa in the hour of victory was seized, tortured, and slain. The dead which the enemy had buried were exhumed and devoured. The beach in the vicinity of the pa presented a horrible spectacle, portions of human bodies lay scattered about, and the dogs fed on human entrails. Ngatiawa lost thirteen chiefs in this fight; these were buried with barbaric honours. Each chief had eight muskets and a quantity of ammunition buried with him, and for each ten slaves were killed, to become servitors in the reinga, or spirit land.

The Waikato never repeated their attack, though they threatened to do so; and the remnant of the Ngatiawa finding themselves too weak to oppose effectually any renewed attack from Waikato migrated with their women and children, and rejoined their relatives at Otaki, Wellington, Queen Charlotte's Sound, and other places. A few forlorn wretches clung to the land of their fathers, stealthily cultivating small gardens in the depth of the forest. A party of fugitives from Pukerangiora sought refuge in the Kaiauai gorge, situated between the Pouakai ranges and Mount Egmont, where they were discovered and slain by the relentless Waikato...

...Ihaia and Tiraurau, chiefs of Ngatiawa have borne testimony to the desolation of the land after the Waikato raid: "All was quite deserted, the land, the sea, the streams and lakes, the forest, the rocks were deserted; the food, the property, the works were deserted; the dead, the sick were deserted; and the land marks were deserted."

In the summer of 1873-4 we paid a visit to Ngamotu Pa and found its aged chief and three or four of his people working in an adjoining garden. We addressed him as Poarama, but he told us that that was no longer his name for he had joined Israel; alluding to a superstition then prevalent among the Maoris. We asked him the name of the chief who defended the pa against the Waikato, and the names of the Europeans who assisted in its defence. The old man's memory seemed at fault, but after a time we gleaned from him that the name of the chief was Warepori, and the names of the Europeans were Barrett, Love, Akerau, probably Akers[39], Tamiriri, probably Wright, Kopiri probably Phillips, and Oliver[40]

You would think that this cataclysmic disaster would pretty much mean the end of the road for Ati Awa but apparently not, for incredibly, the remnants of Ati Awa immediately made a reprisal raid on the Ngati Maniapoto *pa* at Motutawa at the mouth of the Mokau River further north:

"... not long after Waikato had retired from Otaka [the pa of Nga Motu], a strong force of Te Ati-Awa (including some people from

---

[39] "Barrett" refers to Richard "Dicky" Barrett, whom we will meet again shortly. His life story, and most of the events we are discussing, are lucidly and intelligently told in *The Interpreter,* Angela Caughey.
"Love, Akerau, probably Akers" probably all refer to the same person – Jackie Love – for whom the Maori transliteration "Hakirau" is often used.

[40] *The History of Taranaki*, Benjamin Wells, pp7-11.

> Nga-Motu, Puke-tapu, Otaraua, etc.), with contingents from Ngati-Ruanui and the Nga-Mahanga hapu of the Taranaki tribe, who were allied to the Nga-Motu hapu of the Sugar-loaves, started northwards on vengeance bound and proceeded, on arrival at Mokau, to invest Motu-tawa pa".[41]

During this attack the Ngati Maniapoto chiefs Tikawe and Te Whatu-moana were killed:

> "Tikawe's body was put to the usual purposes by the invaders, and his two arms were left on a rock on the south side of the river at a place named Pekanui, as a sign for his relatives."[42]

It is difficult not to think that Ati Awa's decision to attack Motutawa *pa* was not an especially bright one, for the deaths of these chiefs can only result in Ngati Maniapoto seeking *utu* in due course. *Utu* is, after all, the gift that just keeps on giving, a scale of "justice" that keeps see-sawing eternally back and forth.

---

[41] *History and Traditions of the Maoris of the West Coast, North Island of New Zealand, Prior to 1840,* S.P. Smith, p485.

[42] *Ibid*

Chapter 1-4

The diaspora of the Ati Awa

On returning from this little retaliatory jaunt to attack Motutawa pa the remnants of Ati Awa returned home and split into two groups which for convenience we will call:

- GROUP 2 – The Refugees
- GROUP 3 – The Diehards

And to these two groups we must add a third, who really had no choice in the matter:

- GROUP 4 – The Slaves

The story of these groups is somewhat involved and is not usually discussed in great detail. This is, I believe, a mistake, for if we do not understand the story of these three groups, we will never understand why the various protagonists made the decisions which in thirty years' time would lead to the Taranaki War, the opening chapter in the decade of wars we nowadays collect together under the name of the "New Zealand Wars". And equally, if not more important, in following these groups we will be introduced to practical examples which demonstrate many key facets of Maori land "laws", which are also critical to our understanding of the events of the 1860's.

GROUP 2 - The Refugees.

This group comprised the great majority of the Ati Awa survivors of the slaughter of Pukerangiora and Ngamotu, who fearing the imminent return of the Waikatos to seek *utu* for their dead chiefs at Motutawa, migrated south to follow in the footsteps of their Group 1 kinsmen who had joined Te Rauparaha's south-bound party in 1820.

In hindsight some of these decisions are difficult to comprehend. As we have described, Ati Awa was still strong enough to attack Ngati Maniapoto, in a *pa*, on Ngati Maniapoto home-ground, and they did so knowing that as sure as night follows day this is tantamount to issuing Ngati Maniapoto an invitation to attack them in return. Having unnecessarily stirred up this hornet's nest the apparently still powerful Ati Awa force now decided to flee their ancestral lands by migrating south.

It is here that our story truly starts for we now enter the arcane and much debated world of 1800's Maori land lore. We need to start asking questions such as: what happens to land when its residents vacate it? Who then "owns" that land and by what right? Or even more fundamentally, does *anyone* "own" land at this time, in the Maori world?[43]

No individual, or group, has a God-given right to anything that they have not themselves produced. The distribution and "ownership" of land and natural resources that are just "there" and to which no-one has any natural right is therefore a problem as old as time itself. Since there are very few possible options to resolve this dilemma every culture in every country independently evolved a largely identical set of guidelines to deal

---

[43] This is not intended to be a rigorous analysis nor could it ever be. Maori customary land laws are notoriously complex, inconsistent by place and time, full of exceptions and probably impossible to document definitively at all let alone in a few words, which is why the word "lore" is probably more accurate than "law". These simple suggestions are, I believe, reasonable and generally acknowledged as top level guidelines.

with the taking up of land as the nascent peoples of the world evolved and spread themselves out.

When the great canoes of Maori tradition pulled up on the shores of future New Zealand land was claimed as it has been in every age in every culture, by "right of discovery", known in Maori as *take kite*[44] , or as we might more colloquially say in English, a combination of the principles of "finders keepers" and "first up best dressed". Claims to land upon first landfall involved a mad rush to name things, to leave markers and do anything and everything possible to literally "mark out" territory in order for its new owner to recite his many personal connections to the land.

Over time, individuals would accumulate more and more personal connections to, and bonds with, particular pieces of land – a death here, a birth there, an eel weir, cultivation, or confrontation over there – so that a larger tribal area would become an impenetrable, intermeshed, tangled grid of small individual and joint claims to patches of land. As generations passed the ability to recite the existence and deeds of ancestors on the land *(take tupuna)* added further layers of legitimacy to the claim, cementing in place the claim to ownership of the land. It is this seemingly untangle-able web of *intra-tribal* claims to land ownership that would in the future make the European system of buying land an extreme challenge.

Laying claim to land is the easy part. The hard part is holding that land against all new-comers and possible contenders, especially if the land has valuable resources such as food sources on it. Holding on to your land required prove of efficient land usage, which brings us to our first Land Lore:

- **LAND LORE 1** – no matter by what "right" a piece of land is originally claimed that right must be continuously maintained by a principle known as *ahi ka* - "keeping the fires burning" – which, as the name suggests, means the land must be clearly seen to be gainfully occupied and its resources well used. This is a natural

---

[44] The Maori word *take* means, in this context, cause, reason, or "by right of".

and common-sense lore that ensures land is not sitting idle in the hands of those who never intend to use it.[45] The major problem with this lore is defining exactly what level of "occupation" and "usage" is required to fulfil this "fire burning" function,

So far so good. How, then, can land "change hands"? Again it is not complicated:

- **LAND LORE 2** – land can change hands by the simple expedient of conquest by a stronger party, known as *take raupatu*. However the initial conquest must be confirmed by the conquerors actually occupying and using the conquered land – in other words fulfilling the requirement of *ahi ka* – for more than three years before it is acknowledged as definitively "belonging" to them.

- **LAND LORE 3** – Land can be gifted, either within a tribe or to other tribes, in a process called *take tuku*. This is a no-brainer – if you "own" something of course you can dispose of it as you like.

As has been alluded there is nothing specific to Maori culture here. The principle both of land acquisition by conquest, of "if you have the might you have the right", and the "use it or lose it" principle of *ahi ka,* have been universal throughout history. It seems so simple put like this but these basic tenets are the tip of a gargantuan and problematical iceberg and, as we shall see, really offer no clear-cut answer to anything.

It is against this background of land lore and the slaughter of Pukerangiora that the majority of Ati Awa survivors (Group 2) abandoned their homelands and headed south following in the footsteps of their Group 1 kin. They do so because they have no choice, knowing that the likeliest scenario is that the Waikatos will arrive the day after they leave, occupy the land for three years thereby rendering the land officially theirs and Ati Awa officially homeless in perpetuity. There is not a shadow of a doubt that with the slaughter of Pukerangiora and Ati Awa's subsequent

---

45 The under-use or non-use of productive land which Maori refused to sell was of course one of the great frustrations of the early European settlers.

abandonment of their ancestral land, "*mana whenua*"[46] over this land passed to the Waikato for all time, unless and until they came to an alternative arrangement, by peaceful or martial means, with another party. Bottom line, *no one* can, or will, occupy that land without Waikato's say so.

The migration of the Group 2 Ati Awa south took place in the late winter of 1832[47] and involved most of the remaining Ati Awa *hapu* as well as parts of Ngati Mutunga and Ngati Tama[48], totalling perhaps 2,000 people[49].

Among the leaders of this *heke* were the chief Te Puni and his cousins Te Wharepouri and Wi Tako Ngatata, who would in due course feature heavily in the future of New Zealand due to their involvement in the sale of what is now called the Wellington area to the New Zealand Company. And in what is possibly a first in Maori migrations, this migratory group also included a handful of Europeans in the form of some of the European defenders of Ngamotu – Dicky Barrett and Jacky Love, together with their families. It is just one of those strange and seemingly innocuous twists of fates that collectively shape the history of the planet, as we shall see shortly.

In late 1832, after 300 kilometres worth of adventures we need not detail here, Ati Awa Group 2 reached their objective, Te Uruhi, slightly south of Waikanae, to join their Group 1 kinfolk who had occupied the land since their arrival with Te Rauparaha in 1820. At that time Te Rauparaha had "acquired" this land under Land Lore 2, the law of might, and the Ati Awa

---

[46] Authority over the land.

[47] According to McNab *(The Old Whaling Days*, Robert McNab, p42) this migration took place "the following June" after the February 1832 attacks, implying June 1833 rather than 1832. Like many Maori migrations this one was named - in this case *Tama-te-uaua.*

[48] *Taua*, Angela Ballara, p346.

[49] *Te Wanganui-a-Tara*, Angela Ballara, an article in *The making of Wellington*, edited Hamer and McIntyre, p22.

who settled there, having occupied the area for more than three years, were now considered the bona-fide owners of the land from which Te Rauparaha drove the *tangata whenua* tribes. Ballara summarises the situation:

> "At this time the mana of Te Rauparaha over the various parties of newcomers to the Kapiti coast and other fought-over southern regions was still acknowledged, though once he assigned lands to tribes with rangatira status their rights after three years of occupation acquired independent legitimacy."[50]

While this statement verifies the use of Land Lore 2 it also indicates a blurring of the rules because of the clear tension between the "rights" of Te Rauparaha, who did the conquering, and those of the Ati Awa, who fortuitously acquired the spoils resulting from Te Rauparaha's efforts. Ati Awa had gained "their" land not through their own efforts but through someone else's – a clear imbalance of *utu*. While technically Ati Awa may "own" their new land by right of three years occupation, they also very clearly "owe one" to Te Rauparaha for putting them there in the first place. Although Land Lore 2 is still in place it is starting to look more like a nebulous, indefinable shade of grey rather than a lore of black or white.

For some reason the newly arrived Ati Awa Group 2 did not stay long at Waikanae and two years later (1834) a large portion left their longer established Group 1 kin in Waikanae and moved even further south to settle on the north-eastern side of what is now Wellington harbour, around the Waiwhetu area on the east side of the large swampy delta which then existed at the mouth of the Heretaunga (Hutt) river.

But even then the Ati Awa Group 2 had not finished travelling. In a classic demonstration of the chaotic nature and transience of what seems like myriads of disparate groups jostling for an existence based on the never-ending principles of *utu* and kinship, a large portion of Group 2 crossed over to the Wairarapa for "three planting seasons". In accordance with Land Lore 1 they left a few people in Waiwhetu to maintain continuity of

---

[50] *Te Wanganui-a-Tara*, Angela Ballara, p22.

their *ahi ka* "rights" of occupation in that place while the main group was away.

In this nomadic way we see how Ati Awa Group 2 has in its rambles south acquired "rights to", "*mana* over", or "interests in", land in at least three places – their original ancestral lands in Taranaki, in Wellington Harbour and in the Wairarapa. Of course, these "rights" and "*mana*" are not binary or unambiguous, they are amorphous, analogue things, in which these land "claims" are shared with, and/or contested by, many other parties and individuals who will almost certainly have very different ideas about the relative merits of each other's claims to these lands. Such is the byzantine and intractable nature of Maori land tenure – yes, there are "rules", or perhaps more accurately guidelines, but when push came to shove these rules did not, in practice, always provide definitive answers, a conclusion that is easily demonstrated by the constant Maori warfare related to land which existed prior to the first white man setting foot on New Zealand soil. Quoting Ballara again, at this time:

> "Rights were not clearly defined: mana over the land and people had been recently acquired by conquest and was open to challenge."[51]

And that, really, is the overriding Land Lore that trumps all others:

> LAND LORE 0 – All Land claims are analogue in nature and open to challenge, which is why we have been referring to "lores" rather than "laws". They are "guidelines", not "rules", interesting to consider but incapable of determining an absolute resolution that will be accepted by all parties.

There is just one final aspect we need to discuss before we leave the peripatetic Ati Awa Group 2 who seem to be wandering aimlessly about like Moses in the desert.

As early as 1824 groups of Ngati Mutunga and Ngati Tama had also migrated south and were "encouraged" by Te Rauparaha to settle around the western side of Wellington Harbour, while the *tangata whenua* of the

---

[51] *Te Wanganui-a-Tara*, Angela Ballara, p24.

region, Ngati Ira, occupied the eastern side. Thus by 1835 Ngati Mutunga and Ngati Tama have been living in future Wellington for around 11 years and two things have happened. First, according to Land Lore 2 they are now, in theory at least, considered owners of this land. But second, they are in the same position as Ati Awa in Waikanae – they are there only by the grace, goodwill and efforts of Te Rauparaha.

For this reason, and an accumulation of real or perceived offences which through the ever-present principle of *utu* required payback[52], Ngati Mutunga and Ngati Tama felt insecure in their land rights and threatened by a possible attack by Te Rauparaha. Consequently in late 1835 these two tribes migrated from "their" land in Wellington to the Chatham Islands, where they famously – or infamously – performed genocide on the resident Moriori. This is yet another example – two examples in fact[53] – of the tenuous nature of land tenure which, however detailed in principle, could be trumped in an instant by the overriding principle of "might over right".

The relevance of this to our continuing story of Ati Awa Group 2 is that before Ngati Mutunga and Ngati Tama left for the Chathams they gifted "their" old lands[54] around Wellington Harbour to Ati Awa Group 2 and to two *iwi* of the Taranaki tribe, Ngati Tupaia and Ngati Haumia. In this way, Ati Awa Group 2 acquired land around the north-west quadrant of Wellington Harbour, from present day Petone to Ngauranga, while the Taranaki tribes received land around the south-west quadrant, from Ngauranga to Te Aro.

---

[52] Details may be found in *Te Wanganui-a-Tara*, Angela Ballara, p25.

[53] Ngati Mutunga and Ngati Tama moved to the Chathams because of their fear of "might over right" being dealt to them by Te Rauparaha. To avoid this Ngati Mutunga and Ngati Tama in turn migrated to the Chatham Islands and exterminated the Moriori in what is perhaps the ultimate display of "might over right".

[54] Strictly speaking these are really their *new* lands, their ancestral lands being in North Taranaki.

This is an example of Land Lore 3 – *take tuku* – acquisition of land through "gifting". However "gift" is not quite the correct word because in English "gift" has no implication of a motivation beyond that of giving for the pleasure of it. The "gifting" of land in *take tuku,* if we read the fine print, is really just another form of *utu,* for these "gifts" are given for a reason – that of balancing obligations. Both Ati Awa Group 2, and the Taranaki *iwi,* received these "gifts" because they had, in the balance of *utu,* acquired enough brownie points with their departing neighbours to receive them[55]. Thus we have a perfect example of one group of people recognising assistance from another group of people and "rewarding" them to achieve balance. This is an important observation which will be revisited later in this book.

You would think that Ati Awa Group 2 would be over the moon with this unexpected windfall, a.k.a balance of *utu,* but apparently not, for less than six months after Ngati Mutunga and Ngati Tama's departure Ati Awa Group 2 tried to follow them to the Chathams by hi-jacking the whaling ship *Active.* Why they made this attempt is unclear. Perhaps they were fed up with every tribe known to man tramping up and down the west coast. Perhaps, like Ngati Mutunga and Ngati Tama, they did not trust Te Rauparaha. Perhaps they felt Ngati Mutunga's and Ngati Tama's gift of land still under an ill-defined degree of Te Rauparaha's *mana* was more of a poisoned chalice to be avoided like the plague rather than treated as a windfall.

Whatever the reason, this little plot of Group 2 to put a few thousand kilometres between themselves and Te Rauparaha misfired and they found themselves back at square one, waiting in their gifted land for the next catastrophe to occur. Yet again, in all these events, we see egregious examples of Maori being totally unsentimental about either their "ancestral" land, or indeed, *any* land. Land was just a practical resource – square acreage to live on and cultivate.

---

[55] *Te Wanganui-a-Tara*, Angela Ballara, pp24-28, gives a detailed description of how these brownie points were acquired.

Having spent the last four years, from 1832-1836, wandering aimlessly like lost souls, Ati Awa Group 2 and their chiefs Wharepouri and Te Puni finally put down roots on the slightly tainted land gifted to them by the departing Ngati Mutunga and Ngati Tama. They would stay in this new land until one day in late 1839 a strange ship came sailing into Wellington harbour making offers they could not refuse.

Before we leave Ati Awa Group 2 in their newly "gifted" home of Wellington Harbour we should mention that in perhaps early 1834 the European components of the "Ngamotu/Ati Awa Group 2" migration, Dicky Barrett and Jackie Love, and their families, also left the Ati Awa group in Waikanae and set up a whaling station at Te Awaiti, on the eastern coast of the long, thin island of Awapaoa which forms part of the intricate maze of spindly peninsulas and islands that make up the Marlborough Sounds.[56]

So ends our summary of the eight year wanderings of Ati Awa Group 2 – the "Refugees" – from the catastrophe of the slaughter of Pukerangiora and the narrow escape at Ngamotu in 1832 to their final destination of Whanganui a Tara (Wellington Harbour).

We will now rewind and return to the aftermath of these battles in 1832 and take a look at the fate of the second group of survivors.

GROUP 3 - The "Diehards".

This third Ati Awa group is the small remnant of survivors who did not join their Group 2 compatriots in their 1832 migration south but chose to stay put in their ancestral lands in Taranaki. There are two schools of thought regarding the motivations and functions of this group.

One writer refers to this group as the "diehards" and attributes their motives for staying as being no more complicated than the love of their homeland:

---

[56] *The Interpreter*, Angela Caughey, p60.

> "The main migration away from Ngamotu (known as Te Heke Paukena) – almost but not quite – completed the depopulation of North Taranaki. About 300 people, many of them Puketapu people who had escaped the sweep through their own tribal area and joined the Ngamotu, would not be persuaded to give up their homes, preferring death on Ati Awa soil, should that be their lot".[57]

> "After the decision to remove [that is, migrate south] had been decided on ... the whole body moved down to Waitara preparatory to starting. Here they were joined by some of the people of Nga-Motu, but not all; for some decided to remain, and should necessity arise, take shelter on the Sugar Loaf Islands.[58]

The second theory for this group not joining the migration south is that their function was to perform the role of "fire burners" in accordance with the previously mentioned Land Lore 1 principle of *ahi ka* by remaining "at Ngamotu to maintain Te Ati Awa ownership".[59] If this is the case then no doubt these unlucky souls were the elderly or otherwise expendable members of the tribe and their likely fate was complete extermination by the Waikatos to impose their right to the "vacated" land by conquest.

If indeed the function of this group was that of "fire burners" we might wonder exactly the nature of the fine print associated with the principle of *ahi ka*. For instance – how many "fire burners" are required per thousand acres of land to qualify for "occupancy"? One? A thousand and one? And which of the two contending claimants to the land is to make this judgement? The Waikatos or the Ati Awa? These are unanswerable, "how long is a piece of string", questions.

---

[57] *Tales of old North Taranaki*, Murray Moorhead, p9.

[58] *History and Traditions of the Maoris of the West Coast*, S.P. Smith, p488.

[59] *The Interpreter*, Angela Caughey, p53.

In peacetime the principle of *ahi ka* required a tribe to not only continually visit their entire territory but use its resources to maintain claim to that land and its resources. That being the case, how is it possible that a handful of "fire burners" huddled together over a few acres around the islands of Ngamotu could possibly claim "occupation" of the many hundreds of thousands of acres that comprised the Ati Awa ancestral lands? This small band of terrified hypothetical fire burners certainly did not have the "power to hold the land, and to repel intruders", because if they did, they surely would not have been cowering in rags and living in holes on tiny islands. If these "fire burners" could be annihilated in a heartbeat by the Waikatos if they so choose, what exactly was their point?

And unsurprisingly that is exactly what happened, for less than a year after the migrating Group 2 party set off south:

> "The news of the "Tama-te-uaua" migration, in which most of Ngati Awa [Group 2] had departed for Kapiti, reached the Waikato country and emboldened them to attack the few remaining people – nearly three hundred men, women, and children – who remained in the neighbourhood of Nga-Motu".[60]
>
> "Most of this remnant, realising that Waikato would seek revenge for Ngati Awa's attack the previous year on the Ngati Maniapoto pa of Motutawa, removed to Mikotahi, the innermost of the Ngamotu group of islands, an "island" so close to shore it only becomes an actual island at high tide. Mikotahi was a prime site to mount a defence because its uniquely steep sides made it impregnable, meaning a few determined men could hold it against a great number in the days when Maori weapons and old flint muskets were used. The new residents added to the island's natural strength by strengthening the palisading, collecting provisions, and making arrangements for storing water, for there is no spring on this little island, nor could water be obtained within some distance on the main land.

---

[60] *History and Traditions of the Maoris of the West Coast*, S. P. Smith, p497.

In 1833, the year after the departure of the majority of Ngati Awa made their migration south, a Waikato taua occupied the point of land opposite Mikotahi and the adjacent shores, and kept up a musketry fire on the pa, but with little or no result. The place was too strong to take by assault so the invaders sat down to starve out the garrison.

The Waikato made overtures of peace, which the garrison, now much reduced by hunger, agreed to consider, and towards that end admitted a few of the Waikato into the fortifications to discuss the matter. However the garrison detected what they considered signs of treachery in the emissaries, so turned on them and killed a number of them. Negotiations between the besieged and besiegers now proceeded and several of the chiefs of the garrison were taken away to Kawhia and appear to have become vassals, if not slaves, to some of the Waikato chiefs, and did not return to their homes 'until the days of Wairaweke'[61], that is, until Colonel Wakefield arranged to purchase all this coast in 1840"[62]

It is largely for this reason, that by the time Colonel Wakefield's party set foot near Ngamotu seven years later seeking land on which to put colonists, the numbers of these hypothesised "fire burners" had plummeted from their initial number of about 300 to about "30 to 50". And their decision to sell the land to Wakefield makes it quite clear that by 1840 these people did not consider themselves "fire burners", if indeed they ever had. After all, is it likely that this tattered handful of people who had endured such hardship and lived with the daily threat of violent death for seven years specifically for the purposes of keeping the fires burning, would suddenly abandon that role, and hence their presumed obligations

---

[61] *Wairaweke* is the Maori transliteration of "wide awake", the nick-name Maori gave to Colonel Wakefield, the leader of the New Zealand Company party who we shall meet presently.

[62] This is a rationalisation and simplification of the account given in *History and Traditions of the Maoris of the West Coast*, S. P. Smith.

to their entire tribe and relations, by immediately selling that land? It is very difficult to believe.

Notwithstanding the existence of this small group of "diehards" the Ati Awa ancestral lands officially belonged to the Waikato tribes by virtue of *take raupatu*. The Waikatos did not, in this case, choose to follow up that claim by conquest with actual occupation. Why would they? They already had more land than they had people to put on it. And so this beautiful, potentially productive land remained a barren, unoccupied "no man's land" from 1832 until 1840, and for all we know might still be doing so, were it not for the arrival of Europeans, of whom we shall hear a lot more shortly.

GROUP 4 - The Slaves

Our fourth and final group of Ati Awa, those lucky enough to survive the slaughter of Pukerangiora in 1832 and the assault on Mikotahi the following year, were carried off by the Waikatos as slaves, or *taurekareka*.

In the traditional pre-European world the consequences of becoming a slave in Maori society were literally life altering – becoming a slave meant a complete loss of *mana* to the point that even a former chief would be rejected by his own tribe as "damaged goods":

> "To be defeated, captured, and not killed created a deeper stain than being eaten because of subsequent slavery (*herehere*). When the feeling against an enemy chief was so intense as to be termed *ito* or *ngakau*, such a person, if captured, was killed and eaten. Here the act of eating satisfied the additional factor of intense, personal hatred. Apart from such, the victors sometimes preferred to spare captives both for the economic reason of obtaining additional labour and for the personal satisfaction of reducing enemy chiefs of high rank to the degraded position of slaves attending to menial tasks. Once a slave always a slave, for nothing could wipe out the stain. Even if a slave escaped, he could not regain his chiefly status in his own tribe. Under such circumstances, they usually preferred to die with their shame in exile. They were usually treated with

kindness but they were liable to be drawn upon to supplement the food supply."[63]

"People of both sexes who were captured in military campaigns were often spared to perform menial work. In fact, their capture was deliberately undertaken at times as a solution to the labour problem. They were treated as slaves, termed taurekareka, and did not enter into the social grades of the tribe."[64]

However the period between 1830 and 1850 was a time when European influence turned the Maori social structure on its head, creating a flattened social order in which the extreme low status of slaves was raised while the extreme high status of chiefs was correspondingly lowered. This trend towards a more egalitarian social structure would be the cause of much conflict regarding the ownership of Ati Awa land and the validity of the New Zealand Company purchases of Taranaki to be discussed shortly.

This completes our summary of the dispersion of the four groups of the Ati Awa tribe. It is now time to make a substantial diversion to a different place and a very different culture – that of Regency-era Great Britain.

---

[63] *The coming of the Maori*, Peter Buck, pp401-402.

[64] *Ibid*, p338.

Chapter 1-5

Meanwhile, back in England...

We tend to think of New Zealand history as something that happened in isolation from the rest of the world and that the answer to everything we need to know about ourselves is to be found within the shores of these islands. But no country's history exists in isolation – it exists within the framework of the history of the wider world. Consequently we cannot comprehend "New Zealand History" in its proper context unless we have at least a minimal understanding of this wider framework.

"New Zealand History", at least in its written form, is the history of two peoples – Europeans and Maori. It is therefore strange that while we spend a lot of time learning about Maori culture and customs we spend very little time learning about the European culture of the time. Every primary school child can tell you something about Maori mythology but very few can tell you anything about – to quote just a few examples – the Napoleonic Wars, the great social movements, the rise of democracy and evangelical humanitarianism.

The impression one gets is that New Zealanders think of their ancestors simply as 200 year old carbon copies of themselves and that therefore our ancestors thought then as we think now. This is a very big mistake. In 2025 we are (say) seven generations removed from the first European settlers in this country. And of course the same applies for Maori – the signatories of the Treaty of Waitangi are seven generations removed from their current descendants. Think of the enormous changes in mind-sets, values, social constructs and technologies that have occurred just in our own lifetimes. By the time each of us reaches the age of fifty – if not less – we will have seen the "normal" of our youth turned on its head. If we multiply that effect by four to go back 200 years in time it is quite clear that our 1800's ancestors inhabited an entirely different world from our own. If we could go back in time and visit our ancestors of 1830 we would be – literally – incomprehensible to each other – not because we do not speak the same language but because the whole concept of what passes for "normal" is light-years apart. Physically our ancestors may look like us but in every other respect we may as well be talking to aliens from Mars.

With the best will in the world we can never fully understand how our ancestors thought and how they lived. Anyone who claims to understand why their ancestors signed the Treaty of Waitangi or why George Grey made the decisions he made according to 2020's "normality" is being delusional. Having said that, we need to at least try to bridge that mental gap as best we can, for if we cannot mentally inhabit the world of the time we are studying, if we do not understand that every person who ever lived – including ourselves – is a product of their time, if we do not understand that in two hundred years' time we will be judged according to the values of that future time and be found as severely wanting as we currently find our ancestors, then we are kidding ourselves. In short we would be well advised not to pass judgement on the past, because, by definition, we would be casting judgement on ourselves, for we would have done exactly the same in those times. There are no exceptions and this is, or should be, a sobering thought.

Another phenomenon we need to be aware of is what might be called "generational arrogance". Each new generation always, without exception, thinks they know best, that there has never in the history of mankind been a generation as clever or as morally "good" as theirs, that everyone in the past is an idiot, a rogue and a scoundrel, bereft of brain or morality. While that may be good for our egos, it is, sadly, not true – the past is populated by supremely intelligent and caring people and that is why we are all here in the present reaping the benefits of the seeds they sowed. Once again, a little humility goes a long way.

With that preamble we will try as best as we can to enter the world of the other protagonists in the saga of "New Zealand" history, that ill-defined group referred to as "Europeans", which is not-so-secret code for the "English" or the "British". We need to try to understand the thought processes and motivations that brought these people to New Zealand, what made them say goodbye to their old lives and their families, spend literally six months in a leaky boat, and throw their lives to the fate of the Gods.

We have already given some indication of the mammoth social and territorial upheaval caused by the Musket Wars in the Maori World. But that disruption is by no means unique in the world of that time, indeed there were great upheavals simultaneously happening throughout Europe in general and "Britain" in particular. Unlike the Maori situation the disruption in Britain was not caused by a suicidal tendency to annihilate itself[65] but by the massive social and technological upheavals of the late 1700s and early 1800s.

The people who made the key decisions which led to an association between Britain and New Zealand, and the early European colonists of New Zealand, were the product of what is called the "Regency Era", a period that has a number of definitions but which for convenience we shall say the period 1810 - 1840 is as good as any. Simplifying for brevity there are perhaps four key attributes, many of them interdependent, which characterise this era.

First, it was the time of the First Industrial Revolution, a time of huge technological change, of steam engines and steam power, of mechanised spinning machines, of improved iron manufacture, of machine tools, of the replacement of piecework by factories and of manual work by automation – the list of technological advances is practically endless.

---

[65] At least not at this time – in other times "Britain" has of course had its fair share of Civil Wars and fighting amongst the constituent states of England, Ireland and Scotland.

Second, was the exodus of the population from rural areas to the cities, caused by technological changes in sowing and tilling of the land and, even more fundamentally, by a change in the very basics of land usage and ownership – a shift from the communal use of commons to the private and efficient use of land by "enclosure". These changes caused mass unemployment in the country areas which fortuitously filled the need for cheap labour in the cities caused by the industrial revolution. On a social level however it brought a whole new level of misery and destitution to the masses who were famously and infamously used as human fodder to fuel the capitalist machine, to power the "dark satanic mills".

Directly related to the increase in agricultural efficiency was a high population growth fuelled along Malthusian lines by the resulting increased food supplies and (relatively) higher standards of living. It has been suggested that the population of England more than doubled over the period of 1770 to 1850.

Third, it was the era of the wars with France, including the Napoleonic Wars, which involved Britain almost continuously for 23 years from 1792 to 1815, causing an estimated 6 million deaths throughout Europe including 300,000 British casualties alone – no small amount for a war no-one now remembers. The end of the Napoleonic Wars in 1815 was a two edged sword – on the one hand troops stopped dying in war, on the other it meant they were sent home to add to the already huge overpopulation to possibly die in peace from starvation.

Fourth, it was an era of incredible social change in which it seemed that England suddenly developed a social conscience and became aware of the need to be kind to each other. It was, if you like, the "woke movement"[66] of the 1800's, but much more intense because the scope for human improvement was so much greater then than it is now.

---

[66] The official terminology for this phenomenon is the far less user-friendly term of "evangelistic/evangelical humanitarianism".

The early 1800's was an age of rampant evangelical humanitarianism, a world that revolved around Exeter Halls[67], Missionary Societies[68] and powerful and influential humanitarian societies such as the Aboriginal Protection Society (APS). It was a time of huge liberal upheaval, of the abolition of slavery, of extending the electoral franchise to the masses, of defeating poverty and misery in whatever form, not just in England but more generally throughout mankind. Philanthropy, and the gifting of "civilisation" to the world, in the form of taking misery out of the world, was the national ethos of the time. It was, literally, Britain's mission to "save the world".[69]

This sudden need to "do good" was a strange business with unclear and dubious motives. Charles Dickens would later mercilessly parody what seemed to him a fad based on personal vanity and selfishness in his novel *Bleak House*. In today's latest incarnation of wokeness we call this phenomenon "virtue signalling" – nothing changes it seems. Dickens also coined the phrase "telescopic philanthropy", by which he meant that in the scheme of "doing good" the number of brownie points you got was proportional to the square of the distance to those you were "helping". Helping the "natives" of Africa, for instance, received far more adulation than helping the people in the gutter outside your own home. Once again, nothing changes.

The biggest tool in the humanitarian's toolbox of the day was Christianity, at that stage the answer to all life's problems in general and the saviour of

---

[67] "Exeter Hall" is the name of both a literal building in London and more widely a term used to refer to the humanitarian movement prevalent at that time, which often held their meetings at Exeter Hall.

[68] The best known of these in the New Zealand context are the Church Missionary Society (CMS) and the Wesleyan Missionary Society (WMS), both pivotal in the history of New Zealand and of the subject of this book. These societies were organisationally separate from the denominations they represented – for example, the CMS did mission work according to an Anglican faith, but they were not part of the Anglican Church.

[69] It must have seemed a good idea at the time, but posterity has deemed it otherwise.

the "heathen" in particular. In today's secular world it is almost impossible to imagine a time when Christianity reigned supreme and was the rock on which life was built, a commonality joining those in the gutter to the highest in the land. For this reason the Church and the State were to a large extent inseparable since if everyone in a position of power was a devout Christian, as they all were, it followed that all Government policy was automatically based on Christian doctrine. It was a time when the various missionary and religious organisations had huge influence within Government.

British humanitarians could not then know, as we know now but nevertheless choose to ignore, that its efforts for good would all monumentally backfire and that posterity would damn them to Hell and back for their efforts. Intervention rarely ends well and, as history tells us again and again, no good deed goes unpunished.

At this time in British history the business of interfacing and mixing with "aborigines" was uppermost in the minds of the greatest of English intellectuals, statesmen and politicians. Britain was painfully aware and highly sensitive of its dismal record of failures in its contacts with faraway countries and in particular their disastrous outcome for indigenous populations. Acknowledgement of these past mistakes and a commitment to ensuring they were never repeated was the Holy Grail of British sentiment, something that can be readily seen in the highly influential "Report of the Parliamentary Select Committee on Aboriginal Tribes". Released in 1837 this was a report which pulled no punches and even a single paragraph from its 120 page body demonstrates the huge sensitivity of the time to issues of humanity in general and to contact with "aborigines" in particular:

> "The appalling facts which it [the report] discloses, and the judicious suggestions it contains, combine to render it one of the most important documents which has ever come before the legislature. Replete with evidence as to the injustice and cruelty with which the Aborigines have hitherto been treated, and the

pernicious effects which have resulted to them from the intercourse with European nations..."[70]

If we could sum up all these interconnected themes in a single sentence it might be that there was simultaneously a massive desire for the lower classes of Britain to escape the squalor of their current existence, a very bullish entrepreneurial spirit propelling the middle classes to seek prosperity overseas, and an abundance of money in the upper classes to invest in such ventures. In short, there was a huge incentive for people of all classes to emigrate to a new country. The colonisation of America, Canada and Australia was already well advanced and would continue with a passion throughout the 1800s. In the 1830's New Zealand was virgin territory ripe for colonisation, a promised land, or so it seemed. And in the humanitarian spirit of the age this colonisation *must* be achieved not only at no cost to its first-nation inhabitants but in a way that improved them, "civilised" them, educated them and brought light into their darkness.

On to this philanthropic and optimistic stage strode a business concern called "The New Zealand Company", the latest incarnation in a series of similarly named companies that had laboured with scant success in bringing this colonisation dream to fruition. Directing from the wings, as was his custom, was the company's shadowy genius, the brains of the outfit, Edward Gibbon Wakefield.

Edward Gibbon is the best known of a seemingly jinxed family whose various members played a major role in the early colonisation of New Zealand. This seems somewhat unfair for while Edward Gibbon dreamed and schemed in comfort back in England all the heavy-lifting of actually implementing his schemes fell to his luckless and long-forgotten brothers, William and Arthur, and to his son Jerningham. Edward Gibbon himself would not step foot in the country he played such a large part in founding for a full thirteen years after the arrival of the first colonists his schemes caused to be discharged on the desolate shores of Petone in 1840.

---

[70] *Report of the Parliamentary Select Committee on Aboriginal Tribes,* 1837, British Parliamentary Select Committee, Preface.

The Wakefield family, while certainly not poor, was neither "rich" in the context of their day nor titled, and yet against all odds, including a national scandal resulting in a three year vacation at Her Majesty's pleasure in Newgate prison, Edward Gibbon Wakefield managed to rise well above his nominal betters to become an acknowledged visionary in many issues of national importance, most famously that of "systematising" the then totally random business of emigration:

> "Attempts were made by public companies to colonise New Zealand in the years 1825 and 1837, which were resisted by the Government. In 1833, Mr. Edward Gibbon Wakefield published his "View of the Art of Colonisation," the principle of his system being that the new lands of the colonies should be sold in small allotments at low prices to settlers, and the funds thus obtained be expended in carrying out fresh emigrants. This system was adopted by the founders of South Australia, and it was with a view of colonising New Zealand on this plan that on the 22nd of May, 1839, the New Zealand Company was formed".[71]

> "The Company did not so much seek for direct personal gain as for a fresh outlet for British commerce, and a field of emigration for the over-populated districts of Britain in a time of great commercial depression. That object was ultimately attained, but it was in the face of a fierce and powerful opposition".[72]

In the present there is plenty of ammunition to be found in such statements and where one reader may see altruistic, noble intentions, another may see self-serving propaganda while yet another might see these two extremes as not being mutually exclusive. Much has been written about Wakefield and the New Zealand Company but in the interests of brevity let us just say that at worst[73] the New Zealand

---

[71] *The History of Taranaki*, Benjamin Wells, p6.

[72] *Ibid*, p7.

[73] And at best, in the context of its time, there is a strong argument for a very much kinder assessment.

Company were "speculators", no different, better or worse than we might read about in any newspaper we might care to pick up in the present. But for all that, the people behind the New Zealand Company were not villains and they were not idiots – its directors read like a who's who of anybody who was anybody in England[74] and whatever the Company's modern reputation it is clear it meant well for all parties – Maori and European – even if with the cynicism of hindsight we might either laugh or frown at its naivety and self-delusion.

Given that the English air was awash with humanitarianism it was a no-brainer that the New Zealand Company's aspirations and its plans to achieve them were based on the highest of moral obligations – the company simply would not have got off the ground had that not been the case. Whether or not these plans were practical or based on reality is another matter – the Company was after all planning largely in a vacuum, 17,000 miles away from their target settlement[75] and scant on information. While we might say in hindsight there was a lot of misplaced optimism, heads in the sand and crossed fingers involved, it was, by the standards of its day, a well-planned and researched project. In essence it was no different from any modern "start-up" we might see showered with Government money and eulogised in the media for being bold, following its dream and pushing the boundaries into uncharted territories.

The New Zealand Company bent over backwards to involve both the British Government and the Missionary organisations in its schemes but was rejected at every turn. Given the all-prevailing concern for the welfare of aboriginal peoples it is easy to see why this was the case, for logically the best way not to harm first-nation peoples is surely to leave them alone, in which case "colonisation", or the introduction of European – or indeed *any* other culture – in any form or fashion, was anathema. Academically sound though this approach may have been it was a rather

---

[74] "Thirteen of them were members of Parliament, three were aldermen of the city of London, and the majority of the remainder were either princely merchants, or extensive ship owners", *Ibid*, p7.

[75] As the ship sails.

short-sighted view for the "colonisation horse" had already well and truly bolted – by 1840 there were already an estimated 2,000 Europeans in New Zealand and absolutely nothing to stop more of them, either as individuals or as entire boatloads of colonists, descending on New Zealand from any and every country on Earth.

Clearly, New Zealand Company or no New Zealand Company, some action, by someone, in some country, was necessary to control the inevitable settlement of New Zealand, for without some form of control, the random and piecemeal settlement of New Zealand could result in only one of two possible outcomes – Maori would slaughter the settlers or vice versa. In hindsight it seems a huge and unnecessary lost opportunity that neither the British Government nor the Missionaries were prepared to meet the New Zealand Company halfway and work together to come up with the best solution to a festering problem that was simply not going to go away.

Under these unfavourable conditions the New Zealand Company was forced to go its own way and on May 12, 1839, their advance ship, the *Tory,* surreptitiously slipped out of Plymouth bound for New Zealand. Through no fault of its own the New Zealand Company set sail with a huge black mark of condemnation against it and this unrelenting animosity would be the official line taken by every British administrator and missionary they would ever encounter. The New Zealand Company was officially *persona non grata* before the *Tory* weighed anchor from Plymouth and this unnecessary antagonism would be the bane of the nascent colony's formative years.

Chapter 1-6

Beware of strangers bearing gifts

In late 1839 a European vessel sailed into the chaos and upheavals arising from Te Rauparaha's conquests.

It was a small ship, a three-masted barque weighing in at 382 tons and a whole 111 feet long – a little less than two cricket-pitches long. With an armament of eight guns and a complement of just 35 crew and passengers it was not likely to be seen as much of a threat to those watching it glide into Queen Charlotte Sound on September 17, 1839.[76] But change comes in many shapes and guises and the arrival of this innocuous vessel would in its own way be as life-changing and ground-wrenching as Te Rauparaha's recent blitzkrieg from the North.

This ship was the *Tory*, Captain Edward Chaffers, and on board was a small party of men representing an English business concern called the New Zealand Company. The New Zealand Company's business was colonisation, essentially the nineteenth century equivalent of package tours to a foreign country except that you don't get to go home at the end of it. In the nineteenth century many millions of people of all classes left Britain for what they hoped would be greener pastures in every corner of

[76] *An Encyclopaedia of New Zealand*, edited A.H. McLintock.

the world – New Zealand, Australia, America, Canada. For those with money it was a chance to make more money. For those without money it was a chance to escape the abundant misery of England, get back on their feet and start a new life.

The leader of this party was a Colonel William Wakefield and amongst his companions were his 19 year old nephew E.J."Jerningham" Wakefield, 29 year old "naturalist"[77] Doctor Ernst Dieffenbach, 19 year old draughtsman and artist Charles Heaphy, a Maori called "Nati"[78] and 22 year old surgeon Dr John Dorset. This tiny group of what today would seem hopelessly young and inexperienced "men" were the advance party of the New Zealand Company and had been given the thankless and, as they would very quickly find out, almost impossible task of preparing the way for the shiploads of future colonists who, optimistic and far away in England, were buying land from the New Zealand Company which that company did not yet possess. If today this seems hopelessly naïve, judged by the standards of the day it represented the height of organisation, and time would see most of these young men rising with gusto to the challenge and well beyond it.

If ever a man was born under a bad sign it would surely be Colonel William Wakefield. It is simultaneously impossible to imagine the magnitude of the task assigned to the luckless Colonel Wakefield and yet so easy, with 20:20 hindsight, to ridicule and hate him. Here is a man who at the age of 24 went to jail for three years for his part in his more famous older brother Edward Gibbon Wakefield's rather bizarre abduction of a young heiress. While in prison William's wife died, leaving him with a baby girl. He lived in the perpetual shadow of his more intellectual and influential brother Edward Gibbon, and while his brother was basking in fame as the shadowy figure who, like Sherlock Holmes's nemesis Professor Moriarty, was never to be seen but left his fingerprints on everything, younger brother William was the mug sent out to the colonies to do the impossible, buy land from the native people and make sure everything was shipshape and Bristol

---

[77] General purpose "scientist" embracing many disciplines.

[78] Sometimes spelt "Nahiti", "Nyati" and other variations.

fashion so that the settlers could alight after their long journey, walk straight into a house on their allotted property and live happily ever after.

The unlucky Colonel Wakefield would subsequently die at the ripe old age of 47, un-thanked and unappreciated until the last, just eight years after the *Tory* arrived in Wellington, during which time he was relentlessly hounded by justifiably unhappy but nonetheless overzealously merciless settlers, pilloried by newspapers and generally demonised from Wellington to London. Somewhat ironically his life was almost exactly paralleled by those of his arch-nemeses, the equally luckless Governors Hobson and Fitzroy of whom we will hear much more later. All three of these men were sent half way across the world by an ignorant Head Office to perform grandiose but literally impossible tasks in impossible circumstances and unsurprisingly all three failed spectacularly. Hobson, never a well man, would die in office a little less than three years into his tenure. Fitzroy, considered by, or at least alluded to by many, as being mentally "unstable", was to be relieved from office less than three years into his tenure and died by his own hand twenty years later.

It is worth reviewing the state of Maoridom around the Cook Strait area when the *Tory* made its way up Queen Charlotte Sound. In 1839 it was twenty years since Te Rauparaha swept south down the coast of Taranaki subjugating everything in his path as far south as at least Bank's Peninsula. It had been a truly remarkable achievement, unequalled in New Zealand history. Unlike Hongi Hika he had not just swept in, indiscriminately slaughtered and returned home loaded with body parts, slaves and plunder. He had swept in, indiscriminately slaughtered, and created his own private, permanent empire.

In Map 1 we showed the state of west coast Maoridom before Te Rauparaha made his way south. Now it is time to look at Map 2 which shows the same area in 1839. Like all maps of its type it is an approximation – it is absurd, for instance, to think the transition from "Abandoned Land" to land under Te Rauparaha's control can be expressed as the nice, crisp line we have shown. The important point to take away from Map 2 is that the chain of numerous independent tribes which existed in 1820 has been obliterated and replaced by just two parts. Part 1, depicted in green, pink and black is the area under Tainui control, the black area of which just happens to be denuded of its former inhabitants who have fled south. Part 2, depicted in orange, is the area under Te Rauparaha's control, which stretches much further south than shown on this map all the way to Bank's Peninsula.

On Te Rauparaha's orange portion we see some small patches of other colours, representing where certain of the fleeing tribes such as Ati Awa, and opportunists such as Ngati Raukawa have ended up. As we have previously observed, these tribes – various hypothetical "Land Lores" notwithstanding – are, when push comes to shove, guests on Te Rauparaha's land. Te Rauparaha's kingdom is unique and absolute. In the historical annals, while we may from time to time hear about other Ngati Toa personalities such as Rangihaeata and Te Pehi, it is generally all about Te Rauparaha, Te Rauparaha and Te Rauparaha. He is the man and he is the tribe. From 1820 to 1839, thanks to his efforts, the entire coastline has been up-ended. None of the newly arrived tribes have any roots in, or links to, this land; they could be anywhere today and tomorrow they might find themselves on their way somewhere else. They were living life day to day and, if someone was stupid enough to offer them trade goods for land that until recently was someone else's, then bring it on. This, then, was the situation that Colonel Wakefield and his intrepid handful of associates sailed into in September 1839.

Over the next few months the good Colonel and his merry crew purchased great chunks of land on both North and South islands around the Cook Strait area. The process of how this was achieved is described, usually venomously, in a great many books[79] and since much of this is irrelevant to our subject we will largely skirt around it. But there are a few aspects which are not only of passing interest but demonstrate approaches to history that will be useful in the analysis of not just this book but any history book.

---

[79] Eye-witness accounts are given in *Adventure in New Zealand*, E.J. Wakefield; *Travels in New Zealand*, Ernst Dieffenbach; the New Zealand Company records. For secondary sources see for instance *A Sort of Conscience*, Philip Temple; *Fatal Success*, Patricia Burns.

We will not pretend that the Wakefield land purchases were "perfect" as judged by modern standards. Nor, with the best will in the world, could they ever have been. This was uncharted territory for both buyer and seller with both parties looking out for number one, making it up as they went along. As one historian has put it the process was "the epitome of the struggle between an importunate Pakeha and importunate Maori".[80] There are no "innocents" here, just wheeler-dealers on all sides, each with their own self-serving defences in retrospect. Given the manner in which the sellers acquired "their" land – by wholesale invasion as we have described – it is a little churlish to complain about the real or perceived faults of the buyers.

It is difficult to know what William Wakefield was supposed to have done in his position other than precisely what he did.

He arrived equipped with a Maori interpreter, in the form of a Maori called *Nati*, surely quite an achievement given the scarcity of Maori in England at that time. If in practice this "asset" would subsequently prove to be of dubious or zero value that was hardly Wakefield's fault. In addition to *Nati,* the *Tory* also brought a Robert Doddrey "who had been trading on the Coast of New Zealand as storekeeper and additional interpreter".[81] You could not accuse the New Zealand Company of not having tried.

Moreover, and very sensibly, the first thing William Wakefield did on arrival was to find someone who had local knowledge and preferably with influence when it came to buying land. As fate would have it, he found this person in the rotund form of our previously introduced friend Dicky Barrett. Given Barrett's influence with, and marriage into, the Ati Awa tribe who just happened to "own" most of the land around Cook Strait this was an extraordinary stroke of luck and a major coup for the Wakefield party. Surely, on paper at least, there could be no better person to understand the history of the Ati Awa tribe, its tangled recent migrations,

---

[80] *A Sort of Conscience,* Philip Temple, p254. While Temple is speaking here of a specific land transaction it applies equally to them all.

[81] *Early History of New Zealand*, Sherrin and Wallace, p475.

its specific land claims and, you would think, a superior knowledge of the fabled intricacies of the Maori land tenure system. Barrett was a man so highly thought of by Ati Awa that they would later insist that he and his family were granted a portion of the land they sold. If Dicky Barrett would later be mocked by the young whipper-snapper George Clarke Junior for his intellectual simplicity and rudimentary pidgin-English "interpreting" that is irrelevant in the light of his obvious ability to make himself "understood" in the Maori world.

Wakefield arrived equipped with what must surely be one of the most exhaustive, not to mention exhausting, set of instructions ever written – a 5,800 word *magnum opus* from his New Zealand Company masters. Perhaps surprisingly, given the Company's modern villainous reputation, these instructions do not include advice on how to rip off the native inhabitants but instead very much espouse the humanitarian sentiment of the time:

> "We recommend that you should, on every occasion, treat them [Maori] with the most entire frankness, thoroughly explaining to them that you wish to purchase the land, for the purpose of establishing a settlement of Englishmen there, similar to the numerous English settlements on the rivers Thames and Hokianga, and in the Bay of Islands ; or rather on a much larger scale, like the English settlements in New South Wales and Van Diemen's Land, with which the natives of Cook's Strait are very well acquainted. And you will abstain from completing any negotiation for a purchase of land, until this, its probable result, shall be thoroughly understood by the native proprietors, and by the tribe at large. Above all, you will be especially careful, that all the owners of any tract of land which you may purchase, shall be approving parties to the bargain, and that each of them receives his due share of the purchase-money. You will find many of the inhabitants of Cook's Strait, who have visited the Thames and the Bay of Islands, well acquainted with the nature of the exchanges for land which have taken place in those districts, between native owners of land and Englishmen of various classes..."

"The intended reserves of land are regarded as far more important to the natives than anything which you will have to pay in the shape of purchase-money. At the same time we are desirous that the purchase-money should be less inadequate, according to English notions of the value of land, than has been generally the case in purchases of territory from the New Zealanders. Some of the finest tracts of land, we are assured, have been obtained by missionary catechists and others, who really possessed nothing, or next to nothing. In case land should be offered to you for such mere trifles, as a few blankets or hatchets, which have heretofore been given for considerable tracts, you will not accept the offer without adding to the goods required, such a quantity as may be of real service to all the owners of the land. It is not intended that you should set an example of heedless profusion in this respect; but the Company are desirous, that in all their transactions with the natives the latter should derive some immediate and obvious benefit by the intercourse."

"You are aware that numerous vessels resort to New Zealand on their way to England, and that there is constant communication between the islands and the neighbouring colonies of New South Wales and Van Diemen's Land. You will therefore have great facilities for communicating with the Company. We expect to hear from you by every possible opportunity, and to receive frequent reports from the scientific gentlemen. It is indeed expedient that all the journals should be written in triplicate, and that two copies should be forwarded to us by different vessels."

"The tribe from which some land was purchased in 1826, on the Hokianga river by a London Company, (which dispatched an expedition under the sanction of Government, similar to that which you will command,) sent a message to the Directors of the Company to the effect, that unless they took actual possession of the land which they had purchased, it would be resumed by its native owners. The object of the natives is to attract English settlers, by means of whose capital they may obtain goods in exchange for their labour and the natural productions of the country. We, therefore,

> think it desirable that, whenever you can do so without much inconvenience, you should leave some one or more persons in possession of any very eligible tract you may have purchased." [82]

These passages clearly convey the degree of interaction between Maori and Europeans at that time – ships were continually coming and going, Maori themselves were travelling to and from Australia, and the values, concepts and processing of land transactions were evidently well understood, from direct experience of land sales in the North and by osmosis from there to the South.

The cited example of the northern New Zealand tribe who sold land in 1826 is of particular interest. Here is a Maori land seller with the integrity, initiative and understanding to communicate directly with the Company saying that despite the land not being occupied within fourteen years of purchase they still consider the Company to be its owners. Clearly, as early as 1826 this tribe understood that the land they sold was gone for good, a sale in perpetuity for the exclusive use of the buyer, giving the lie to the theory sometimes argued by modern historians that Maori of that era considered "selling" land not as permanent alienation but merely as permission to use it. Neither have these vendors invoked the Maori land lore of *ahi ka* discussed previously, which requires constant land use for retention of ownership – they have waited a whole fourteen years before going to what surely must have been considerable trouble to explain the situation to the buyer half a world away. Their understanding of the agreement, and their efforts to honour it, does them great credit.

It is a reminder that however early land purchases may be perceived in modern times, in most parts of New Zealand they generally proceeded in an orderly fashion, without rancour and with honour. The level of difficulty and violence associated with the land purchases which are the subject of this book are atypical and largely limited to the displaced Taranaki tribes. In the study of history we need to constantly remind ourselves that it is generally a study of exceptions, a study of the one

---

[82] See for instance, BPP (British Parliamentary Papers), 8th April 1840, pp22-27.

thing that went "wrong" to the exclusion of the hundreds - if not thousands – that went "right". History is a pessimist's dream.

Some further advice in Wakefield's instructions proved less reliable:

> "We have reason to believe, that you may rely on the good faith of the natives, in any transactions for the purchase of land."

In this respect William Wakefield was to be disappointed, as we shall see.

No doubt portions of Wakefield's instructions can in hindsight be considered as naïve and/or ridiculous. None the less, they had been written based on hard-earned and practical knowledge gleaned over a fourteen year period by the various precursors of the New Zealand Company[83]. The New Zealand Company were not Johnny-come-latelies with big dreams. If their knowledge was imperfect – and how could it not be given the communication issues of the time – it was very much better than most.

In addition to his written instructions we can probably assume that Wakefield would have been rigorously briefed on what was known in England regarding the system of Maori land tenure. But given that this byzantine subject was barely understood by any European at the time, and was still being debated and unravelled over a century later, we can hardly blame him for walking into a minefield. Chances are high that, if we were to ask a hundred Maori of the time who "owned" what land, you would get (at least) a hundred different answers.

Over the next five months the Wakefield party negotiated with various groups of Maori for major land purchases on behalf of the New Zealand Company:

---

[83] The first colonising expedition was the abortive mission of the 1825 incarnation of the New Zealand Company, which left England in August 1825 in the *Rosanna* (Captain Herd) and the *Lambton* (Captain Barnett). It was this expedition which made the land purchase at Hokianga referred to in William Wakefield's instructions.

- The Wellington Deed (27 September, 1839)
- The Kapiti Deed (25 October, 1839)
- The Queen Charlotte Sound Deed (8 November, 1839)
- The Taranaki Deeds (two of, 15 February, 1840)

We now know – as Wakefield did not – that New Zealand comprises about 65 million acres. Although there is abundant evidence to prove otherwise, some of which is presented in this book, the received and accepted wisdom is that Maori revered this land with a spiritual passion unmatched by any culture before or since. It is also constantly stated that Maori knew, named and marked every square centimetre of the land, and that may well be so.

Be that as it may, in 1839, to European eyes, the very great majority of this 65 million acres of land was rubbish – literally unusable, waste land, of no use to anyone, Maori or European. The lion's share of it was covered with mountains, unusable hill ranges, swamps and impenetrable vegetation. Thus when Wakefield bought this land he did so on the basis of buying a job-lot, sight unseen, like a man buying the contents of a deceased estate, or a storage unit whose users have defaulted on the rent. Like the man standing in front of a storage unit bidding for its contents he may be able to glimpse a few things he can recognise and put a value against but most of it is unknown. It is a gamble, an act of faith.

Thus when Wakefield buys land – or thinks he is buying land – he is buying a pig in a poke. He must therefore buy in bulk and hope against hope that there is something of value, a hidden gem somewhere among the mountains of dross.

It does not help that he has been given a bum steer by his masters – his instructions are to buy land around Cook Strait. Of all the places to acquire land in New Zealand this area is in fact among the worst. The land south of Cook Strait is a maze of water channels and almost totally useless. Among its hundreds of thousands of acres of theoretical land the future Nelson settlers will find to their horror that there is virtually none that is of any use. The future Wellington may have been one of the very few substantial and useful harbours in the entire set of islands but as far as usable land goes it too is virtually useless – the first settlers of Wellington will be flooded out of the first choice of town site and will be looking for additional land elsewhere as soon as they first step off the boat. The future New Plymouth settlement is selected from a very short list of a very bad lot, founded on the merest scrap of usable land in Taranaki, and it is harbourless to boot. Like the Wellington settlers they will be looking for additional usable land as soon as they step off the boat. All of the actual usable land in the Cook Strait area is in small, isolated patches with no communication other than by boat.

If that was not bad enough, the recent tribal upheavals in this particular area mean that both the places that have been abandoned by Maori, and the places they have subsequently settled, are distinguished by probably the most complicated, tenuous and disputed ownership claims in the country. And to cap it all off these various claimants are scattered far and wide from Taranaki to Queen Charlotte Sound and have multiple, disputed real and opportunistic claims in multiple places.

In modern times, once again with the infinite wisdom of hindsight, we may either revile Wakefield for his stupidity in thinking he could unravel the unravelable, and/or accuse him of moral bankruptcy in not immediately setting the *Tory* on a course back to England to stand, cap in hand, before his masters proclaiming either the impossibility or the ethical wrongs of trying to barter with a group of people with whom it is impossible to barter. But the point is moot – whatever Wakefield did or did not do there were queues of other potential buyers lining up to buy land if he failed. Indeed, on paper at least, a good proportion of New Zealand had *already* been "bought" multiple times by Australian speculators. In 1839 it was not a matter of *if* New Zealand would be colonised, of *if* land would be purchased, but *who would do it.*

Mountains of paper have been generated on the subject of these transactions so we will only skim over the areas that bear on our ultimate subject – the land ownership of Taranaki. We will however spend a little time discussing the Wellington purchase, first because it enables us to draw further conclusions about the nature of land law in those times, and second because it is an almost precise dress-rehearsal of the "Wiremu and

Teira" scenario that will unleash the New Zealand Wars twenty years in the future and which we shall discuss in detail in a later section.

First let us make some observations about the Maori situation in *Whanganui a Tara* – the Maori name for what would become Wellington Harbour – at the time of Wakefield's arrival. The *Tory's* naturalist, Ernst Dieffenbach remarked:

> "All my companions were Europeans, as I could not obtain the services of any natives. This, however, was of no consequence, as they [the "natives"] knew the valley as little as myself, never having penetrated far for fear of the Nga-te-Kahohunu [Ngati Kahungunu] tribe, the former proprietors of the place, and their greatest enemies."[84]
>
> "The natives were awfully afraid of the Wairarapa people [Ngati Kahungunu], against whom they had lately fought, and while we slept with our feet near the fire, they sat crouched, with our guns in their hands, listening to detect any possibly approaching footsteps, for they were on the debateable land of the two tribes.[85]

Clearly these statements confirm what we have already established – that the situation of all of these newly-arrived tribes who floated in on the coat-tails of Te Rauparaha was tenuous at best. They knew little of "their" land other than the few coastal acres on which they were huddled. They were living in daily fear of their lives and might lose "their" land on any given day by the same method they supposedly "acquired it"– by *take raupatu*, or right of conquest – in this case by the Wairarapa tribes.

It is also clear that, far from being innocent of European ways, at least some of the Ati Awa were extremely worldly – they had been to Australia and seen first-hand the disastrous effects that land loss and the influx of Europeans had had on their Australian counterparts, the Australian

---

[84] *Travels in New Zealand – Vol 1*, Ernest Dieffenbach, p70.

[85] *Notes on Port Nicholson and the Natives in 1839*, Charles Heaphy, from *Transactions and Proceedings of the Royal Society of New Zealand*, Vol 12, 1879, p34.

Aboriginal people. There can be no doubt they understood the implications of what they were doing:

> "The natives in Port Nicholson belong to the large nation of the Nga-te-awa (river people), and are about 1500 in number. They are subdivided into several smaller tribes, living in the different coves of the harbour. The present natives are not the ancient inhabitants of the place, but seized it from a tribe called the Nga-te-Kahohunu [Ngati Kahungunu], after they had themselves been driven from their ancient homes at the foot of Mount Egmont. They received us at our arrival with every mark of friendship, listened to and discussed the subject of our coming among them with great discretion and good judgment, and agreed at last to sell the land; not, however, without a lively opposition having been offered by a chief, Puakawa (Bitter Sowthistle), who, with simple and solemn eloquence, warned his people of the cupidity of Europeans, pointed to the fate of the Tasmanians and Australians, and pictured a similar fate as awaiting his own people: the Europeans promised brotherhood to them, he said, but they were men who spoke with the lips only (tangata ngutu kau). This chief, however, was outvoted; partly through the impression which our trade had made on the rest, - partly, I believe, by a higher motive, the desire of acquiring civilization, protection, and instruction from a European colony. Poor Puakawa!"[86]

We hear a lot about the skulduggery of the wicked Wakefields but we hear little about the lack of scruples and dubious dealings of the Maori participants in these land transactions. Here are some observations regarding the actions our old friends Te Wharepouri and Te Puni, the two main Maori representatives who negotiated with the Wakefields for the Wellington sale – which included land which belonged not to them but to the Taranaki hapu Ngati Tupaia and Ngati Haumia, who were understandably less than pleased:

---

[86] *Travels in New Zealand - Vol 1*, Ernest Dieffenbach, pp91-92.

> "Shortland had been following the action and knew that the [Taranaki hapu] chiefs at Te Aro insisted the land belonged to them and not to [Ati Awa chiefs] Te Wharepouri and Te Puni and the other chiefs who had negotiated with the company. When this latest unrest erupted, Shortland confronted Te Wharepouri and Te Puni with this. They confessed they had no right [to sell the Taranaki hapu land], then Te Puni said, "But how could I help it, when I saw so many muskets and blankets before me?!""[87]

This surely calls for another Maori Land Lore – or more accurately a "Universal Law" – which is:

> **Land Lore 4** – Like everything in life, in all cultures, all transactions, of land or of anything, are subject to the usual foibles of human nature, which regrettably includes dishonesty and greed.

But if Wharepouri could on this occasion be accused of dishonesty then he at least somewhat redeemed himself by the display of honesty and honour he showed when in due course he found his former dwelling place inundated with European settlers. Historian Ann Parsonson tells us:

> "Te Wharepouri, however, was not expecting many pakeha. After he watched the first settlers crowd on to his beach, he went sadly to tell Wakefield that he thought he would return to Taranaki.
>
> > "I know that we sold you the land, and that no more White people have come to take it than you told me. But I thought you were telling lies, and that you had not so many followers. I thought you would have nine or ten, or perhaps as many as there are at Te-awa-iti. I thought that I could get one placed at each, as a White man to barter with the people and keep us well supplied with arms and clothing; and that I should be able to keep these White men under my hand and regulate

[87] *The Interpreter*, Angela Caughey, p162.
Te Puni's quote is from BPP, Vol2, 1844, Appendix 2.

their trade myself. But I see that each ship holds two hundred, and I believe, now, that you have more coming. They are all well armed and they are strong of heart, for they have begun to build their houses without talking. They will be too strong for us"

Te Wharepouri had thought Wakefield a braggart."[88]

One might logically think that if ever there was a clear, definitive statement that Wharepouri regarded the sale of Wellington as a permanent alienation of land, this would be it. To his eternal credit he disputes absolutely nothing about the sale. He does not demand more payment. He does not renege on any part of the deal. He admits his land is gone and he is off to Taranaki. He agrees that Wakefield has been scrupulously honest in warning him of the numbers of settlers, and therefore of the possible potential outcomes of his entering into the sale. He admits he has made a mistake and more importantly he takes responsibility for his own actions. Good on him.

After the Wellington Purchase the *Tory* sailed via Port Underwood to arrive at Kapiti to meet with Te Rauparaha to purchase any Ngati Toa claims to land on both sides of Cook Strait. After much wrangling a deed was signed and the purchase goods distributed. Somewhat predictably the intent and extent of this deed would later be disputed and lead in 1843 to the so called "Wairau Affray".

Having, as they thought, bought out the Ngati Toa interests in the various land purchases the Wakefield travelling land purchasing extravaganza now headed south to purchase the Ati Awa land claims to not only the recently conquered lands around Cook Straight but also the Ati Awa ancestral land of Taranaki itself. This was always going to be a tall order because, as we have seen, the Ati Awa tribe was now split up and scattered into four groups spread from Taranaki itself to Queen Charlotte Sound.

---

[88] *He whenua te utu (The Payment will be land),* Ann Parsonson, p197 (Parsonson is quoting *Adventure in New Zealand – Vol 1,* E. Jerningham Wakefield, p202).

Wakefield was already on good terms with the Ati Awa group in Wellington, having recently completed the purchase of the Wellington area from them. His immediate mission was therefore to cross two more of the Ati Awa factions off his list – the two sub-factions of Ati Awa Group 1 – both those who had settled at Waikanae and those who had settled in Queen Charlotte Sound.

To this end the *Tory* made the short crossing from Kapiti to Waikanae, picked up some Waikanae Ati Awa chiefs who had been authorised to sign on behalf of that faction, and headed south to Queen Charlotte Sound to purchase the land claims of these two Ati Awa factions with a single deed. This "Queen Charlotte Sound Deed" was the first to include purchasing of the Taranaki area itself and is thus especially relevant to our story. Various aspects of this deed and its signing will appear over the next few chapters but for now we will only discuss the single, vital aspect of the Deed's validity.

We have already quoted acclaimed historian Ann Parsonson as acknowledging Wharepuni's complete understanding of the consequences of signing the Wellington Deed. Therefore it comes as somewhat of a surprise to note her view of the Queen Charlotte Sound Deed signing, of which she remarks:

> "It may therefore be said with complete certainty that at the time they signed the deeds, neither Ngati Toa nor Ati Awa had the least notion that the result of their action would be to transfer to the pakeha overriding and exclusive rights to their lands."[89]
>
> "As Colonel William Wakefield, the company's chief agent, toured their settlements, they put their names to three deeds, which, on the face of it, transferred to the company all the lands they had held in generations past, or had settled in recent years in both islands. Te Rangitake (sent by the elder Waikanae chiefs to escort Wakefield to Queen Charlotte Sound) put his mark on the deed drawn up there

---

[89] *He whenua te utu (The Payment will be land),* Ann Parsonson, p197. In this case Parsonson is speaking of the Queen Charlotte Sound negotiations.

> on 8 November 1839. Clearly it never occurred to him or to the other chiefs that these pieces of paper might make them guests on their own lands, for such written transactions, involving vast tracts, were quite outside their experience."[90]

Such anomalies surely cannot pass without discussion, for two reasons. First they pass judgement on the validity of the Taranaki purchases which are pivotal to our story and it would be remiss to ignore the opinion of someone as justifiably esteemed as Parsonson. Second, in a more generic sense they demonstrate what seems to be the almost obligatory modern paradigm which sees New Zealand history as a narrative of heroes and villains. For these reasons we are obliged to take a short detour to examine these points.

Parsonson offers no evidence to support her "complete certainty" regarding the supposed unintelligibility of the Queen Charlotte Deed. But an evidence-based enquiry on the subject would conclude the precise opposite – that it can be said with "complete certainty" that signatories of all deeds knew *exactly* what they were doing. The evidence is everywhere – you cannot move without tripping over it.

If we were talking of a land purchase in 1815 such claims might have a microscopic grain of validity. But by 1839 Maori in general had been dealing with European for at least 20 years and the Ati Awa tribe in particular had had European traders living in their midst – in the form of Dicky Barrett and Jackie Love – for 12 years – since 1827. Parsonson herself has conveniently provided us with evidence demonstrating Wharepouri's complete understanding of what he was doing in signing the Wellington deed.

Wharepouri subsequently went in person to Waikanae to explain to the Ati Awa chiefs there what the negotiations were all about – although unless they had been deaf, dumb and blind for the last twenty years the Waikanae chiefs would have been thoroughly familiar with the concept of

---

[90] Biography of Wiremu Kingi, *Dictionary of New Zealand Biography*, Ann Parsonson, p499.

land sales anyway. As we have seen with Puakawa, some Maori had seen the consequence of European colonisation first-hand through their visits to Sydney and beyond – indeed, around the same time that Wakefield was making his purchases Ngai Tahu chiefs independently sailed to Sydney and negotiated the sale of their ancestral lands.[91] In 1839 it was 19 years since Hongi visited London and 16 years since Ngati Toa chief Pehi Kupe did the same. The *Tory's* passenger and intended Maori interpreter, Nati, had just arrived fresh from spending two years living with Edward Gibbon Wakefield. We could go on and on. In 1839 both dealing with Europeans and selling land was old hat.

Every documented Maori/European transaction since 1814, whether for a pig, a basket of potatoes or a million acres of land, shows Maori to be masters of negotiation and of the principles of supply and demand. Negotiation and deal making was just another day at the office, either Maori to Maori or Maori to European. The all-pervasive system of *utu* meant that everyone in the Maori world was constantly weighing up mental ledgers of balance and making quite sure they were always on the winning side of it – and like everyone else in the world from time immemorial Maori made *good* deals otherwise they would not have made them at all.[92]

In this context Parsonson's suggestion that it is acceptable to receive payment and then claim ignorance and shock that something is required in return seems like retrospective wishful thinking to support a narrative. And it would have been abundantly clear, as it was in Wharepouri's case in Wellington, that that "something" was land – what else was there to bargain for?

---

[91] While this and other sales of its ilk were subsequently overturned they never the less demonstrate the agency, initiative and willingness of Maori to sell land, their understanding of what such transactions meant and the low transactional value Maori placed on land according to their own values.

[92] Logically it is axiomatic that no-one in the history of mankind has *ever* made a bad deal – no-one gets up in the morning thinking – "today I think I will make a bad deal".

William Wakefield says of the Queen Charlotte Sound transaction:

> "2nd November – The natives here, some of the ancient possessors of Taranaki, are very desirous that I should become the purchaser of that district, in order that they may return to their native place without fear of the Waikato tribes."[93]

This tells us that the Maori sellers understood the two interconnected aspects of the deal – first that they were selling land and second that they would be awarded reserves – for how could they "return home" (to Taranaki) unless they were granted reserves, and why would they need reserves if they had not sold the remainder of the land?

The signatories of every deed craved Wakefield's goods and *theoretically* they had the land to trade for it. This theoretical land in Taranaki however had one enormous catch to it – it could not be occupied because it was still under the *mana* of the Waikatos. This theoretical land was in practice worthless until someone – the Europeans – made it safe to return to. For Maori the sale of Taranaki was a spectacular and never to be repeated deal and one which anyone in the same position would jump though flaming hoops to sign. It is a no-brainer – what would you rather do – get all the land you need[94] back *and* a pile of coveted European goods, or not get any of your land back and lose out on those coveted goods? You would have to be crazy not to sign.

Similarly Parsonson's claims about "written transactions" are untenable and/or irrelevant. Maori had been making transactions without paper for millennia – they did not need "pieces of paper" or signing processes to know what was right and wrong or to make eternally binding agreements.

---

[93] AJHR, 1859, E2, p2. While some may automatically object to quoting Wakefield as the presumed villain of the piece that is not history. In law both the prosecution and defence have their day in court and there is no reason to presume Wakefield is anything less than honest in his statement.

[94] This is what the reserves were for.

They signed pieces of paper not for *their own* benefit but because they knew that signing was important to the Europeans.

After this philosophical diversion let us return to the Wakefield party in its land buying spree.

With the signing of the Queen Charlotte Sound Deed the New Zealand Company had now negotiated with three of the four Ati Awa groups, who had either signed deeds transferring their claims to land ownership or at least come to an agreement in principle. It was a work in progress – there were still some loose ends to sort out but things were looking promising. There was now just one Ati Awa faction left to negotiate with and in theory they should be the easiest. In Jerningham Wakefield's words:

> "...We had now obtained the rights and claims of a large proportion of the owners of land on both sides of Cook's Strait.
>
> The Kawia claimants by conquest [Ngati Toa/Te Rauparaha][95], and the Ngatiawa or actual occupants[96], had both been satisfactorily dealt with in a general way. It remained to satisfy the tribes resident along the sea-coast of the northern shore, between Waikanae and the Sugar-loaf Islands. Colonel Wakefield left it to future times to deal with the Ngatiawa of Waikanae, many of whose chiefs had been concerned in this last affair, and who had seemed moreover well inclined to join in the transaction on the occasion of Colonel Wakefield's recent visit to them. He also postponed to a less disturbed season the idea of dealing with the Ngatiraukawa. And he resolved next to proceed to Taranaki, in order to satisfy the now scanty occupiers of that extensive and

---

[95] In other words, the Kapiti Deed had bought out the "*mana*" of the Ngati Toa, who, while not themselves residing on the conquered land, were never-the-less owed compensation for making occupation by others possible.

[96] In other words, the Queen Charlotte Sound Deed had bought out the Ati Awa "ownership" rights of the Cook Strait lands, which although conquered by Ngati Toa, now belonged to Ati Awa by virtue of three-plus years of occupation. This same deed also bought out the rights of these two factions to the Taranaki ancestral land.

> fertile region, by the mediation of Barrett and the ambassadors from Port Nicholson.[97]

Whatever we may say in the present about the New Zealand Company no one can say that they did not understand precisely what they needed to do to make an honest and indisputable purchase. They went to extreme efforts to do the right thing, chasing down every last handful of possible claimants. If it would all later go horribly wrong it was certainly not for want of trying.

---

97 *Adventure in New Zealand – Vol 1*, E. Jerningham Wakefield, p137.

Chapter 1-7

The buying of Taranaki - Take 1

On 11 November, 1839, the *Tory* quit the area of Cook's Strait and headed north along the west coast of the lower North Island to arrive off the Ngamotu Islands, with the intent of negotiating with the handful of Group 3 "Diehards" and buying out their rights to the Ati Awa ancestral land. Again we can do no better than to quote Jerningham Wakefield verbatim:

> "We at length anchored to the north of the middle Sugar-loaf Island, on the morning of the 27th [November 1839], in eight fathoms. A long swell from S. W. made us roll very heavily.
>
> A volcanic peak at Sugar-loaf Point shoots up to the height of 500 feet. Two islands lie at the distances of one and two miles respectively to the westward; and several islets and extensive reefs are scattered about on the southern side of the point. Barrett went off in a whale-boat, accompanied by E Ware and Tuarau, the two young deputies from Port Nicholson;[98] but he found the surf too heavy for landing. They succeeded in making themselves known to

[98] "E Ware" (Te Whare) was the eldest son of prominent Ati Awa chief Te Puni who together with Wharepouri was central to the sale of Wellington to The New Zealand Company. Tuarua is described by Jerningham Wakefield as "a nephew of former head chief of the Ngati Awa tribes" (*Adventure in New Zealand – Vol 1*, E. Jerningham Wakefield, p99)

some natives on the beach, two of whom swam off through the surf, and came on board the Tory.

An interesting scene now took place: Maori custom had prevented any communication in the boat; and even for some time after they had got on board, all four sat weeping on the deck, with their heads buried in their mats.

One of the two strangers at length rose, and after the ceremony of rubbing noses had been performed by all, he related in a recitative dirge, beautifully affecting in its tone and expression, the hardships and dangers which had been endured by those on shore since the retreat of the main body of their relations [the Group 2 "Refugees" who migrated south in 1832]. Their numbers, he said, had been woefully diminished by the predatory incursions of the Waikato war-parties. They had repeatedly been besieged in their strongholds on the peak or the islands; and, unable to trust themselves so far from places of refuge as to cultivate to any extent, had lived in a great measure on fish and fern-root. "But," he said, "though we muster now no more than threescore, we have determined to remain on our dear native land, and to struggle on through fear and hunger. We are glad to see our brothers from Port Nicholson, and our old White friend [Dickey Barrett]."

Tuarau answered them in an encouraging strain; telling them how he had brought White men to pay them for their land, and to protect them from their enemies; and how a like protection had been needed and secured by his fathers in the south. He drew a short sketch of our progress and intentions, and then delivered the advice of Epuni and Warepori, that they should sell Taranaki to their good pakeha, or White man.

The next morning we landed Barrett and his train, including Tuarau. It was declared impossible to collect the different chiefs connected with the district of Taranaki in less than a week, as some of them resided far off. Colonel Wakefield, therefore, determined to leave Barrett here to prepare the natives for the sale, and to proceed himself at once to Hokianga and Kaipara, two harbours in the north

> of the island, where he had to discover and take possession of certain districts which had been acquired by the Company from former purchasers before we left England. Dr. Dieffenbach was also persuaded by my uncle to land here, and seize the opportunity of examining Mount Egmont and the surrounding country, so highly interesting to the geologist, and of which so little was yet known from authentic sources. The surf was still exceedingly high on the beach; but the whale-boats landed Dicky and all his goods and chattels, animate and inanimate, by an early hour in the afternoon, and we weighed anchor and stood to the northward, before a fine fresh breeze."[99]

Thus on November 29th 1839 both William and Jerningham Wakefield, along with Dr Dorset, Charles Heaphy and Doddrey the storekeeper, set off in the *Tory* on what they imagined would be a quick jaunt north to sort out some minor company affairs in Hokianga and Kaipara, leaving Dicky Barrett and Dieffenbach at Nga Motu to gather the relevant chiefs with whom to negotiate for the purchase of Taranaki.

This well-conceived plan went horribly wrong when the *Tory* was badly damaged after running aground on its entry into Kaipara on December 19th. The trials and tribulations resulting from this were many and varied but need not concern us. Eventually, after about a month stranded at Kaipara, the majority of the Wakefield party made their way back to Taranaki, not in the *Tory*, which was still under repair at Kaipara, but in the *Guide*, a 150 ton Whaler "swarming with cockroaches" and manned by a particularly motley crew. Unbeknownst to the travellers, they arrived at Taranaki two days after a Captain Hobson arrived in the Bay of Islands and five days before a famous Treaty gained its first signatures at Waitangi.

> "We at length managed to come in sight of the Sugar-loaf Islands on the 1st of February, and anchored to the north of the inner one, Moturoa, or "High Island," in the afternoon. Barrett came off from the island and piloted her to the anchorage. The Acquilla cutter came in

---

[99] *Adventure in New Zealand – Vol 1*, E. Jerningham Wakefield, pp146-148.

> from the southward and anchored about the same time. Mr. White was on board; and Barrett told us that he had been here once before, since he left Kaipara, trying to buy the Taranaki district, but had been foiled by Dicky's superior influence... Mr. White had, on his former visit, asserted his claim to the district; as founded on his purchase of the rights of a large number of inhabitants of Taranaki, originally made captive by the Waikato tribe, but now freed at Hokianga, Kaipara, and other places since their masters had embraced the Christian religion".[100]

The "Mr White" referred to here was the veteran Wesleyan missionary William White, who having arriving in New Zealand in 1823 quickly managed to alienate and antagonise most of his fellow missionaries and was finally dismissed from missionary service in 1836 for his trading activities and predilection for Maori women. For all his flaws White was a formidable personality, always with an eye for the main chance and who in 1840 was still wearing his missionary garb and leveraging his prior missionary influence to wheel and deal his way to prosperity. His threatened purchase of Taranaki was just another in a long line of entrepreneurial bluffs.

It is apparent that even though the Waikato tribes had not occupied Taranaki in the eight years since they drove off its original inhabitants Taranaki was still very much under their control or "*mana*":

> "...Barrett now related to us all that had occurred since we left him here. In the first place, constant rumours had been brought down the coast of fresh invasions projected from Waikato. In readiness for these, he had removed all his family and goods to the island, and the natives had stored it with firewood and potatoes."[101]

It is also evident that as early as January, 1840, former slaves released by their Waikato masters were returning to their homelands, which in this

---

[100] *Adventure in New Zealand – Vol 1*, E. Jerningham Wakefield, p167.

[101] *Ibid*, pp167-8.

case appear to be somewhere south of Ati Awa territory, perhaps members of the Taranaki and Ngati Ruanui tribes:

> "Numerous parties of released slaves had passed along from the northward to their native places further south, spreading all the missionary doctrines; and never omitting to preach the uncharitable one of calling all White men rewera, or "devils," who were not missionaries, or to warn the natives against selling their lands to us, who would, they said, drive them away to the mountains.[102] A variation of this calumny was that we were Pikapo, (the Maori corruption of episcopoi, or Roman Catholics,) and would therefore infallibly cut their throats or drive them away. Some white missionaries, and also some lay white traders from Kawia and other places to the north, had on more than one occasion headed these agitating parties; and had distinguished themselves by vehement support of these statements and determined attempts to obtain the land for themselves."[103]

It seems that in their absence the status of the returning Ati Awa Group 4 "Slaves" had become greatly elevated thanks to the new social order demanded by the doctrine of Christianity. This new status was, however, not necessarily recognised by their tribal kin who insisted these former slaves had "lost caste by servitude".

Negotiations with the Group 3 Ati Awa, the Diehards who had remained at Ngamotu, confirmed that they did not in fact perceive themselves as "fire burners", on the contrary they distinctly dissociated themselves from both the returning Group 4 slaves and the bulk of the tribe (Ati Awa Group 2) who "took refuge" and fled south via migration:

---

[102] Further evidence of Maori understanding of what selling land and signing deeds meant.

[103] *Adventure in New Zealand – Vol 1*, E. Jerningham Wakefield, p168.

"The natives residing at Nga Motu, or "the Islands", as the land abreast of them is called, refused to acknowledge this claim [of the Group 4 Slaves]; saying very truly, that they [the Group 3 Diehards] who had never lost caste by servitude, or taken refuge in a distant land from the persecutions of their enemies, like the slaves to the north or their relations in Cook's Strait, had the best right to sell the district. They had also declined Mr. White's offers to buy their claims; stating that they had promised to sell it according to E Tiki or Dicky's recommendation, and that they meant to keep their word."

In short, Barrett's influence and perseverance had effectually conquered numerous efforts made to outbid us in this purchase. Too great praise could not be given to him for the zeal which he had shown in supporting our interests, or his disinterestedness in refusing the offers of some of these parties, even though we had much exceeded the time we had named for our return, and the natives were becoming daily more impatient for the conclusion of the bargain.

The next morning a native brought off from the main, where Mr. White had landed, letters to Barrett and to Colonel Wakefield. The latter was opened by Dr. Dorset, as acting agent. They both contained a statement from the worthy ex-missionary [White], that "he had bought the land bounded by the Wanganui and Mokau rivers, and a line between their sources, from the Waikato and Ngatimaniapoto tribes; and that if we persisted in buying this district from the resident natives, those former conquerors had determined to recommence hostilities, or to claim the protection of the British Government in securing their rights.""[104]

Given that these letters from White arrived on what seems like 2 February 1840, just five days after Hobson's arrival in the Bay of Islands, White's invoking of the "protection of the British Government" is a demonstration not only of how fast news travelled but of how the ramifications of

---

[104] *Ibid*, pp168-9.

Hobson's arrival had been instantaneously understood by Maori and used to their advantage:

> "The natives [Group 3 Diehards] were very angry on hearing the contents of these letters, and we had some trouble in preventing them from going to break up the boat in which Mr. White had landed. As we landed, he retired from the beach, where he had been preaching and praying with some of them, to a less conspicuous situation. A Waikato chief, who had come in the cutter with him, reassured us and the resident natives. He said that White had given some tobacco and a few blankets to the Waikato as payment for those whom they lost at Taranaki, which any one buying this land would have to do in accordance with native custom. "But," said he, "we have not sold your land; more than half the Waikato are missionaries now, and these will join with you, as brothers, against any invasion from their heathen countrymen."" [105]

Wakefield notes what many other accounts confirm – that the hostility shown by the Missionaries to their non-missionary European brethren has been duly absorbed by their Maori converts:

> "The conduct of the native teachers [of Christianity] caused great indignation in my mind. I began to believe that this continued opposition to our proceedings really originated from the white missionaries; and being now able to make myself understood pretty well, told the natives my candid opinion of the unchristian tendency of these underhand proceedings. But I took care to tell them that the rangatira, or "chief" missionaries, would come out with the settlers, and behave very differently from those who incited them against us. I also explained to them, that many of these bad missionaries were shoemakers or tailors, who received money from people in England to preach the Gospel to them, but not to make them enemies to white people; and that the clergymen who were to

---

[105] *Adventure in New Zealand – Vol 1*, E. Jerningham Wakefield, pp169-170.

accompany the settlers would preach to them and the white people together in one church."[106]

The problematical Mr White seems by now to have taken the hint and moved on to his next dream and scheme. Barrett and Wakefield's negotiations with the Nga Motu remnant continued into mid-February:

"14th [February 1840] - The natives [Group 3 Diehards] came on board [the *Guide*] to-day, and after some hesitation on account of a desire for more fire-arms, agreed to sign the deed on the morrow.

Feb. 15th. This morning I took the deed, drawn up like the former ones, ashore. Barrett translated it, and explained its provisions. Forty-seven signatures were then appended to it, including the women and the children, whom the chiefs compelled to come and touch the pen, as they would be the future chiefs. Two or three young men, who had acquired the knowledge of writing, signed their names in full. The others made a cross opposite to their names, as had been done on former occasions.

A party of fifty or sixty natives, who had arrived from a settlement further south, now expressed a desire to sell another tract of land adjoining that sold by the Ngamotu chiefs; and a large number of them signed a second deed after a short negotiation. The goods were then landed in whale-boats through the surf.

The Ngamotu natives got quietly through the distribution of their share; but those from the southward, who were extremely wild and uncouth in their manners and appearance, although professing to be strict mihanere, or "missionaries," could not affect it without a scramble. A small stream divided the two parties. As soon as the southern party began to show a disposition to scramble, one of the chiefs of the Ngamotu tribe raised an exciting shout, and cheered his followers on to take advantage of this confusion, in order to partake of the spoil of their neighbours, after they had stowed their own away.

[106] *Ibid*, p173.

They came rushing on along the hundred yards of beach which separated the two parties, flourishing their arms. The readiness with which the others, close to whom I was sitting on a sand-hill, dropped their own disagreements and threw themselves into a defensive attitude, was well worthy of admiration. Along their own side of the little rill, the most stalwart warriors knelt, protruding forward their sharp wooden spears, or grasping the tomahawk firmly, ready to spring upon the assailants. Behind these, others loaded the few guns in their possession, and quietly took up a station, while behind them again the women and children handled a weapon as they bent over some heaps of goods. And all this in perfect silence; the occasional yells of the charging party alone being heard, as they closed rapidly in.

I was so taken up with admiration at the classical attitudes of some of the defenders, who all remained still as statues, gazing stedfastly on the advancing enemy, after they had once taken their position, that I had not thought of getting further from the conflict until the moment of meeting seemed close at hand. The assailants were all seeking the weakest point as they approached; the guns were pointed on both sides; each muscle of the defenders seemed straining with preparation for the shock; and I suddenly thought of my own dangerous position, and flung myself flat on the ground, expecting to hear a volley and the whistling of bullets over my head.

Barrett, however, had tripped up one of the assailants and pinioned another at this critical moment; Worser and the women of his train had also suddenly rushed between the threatening ranks of their relations; and after some squabbling and earnest persuasion of the most refractory, peace was re-established. The Ngamotu seemed to treat the affair as a mere joke; but the others were more than suspicious, and, sullenly packing their goods on the backs of the women and slaves, departed homewards at nightfall, without the usual farewell. A strong party of vigilant warriors closed the rear of the caravan as it crossed the sand-hills inland of Paretutu.

The two purchases extended from a spot half-way between the mouth of the Mokau river and the Sugar-loaf Islands, to a river called Wangatawa, south of Cape Egmont; and inland, to the summit of the mountain, and thence to a spot on the banks of the Wanganui river, high up its course.

Had we been provided with a handier vessel and good crew, we should have proceeded to extend the transaction by treaties at Mokau, and at Patea between Cape Egmont and Wanganui; the chiefs of those places having been prepared for such an arrangement by deputations which had travelled to Ngamotu in order to treat with Barrett during our absence.

We were forced, however, by the inferior sailing-qualities and appointments of the Guide, to renounce these expeditions on a dangerous lee-shore; and turned her head towards Port Nicholson on the evening of the 16th. The whole menagerie from Moturoa was transferred on board; three Mokau chiefs accompanied us, in order to urge upon Colonel Wakefield the purchase of their country; and we bade farewell to our friends at "the Islands", promising that they should soon have pakeha to live amongst them."[107]

The debacle of the scramble for goods, and the intuitive decision of one tribe to plunder the goods of the other, reveal a tribal character that does not bode well for an agreement of any longevity or on which honour can be relied upon.

With this deed signed the New Zealand Company believed it had ticked the final box in disposing of all native interests in what was the Ati Awa traditional territory in Taranaki. And, as an unexpected bonus, it had also purchased land south of that, in what was once the territory of the Taranaki tribe. But if William Wakefield thought this was the end of the story he was very sadly mistaken for the story had in fact only just begun and what lay ahead would be very long and very painful.

[107] *Adventure in New Zealand – Vol 1*, E. Jerningham Wakefield, pp179-182.

Chapter 1-8

Beware of strangers bearing treaties.

On January 29, 1840, four months after the *Tory* carrying the Wakefield party slunk into Queen Charlotte Sound, another ship, the *Herald,* Captain Nias, slunk into the Bay of Islands. And, like the *Tory,* this ship also numbered among its passengers a small group of men who would essentially change New Zealand forever.

The leader of this group was Captain William Hobson and, like William Wakefield, he was a man with a very specific mission. The British Government had been blindsided by the *Tory's* departure and the New Zealand Company's calling of their bluff that it represented. They panicked, and in a classic "taxi, follow that car" moment, but with ships, they went into damage control mode, cobbled together a disparate posse in the form of Hobson and some flotsam and jetsam he picked up at Sydney en-route, to deal to the depredations of the scumbag rapscallion Colonel William Wakefield.

It is important to realise that, contrary to popular contemporary opinion, Hobson's arrival, and Britain's future involvement in New Zealand, had nothing to do with that dreaded word "imperialism". In 1840 Britain needed New Zealand like it needed a hole in the head and, if it had a choice, the British Colonial Office would have rather poked bamboo under its fingernails and eaten ground glass than get involved with the nothingness that was New Zealand at that time. But the British

Government did not have a choice, for there was a bunch of evangelical humanitarians who would tear them limb from limb if they did not do their philanthropic duty, do the decent British thing, and save the "noble savages" from "civilisation".

And Hobson's arrival had nothing to do with advancing the "colonisation" of New Zealand. Britain's panic-stricken and belated official presence was, in fact, quite the opposite – to put in place some *control over* colonisation – from Britain or from anywhere. Arthur Thomson, generally regarded as New Zealand's "first historian", put it this way:

> "[British] Ministers took this step with much regret, and Lord Normanby informed Captain Hobson that her Majesty's government had deferred as long as possible the colonisation of New Zealand, because the approximation of civilised with uncivilised men had hitherto proved destructive to the latter, and the white man's progress in the New World had been over the dead bodies of the aborigines."[108]

Britain's only intention in despatching Hobson was to "do good", where "good" was the state of the art in humanitarianism at that time. Britain had absolutely nothing to gain except yet another problem child to manage whose only possible consequence was pain, heartache and expense. In today's world, where the very thought of trying to help someone of a different culture is seen as being outrageously patronising, Hobson's arrival would be cited as a classic example of "white saviour complex". But as the saying goes "no good deed goes unpunished" and true to form "Britain", and "Europeans" in general, have subsequently been damned to Hell and back for what was intended to be a noble and magnanimous gesture.

But there was a rather large legal fly in the ointment to Hobson's, and Britain's, cunning, philanthropic plan. No country – now or then – can interfere in the business of someone else's country. That was, is, and always will be, a golden rule of international diplomacy. Britain had no legal jurisdiction over British subjects living in what was then a non-

---

[108] *The Story of New Zealand – Vol 2*, Arthur Thomson, p10.

British "country" such as New Zealand – it could neither prohibit British subjects from going there nor have any power to control them once they got there.

There was only one way Britain could prevent, or at least control, the colonisation of New Zealand and that was for New Zealand to become a British "possession". That outcome would in fact be a double whammy, for if New Zealand became a British possession not only could Britain control British subjects already there but it could also control the future influx of people from *anywhere*:

> "...the settlement of Europeans in New Zealand could not be prevented after the year 1838 without a fleet to blockade the coasts, and as this was impossible, it was better to have a British colony formed in the country, than a number of republics similar to that flourishing at the Bay of Islands. The missionary opposition [to this plan] was a pious attempt to work a miracle. Such philanthropy, although honourable to the hearts of men, is discreditable to their judgments; and from similar ill-judged attempts to do good, much evil has often arisen in this world."[109]

For this reason Hobson arrived in the Bay of Islands not just as a Captain in the Royal Navy but as prospective Lieutenant-Governor of a fictitious sovereign nation referred to by Europeans as "New Zealand". The actual inhabitants of this "country" were the Maori people who would have been amazed to know that they were a single nation and that they lived in a thing called a "country" or were a united "nation". For "New Zealand" at the time of Hobson's arrival was not a nation but a patchwork of 300 plus amoeba-like tribes or "principalities" jostling against each other. As we have seen, at any time the relationship between these tribes was one of tension, ranging from simple competition through contempt to outright warfare. Like all good amoebas they swelled and receded, joined together, and split off as required. New Zealand, at that time, was not a country, or a nation, but 300 balls of humanity in the air being juggled.

---

[109] *Ibid*, p7.

This was not Hobson's first time in the Bay of Islands, having visited for a month or so in 1837 in his nominal capacity of naval captain. As a result of his observations at that time he penned a report recommending the establishment of "factories"[110] in New Zealand. It was actually a pretty sound idea, at least at the time of his report, and probably to his utter amazement would ultimately result in his remarkable elevation from one of hundreds of non-descript Royal Navy captains to the exalted position of Lieutenant-Governor of this hypothetical "sovereign nation" of New Zealand. For someone who joined the Navy at the tender age of 11 and after 37 years of hard and unrewarding service had only reached the rank of Captain this surely represented winning the jackpot.[111]

Like Wakefield before him Hobson arrived in New Zealand armed with copious instructions from his master, in this case the "Colonial Office", the British Government departmental body charged with managing Britain's various far-flung international interests. Although these instructions were the output of many people and generated by the processes and machinery of this necessarily bureaucratic office, they are known to posterity as the "Normanby Instructions", named for the then Secretary of State of the Colonies, Lord Normanby.[112]

Perhaps amazingly, despite being a creation of a grinding, bureaucratic machine, "The Normanby Instructions" emerge as a model of their kind.

---

[110] "Factories" in the parlance of that time and in this context were essentially small self-contained trading enclaves recognised by the Government of the country in which they were situated as a specialised, miniature "sovereign state". Such enterprises were ideally on the coast and therefore ideal for the distribution of goods.

[111] In this respect Hobson's career trajectory echoes almost precisely that of a future New Zealand Governor, George Grey, who in 1840 also penned a report airing his views on indigenous colonisation which would result in his rocketing to fame as Governor of South Australia and, ironically, eventually filling Hobson's shoes as Governor of New Zealand.

[112] Otherwise known as Constantine Phipps, First Marquess of Normanby

As well as literal instructions they provide a coherent summary of the reasons for the Hobson mission, and moreover they do so in a humane and highly personal way. Whatever its provenance, no matter how many drafts were written or by whom, the document emerges not as a "memorandum" from a Government Department but as a personal letter from an individual who is clearly fastidiously moralistic, deeply concerned for the plight of the Maori people, highly intelligent and deeply humane, someone who understands the contradictions in what he is requesting and who tempers them with the highly possible reality that what he asks for may not in fact be achievable. The overriding impression is of a man grappling not with British Colonial policy but with a much regretted but necessary evil. While recognising that the expression "Hobson's Choice" is not derived from William Hobson, it is perhaps ironic that Lord Normanby's instructions are, none the less, documenting a "Hobson's Choice" for both the British and the Maori people. [113]

Amongst other things, Normanby's instructions had to grapple with the issue of Britain's previous acknowledgement of New Zealand as a sovereign nation. This ludicrous outcome was the result of an 1835 request from the "United Chiefs of New Zealand", a mythical entity hastily dreamt up by the well-meaning British Resident to New Zealand, James Busby, in response to the real or perceived threat of French presence in New Zealand in the form of the amiable and optimistic Baron Charles de Thierry. Busby's request should have been recognised for its good intentions but, in the nicest possible way, diplomatically declined for its stupidity. Instead it was treated by British politicians in the same way as a request for a lolly by a petulant child to an indulgent parent.

The bizarre decision for Britain to acknowledge sovereignty to the mythical "United Chiefs" dramatically demonstrates the way in which Maori, or more accurately, any "native", had always been perceived in Europe at that time – as children who must be looked after and humoured.

---

[113] Historian Peter Adams emphasises the importance of recognising this dilemma by titling his book *Fatal Necessity* – a masterful two-word summary which captures the "damned if you do and damned if you don't" inevitability of Britain's involvement in New Zealand.

This acknowledgement of sovereignty was not the considered act of one adult dealing with another adult but the equivalent of extravagantly praising a three year old for tying their shoe lace. On the one hand it is easy to see how this happened – human beings are, after all, supposed to be kind and forgiving of those of lesser understanding and in that light the acknowledgement of sovereignty can be seen as an example of what was intended to be a fatherly encouragement to a foreign culture which was then a "child" in international diplomacy. But as history overwhelmingly confirms, kindness nearly always backfires and such would be the case in a few years' time when Britain became involved in New Zealand against its better judgement.

In 1835 harder hearts and better brains should have, but did not, prevail and Britain duly acknowledged the sovereignty of this seething mass of amoebas collectively known to Europeans as New Zealand. After all, what possible harm could it do to humour the "natives" who in 1835 you had every reason to believe you would have nothing further to do with? By 1839, when Britain was finally forced to, and was on the verge of, interceding in New Zealand, it was not politically acceptable to simply revoke or ignore this bizarre recognition of sovereignty, requiring Normanby to go to great pains to address this inconvenient conundrum in his instructions to Hobson.

In one breath Normanby stresses Britain's previous diplomatic recognition of New Zealand as a sovereign state while in the next he describes the practical reality and stupidity of such a notion by describing Maori as:

> "...a people composed of numerous dispersed and petty tribes, who possess few political relations to each other, and are incompetent to act or even deliberate in concert".

On the subject of sovereignty he continues:

> "But the admission of their rights, though inevitably qualified by this consideration, is binding on the faith of the British Crown. The Queen, in common with Her Majesty's predecessor, disclaims for herself and Her subjects every pretension to seize on the Islands of New Zealand, or to govern them as a part of the Dominions of Great Britain unless

the free intelligent consent of the natives, expressed according to their established usages, shall first be obtained. Believing, however, that their own welfare would, under the circumstances I have mentioned, be best promoted by the surrender to Her Majesty of a right now so precarious and little more than nominal, and persuaded that the benefits of British protection and laws administered by British judges would far more than compensate for the sacrifice by the natives of a national independence which they are no longer able to maintain, Her Majesty's Government have resolved to authorise you to treat with the aborigines of New Zealand in the recognition of Her Majesty's sovereign authority over the whole or any part of those Islands which they may be willing to place under Her Majesty's dominion. I am not aware of the difficulties by which such a treaty may be encountered. The motives by which it is recommended are, of course, open to suspicion. The natives may probably regard with distrust a proposal which may carry on the face of it the appearance of humiliation on their side and of a formidable encroachment on ours: and their ignorance even of the technical terms in which that proposal must be conveyed, may enhance their aversion to an arrangement of which they may be unable to comprehend the exact meaning or probable results. These, however, are impediments to be gradually overcome by the exercise on your part of mildness, justice and perfect sincerity in your intercourse with them...

You will therefore frankly and unreservedly explain to the natives or their chiefs the reasons which should urge them to acquiesce in the proposals you will make to them. Especially you will point out to them the dangers to which they may be exposed by the residence amongst them of settlers amenable to no laws or tribunals of their own and the impossibility of Her Majesty extending to them any effectual protection unless the Queen be acknowledged as the Sovereign of their country, or at least of those districts within or adjacent to which Her Majesty's subjects lands or habitations."

With the issue of sovereignty covered, Normanby proceeds to the thorny issue of land ownership:

> “It is not, however, to the mere recognition of the sovereign authority of the Queen that your endeavours are to be confined, or your negotiations directed. It is further necessary that the chiefs should be induced, if possible, to contract with you, as representing Her Majesty, that henceforward no lands shall be ceded, either gratuitously or otherwise, except to the Crown of Great Britain. Contemplating the future growth and extension of a British colony in New Zealand, it is an object of the first importance that the alienation of the unsettled lands within the limits should be conducted from its commencement upon that system of sale of which experience has proved the wisdom, and the disregard of which has been so fatal to the prosperity of other British settlements. With a view to those interests it is obviously the same thing whether large tracts of land be acquired by the mere gift of the Government or the purchases effected on nominal considerations from the aborigines. On either supposition the land revenue must be wasted, the introduction of emigrants delayed or prevented, and the country parcelled out amongst large land owners whose possession must long remain an unprofitable, or rather pernicious waste. Indeed in a comparison of the two methods of acquiring land gratuitously, that of grants from the Crown, mischievous as it is, would be the less inconvenient, as such grants must be made with at least some kind of system, with some degree of responsibility, subject to some conditions, and recorded for general information. But in the case of purchases from the natives even these securities against abuse must be omitted, and none could be substituted for them. You will immediately on your arrival announce, by proclamation addressed to all the Queen's subjects in New Zealand that Her Majesty will not acknowledge as valid any title to land which either has been, or shall hereafter be acquired in that country which is not either derived from or confirmed by a grant to be made in Her Majesty's name and on Her behalf.”

His requirement for observation of the highest moral standards, and the preservation of what is termed "The honour of the Crown", is unequivocal:

> "All dealings with the natives for their lands must be conducted on the same principles of sincerity, justice and good faith as must govern your transactions with them for the recognition of Her Majesty's sovereignty in the Islands. Nor is that all: they must not be permitted to enter into any contracts in which they might be ignorant and unintentional authors of injuries to themselves. You will not, for example, purchase from them any territory the retention of which by them would be essential or highly conducive to their own comfort, safety, or subsistence. The acquisition of land by the Crown for the future settlement of British subjects must be confined to such districts as the natives can alienate without distress or serious inconvenience to themselves."

Normanby gives a wealth of administrative details which might seduce the casual reader into thinking that his document constitutes a plan. It does not, and to his credit Normanby is honest enough to say so:

> "I have thus attempted to touch upon all the topics on which it seems to me necessary to address you on your departure from this country. Many questions have been unavoidably passed over in silence, and many others have been adverted to in a brief and cursory manner, because I am fully impressed with the conviction that in such an undertaking as that in which you are about to engage much must be left to your own discretion and many questions must occur which no foresight could anticipate or properly resolve beforehand."

Finally Normanby passes the responsibility for mission control across to Hobson:

> "Reposing the utmost confidence in your judgement, experience and zeal for Her Majesty's service and aware of how powerful a coadjutor

and how able a guide you will have in Sir George Gipps[114], I willingly leave for consultation between you many subjects on which I feel my own incompetency at this distance from the scene of action to form an opinion."

Hobson's bluff has been called and the report he made in 1838 has come home to roost. His earlier factory suggestion, an academic recommendation made with all the confidence of someone who at the time of writing had no responsibility for its implementation, and whose practicality has now been overtaken by events, has landed him in a position whereby he has been given full responsibility for masterminding the resolution of a much larger problem.

Lord Normanby has provided the bones of what might be described as a mission "strategy" and passed the baton to Hobson who must come up with a cunning tactical plan to achieve what Normanby freely admits will be difficult if not impossible to achieve. No pressure then. As it happens, once again in that time honoured manner of top-level decisions, having passed Hobson the "baton from Hell", six months before Hobson arrives in New Zealand Lord Normanby will be replaced in the position of Secretary for the Colonial Office by Lord Russell.

Normanby's brief to Hobson is, at least as regards sovereignty, infinitely flexible. Hobson is instructed to:

> "...treat with the aborigines of New Zealand in the recognition of Her Majesty's sovereign authority over the whole or any part of those Islands which they may be willing to place under Her Majesty's dominion"

Hobson could, for instance, at his discretion, choose to "treat with the aborigines" for 10 acres or 10 million acres, in any place, at any time.

---

[114] Gipps was then Governor of "New South Wales". The plan was that any land Hobson might gain sovereignty to in New Zealand would fall under the umbrella of "New South Wales", making Hobson Lieutenant-Governor of the New Zealand portion of "New South Wales", reporting to Gipps as Governor of the entire New South Wales colony.

Given his 1838 report recommending the establishment of trading factories in New Zealand Hobson is assuredly more than open to – indeed probably more inclined to – the option of a very limited cession of "sovereignty" in a few selected places.

If Hobson has a long term plan when the *Herald* drops anchor in the Bay of Islands on 29 January, 1840, it is not immediately apparent and subsequent events will show that he did not really have one. His employer has given him an infinitely flexible brief of desirable and philanthropic outcomes that regrettably come with an infinitely inflexible list of philanthropic caveats. Given the speed of the New Zealand Company's operation and the scope of their vision, being tantamount to a planned, wholesale, peaceful invasion of New Zealand with organised settlers rather than a smattering of random individuals, we can probably speculate that Hobson has abandoned his original recommendation of establishing small pockets of land acquired on an as-required basis for his "factory" system. With the New Zealand Company buying up great tracts of land even as Hobson arrives something much more drastic is required and it is required immediately.

Hobson is evidently a man of action, for the day after his arrival:

> "... two commissions were read; one under the Great Seal extending the limits of New South Wales to include New Zealand; the other under the royal signet, appointing Captain Hobson lieutenant-governor over such parts of New Zealand as shall hereafter be added to her Majesty's dominions. Two proclamations, afterwards printed at the missionary press at Paihia, were at the same time promulgated. The first asserted her Majesty's authority over British subjects in the colony, and the second announced that the Queen would acknowledge no titles to land but those derived from Crown grants, that purchasing land from natives after this date was illegal, and that a commission would investigate into all the land purchases already made. This last announcement startled the whole

> community, being a death-blow to men who had purchased principalities for baubles."[115]

Within a week of his arrival Hobson had set in motion the most extreme interpretation of Lord Normanby's instructions, immediately dismissing the least controversial approach of negotiating for sovereignty over small, selected portions of the country, and going straight for the jugular by negotiating sovereignty over the whole of New Zealand.

It is an outstandingly audacious move that makes the New Zealand Company's actions seem the epitome of organisation and thoroughness by comparison. William Wakefield has spent the best part of four months bouncing like a ping-pong ball backward and forward between Queen Charlotte Sound, Port Nicholson, Kapiti, Taranaki, Kaipara and Hokianga, trying his darndest to do due diligence and wrecking his ship in the process. The reward for his efforts will be to be castigated and vilified for eternity. Hobson swans into the Bay of Islands and within a week, while barely leaving his cabin, has got the first marks on what will soon become dignified by the title "Treaty of Waitangi".

While Hobson, and posterity, will ruthlessly question the Maori understanding of Wakefield's deeds of purchase, and indeed of every land transaction to Europeans prior to his proclamation of January 14, 1840, Hobson has this to say of the signing of his own piece of parchment when questioned by young missionary CMS printer William Colenso:

> "**Mr. Colenso:** "May I ask your Excellency whether it is your opinion that these Natives understand the articles of the treaty which they are now called upon to sign?"
>
> **The Governor** [Hobson]: "If the Native chiefs do not know the contents of this treaty it is no fault of mine. I wish them fully to understand it. I have done all that I could do to make them understand

---

[115] *The Story of New Zealand – Vol 2*, Arthur Thomson, Vol 2, p17.

> the same, and I really don't know how I shall be enabled to get them to do so. They have heard the treaty read by Mr. Williams."[116]

If this recollection of Colenso's is correct it would seem that the standards for agreements with Maori vary wildly depending on who you are.

In 1972 historian Ruth Ross gave a brutal summary of the Treaty process:

> "However good intentions may have been, a close study of events shows that the Treaty of Waitangi was hastily and inexpertly drawn up, ambiguous and contradictory in content, chaotic in its execution. To persist in postulating that this was a "sacred compact" is sheer hypocrisy".[117]

Ross's withering summary was famous in its day to the point of cliché. But, eminently quotable though it may be, she is absolutely wrong. The Treaty may indeed have "been hastily drawn up" and its execution may have been "chaotic", but she misses the point entirely. The end result of what may indeed have been a less than ideal process was, for the situation and time, a model of simplicity and clarity which could hardly be bettered had it been written by a team of crack constitutional lawyers. In 180 years no one has ever questioned the meaning of a single word or intention of the *English* version of the Treaty.[118]

If any further evidence were required to prove the absurdity of the claim that prior to the Treaty New Zealand was either a "country" or a "sovereign nation" we need look no further than the Treaty signing process itself. If New Zealand was indeed a sovereign Maori nation on February 5, 1840 then the Treaty signed the day after would have required only a single Maori signature by the recognised representative of that presumed nation. Instead, because no such nation or representative

---

[116] *The Authentic and Genuine History of the Signing of the Treaty of Waitangi*, William Colenso, p33.

[117] *Te Tiriti o Waitangi, Text and Translations*, Ruth Ross, article within *New Zealand Journal of History*, 1972, Volume 06, Number 2, pp129-157.

[118] The Maori version is a different subject, beyond the scope of this book.

existed, the signing of the Treaty at Waitangi on 6 February, 1840 is just step one in an epic multi-month process scouring the length and breadth of New Zealand that will eventually net over 500 signatures.

The following week Hobson's great travelling Treaty signing extravaganza is repeated at Hokianga and on the basis of his success here he proclaims partial cession of Northland:

> "I considered on the conclusion of the Treaty of Waitangi the sovereignty of Her Majesty over the northern district, was complete. I therefore propose to issue a proclamation announcing that Her Majesty's dominions in New Zealand extend from the North Cape to the 36th degree of latitude. As I proceed southward and obtain the consent of the chiefs, I will extend these limits by proclamation, until I can include the whole of the islands."[119]

Over the next few months the Treaty "box-ticking" exercise is taken up by various missionaries and other hangers-on who scour the country touting for additional signatures, an exercise at least as debatable as that of Wakefield's and with zero documentation. However before the signature gathering process is complete Hobson is panicked into proclaiming cession of the sovereignty of New Zealand to Britain in order to shut down the incipient rival "settler government" being set up by the Wakefield settlers at Port Nicholson. Cession of the North Island is justified on the basis of signatures to the Treaty while that of the South Island is initially justified on the basis of "discovery".

With the cession of the islands of New Zealand to Britain we enter an entirely new world for all parties. Life will never be the same for the Maori people, for the estimated two thousand Europeans who have made New Zealand their home prior to 1840, or for the Missionaries of all persuasions who have ruled the roost since 1814.

So what did this bright, shiny new Treaty mean for Ati Awa and the various other tribes jostling for space and bickering amongst themselves along the southern west coast of the North Island? To many of them it

[119] Despatch Hobson to Sir George Gipps, 17 February, 1840.

meant they received some red blankets for reasons they did not understand. For others it may have been a vague realisation that things were changing, that the days of the "traditional Maori" were numbered and that their simple and well-ordered lives would in future become meshed in some way with those of Europeans. The exact future was unclear and it was a lottery for everyone, Maori and European alike.

While the Treaty would assume more importance as the decade of the forties progressed, in 1840 it was a minor distraction to most Maori. In 1840 Hobson's visit had two key implications for Maori. The first of these had nothing to do with the Treaty itself but with Hobson's commitment to investigate land purchases, the largest and most controversial of which were the Wakefield purchases in Wellington, Queen Charlotte Sound and Taranaki. The second and most important implication of the Treaty was not to be found in a word-for-word legal dissection of its contents but as a document of hope and the coming together of two peoples under a new, brighter regime based on European laws and values, the most important of which was the concept of peace. This second implication was really just the formalisation of a trend that had been a steady work in progress for 26 years – the uptake by Maori of European Christianity.

Chapter 1-9

Beware of strangers bearing Bibles.

In the two thousand years of its existence Christianity has been many things and not all of these things have been good. It has often – perhaps always – "meant well", at least according to its own definition of "well", but it has in the process caused enormous collateral damage, some of which we are still trying to repair, some of which, like most history, can never be repaired.

But there are two sides to Christianity and indeed to any religion – the "spiritual" side and the "practical" side. In modern day New Zealand we might say we are a "Christian" country even though only a small percentage of the population believe the basic spiritual tenets of the religion itself. We say this because we live our practical day to day lives according to common sense rules which are articulated in the Bible and especially in the New Testament. The concepts of peace and love, of turning the other check, of treating others as you would have them treat yourself, the Ten Commandments, never let the sun go down on your anger, and so on.

These are simple rules and of course not unique to Christianity – they appear in many religions in some form or fashion. The point is, even if the great majority of New Zealanders care nothing for Fathers, Sons and Holy Ghosts, the Bible is the book of rules which has underpinned "Western Civilisation" ever since there has been a Western Civilisation. In many ways the Bible *is* Western Civilisation. From these Biblical guidelines are derived not only the day to day conventions of how we interact with each other but also the codified secular laws that define the limits of our behaviour. Like all ways of living it is a construct, but it is a construct that has stood the test of time, albeit being constantly challenged.

Like every other society in history Maori developed its own set of rules, standards or constructs that ensured its survival and prosperity. Because there are a very limited number of sets of rules that result in survival the constructs developed by all groups throughout history must by definition all be variations on a basic theme. Every society, be it a small tribal group or an entire major civilisation such as Rome or Egypt, evolved constructs that involved an appeal to, or fear of, supernatural "beings", entities we might call "gods" or at least "spirits". In this respect Maori were no exception:

> "The early missionaries and other contemporary observers were all agreed that the Maori had no conception of a supreme deity, but that he recognized a number of beings generally referred to as '*atua'*, who exercised their powers in their own special departments. Bishop Herbert Williams, in his paper "Some Account of the Maori Beliefs", says:
>
> > "This word "atua" is commonly translated by the word "god" but there is grave danger of mistake if "god" be accepted as an equivalent for "atua", and, as [pioneer anthropologist Elsdon] Best has pointed out, it is unfortunate that the early missionaries adopted the word for the God of the Bible".
>
> An 'atua' was a supernatural being who, in his relation to mankind, was generally of a malevolent disposition. Many of these 'atua' were considered to be personification of natural objects and the forces of nature, over which they were supposed to preside. The Maori regarded the 'atua' with terror – or perhaps the word "awe" would better describe his feeling – but he did not worship him.
>
> When a Maori entered upon an undertaking which came within the scope of the authority of any 'atua', such 'atua' had to be rendered harmless by the aid of powerful spells or 'karakia'. The large majority

of 'karakia' that have been collected contain nothing in the nature of a petition, but consist simply of a form of words. The efficacy of them depended entirely upon the correct and unbroken recitation of the form, which was accompanied by certain ceremonies.

In some cases lustrations were performed, it often being necessary also to procure certain objects and present them before the 'atua'. In addition to these important 'atua', it appears that the Maori believed in the existence of hordes of minor sprites who were at the beck and call of those who were initiated, to carry out their behests.

Some authors who have written about the Maori religion, speak of the worship of ancestors but it has been pointed out that the word "worship" is inapplicable to describe the Maori attitude towards his gods, and Bishop Herbert Williams thinks that evidence is wanting to prove that the Maori regarded his deceased ancestors as 'atua'. He certainly dreaded the spirits of the deceased, but this dread was by no means the same thing as deification. If, on the other hand, the theory is held that the Maori regarded his ancestors as 'atua' it must be acknowledged that these ancestor "godlets" were confined to the lowest form of 'atua', and "ancestor-worship so-called, occupied but a lowly position among the Maori folk.""[120]

Yet again we see that there are more similarities between so-called disparate societies than there are differences, for with the change of a few words the description above could apply equally well to European paganism or to the supernatural beliefs of every other society in the world until very recent times.

While Europeans of the time would have termed this belief system "paganism" or "heathenism" rather than "religion" any belief system or construct that invokes an unseen being or beings is a "religion" nonetheless. And clearly these constructs, perfected over a period of over

[120] *The Advance of the Missionaries*, H.C. Fancourt, pp2-3.

5,000 years[121], served Maori well, for they had maintained a balance and order that achieved not just survival but population growth.

It is into this "pagan" world that the first European missionaries arrived carrying big black books and wearing beaver-skin hats. Their purpose was simple – to save the world – or at least the souls of the world, whether the world liked it or not. Missionaries of many persuasions have been doing this for centuries, in every corner of the world, bringing, so they believed, lightness to the dark.

The first missionaries arrived in New Zealand in late 1814, sent by an English society founded in 1799 called the Christian Missionary Society (CMS). These CMS missionaries were adherents of the Anglican[122] variant of Christianity and established themselves in the prime position of the Bay of Islands amongst the Nga Puhi people. The next missionary group to arrive in the early 1820's was the Wesleyan faction of the Methodist churches – the so-called "dissenters" from the "true" (Anglican) church. After being forced to leave Whangaroa in 1828 the Wesleyans set up headquarters in Hokianga directly across from the Bay of Islands on the West Coast of the North Island among a different group of Nga Puhi.

The missionaries arrived at a transitionary phase in Maori history, spanning the era when Maori warfare was changing from its more benign form involving traditional weapons to the outright slaughter that occurred while the imbalance of musket ownership was resolved.

The early missionaries were playing a very long game, for while Maori instantly grasped the temporal, material and trading benefits that European presence brought them they were very happy with their existing Gods, thanks very much. To their credit the missionaries took a cautious approach and concentrated more on material and social progress, or as

---

[121] A typical length of time mooted for the progressive migration of the people who in the 1800's would become known as Maori to reach New Zealand, see for instance, *The Quest for Origins*, Kerry Howe, throughout.

[122] The Anglicans, being the mainstream denomination at that time, were also known simply as "church", transliterated to Maori as *haahi*.

they called it "civilisation", rather than spiritual progress, and in this they had some success in discouraging habits "abhorrent" to their "Christian" sensibilities, such as cannibalism, slavery, infanticide and polygamy.

It was to take about fifteen years of hard, unrewarding work before the missionaries saw any spiritual rewards from their labours and it is often mooted that it was the mayhem caused by the Musket Wars which finally tipped the balance into Maori accepting the "Word of God". The theory is that the introduction of muskets into traditional warfare threw a very large spanner in the traditional Maori system of *utu* which made it no longer tenable. If *utu* can be represented by the well-known blindfolded scales of justice then when implemented with traditional weapons *utu* resulted in a mild and perpetual gentle rocking back and forth of the scales which taken over time averaged out to level. But in the context of an imbalance of weaponry as caused by the selective introduction of muskets, the scales went clang to the bottom on one side, never to return because there was no tribe left to make it so.

Thus it was in large measure the mayhem caused by the Musket Wars, and the recognition that the European God brought not just peace but wealth, prosperity and technology that their own gods and systems could not, which forced Maori to reassess their traditional constructs and find them wanting. If it was Western technology in the form of muskets which "caused" the problem then it was Western religion with its message of peace which was to provide the solution.

It was in the early 1830s that the "penny" of Christianity finally began to drop among Maori, and when it dropped it did so with a vengeance, as if after fifteen years of chipping away at a megalithic dam with a tiny hammer the dam had finally burst, enveloping the entire island in an unstoppable torrent. From 1835 the prospect of peace, combined with the wonders of literacy and of printed material – which was inevitably Biblical – and the dispersal back into Maoridom of Maori schooled by Missionaries, carried the Christian message southward throughout the island.

In today's terminology Christianity "went viral", and the message, coming from Maori rather than European, spread through the masses like wildfire.

Urgent appeals began to arrive from far-off tribes for missionaries to live amongst them. Everywhere missionaries went they were mobbed for the smallest printed scrap of scripture and for instruction. *Raupo* chapels popped up everywhere – in 1835 the chief Haupokia, who only three years previously had been part of the slaughtering party at Pukerangiora, was building a chapel for use by the incoming Wesleyan missionary, John Whiteley. Christianity, and its accompanying accoutrement of literacy, was embraced everywhere with a zeal that can only be described as fanatical. It was like Beatlemania but with Bibles.

From 1835 both Anglican and Wesleyan missions extended their operations southwards, into the Waikato, the Hauraki Gulf area, Tauranga and the western coastal areas. Whereas hitherto these two missionary groups had worked together amicably they were now in danger of encroaching on each other's turf and there was some friction as the two groups decided who was to get what patch. After some toing and froing, in 1837 it was agreed that the Wesleyans would minister to the area around Kawhia, servicing the key area of the Waikato and Ngati Maniapoto tribes, while the Anglicans would service the area from Wanganui south. In some areas, such as around the Waipa delta, Maori were either spoiled for choice, or possibly confused beyond measure, by having a choice of *three* denominations[123] – Anglicans, Wesleyans and a relative new-comer, the Catholic Church, stationed at Rangiaowhia.

From the distance of a hundred and eighty years it is easy to be of two minds about the missionaries. On one hand it is impossible not to be in awe of the trials, hardship, personal sacrifice and utter selflessness that these handfuls of men and their luckless families endured, tramping thorough swamps, bush and raging rivers, with wives and children dying left and right. On the other hand it is very easy to confuse selflessness with selfishness and benevolence with arrogance. When push comes to shove the Missionaries were doing all this for purely selfish reasons, for

---

[123] To which we could add a forth if we include North German Missionary Society missionary Johann Riemenschneider, situated at Motukaramu between 1844 and 1848.

something *they* believed in and something *they* thought Maori needed. It is the type of hypocrisy that is not only still alive but healthier than ever today. Today we wrinkle our brows at Europeans for having the gall to think their "civilisation" was superior to everyone else's and ramming it down their throats, and we clamour for "decolonisation" to make it all better. But in the same breath we are in the present very quick to do precisely the same, to judge other cultures and countries and find them wanting – on the treatment of women, education, environmental issues for example – and impose these Western values on them and intervene to make that happen. Yet again we see that nothing ever changes – hypocrisy still rules supreme, no one ever learns from history and humans are still as stupid as ever.

It is difficult to know exactly what the missionaries' end game was, or even if they had one. We might wonder how they saw themselves, and the Maori people, by, say, the year 1900. Were they trying to create their own little kingdom in their own image, a country in which they were the only Europeans and the entirety of Maori were all perfect "missionary clones", clinging to every word of the Bible with true missionary zeal? Were they trying to create some utopian Biblical paradise unlike their Godless home country of England, which after 1,200 years of exposure to Christianity had long lost its novelty and sheen and reduced the great majority of the population to paying lip service to Christianity at best? For this indeed was the mythical world the missionaries actually did create, a Maori nation of "perfect", robotic Christians, with all the fanatical fervour and naïve zeal typical of neophytes, analysing to death the meaning of every word of the Bible, thinking that this façade was the way the real world actually worked.

For all their supposed "good" intentions it is clear that the missionaries totally misled Maori by creating in their minds a beautiful, fantasy world which had no basis in reality, a utopian paradise which must inevitably come crashing down and cause bitter resentment and a sense of treachery when it did. Maori were hoodwinked by the missionaries who did not tell them the truth of how European "Christians" *really* lived and instead introduced Maori to fantastic Biblical tales of Kings, lost tribes, and worlds in which everything was always sweetness and light, worlds a

European Missionary may have been able to put into perspective and perceive as allegories but which to the Maori mind played out as reality. It is this facile understanding of the Bible, and the promises and models of living that it portrayed, which was in no small way responsible for the New Zealand Wars.

To return from this more general discussion to the specific subject of this book the reason we have had this aside on the introduction of Christianity among the Maori is that amongst many other things Christianity required:

- There shall be no slavery.
- Although there may still be hierarchy – Kings, Queens, Governors, etc – inherently all men are equal.

These were both mind-blowing concepts to 1830's Maori society in general and to the "chiefly" class in particular. Adopting Christianity had implications that rocked Maori society to its very core. For instance, if your tribe was Christian you must not only *release* any slaves you have taken in battle but *receive* slaves back into your tribe and treat them like yourself rather than as the untouchables they would have been in pre-Christian times

But there was more – for many of these slaves – in particular those taken by the Nga Puhi and who had therefore been exposed to and possibly schooled by the Missionaries in the Bay of Islands – returned to their original homes not as outcasts but as the most literate, Europeanised, lionised people in the tribe. The chief, whose rule and *mana* had once been absolute, now had to watch "his" people hanging on the every word of a mere *slave*. It was a turning on its head of the Maori caste system – slaves had gone from zero to hero while the Chief's *mana*, if still present, took a serious nosedive. Welcome to the new age of the individual and egalitarianism in Maori society. As we shall see in later chapters this reversal of the caste system in the Maori World between 1835 and 1860 would also play an essential role in causing the New Zealand Wars

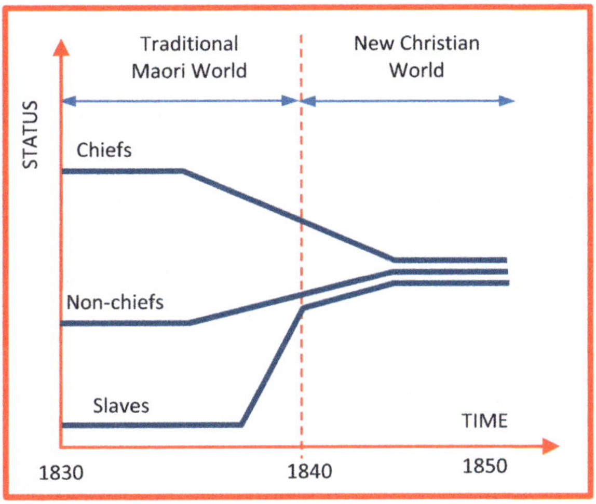

Graphical representation of the upending of caste caused by the adoption of Christianity.

Returning to our summary of the diaspora of the Ati Awa, it was in this way, and in this hugely elevated status, that the Ati Awa Group 4 Slaves taken after the Waikato onslaught of Pukerangiora in 1832 and Mikotahi in 1833 returned to their ancestral lands of Taranaki with the arrogance of higher beings.

W.A. Chambers, in his excellent biography of Wesleyan missionary Samuel Ironside, describes the return of one contingent of these slaves as they trekked south along the west coast of the North Island from their place of captivity in Kawhia to their former home of Taranaki in the last half of June, 1840, four months after Barrett negotiated the sale of Taranaki on behalf of the New Zealand company:

> "... further information was required about the Taranaki area, from which many of the slaves held by the Kawhia and Waikato tribes had come. To obtain this information, and to accompany a band of approximately 200 freed slaves returning to their home lands in Taranaki, Samuel Ironside, John Aldred and George Buttle were

> selected to set out from the Ahuahu mission station on an overland winter journey to Wanganui..."[124]

This return of slaves to Taranaki was, to say the least, problematical for Colonel Wakefield and the New Zealand Company and marked the point at which the Taranaki purchase started to unravel. Just four months previously Wakefield had congratulated himself on satisfying what he thought were the last possible claimants to Ati Awa land at Taranaki – the Group 3 "Diehards". With the arrival of the Group 4 slaves in their shiny new elevated status he was back to square one – he can satisfy ten thousand people but it only takes a solitary objector to make the whole exercise null and void and these returned slaves were full of them.

And if that were not enough it was also becoming apparent that not everyone in the Waikato/Ngati Maniapoto confederation which laid waste to Taranaki just eight years previously at Pukerangiora was thrilled with the supposed sale of what they considered *their* land to the New Zealand Company. If anyone was to receive guns and goods for the purchase of Taranaki it should be *them*, and certainly not the defeated and wretched Group 3 Diehards who the Waikatos were kind enough not to obliterate – that was not cricket in anyone's language.

The Waikato chief Muriwenua thought he still had claims in Taranaki for which *utu* in some form must be obtained, and his war party shadowed the contingent of released slaves as they made their way south:

> **Saturday 13 June:** "...Arrived at Mokau in the evening where we met with Muriwenua and his party who had left his Kainga (village) for the purpose of visiting Taranaki, whose inveterate enemy he had been for years, and by whom for as many years he has been dreaded. Thither he has at different times conducted his warlike tribe, to scatter, tear, and slay, and there he has left many to slumber in the dust. The report was that many years ago he lost some of his bravest and best men, being not only fought against by the natives but by several Europeans also, who were then living there at a whaling station and who had several

[124] *Samuel Ironside in New Zealand*, W.A. Chambers, p74.

> large guns. These circumstances it is said were still fresh to his memory and he was going to be avenged by killing as payment for them (their native custom), others that he claimed Taranaki, and as they had sold it was going for part of the payments, others that he is going to make peace"(Aldred)
>
> **Saturday 13 June:** I shall never forget the weeping, wailing, and shouting of the poor slaves as we came out on the brow of a hill, near Mokau, and had a view of grand old Taranaki [Mt Egmont] 9000 feet high with his sugar loaf crown: a sight these hundreds of poor fellows had lost all hope of ever seeing again." (Aldred)

Eight years after the battle at Ngamotu in 1832, and seven years after the skirmish at Mikotahi at which some of these returning slaves may well have been captured, the remnant of the Ngamotu "Diehards" clearly still lived in daily fear for their lives. They may be "Diehards" but for all that they clearly understand that they remained alive only by the goodwill of their conquerors, the Waikatos:

> **Thursday 18 June:** "Our journey, for the last three or four days has been over a large extent of fine fern land, watered by several splendid rivers – but not a single inhabitant, they have all been destroyed or dispersed by the sanguinary feuds and quarrels with the natives...
>
> A few years back this district was thickly populated – this is evident from the number of fortifications in ruins and from the vast quantity of pigs running wild in every direction, left by the people in the hurry of their flight. We arrived just before nightfall at Nga Motu north of the Cape Egmont of Captain Cook. As we neared the native settlement at Nga Motu we could see the few people, taking alarm at our numbers, run across the beach into the tide way, scramble on board the canoes, and paddle off in all haste to the outermost rock, in caves of which they had their sleeping place, only coming on shore by stealth to plant and gather their food. No signals of ours could induce them to come to us." (Ironside)

Luckily the threat of Muriwenua's war party turned out to be a damp squib – it seemed everyone was getting old and/or could not see where – or even if – they fitted within the new, confusing Christianised social order:

Saturday 20 June: "About breakfast time Muriwenua was seen near us. He was received in the usual way by a sort of dance" (Aldred)

> ..."and proceeded to state that it was their desire to make peace but hoped they might be allowed to fire off their guns in memory of the dead belonging to them who had fallen in battle. This was allowed by the Taranaki natives – plenty of powder was wasted away and this affair ended."(Ironside) "While this was going on, Muriwenua sat insensible. He might have been reverting to former days of war and bloodshed and to those of friends who had been slain near the spot. The chiefs on both sides made speeches, all expressive of peace, with the invitations to their respective kaingas. It was an interesting sight." (Aldred)[125]

Thus the Taranaki slaves reappeared out of nowhere, not as slaves but as conquering heroes bringing peace and hope. This was a fine, humanitarian outcome indeed, but one which came with a lot of question marks. What did these slaves expect would happen next? Did they think they could pick up the pieces from where they were so rudely interrupted seven or eight years ago, free of the constant fear the "Diehards" had been living under for the past eight years? Or did the "Diehards" have to shuffle together and make room for 200 more people on the top of Mikotahi and Moturoa?

This rather wonderful quote from Ngati Maniapoto chief Haupokia to his former slave Katatore, on the latter's post-release assumption of high airs, puts the matter of ex-slave status into perspective:

> "It is since your return [as a released slave to Taranaki] that you have become a tall man; you have to thank me for your being so tall. But I did not send you here to quarrel with the Europeans; I sent you expecting you would be friendly with them; and why should you not? ... it is by having Europeans with you that you are now great. You have to thank Christianity for this – if it had not been for

---

[125] *Samuel Ironside in New Zealand*, W.A. Chambers, pp74-76. "Aldred" and "Ironside" refer to the authors of the journals quoted within this book – the Wesleyan missionaries John Aldred and Samuel Ironside.

> Christianity you would not have been here, you would not have had land to contend about either with Europeans or anyone else – all your land would have been taken from you by us, and you would now have been in bondage."[126]

It is also simultaneously a good example of how one significant portion of Maoridom felt about the role of Europeans in making it possible for Taranaki natives to return, the ingratitude of the Taranaki tribes for this inestimable and undeserved boon, and the utter amazement on the part of the Waikatos that the Europeans were so stupid as to let the Taranakian's walk all over them.

Which brings us neatly to the question of *utu*. To Haupokia it was a no-brainer – two weeks ago these people were slaves and now, through no action of their own, they are not only free men and women, not only hugely elevated in status, but back in their ancestral lands. Even a stupid and benevolent European can tell you that a "debt" is owed somewhere here – it is not rocket science. Surely, with the infinitely finely tuned sense of *utu* for which Maori are famous, this debt must go somewhere on the great mental ledger of who owes whom what?

The most obvious candidates for repayment of this *utu* are the missionaries who have toiled tirelessly for twenty-five years to introduce the religion which has resulted in the slaves being freed. Or perhaps *utu* is owed to "Europeans" in general who have not only developed the religion which freed them but bought the lands and brought the peace which have made it safe to return? Or is it only Maori who qualify for admission to the *utu* ledger, and every benefit that derives from a European source is a freebie? Well no, not quite, for we see that Haupokia, for one, sees the imbalance of *utu* very clearly. Perhaps this principle of "racially selective *utu*" is peculiar to Taranaki Maori?

And what, if anything, does this mean for Dicky Barrett's purchase of Taranaki on behalf of the New Zealand Company, during which, of course,

---

[126] Quoted from *He Whenua te Utu*, Ann Parsonson, p244, which cites the source as "Quoted in Whiteley to the Secretaries, 15 August 1844, MMS, p.13."

he purchased a land still controlled by the Waikato tribes, a situation the New Zealand Company would have to resolve at its own expense? After eight years of Taranaki being deserted and controlled by the Waikato tribes how could Barrett have possibly predicted not just the return of the slaves but their elevation to a station inconsistent with Maori *tikanga*? The *reductio ad infinitum* argument is that, were it not for European intervention, the slaves would never have been released and Taranaki would still be under control of the Waikato tribes to this day.

Chapter 1-10

The buying of Taranaki - Take 2.

While the New Zealand Company may have been the first and most important cab off the rank heading towards New Zealand it was by no means the last. Escape from England to the as yet little known but presumed greener pastures of New Zealand seems to have been high on the agenda for many people, resulting in a wave of smaller colonising associations and projects being established in the wake of, and on the coat tails of, the New Zealand Company's pioneering efforts. These smaller scale colonising projects had no desire to emulate the New Zealand Company's more grandiose plans of buying huge amounts of land but had the more modest goal of creating single cities of a particular class, religious or territorial character. These smaller associations would over the decade of the 1840s be responsible for the nascent settlements of New Plymouth, Dunedin and Christchurch.

Given our previous emphasis on the movements of the Taranaki tribes it will probably come as no surprise that the settlement that will feature most prominently in our story is that of "New" Plymouth and that it was intended as a settlement for colonists from the south-west of England around "Old" Plymouth. The commercial entity behind this settlement project, the Plymouth Company, was formed at the astonishingly early date of January 25, 1840, before Hobson had even arrived in New Zealand and a mere four months after William Wakefield arrived in the *Tory* – in other words at a time when the entire situation in New Zealand was a complete question mark as to land ownership and governance. In what can only be described as an audacious gamble the Plymouth Company agreed to buy 10,000 acres[127] of hypothetical and as yet unknown land from the New Zealand Company when for all anyone in England knew William Wakefield and his optimistic crew could have been roasting in an *umu*.

The Plymouth Company as an individual entity was short-lived due to the failure of its bank, which forced them to merge with the New Zealand Company in May 1840. The settlement of New Plymouth henceforth ceased to be a private venture and defaulted to becoming the second "New Zealand Company" settlement (after Port Nicholson/Wellington).

On 13 August 1840 the *London*, Captain Shuttleworth, sailed from Gravesend carrying the Plymouth Company's Chief Surveyor Frederick Alonzo Carrington, who arrived in Wellington with his family on 12 December, 1840. His immediate task was to determine precisely where amongst the New Zealand Company's newly acquired lands "New Plymouth" would be sited, and from there to survey the new town in detail prior to the arrival of boatloads of its new residents.[128]

While Carrington was in transit between Gravesend and Wellington two major events had occurred unbeknownst to him. First, the New Zealand Company had sent what seems to be a not very well organised exploratory expedition of its own to study in detail its most recent acquisitions in Taranaki. Among this group was our old friend from the *Tory*, draughtsman and artist Charles Heaphy, and a Mr Stokes[129], who reported of Taranaki:

> "[we] descended to the pa on the other side, which is a small collection of huts, without even a fence, and containing very few natives...

---

[127] An additional 50,000 acres were purchased from the New Zealand Company on 26 August, 1840.

[128] *Early Wellington*, Louis Ward, p74.

[129] Immortalised in the toponym Stokes Valley, in the Hutt area.

> ...On the farthest island [of Ngamotu] the natives keep their property and provisions, to secure them from a sudden incursion of the Waikato tribes... All their time of late has been occupied with the erection of houses, even to the neglect of their potatoe grounds. They speak of nothing else but Port Nicholson and the settlers there, and all their questions are directed to that point."[130]

The "houses" to which Stokes refers are those Dicky Barrett had requested that the Group 3 Diehards build for the reception of the anticipated European settlers and are pictured in Heaphy's well-known painting. According to Stokes' report these same die-hards were keenly awaiting the arrival of the Europeans who would finally, after eight wretched years of watching their backs, rid them of the ever-expected wrath of the Waikatos.

The second thing that had happened is that a month before Carrington set foot in Wellington the "pioneer vessel" *William Bryan* had sailed from Plymouth with about 150 settlers, en-route to the fabled settlement of "New Plymouth". It was the *Tory* situation all over again – the settlers were on their way before there was any land to put them on – so no pressure on Carrington then to get his town located and mapped out.

It was almost a month after his arrival in Wellington, on 8 January, 1841, before Carrington – accompanied by Dicky Barrett – set out in the *Brougham* to explore the short list of options for the site of future New Plymouth. The first stop on this jaunt was Taranaki – or more specifically the easily accessible parts of it – the Nga Motu area and land further north adjacent to the small Waitara River. Carrington, recalling this visit, says:

> "When first I visited this part of New Zealand there were not more than some fifty or sixty natives[131] throughout the district. These few

---

[130] *The History of Taranaki*, Benjamin Wells, p49.

[131]Another member of the party, R.H. Aubrey, put the number at "of at least one hundred". Whatever the exact number it appears that the population had swelled somewhat since the New Zealand Company's visit six months earlier, presumably through the return of slaves.

dejected beings were living immediately on the shore close to the Sugar Loaf Islands, so that they might be ever ready to flee to these rocky islets from the impending danger with which they were incessantly threatened by their implacable enemies, the Waikatos; they existed upon fern-root and fish, without garden or plantation of any kind, and their clothing was in keeping with their servile wretchedness. No sooner had they learned, through an interpreter, the object of my visit, than in speeches and gesture I was importuned to bring white people and dwell among them; the whole district was abandoned – they invited me to take it, so that they might be protected from their dreaded enemies, the Waikatos, who, some eight years before, under Te Whero-whero, a leading chief, had barbarously tortured and slaughtered, dispersed and carried away captive the greater portion of these, the Ngatiawa people. So great was the slaughter, dispersion, and captivity of these people, that, after eight years had elapsed, only some fifty or sixty of them had returned to a point on the coast where, by nature, they could at all times be secure from surprise."[132]

Evidently a small number of Maori had also returned gingerly to the Waitara area and even a year after the signing of the Treaty of Waitangi were still living in fear of the Waikato:

> "The wretched beings farming it [the banks of up-river Waitara River] appeared much surprised to see us pounce upon them in so unexpected a manner; but the sight of Mr. Barrett soon dispelled any fears they may have entertained respecting their personal safety."[133]

After their brief visit to Taranaki the *Brougham* headed south to check out other possible options for siting New Plymouth within the New Zealand Company's suite of lands. They visited Tasman Bay (then called Blind Bay)

---

[132] *The Land Question of Taranaki*, F.A. Carrington, p10.

[133] Journal of Mr. R. H. Aubrey, as quoted in *The History of Taranaki*, Benjamin Wells, p55.

and Queen Charlotte Sound, but finding nothing that ticked all the boxes,[134] returned to Wellington on 24 January, 1841. By this process of elimination of a very short list of very bad options Taranaki became Carrington's choice for the site of New Plymouth by default and on 12 February, 1841, Carrington returned to Ngamotu in the *Brougham*, landed his "staff and party" and began the tedious business of surveying what was essentially a wilderness and transforming it into something resembling a town.

His one disappointment with the area was the lack of a harbour but on the plus side he felt that this drawback was amply compensated for by the fertility of the Waitara district, which he referred to as "the garden of this country". He set the site for the town of New Plymouth a few miles north of Nga Motu, between the Huatoki and Henui rivers, and went about the detailed business of surveying an entire town with all its amenities.[135]

Carrington was not a moment too soon, for less than six weeks later, on 30 March, 1841, the "pioneer vessel" *William Bryan*, the first of an eventual six Plymouth/New Zealand Company ships, anchored off Ngamotu carrying 134 rookie settlers. Five months later, on 3 September, 1841, the budding settlement was further augmented by the arrival of the *Amelia Thompson* with a further 187 passengers, followed by the *Oriental* with 130 more on 7 November, 1841.[136]

Thus by the end of 1841 the area around Ngamotu and further north around the coast had undergone a transformation of epic proportions. This once deserted district with its few handfuls of native residents living in fear and trepidation around Ngamotu, scrambling back to the islands

---

[134] Angela Caughey in *The Interpreter* has a theory suggesting that Barrett sabotaged this excursion to the upper South Island in order to force Carrington's decision towards Taranaki, his former home and that of his wife's tribe.

[135] *The History of Taranaki*, Benjamin Wells, p58.

[136] New Plymouth Genealogy Society Inc. records.

every time a fire was spied in a northerly direction, was now a veritable hive of activity as over 400 Europeans beavered away trying to make some order from the chaos that must be the inevitable result of being deposited rudely on the shores of Ngamotu with 400 sets of assorted chattels.

It was not the sort of change that could go unnoticed and there are two sets of people whom we might guess would be particularly interested – the Waikatos, who drove the "original owners", the Ati Awa, off the land, and the Ati Awa themselves.

Let us take a step back and summarise the situation in Taranaki towards the end of 1841.

In November, 1841, when the *Oriental* deposited its passengers at Ngamotu:

- The Treaty of Waitangi, and the peace that results from a European presence and governance, has been in place for a year and a half.
- European Christianity has been a dominant force in the Maori world for five plus years, with a consequent rapid and marked reduction in warfare.
- It is 21 years since Ati Awa Group 1 migrated south with Te Rauparaha to settle around Waikanae and Queen Charlotte Sound.
- It is 10 years since Ati Awa Group 2 migrated south in the wake of the slaughter of Pukerangiora and wended its way south, eventually settling around Wellington harbour.
- It is the best part of two years since Ati Awa Group 3, the Ati Awa Group 3 "Diehards", sold Ati Awa land to the New Zealand Company. There is no record of either Group 1 or Group 2 Ati Awa objecting to this sale during this period.
- It is about a year and a half since Ati Awa Group 4, the slaves, have been freed and some have returned "home" after their eight year absence serving their Waikato masters. However, judging from Carrington and Stokes' comments, the number of these returned slaves to Ata Awa territory is actually quite small – probably in the order of 50 by January 1841.

- While the Waikato tribes have not seen fit to occupy the district – whatever the word "occupy"[137] means and to whom – despite all sections of the Ati Awa having sold their assumed remaining rights to the land of Taranaki, there is absolutely no doubt that Waikato *still* have *manawhenua* over the entire Taranaki area by right of conquest.

If this last point was not immediately obvious it became indisputable on considering what happened next.

In August, 1841, Governor Hobson, after eighteen months in the colony, made his first visit to its largest settlement by far, that of Wellington, where he was received with customary and well-deserved frigidity by its New Zealand Company inhabitants. Jerningham Wakefield reported of this visit:

> "Captain Hobson, however, had carefully nursed a great chief, who was in opposition to some of the Company's land-claims. He brought with him Te Werowero, the Waikato chief, who had formerly conquered Taranaki from the Ngatiawa; and when Colonel Wakefield spoke to the Governor about the settlement of New Plymouth, his Excellency introduced Werowero as the "sole owner of Taranaki."[138]

In this way, in one fell swoop Hobson confirmed his deep-seated and implacable contempt for the New Zealand Company by repudiating their purchase of Taranaki while simultaneously confirming that sole ownership of the entire de-populated Taranaki area – not just the Ati Awa area but the entire strip of coast extending from Ngati Tama territory in the North to Ngati Rauru territory in the South – lay with the Waikatos.

---

[137] Would, for instance, the existence of 30 Waikatos in an area of a few acres, fulfil this purpose, as it is said that the existence of 30 Group 3 "Diehard" Ati Awa at Ngamotu is supposed to?

[138] *Adventure in New Zealand – Vol 2,* E. Jerningham Wakefield, p49.

In November, 1841, Hobson wrote to his Colonial Office masters back in England:

> "At Taranaki the powerful tribe of the Waikatos threatens to dislodge the settlers, as they did not buy the land from them, who claim it in right of conquest. The Natives of Wanganui have followed a similar course with those of Porirua. I have reason, however, to hope that a payment of money will induce these people to forego any further opposition: and the principal chief of the Waikato tribe, Te Wherowhero, has already consented to accept compensation to the value of £250 for the claims of his tribe on the lands of Taranaki."[139]

> "I certainly admit that a people, who are in the highest degree jealous of their territorial rights, and amongst whom those rights are very imperfectly defined, are not unlikely to resort to force sooner or later, rather than suffer the occupation of lands, which may have been fairly bought from one tribe, but are claimed with great apparent justice by another. I take, for instance, the Waikato tribe, under the Chief Te Wherowhero, who are extremely powerful. They conquered and drove away the Ngatiawas from Taranaki in 1834 [sic 1832], leaving only a small remnant, who found refuge in the mountains of Cape Egmont; and having pretty well laid waste the country, and carried off a large number of slaves, they retired to their own district on the banks of the river Waikato.

> It appears that in 1839 Colonel Wakefield visited the country and bought a considerable portion of it from the few Ngatiawas who had resumed their habitations on the retreat of Te Wherowhero. Now Te Wherowhero claims the country as his by right of conquest, and insists on it that the remnant of the Ngatiawas are slaves; that they only live at Taranaki by sufferance, and that they had no right whatsoever to sell the land without his consent. In illustration of his argument, he placed a heavy ruler on some light papers, saying:

---

[139] Extract from Despatch from Governor Hobson to the Secretary of State, 13th November, 1841, (AJHR 1860, E2-No 4, p5)

> "Now so long as I choose to keep this weight here, the papers remain quiet, but if I remove it, the wind immediately blows them away; so it is with the people of Taranaki."

And alluding to Te Wherowhero's power to drive the Ati Awa off what he considers *his* land Hobson continues:

> "Te Wherowhero certainly has a claim to the land, but not a primary one, as the received rule is, that those who occupy the land must first be satisfied. But he is the most powerful chief in New Zealand, and I fear will not be governed by abstract rights, but will rather take the law into his own hands."[140]

It took less than a month for Hobson's suspicions to be proven correct:

> "In December, 1841, a party of Waikatos under the chief Te Kaka, paid a visit to New Plymouth respecting their claim, causing considerable alarm to the unsophisticated settlers by their warlike bearing. Their war dance is thus described by Mr. T. W. Shute, a well-known pioneer, in a letter to a friend at Plymouth: –
>
>> "New Plymouth, December, 1841.
>>
>> This day we have had a much finer sight than ever you saw on the Hoe with soldiers. A part of a strange tribe of natives have arrived here, and something appears to have occurred which does not please them. They were all armed with double-barrelled guns, and met the natives residing here in a place appointed for the purpose. When they came in sight of the place they began to run, and a Ngatiawa chief ran to meet them, casting a stick, taiaha, towards them. When they came up as far as the boundary, they sat down for a little time, and then got up at the command of their leader and commenced the war dance. The chiefs then commenced speaking to each other, one at a time, at the end of which they engaged in a feast. The food consisted of a

---

[140] Extract from Despatch from Governor Hobson to the Secretary of State, 15th November, 1841 (AJHR 1860, E2 - No 5, p5).

large quantity of potatoes, cooked for the occasion, with meat, fish, rice, pease [sic] and Indian corn, dished up in three-legged iron pots. The piece de resistance consisted of a pig, split down like a fish, and cooked whole. You may be sure it was a fine sight. The Waikato is one of the largest tribes of the island. We have but 150 of the original tribe of this district here, the others having been killed in war or taken captive, and it is only since we have been here that these have returned from captivity."

By means of trifling presents this party was induced to return in peace to Waikato, where shortly after the Governor prevailed on Te Wherowhero to part with his claim to the land..."[141]

The transaction referred to by which Hobson "prevailed on" the Waikatos to relinquish their claims to Taranaki reads:

"DEED OF SALE FROM TE WHEROWHERO TO HER MAJESTY, 31ST JANUARY, 1842

Know all men by this paper, that we, chiefs of Waikato, do let go and sell these lands of ours to George Clarke, the protector of natives, for Her Majesty, the Queen of England, her heirs and successors, whether male or female; the land, and all things that are on or under this land, we sell to George Clarke, the protector of natives, for an estate for the Queen, her heirs and successors, whether male or female, forever.

The beginning of the northern boundary is at Tongaporutu, the western boundary is along the seashore between Tongaporutu and Waitotara, the southern boundary is from Waitotara inland by Piraunui.

We receive these payments on behalf of the tribes of Waikato for their interest in the said lands, namely, one hundred and fifty pounds in money, two horses, two saddles, two bridles, and one hundred red blankets...

"E Kati[142], Te Wherowhero.

---

[141] *The History of Taranaki*, Benjamin Wells, pp76-77.

Witness: J. Coates, George Clarke, Sub-Protector."[143]

That this enormous area of land – which included not just the Ati Awa land but the ancestral land of the Taranaki, Ngati Ruanui and Ngati Rauru tribes – was sold[144] for the modest total sale price value of £400-500 is illuminating. Apparently a full two years after the signing of the Treaty of Waitangi, and after considerable interaction with Europeans in general and the Governor specifically, Te Wherowhero, and presumably Maori in general, still placed an incredibly low value on land. To be honest Hobson's second purchase of Taranaki makes Wakefield's first purchase seem like the height of generosity.

However not everyone in the Waikato camp was thrilled by Te Wherowhero's sale of land to Hobson:

> "In an interview which the Governor held with Awaitai[a] (William Naylor) and Te Maihoa (Broughton) these Chiefs expressed themselves highly dissatisfied with the conduct of Te Wherowhero who they complained was aggrandizing himself at their expence [sic] they particularly cited his sale of Taranaki to the Govt for which he recd payment to the value of £500 no share of which they had been given although instrumental to its conquest."[145]

Hobson's second buying of Taranaki was no doubt a good start but if he thought that any sale in the Maori world was definitive and that he could walk away congratulating himself he was very much mistaken. Three years after Hobson's "purchase to end all purchases" there was still an element of doubt as to the intentions of the Waikatos, as this letter from missionary Samuel Ironside to Land Commissioner Spain suggests:

---

142 "E Kati" is Te Wherowhero's brother.

143 AJHR 1860, E2-No.6.

144 Or perhaps more accurately "had an encumbrance removed".

145 *Journal of Ensign Best*, Abel Best, edited N. Taylor, p357.

> "With reference to the settlement of the land claims question in the New Plymouth district, I have no hesitation in stating my sincere conviction that to compensate the natives residing in the neighbourhood for the lands claimed by the New Plymouth Company, would be very injudicious and might lead to disastrous results, which we should all deprecate. The Waicato [sic] chiefs who conquered Taranaki have not acknowledged, and do not acknowledge the right of the Taranaki people to sell the land on which they reside merely on sufferance ; they look with jealousy on the proceedings of the returned slaves, still call the country their own, and I fear that compensating them, the Taranaki natives, would foster the jealousy and suspicion of their former masters, rouse their ire, and lead to an open rupture between the tribes: I may be wrong, but that is my opinion."[146]

And as we shall see in later chapters even as late as 1849 Ati Awa were *still* living in fear of the Waikatos swooping down on them from the north.

It is just more of the same in the world of 1800's Maori land ownership – you could spend ten years traipsing the length and breadth of New Zealand collecting ten thousand marks on a land sale deed, only to have someone turn up the day after complaining they were not included. Any attempt to alienate land was a hiding to nothing.

Be that as it may, by February, 1842, the entire coastal area of Taranaki – encompassing – in order from North to South – the former lands of Ngati Tama, Ngati Mutunga, Ati Awa, Taranaki, Ngati Ruanui and Ngati Rauru – were *theoretically* in European hands, either by virtue of the New Zealand Company's first purchase(s), Hobson's second purchase, or a combination of both.

---

[146] Letter Samuel Ironside to Commissioner Spain, 31 October, 1844 (BPP, 8 April 1846, p72).

Chapter 1-11

Spain and Fitzroy play snakes and ladders.

Seven months after the signing of this deed Hobson was dead. Never a well man, and chronically ill from within a month of his arrival in the country, he died on 10 September, 1842, through a combination of natural frailty and the burden of the task he talked his way into. Today he is remembered by the vast majority of New Zealanders only as a name associated with the Treaty of Waitangi and by historians as a man ill-suited for a job in which anyone would fail.

While a replacement Governor was appointed through the official selection process back in England Hobson's role was temporally assigned to his former Colonial Secretary, Willoughby Shortland, a man whose chief claim to fame was to achieve something formerly thought impossible – being even more unpopular than Hobson. But to give him his due his was purely a caretaker role and therefore he may be somewhat forgiven for a strategy of being reactive rather than proactive, of twiddling his thumbs and doing as little damage as possible before his formal successor arrived.

The most momentous event to occur during Willoughby's 15 month interregnum came on 17 June, 1843, in the form of the so-called "Wairau Affray", a land related altercation between Te Rauparaha and his volatile nephew Rangihaeata on the one hand and New Zealand Company officials and settlers on the other, in which nineteen of the latter, including William Wakefield's brother Arthur, were captured and massacred. The reactions to this were all you would expect and followed the eternal principle of *utu,* which while different words may be used to describe it, always has and always will govern human nature in all cultures, to a greater or lesser extent – the European settlers clamoured for immediate revenge and Maori immediately abandoned the area and hightailed it to Kapiti to prepare for said revenge which according to tradition *must* follow.

Perhaps wisely Shortland decided this was above his caretaker's pay grade and put this one in the "too hard basket" to await the no-doubt far greater wisdom of his successor who would have to live with the consequences of his own actions.

The other significant, if less dramatic, occurrence over this period was the operation of the various Land Commissioners. On 30 January, 1840, the day after his arrival in the Bay of Islands, Hobson proclaimed his intention to ban sales of Maori land to individuals and to investigate the validity of such sales that had taken place prior to 14 January, 1840. The resulting retrospective investigation into the validity of the so-called "Old Land Claims" of a lesser nature began in early 1841, conducted by a "New Zealand Land Commission" comprising three commissioners specially appointed for that purpose by the New South Wales Government. The considerably more onerous task of investigating the far more complex and gargantuan claims related to the New Zealand Company purchases, however, fell to a luckless individual appointed by the British Colonial Office, one William Spain.[147]

---

[147] See for instance - *A difficult and Complicated Question: The New Zealand Company's Wellington, Port Nicholson, Claim*, Rosemary Tonk, an essay in *The making of Wellington*, edited Hamer and Nicholls.

Spain duly arrived in New Zealand on 24 December, 1841, but did not begin his formal investigations until 15 May, 1842, in Wellington, a full two and a half years after the purchases he was to investigate were made. During this time the land purchased by Wakefield's Wellington Deed had changed from a harbour containing possibly two hundred Maori scattered around the entire coast line to several thousand Europeans and the vast array of chattels, capital and enterprise they brought with them. In that time European occupation had caused an explosion in land value and – surprise, surprise – the original Maori vendors had decided they had been diddled and were clamouring for more payment. More than that, these vendors now had the full, righteous moral high-ground provided by the missionaries as well as the official Governor appointed "Protectors of Aborigines", who, being ex-missionaries, were essentially an extension of the same thing. Spain's job was a thankless, miserable one that you would not wish upon your worst enemy.

Like so many of these early official appointments to New Zealand, Spain's position was a poisoned chalice, doomed from the start if not to complete failure then to toil, heartache and bitterness. William Spain was a man described in terms of faint praise by most accounts – words like "stolid" and "pedantic" are used – but these, surely, are precisely the characteristics required for such a dreary, petty, thankless task of what was essentially herding cats and unravelling hearsay of what may or may not have been understood by who in what language three years ago.

We need not go into the details except to say that Spain seems to have acquitted himself admirably and thoroughly to a fault, and that his fairness and impartially was amply demonstrated in his finding of many faults in the Company's Wellington purchase, failings which the New Zealand Company was obliged to mitigate, if and where that was possible. Spain was between a rock and a hard place. Sending thousands of Europeans back home to England was not an option[148] and so the outright abandonment of the New Zealand Company's claims was off the menu.

---

[148] This option was as unpalatable to Maori as it was to European – they wanted the money.

The weapon of choice – or rather the *only* possible weapon available for mitigation of land disputes – was additional compensation for the original vendors.

By the time Spain completed his investigation of the New Zealand Company's Wellington purchase and moved to New Plymouth to investigate the Company's Taranaki purchases it was May, 1844 – over four years since those purchases had taken place. During that time the area had been transformed from a desolate wilderness containing some fifty native "residents" huddled in fear around the islands of Ngamotu to a well-developed European township containing some one thousand residents and with scores of European farms scattered along the coast from Ngamotu to Waitara.

Thanks to the return of the slaves from Waikato the native population of Taranaki had swollen somewhat and Spain's court of investigation took place before "a large assemblage of natives" numbering "about 300".[149]

If Spain had arrived in New Zealand as a complete rookie in matters related to Maori Land Lore, by the time he arrived in Taranaki he was surely the absolute oracle on the subject. For the past two years he had lived and breathed the unfathomable intricacies of Maori land lore and analysed and dissected it in excruciating detail. He had met with, heard depositions from, debated with and negotiated with literally hundreds of Maori claimants of many tribes and many ranks. He had been badgered and hindered by his so-called "assistants", Government appointed "sub-

[149] *The History of Taranaki*, Benjamin Wells, p106.

protectors" such as George Clarke Junior, at every step[150]. He has heard every argument for every party, was more knowledgeable, and has more experience at the coalface and on a greater scale then any missionary of the past or any armchair theorist of the future.

In marked contrast to Spain's previous laborious proceedings in Wellington his Taranaki investigation was short and sweet – less than a week long, from 31 May until 6 June, 1844. On 8 June he made a verbal pronouncement of his judgement to the assembled natives and a few days later he filed a lengthy interim written report to his new boss, Governor Fitzroy, the crucial conclusion of which was that he had awarded the New Zealand Company 60,000 acres of land in Taranaki.[151]

Let us pause a moment to comment on the recipient of this letter, Governor Fitzroy, the recently arrived replacement for the deceased Governor Hobson and his interim replacement, Willoughby Shortland.

Robert Fitzroy had at least four things in common with Hobson. First he was a Royal Navy Captain. Second he had also visited New Zealand previously, in 1835 as captain of the *Beagle* on the famous voyage carrying the soon to be even more famous Charles Darwin, author of the equally famous and seminal work *Origin of Species*. Third, in what seems to be a

---

[150] Spain says of Sub-Protector George Clarke Jr – "Another difficulty I had to contend with arose from the little confidence the elder natives placed in Mr. Clarke, whom they used frequently to describe as a mere child, who was incapable of teaching them, or affording them advice. A Protector intrusted with this duty had it in his power, from the facility of intercourse with the natives, and capability of conversing with them in their own language, materially to assist an officer in my situation. But Mr. Clarke seemed to consider this no part of his duty, and often retarded my operations to an extent that caused me much embarrassment and annoyance." (*Copies or extracts of despatches from the Governor of New Zealand, enclosing or having reference to reports and awards made by Mr. Spain Commissioner of Land Claims, upon the titles of land of the New Zealand Company*, BPP, Iss 103, 8 April 1846, pp10-11).

[151] Spain's full report can be found in Appendix 1

required part of the resume of any British official of the time, he hated the New Zealand Company, and settlers in general, with a passion possibly exceeding all his predecessors combined. Fourth he had been sent on an impossible mission that was doomed to failure and which would elude someone with the wisdom of Solomon.

But that was not all. In addition to these traits in common with Hobson he had some peculiarities all his own. While all Englishmen of his time and class were highly religious Fitzroy was in a class of his own – he was a religious zealot on a par with, if not more than, an actual missionary. While there is nothing wrong with that it is surely courting disaster to have a man of this ilk in charge of a country whose European inhabitants' religious inclinations were of a more nominal, humanly achievable and pragmatic nature. But perhaps even more fatally he was a man of great volatility and whose very sanity was questioned by some.

Fitzroy arrived on 24 December, 1843, to a country in turmoil. What passed for the Government was bankrupt. He had a decision to make regarding the resolution of the Wairau Affray which must by definition make enemies of one faction or the other and/or put the country into a state of open warfare between the races. And although he did not yet know it, in a few months' time he would have a disgruntled, axe wielding, flagpole hating Maori called Hone Heke to deal with.

On 12 February, 1844, Fitzroy confronted the issue of Wairau at a meeting with Te Rauparaha at Waikanae. Since the Wairau event was then eight months in the past his actions were a farce and a foregone conclusion – if there has been no *utu* sought by the Europeans for the death of their countrymen at Wairau by then there never would be. Maori already saw the hallowed principles of British justice as a pushover and a joke. As we have observed, Fitzroy was on a hiding to nothing and his decision would simply determine to which of the two races his name would become anathema. On the subject of Wairau Fitzroy concluded:

> "I, the Governor of New Zealand, have made my decision. In the first place, the White men were in the wrong. They had no right to survey the land which you said you had not sold until Mr. Spain had finished his inquiry; they had no right to build the houses they did

on that land. As they were, then, first in the wrong, I will not avenge their deaths...But though I will not avenge the deaths of the Pakehas who were killed at the Wairau, I have to tell you that you committed a horrible crime, in murdering men who had surrendered themselves in reliance on your honour as chiefs. White men never kill their prisoners. For the future let us live peaceably and amicably – the Pakeha with the native, and the Maori with the Pakeha; and let there be no more bloodshed."[152]

Whatever the wisdom of this pronouncement, the moment these words left Fitzroy's lips he instantly and simultaneously lost not only the support and goodwill of his European constituents but the respect of the Maori people. The meeting marked the beginning of the end of what proved to be Fitzroy's brief and unsatisfactory sojourn in New Zealand.

Such was the man to whom Commissioner Spain optimistically forwarded his report on his investigation on the New Zealand Company's purchase of Taranaki. Spain, no doubt, heaved a huge sigh of relief at having crossed the last of these miserable, interminable Gordian knots that the New Zealand Company deeds represented off the list. A few months later he was therefore gob-smacked to find out, second-hand, that Fitzroy had no intention of abiding by his judgement. Writing to Fitzroy with admirable restraint Spain says:

"It was with considerable surprise that when at Nelson, in August last, I received the first intimation of your Excellency's disallowance of my decision at Taranake [sic], from the principal agent to the Company, who showed me a letter which, from its tenor and superscription, he had no doubt was dictated by your Excellency, but bearing no signature, in which your Excellency informed Colonel Wakefield that it was not your intention to comply with my recommendation regarding the New Zealand Company's purchase of land at Taranake; and that you should cause a further investigation to be made as soon as possible; also stating that a large number of

---

[152] *Nelson Examiner and New Zealand Chronicle*, 2 March 1844.

natives would be set aside by me (namely, those who were absent or in captivity at the time their lands were said to have been sold), whose claims you felt bound to recognize and maintain. By the same post, I had the honour to receive a letter from your Excellency, requesting me to meet you at Taranake, on the 1st October then following, and to have with me the evidence taken at my court in June last; but wholly silent as to the fact of your Excellency having reversed my decision."[153]

Let us see if we can shed some light on how and why Fitzroy made his decision.

Three weeks after Spain gave his judgement everything seemed sweetness and light in Taranaki:

> "An overland mail from Taranaki arrived in Auckland on Tuesday last [2 July, 1844], and we are happy to hear that all is going on well in that district; Mr. Spain was settling the land disputes entirely to the satisfaction of both Natives and Europeans."[154]

Two weeks later however the situation was looking somewhat less rosy:

> "Since the report reached us of the amicable adjustment of the land claims by Mr. Spain at Taranaki which we stated last week, other and more recent accounts have arrived, wherein it appears that a body of about thirty natives have commenced a wanton and destructive attack on the property of the Europeans in that district; alleging as a reason for their outrageous conduct, that the decisions of the Commissioner are unjust, and that they have a claim on the land; various reports are circulated as to the amount of damage done, some

---

[153] Spain's final report as cited in BBP 8 April 1846, pp46-64, this quote from p61.

[154] *The Auckland Chronicle*, 11 July, 1844, p2.

estimating it above £1000, but all agree that a great deal of property has been destroyed..."[155]

Fitzroy's subsequent account of his response to this situation sounds very dramatic, a matter of life and death, a national emergency. He was immediately on his way to the scene of the action, together with an assortment of missionary advisors:

> "...after Mr. Spain's departure [after giving his judgement], which took place in a few days, an express was sent off to the Governor, at Auckland, asking for military assistance in the most pressing terms, as the only security for life itself. The Governor immediately despatched a confidential person with special instructions overland to Taranaki, and himself embarked on board Her Majesty's ship "Hazard," and hastened thither. The Bishop [Selywn] also repaired to the scene of difficulty with the utmost celerity, travelling from Auckland by Kawhia to Taranaki in eight days; while Mr. Whitely [Whiteley], the Wesleyan missionary at Kawhia (sixteen years resident in that part of the country), preceded them. Mr. Spain's award was made known in the middle of June, and on 3rd of August a large meeting of English and Natives were assembled at New Plymouth to hear the final decision."[156]

Newspaper coverage of this emergency meeting however painted a far less serious picture:

> "On landing, it was intimated to the Governor that a deputation had been appointed at a public meeting of the inhabitants to wait on him with a list of grievances which they labored under, when Captain Fitzroy appointed half-past two to meet them, at which hour a numerous body assembled in the large room of the Devon Hotel. On the Governor requesting the deputation to inform him of their grievances, Mr. Flight (who acted as chairman to the committee while

---

[155] *Auckland Chronicle and New Zealand Colonist*, 18 July, 1844, p2.

[156] Memorandum By Governor Fitzroy on the Taranaki Land Question, dated 2nd December, 1844, taken from AJHR, 1860, Session 1, E-02, p13.

taking the evidence) proceeded to address the Governor on the conduct of the natives to the white population, and read the evidences of about 15 settlers who could not obtain their land, whose houses the natives had repeatedly threatened to burn, and whose wives and relatives had been frequently and grossly insulted ; and concluded by observing that it was the firm conviction of the settlers that they would never be able to retain any of their land without efficient protection from Government, and that the present forbearance of the whites could not last much longer, and in case assistance was refused, a collision must take place. The Governor enquired if we had made known our grievances to the Police Magistrate.

Mr. Flight replied that most of them had been made known, but that he uniformly told them he could not interfere. The Governor then enquired of Capt. King, if he had reason to believe the evidence produced to be substantially correct. Capt. King replied that he thought it was strongly worded. Mr. Flight repudiated the idea of the evidence being colored, and affirmed it to be much less than the truth, and after some desultory conversation the Governor addressed the meeting...

...He knew Mr. Spain's decision – as no doubt we all did – and had no hesitation in saying that he (Mr. Spain) has most decidedly made a mistake, which he could not and would not confirm ; and he said this without any reflection on him, as he believed Mr. Spain had acted conscientiously according to his opinion of the case. But it was absurd to suppose because the natives had been taken away from their country that they had lost all claim to the land on which they were bred and born. People talked about their being slaves, but he denied that they were like the poor negro who was carried away from his country in childhood and educated in slavery. But these people were of the same habits and customs as their masters, and was it to be said, after diffusing the benefits of the gospel among their masters the Waikatos, and thereby inducing the Waikatos to set them free, was it to be said to them "we have induced your masters to let you go, but mean to take your land?" No! They are like men holding land in England, serving on board an English frigate, and being taken

> prisoners to France, would it not be hard to tell them, when they returned, that they had forfeited their land"[157]

Clearly Fitzroy's reversal of Spain's judgement had nothing to do with defusing a situation "as the only security for life itself", not an example of *realpolitik* for the purposes of avoiding bloodshed, but a purely moral one – for the sole purpose of "doing the right thing" as seen in his own, European eyes[158] – a fine and noble thing if the decision is indeed correct.

Indeed on the basis of the in-fighting and differences of opinion between the Taranaki officials it seems that their "problem" had been greatly exaggerated and that by alarming Fitzroy they had shot themselves in both feet by forcing him to reconsider Spain's decision. It is tantalising, if futile, to consider that had they not cried wolf quite so loudly Fitzroy may have just let Spain's judgement stand.

Fitzroy's "special instructions" despatched by a "confidential person" are somewhat puzzling. What were these, and if he was so sure of his decision to overturn Spain's decision why did he not just say so in this despatch and save himself, Selwyn and Whiteley the extreme trouble of rushing to do so in person? The implication is that Fitzroy only made his decision very late in the piece – perhaps even on the spot – and possibly under the influence of Selwyn. Again, we can only conjecture.

In August, 1844 Fitzroy was a rookie, seven months in the country and preoccupied by problems in the Bay of Islands related to Hone Heke. His naivety and lack of ability to reason is on full display in his attempt to compare the Taranaki situation to that of a captured English sailor. First

---

[157] *New Zealand Gazette and Wellington Spectator*, 14 August,1859, p2.

[158] Keith Sinclair (*The Origins of the Maori Wars*, p114) has what may or may not be a contrary view, confusingly suggesting that Fitzroy's decision was both because it was "right" *and* because it was "politic". ("He [Fitzroy] refused to use force and bloodshed in defence of a defective purchase and an unjust decision. His decision to abandon the [New Zealand] Company purchase was politic and, as we shall see, just"). Fitzroy made precisely the decision he personally wanted, which, as it happened, happily eliminated the unknown probability of violence that the alternative decision *may* have caused.

his "analogy" is not within a bulls-roar of the Taranaki scenario and second he is trying to apply (incorrectly) English principles to a Maori situation. While he is clearly well-meaning he is equally clearly out of his depth.

Fitzroy summarised his cunning plan to override Spain's now abandoned judgement in a letter to the New Zealand Company's agent in New Plymouth, the crux of which was that all Taranaki settlers must remove themselves to "a small block of land" to be bought from Maori for that purpose.

Fitzroy's plan was possibly a very good one, but for all that, whether he realised it or not, his decision was an absolute catastrophe for future New Zealand, guaranteeing a world of pain for his gubernatorial successors as well as generations of New Zealanders in perpetuity.

In overturning Spain's decision he had in effect erased the twenty-plus years of history from 1820 to 1844, everything we have gone to such pains to summarise so far in this book. Fitzroy refused to recognise the complicated chain of events and upheavals that had resulted in the change of status in the ownership of Taranaki and upon which Spain based his decision. He arbitrarily reset "year zero" for determination of ownership of Taranaki from 1820 to 1844, paving the way for a series of events which would not otherwise have happened and which would in less than 20 years' time play a major part in initiating the New Zealand Wars.

In November, 1844, Fitzroy's "small block of land" to which the settlers of New Plymouth were to be reined into was duly purchased from the Ngati Te Whitu *hapu*:

> "A meeting was accordingly held of the natives principally concerned, when, after some difficulty in obtaining the quantity of land which his Excellency was desirous of purchasing, to enable him to place all the Europeans who occupy land in this settlement in quiet and indisputable possession, and, after much discussion, he succeeded in

> obtaining their consent to sell about 3,300 acres[159], with an understanding that their cultivations should be reserved.
>
> Messrs. Whitely [Whiteley], Forsaith, myself and a surveyor, with a party of the natives, then perambulated the boundaries of the block of land treated for; after which a deed was prepared and signed by eighty-four natives being within fourteen of the whole number of adults in the tribe"[160]

What with the New Zealand Company's original purchase from the Ngamotu remnants, and Hobson's purchase from the Waikatos, this particular piece of land had now been purchased three times.

---

[159] Generally referred to as 3,500 acres in most accounts.

[160] Letter from Donald McLean to Chief Protector of Aborigines, 17 December, 1844 (BBP, 8 April 1846, p143).See also *He Whenua Te Utu*, Ann Parsonson, p236-242, for a good account of these events.

Page 153

The location of the Pukerangiora and Otaka pa attacked by the Waikatos in 1832, shown on a modern aerial view to put things into perspective for modern readers. Also shown are the sites of the Manukoriki and Puketapu pa, which are important to note as being areas vacated by the various migrations and Waikato slave-taking subsequent to these raids, and the Waitara River, a major demarcation line of the Taranaki area.

Although this modern view shows the area largely denuded of bush, in 1832 it was predominantly covered by bush and trees down to the bush-line approximately as shown by the dotted yellow line. Given the tiny amount of clear land, and the dense tangle of valley-lets caused by the flow-off from Mt Taranaki which we see in this modern photo, it is not difficult to predict that land procurement would become a major problem for early European settlers.

Pages 154 and 155

***MAP 1** – Showing the approximate position of the west coast tribes circa 1800, prior to the upheaval that would result from Te Rauparaha's migration south in about 1820.*

***MAP 2** – Showing the approximate distribution of mana whenua at the time of William Wakefield's arrival in late 1839. The area in orange is under the mana of Te Rauparaha while that in green, pink and black is under the mana of the Tainui tribes.*

Page 156

A composite drawing showing what is known of the Otaka Pa siege by the Waikatos. The basis is a detail from a map drawn by Frederick Carrington dated 1842.

The remains of Otaka Pa were evidently still visible ten years after the event and are recorded by Carrington. Other snippets of detail related to the engagement itself have been added from Map 7 of S. Percy Smith's classic, "History and Traditions of the Maoris of the West Coast". The high-tide line is that shown in Carrington's map, which differs from that shown in Smith's picture.

This area of what is now New Plymouth is much changed since the siege of 1832. Breakwaters, docking and port facilities have been added, land has been reclaimed and the detailed coast line heavily modified and linearly trimmed, losing what was once the "island" of Mikotahi in the process. The only area that resembles its 1832 state is Moturoa Beach itself and the site of Otaka Pa is in the playground just behind it. If these maps are correct Otaka Pa would have been in the order of 350 by 50 meters, roughly the area of two rugby fields.

Page 157

A simplified summary of the diaspora of the four Groups of the Ati Awa.

Page 158

Top: *Te Rauparaha in 1839, probably then in his seventies, as sketched by nineteen year old New Zealand Company draughtsman Charles Heaphy (Credit: Alexander Turnbull Library, Ref:A-146-008).*

Te Rauparaha was the unwitting architect and enabler of European settlement in the lower half of the North Island and the top of the South Island, and ultimately the source of the land ownership confusion that would eventually create the spark, if not the logs, which fuelled the conflagration currently referred to, rather erroneously, as "The New Zealand Wars".

Bottom Left: *(Colonel) William Wakefield, Edward Gibbon's younger brother by 5 years, in what appears to be the only extant likeness of him, made thirteen years before he set foot in New Zealand (Credit: Alexander Turnbull Library, Ref: A-087-014).*

If Edward Gibbon was the brains then William was the luckless lackey tasked with turning his pipe-dreams into reality. William died in 1848 at the age of 47 after eight years of harassment by colonists who heaped scorn on him for his inability to pull non-existent rabbits out of invisible hats.

Bottom right: *Edward Gibbon's only surviving child, Edward Jerningham Wakefield, who accompanied his Uncle William to New Zealand in the Tory in 1839 (Early History of New Zealand - Sherrin and Wallace, p479).*

His lasting legacy is his classic work "Adventure in New Zealand", written on his return to London in 1844 after being ignominiously upbraided by new Governor Robert Fitzroy. Returning to New Zealand in 1850 he engaged in politics with spasmodic success, slid into a decline of drunkenness and died in obscurity and poverty in 1879.

NGATI MUTUNGA TRIBE
North
Ati Awa Tribal
Boundary
Ngati Rahiri
hapu
of Ati-Awa
Waitara River
Manukoriki Pa
ATI-AWA
TRIBE
Pukerangiora Pa
Puketapu Pa
Approximate
Bush-line
South
Ati Awa Tribal
Boundary
Otaka Pa
Mikotahi "Island"
Nga Motu/Sugarloaves
TARANAKI
TRIBE

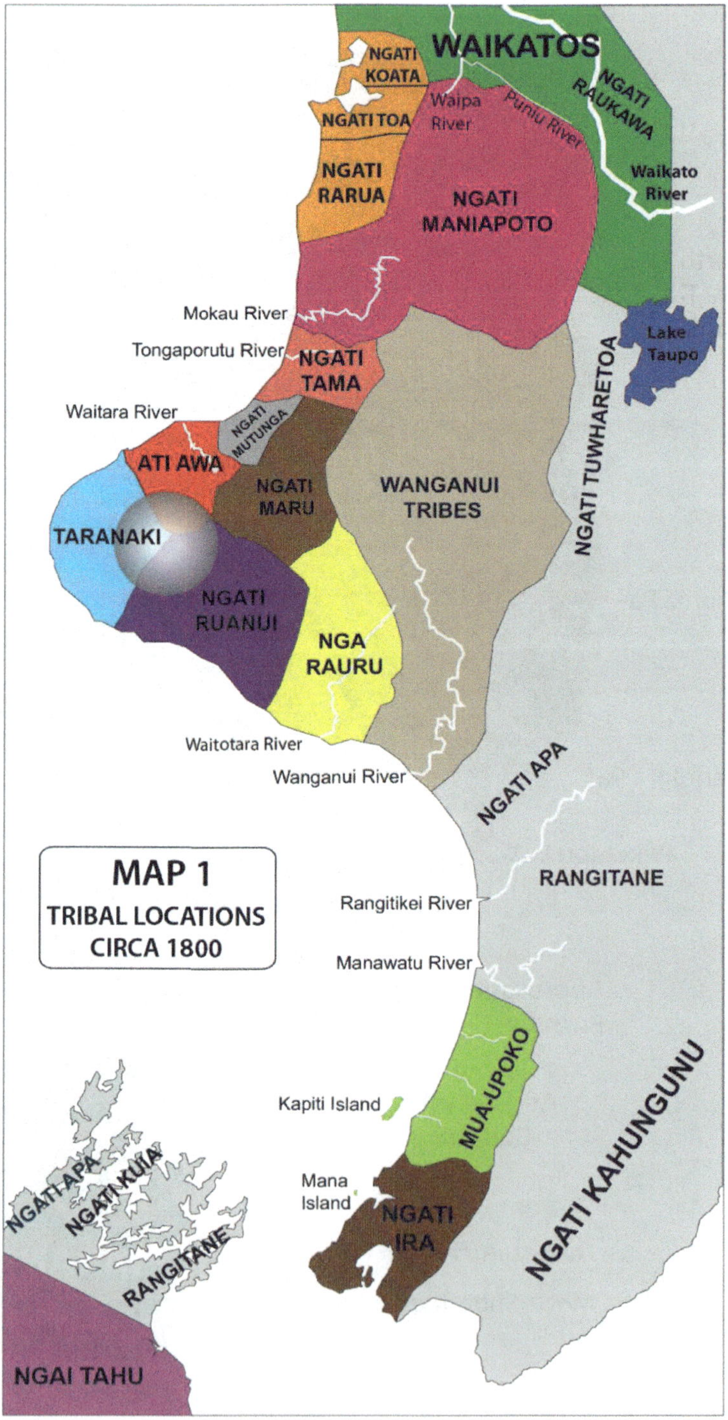

MAP 1
TRIBAL LOCATIONS CIRCA 1800

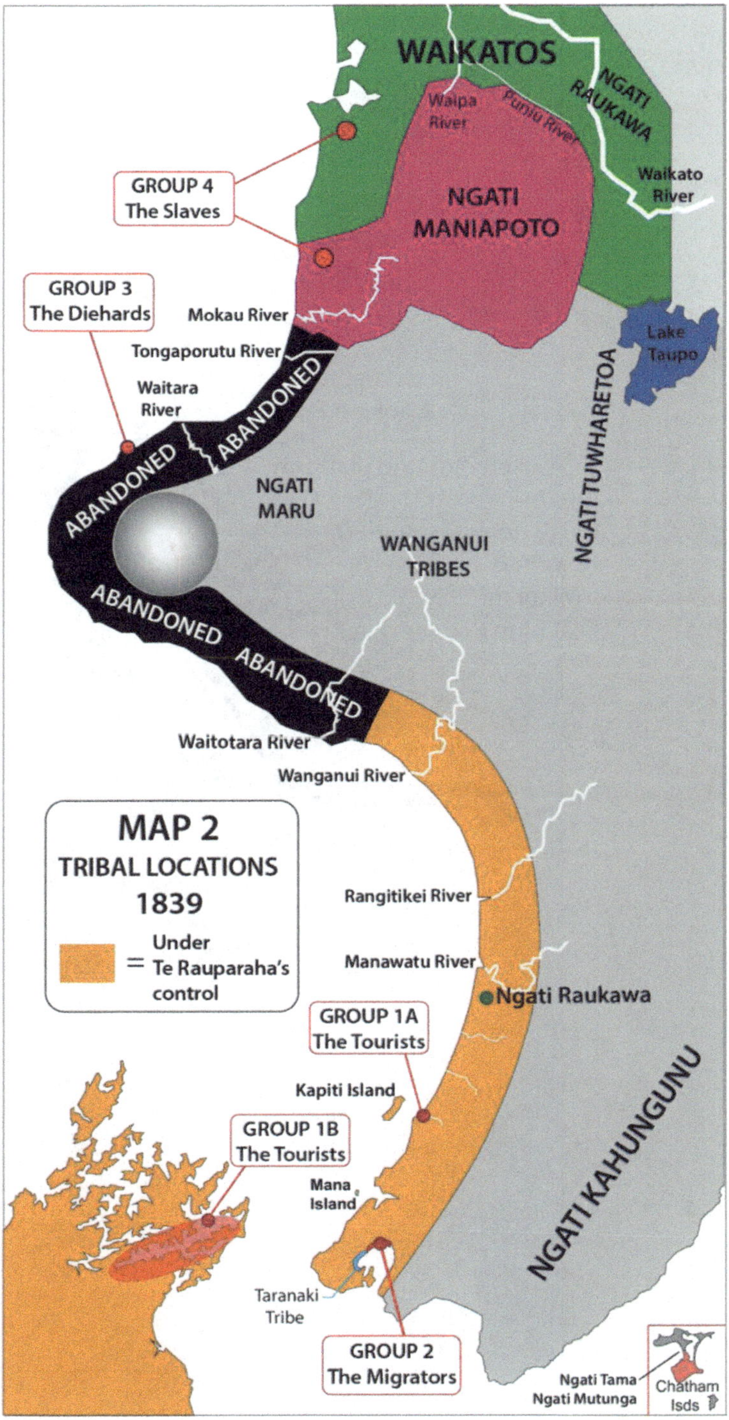

WAIKATOS
NGATI RAUKAWA
Waipa River
Puniu River
Waikato River
GROUP 4
The Slaves
NGATI MANIAPOTO
GROUP 3
The Diehards
Mokau River
Tongaporutu River
Waitara River
Lake Taupo
NGATI TUWHARETOA
ABANDONED
ABANDONED
ABANDONED
NGATI MARU
WANGANUI TRIBES
ABANDONED
ABANDONED
Waitotara River
Wanganui River
MAP 2
TRIBAL LOCATIONS
1839
= Under Te Rauparaha's control
Rangitikei River
Manawatu River
Ngati Raukawa
GROUP 1A
The Tourists
Kapiti Island
GROUP 1B
The Tourists
NGATI KAHUNGUNU
Mana Island
Taranaki Tribe
GROUP 2
The Migrators
Ngati Tama
Ngati Mutunga
Chatham Isds

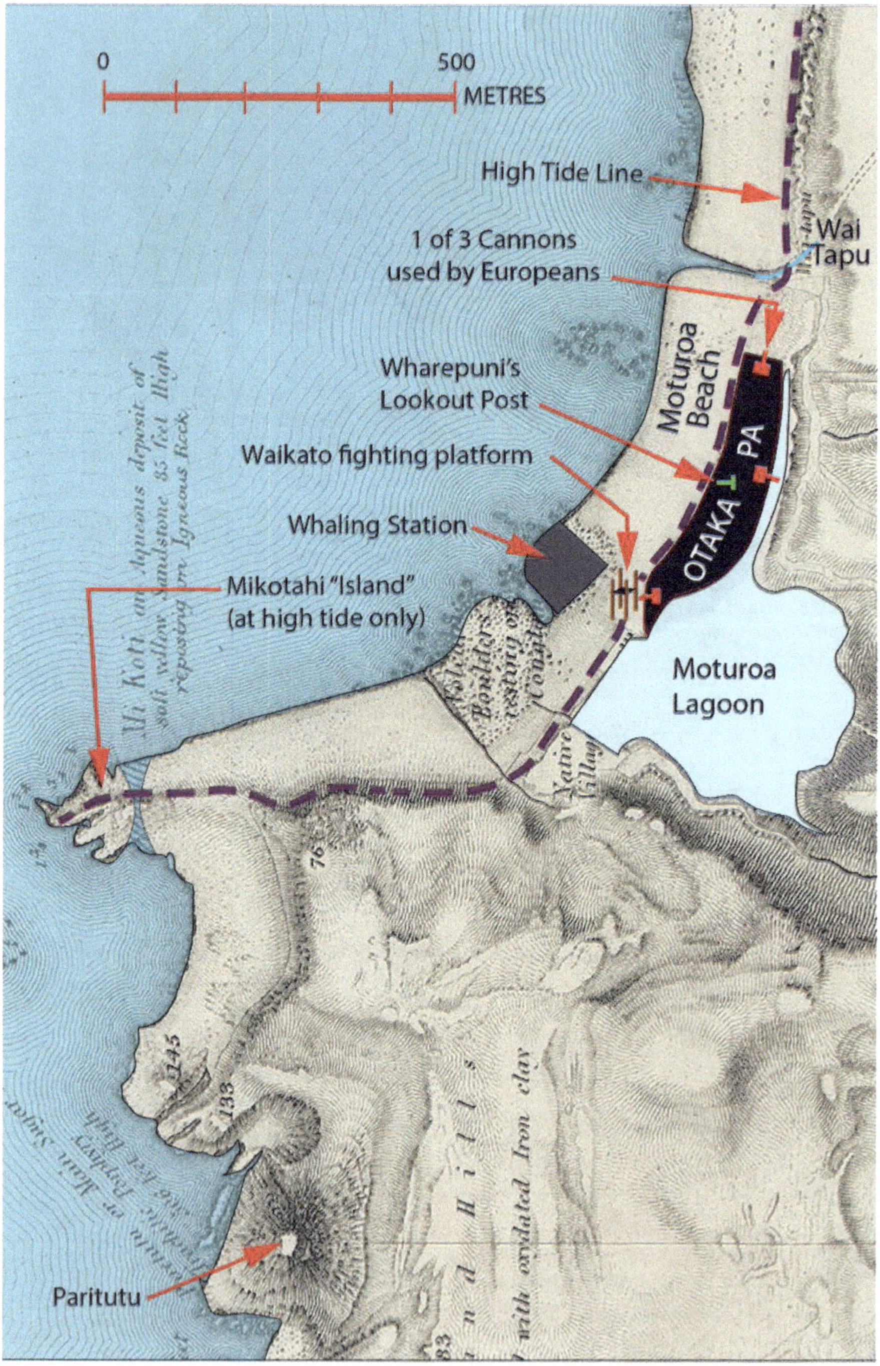
0
500
METRES
High Tide Line
1 of 3 Cannons
used by Europeans
Wai
Tapu
Moturoa
Beach
Wharepuni's
Lookout Post
Waikato fighting platform
OTAKA PA
Whaling Station
Mikotahi "Island"
(at high tide only)
Moturoa
Lagoon
Paritutu

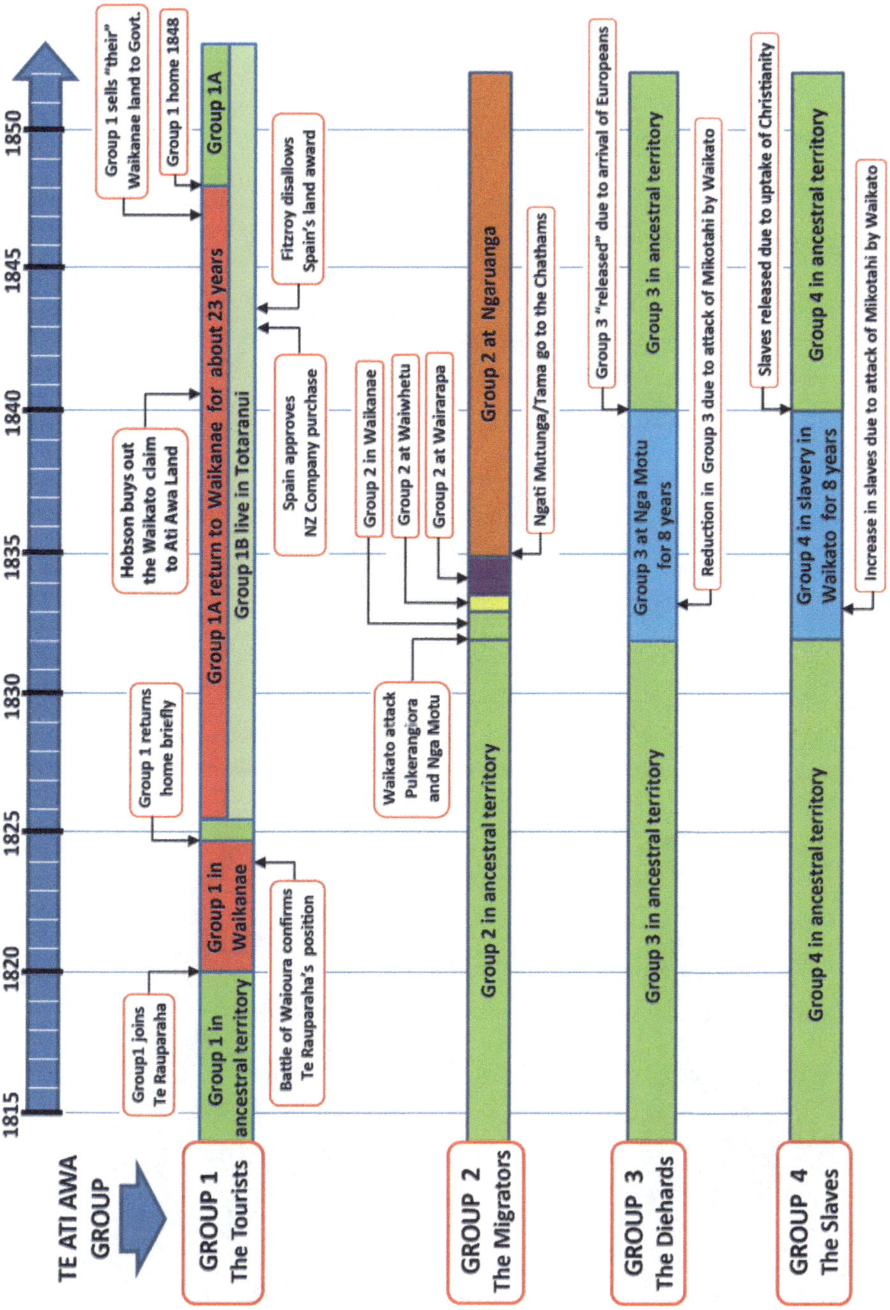
TE ATI AWA GROUP
1815
1820
1825
1830
1835
1840
1845
1850
GROUP 1 The Tourists
Group 1 in ancestral territory
Group 1 in Waikanae
Group 1A return to Waikanae for about 23 years
Group 1B live in Totaranui
Group 1A
Group1 joins Te Rauparaha
Group 1 returns home briefly
Hobson buys out the Waikato claim to Ati Awa Land
Group 1 sells "their" Waikanae land to Govt.
Group 1 home 1848
Battle of Waioura confirms Te Rauparaha's position
Spain approves NZ Company purchase
Fitzroy disallows Spain's land award
GROUP 2 The Migrators
Group 2 in ancestral territory
Group 2 at Ngaruanga
Waikato attack Pukerangiora and Nga Motu
Group 2 in Waikanae
Group 2 at Waiwhetu
Group 2 at Wairarapa
Ngati Mutunga/Tama go to the Chathams
GROUP 3 The Diehards
Group 3 in ancestral territory
Group 3 at Nga Motu for 8 years
Group 3 in ancestral territory
Group 3 "released" due to arrival of Europeans
Reduction in Group 3 due to attack of Mikotahi by Waikato
GROUP 4 The Slaves
Group 4 in ancestral territory
Group 4 in slavery in Waikato for 8 years
Group 4 in ancestral territory
Slaves released due to uptake of Christianity
Increase in slaves due to attack of Mikotahi by Waikato

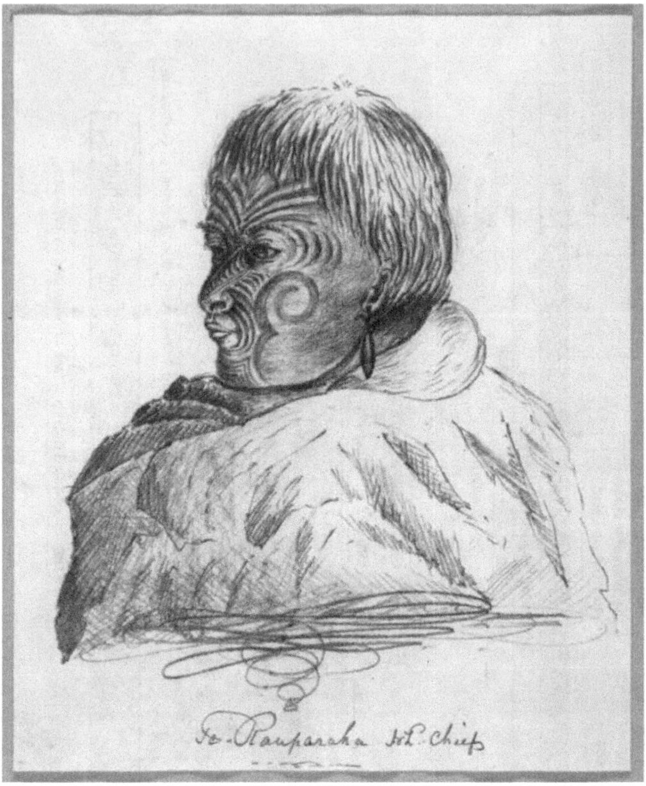
Te Rauparaha

Chapter 1-12

The makings of a spark.

Traditionally the generation of a spark requires the banging together of two hard objects – two hard rocks, two hard heads, or in a more modern implementation, a flint and steel. In this chapter we introduce the man who would become one of the two hard rocks that generated the spark that ignited the New Zealand Wars.

It is one of the great paradoxes of history that many of the most momentous and world-changing events have been brought about by the actions of obscure and otherwise totally unmemorable individuals. Such is the case with the small cast of the play "The creators of the New Zealand Wars", all of whom were relatively unimportant before the event and all of whom disappeared into total obscurity after it. This was their fifteen minutes of fame and their names are now known only to historians.

We have already been briefly introduced to our first cast member, many pages ago, in our summary of the various migrations of the Ati Awa. This man is most often referred to today by his baptismal name of Wiremu Kingi, the Maori transliteration of "William King". For someone whose actions had, and continue to have, such extreme consequences we know precious little about him. He was an enigma, a man of few words – especially, and most infuriatingly, when they were most needed – a man who preferred to hide in the background and delegate his battles to others.

The future Wiremu Kingi was born to father Reretawhangawhanga and mother Te Kehu in the final years of the 1700's.[161] At that time his name was Te Rangitake but he seems to have been generally known in his youth as Whiti, sometimes also written as Witi, Wite or even White. The first 30 years of Whiti's life are a blank page and he first bursts into a fleeting existence, as noted elsewhere, with a very brief reference to his having been part of the 1820 migration of the Group 1 Ati Awa with Te Rauparaha to the Kapiti area.

In the first four decades of the 1800's we hear regular references to his father Reretawhangawhanga, who is described as "paramount chief" of Ati Awa, but we hear little of his soon-to-be transiently famous son, Whiti. Since Reretawhangawhanga is said to have joined Te Rauparaha in his raids to the South Island it is likely, but unprovable, that his son Whiti, who would then have been in his thirties, accompanied him on these sanguinary exploits.

With the arrival of the *Tory* in late 1839 we get a small flurry of passing references to him. His mark appears at the top of the New Zealand Company's Queen Charlotte Sound Deed, with the name "Wite" written alongside. Describing the shambolic division of goods among the signatories of this deed Jerningham Wakefield writes:

> "On my way, I met E Witi, one of the chiefs of a tribe which had effected a quiet division; and he reassured me by telling me that no harm would be done to the White people, and that I had better go up in the rigging and look upon the way in which the natives divided their goods."[162]

---

[161] The *Dictionary of New Zealand Biography* – Volume 1, p499, suggests "the last years of the 18th century".

[162] *Adventure in New Zealand* - Vol 1, E. Jerningham Wakefield, p136.

Missionary Samuel Ironside says of the same event...

> "In 1839, Colonel Wakefield, the agent of the New Zealand Company, purchased the district [Taranaki] from the exiles [Ati Awa of Taranaki] in Cook's Straits, and from the remnant in occupation [the Group 3 "Diehards"]. The chiefs all signed the deed of sale. Among the parties to the sale was Wiremu King, who is now so violent and rebellious. He was then called E Witi. He was very active in furthering Colonel Wakefield's wishes. He wrote to Taranaki, telling the few in occupation to receive Colonel Wakefield and further his views in every way. They were all too glad to sell the land, and get payment for it, as they dare not return to occupy it for fear of Waikato."[163]

Other comments which shed light on both the Queen Charlotte Sound Deed and Kingi's place in the pecking order of Ati Awa hierarchy include:

> "Sunday, 27th October, 1839 - I [William Wakefield] went to Waikanae, taking with me E Patu, the son of Toroa, the two principal chiefs of that place and of Queen Charlotte's Sound: The three chiefs of the Ngatiawas, whom I had brought from Waikanae, declined proceeding with me to Queen Charlotte's Sound...They pleaded, with justice, the danger to their families during their absence, from their neighbouring enemies, but deputed one of their sons [E Whiti = Wiremu Kingi] to accompany me, who is empowered to act for them.
>
> Thursday, 31st October...we crossed the strait this morning... my companion and myself with the Waikanae chief [E Whiti = Wiremu Kingi], had to go through the ceremony of shaking hands with everyone in the settlement...After this operation, a tangi commenced in honour of the chief's arrival...E Whiti remained to talk about the land.

---

[163] *Empire* (Sydney Newspaper), 21 May, 1863, p5.

11th November. Being under a promise to take back the chief E Whiti, and the missionary who had been a witness to the late sale, to Waikanae, we sailed for this place yesterday..."[164]

"Much difficulty occurred, both during these discussions and at the distribution of the goods, in consequence of the absence of chieftains of great influence to take the lead in treating and speaking for the others...I met E Witi, one of the chiefs of a tribe which had effected a quiet division..."[165]

"The Waikanae chief Reretawhangawhanga told Spain that he remembered his son, Wiremu Kingi te Rangitake, and Himiona returning from the sound after the deed was signed, but he believed that only Arapaoa, the large island near the entrance to the sound, had been sold. Another Te Atiawa witness, Ngapuka, also stated this belief.[166]

"I am quite amused in the morning to see the principal chief of the place, Reretawhangawhanga, learning to read and write his letters. He is an old man with a long grey beard."[167]

"The third tribe, the Ngatiawa, lived at Waikanae under the leadership of Te Reretawhangawhanga, who largely exerted his authority through his son, Te Rangitake." [168]

These comments provide conflicting views of Kingi's status at this time. Although he was a significant enough guest to be afforded a tangi, and his name appears at the top of the signatories of the Queen Charlotte Sound

---

[164] Selected extracts from despatches of William Wakefield, taken from AJHR 1861, C1, p163.

[165] *Adventure in New Zealand* – Vol 1, E. Jerningham Wakefield, p136.

[166] Waitangi Tribunal Report WAI 785, p202.

[167] Letter written by Octavius Hadfield to his brother Charles, 19 December, 1839. (*Octavius Hadfield*, Barbara McMorran, p163).

[168] *Octavius Hadfield*, Barbara McMorran, p19.

Deed, both William and Jerningham Wakefield's reports suggest he was subordinate to three other chiefs and was expendable while the real chiefs dealt to the crisis of the moment, that of dealing to the threat of imminent battle with Ngati Raukawa. This could also be an indicator of split leadership in which the warrior generation chiefs dealt to matters of war while the younger generation son handled matters of diplomacy and interfacing with the new world of Europeans. Another quote suggests his father was specifically recognized only as principal chief of the Waikanae group, not paramount chief of Ati Awa as a whole, which would mean that this would be the extent of Kingi's authority on his father's death. And yet another quote suggests that while the father was indeed titular "chief" of his *hapu* (Manukorihi) he had delegated day to day leadership to his son.

It was about this time that Christianity began to make its mark in the Kapiti area and it did so via a rather random and surprising sequence of events. It has already been noted that the transmission of the Christian message southward was largely the result of missionary influenced Maori returning home rather than of European Missionary personnel themselves. The particular Maori individual responsible in large part for the introduction and uptake of Christianity amongst Maori along the Kapiti coast was a released slave called Ripahau[169], originally of the Ngati Raukawa tribe, who arrived in the area in early 1838 bearing not one but two precious gifts – a few pages of St Luke's Gospel and the ability to read and write.

While not well received by his Ngata Raukawa kinsmen at Otaki, Ripahau struck up a friendship with Te Rauparaha's only surviving son Katu and Katu's nephew Matene Te Whiwhi, to whom he taught the rudiments of reading and writing. Interestingly Ripahau himself was not a Christian at this point but he seems to have had an awareness that he held something precious if only he could figure out what it was. It is yet another example

---

[169] Sometimes called Matahau and later baptised as Hohepa (Joseph).
See *The Wounded Lion*, Christopher Lethbridge, pp44-6, and *The Advance of the Missionaries*, Hilda Fancourt, pp83-89, for a good summary of the original sources related to Ripahau.

of the feeling among Maori of the time that their traditional way of life had failed them and which generated a thirst and curiosity for alternatives. Nowhere is this spectacular seismic shift between the warrior oriented social order of the fathers and the rejection of that order by their sons better exemplified than by a comparison between the knarly old chief Te Rauparaha, slaughterer of thousands, and his Christian, thoroughly Europeanized son Katu, later to be better known by his baptismal name of Tamihana.[170]

To cut a long story short, inspired by the teachings of Ripahau the young Katu Te Rauparaha and Matene Te Whiwhi journeyed to the CMS Missionary Station in Paihia to request the presence of a missionary in the Kapiti area. This request in due course resulted in the newly arrived and chronically unwell CMS missionary Octavius Hadfield arriving in the Otaki/Waikanae area in November, 1839, an event which would prove to be pivotal in Whiti's life.

Six months later, Whiti's willingness to engage with Europeans was further demonstrated by the adding of his mark to yet another one of those inscrutable European pieces of paper:

> "... in May 1840, Te Reretawhangawhanga and Te Rangitake drew their moko as signatures at the head of the Waikanae names of the Treaty of Waitangi..."[171]

From 1840 to about 1846 we hear little more of Whiti than random snippets, such as this short but glowing 1842 reference from New Zealand Company Native Reserves Commissioner, Edmond Halswell:

---

170 Most often interpreted as "Thompson", sometimes as "Sampson".

171 Wiremu Kingi's biography in *Dictionary of New Zealand Biography*, Ann Parsonson, p499. In contrast with Parsonson's dismissal of the very simple Queen Charlotte Sound Deed she is silent on the possibility of Whiti misunderstanding the far more complex document that is the Treaty of Waitangi, or his unfamiliarity with written documents.

> "E Witi is by far the most powerful and influential chief in the whole of Cook's Straits, and both sides of the Northern Island from East Cape and Waikato; he is a very excellent man. Warepori set off some time ago to meet a party of Waikato people at Taranaki; on arriving at Waikanae he was stopped and sent back by E Witi."[172]

This seems to suggest that in the scheme of the Ati Awa world Whiti outranked Wharepouri, whom we have already met as one of the "senior" chiefs of the Group 2 Ati Awa in Wellington.

In 1844 we see Whiti involved with Commissioner Spain's investigation into the New Zealand Company's Wellington purchase:

> "Wiremu Kingi, the principal young chief of the place, then spoke ; he said the sum was too small, they could not accept it; he wished to know whether any reserves would be made for them, saying that the reserves allotted them by the Company were wholly unfit for their use, being swampy or covered with water; he wished to know whether these reserves would be changed...On preparing to leave, Wiremu Kingi requested us not to be in haste ; that if they could be sure of having certain lands reserved, which he named, they would take the payment."[173]

This quote suggests that Kingi was not just principal chief of his own *hapu*, or even just of the collective of Group 1 Ati Awa resident at Waikanae, but that he was also principal chief of Group 2 Ati Awa resident at Waiwetu, Wellington – "the place" referred to in the text.

---

[172] *History of New Zealand* - Vol 1, George Rusden, pp279-280.

[173] Minutes of Proceedings in Commissioner's Court, Port Nicholson,
Friday 15 March 1844 (quoted from Copies of Despatches, BBP, 8 April 1846, p26). Once again we see Whiti's unequivocal understanding of the concept of permanent land transfer, its associated requirement of reserves and the natural haggling involved in such deals, including, in this case, having his bluff called.

In the years between 1842 and 1844 two life-changing events occurred in Whiti's life. First he was baptised by resident Anglican missionary Octavius Hadfield, obtaining the baptismal name of "Wiremu Kingi" by which he is most commonly remembered. Second, on 26th September, 1843, his father Reretawhangawhanga died and the newly renamed Kingi finally assumed the authority of his father – whatever that may have been – by virtue of hereditary title.

His recently acquired baptismal name of Kingi was, by accident or design, now strangely appropriate, for he was now "king" of his Ati Awa domain, although the actual extent of that domain remains unclear.

Clearly Kingi was now a very big wheel in the Ati Awa hierarchy but whether that makes him supreme commander over the entirety of the disparate and far-flung factions of that tribe is hard to say. It is a point of confusion that remains to this day and his ill-defined status is in no small way a contributor to the "spark" that ignited the New Zealand Wars.

Historian Keith Sinclair's take on Kingi's authority is as follows:

> "It is usually accepted by modern historians, and was often said in the eighteen-sixties, that Wiremu Kingi was also the ariki of the entire Atiawa tribe. For example, a correspondent of the Auckland Examiner on 29 February, 1860, wrote that "Wm. King is the head man of the tribe now." It is certainly true that, among the Maoris, Wiremu Kingi was the best known of the Atiawa and was far more influential than any other chief of his tribe. His father also was one of the most renowned chiefs of his day. But for all practical purposes there was no single chief of the Atiawa. Many of the tribe were still scattered. Of those in Taranaki, the few who had remained there throughout, those who had returned from slavery in the Waikato, and those who had returned from exile in places other than Otaki, most had not known Wiremu Kingi. They had spent twenty years away from the complex of tribal authority, and tended to recognize only individual leaders."[174]

---

[174] *Some Historical Notes on an Atiawa Genealogy*, Keith Sinclair, JPS, 1951.

On the death of his father Kingi was no longer a young man himself – somewhere in his late 40s – and his life and actions bear a remarkable similarity to his Ngati Toa contemporary and generational equivalent, Katu/Tamihana Te Rauparaha. He had been raised and lived in a classic Maori traditional society, lived through and survived the most tumultuous period in Maori history and possibly killed his fair share of whomever his enemies were at the time. For all that there is a sense that his father's death marked the end of an era which Kingi had never entirely entered into, a world he accepted out of respect for his father rather than because his heart was in it.

His father came from a different time and world, an uncomplicated time of a warrior code and constant warfare. By 1840 that world was history and his son knew it. Like Katu Te Rauparaha he understood he was now part of a much larger, rapidly changing and more complicated modern world, in a time of relative peace, of Christianity and of having to find a workable compromise between the Maori and European worlds. With his father gone, Kingi stepped up to his pre-destined but very different role and took firm control. The "boy" Whiti had become the "man" Kingi.

In early June, 1844, Kingi travelled from Waikanae to New Plymouth to attend Commissioner Spain's investigation into the New Zealand Company's purchase of Taranaki. You would think that Kingi, the assumed "principal chief" of the area under discussion, would be the lead advocate in its defence, but strangely he is not recorded as making any contribution in the defence of "his own" ancestral land while other lesser Ati Awa do.

This would not be the last time Kingi was his own worst enemy through an inability or unwillingness to communicate, although to be fair, the entire proceedings of Spain's court at New Plymouth were notable for an extreme reluctance on the part of *any* of the assembled Maori to make any contribution or comment whatsoever. At New Plymouth Spain was working in a vacuum to an unresponsive house and he was getting

---

Volume 60, No.1, p59.

nothing back. Kingi seems to have had an unhelpful personality, and communication, at least in that particular setting and context, was evidently not his forte. Yet perversely, while he is not recorded as saying a word in his defence at the appropriate time in Spain's court, as soon as Spain verbally presented his judgement to the assembled masses on 8 June, 1844, Kingi was within hours on the end of a pen writing a letter of complaint to Fitzroy in which he states that Taranaki Maori "hearts are dark by reason of Mr. Spain's words" and that "Waitara shall not be given up; the men to whom it belongs will hold it for themselves."[175]

We can empathise with Kingi's plea and it is no doubt difficult to accurately and completely express one's thoughts in a short letter using the newly acquired medium of writing to a person of an entirely different language and culture. But it is difficult not to think he has left his run about twenty-five years too late and that he is unfamiliar with the concept that actions – or lack of them – have consequences. His words are specious and none of them stand close scrutiny. He says "It was love for the land of our forefathers that brought us back to those lands" and while that may be so he fails to acknowledge that the only reason he is able to "go back to those lands" is thanks to a combination of the peace brought by European settlement and the European money paid to the Waikatos. In what is a recurring theme, when it comes to interaction with Europeans Kingi forgets the principle of *utu* – that he "owes one" – and a *very, very big* one – to the Europeans.

The thrust of his letter is that the "Europeans" can have whatever land has been "justly purchased" and that while he agrees much of Taranaki *has* been sold, Waitara has not. It is a great shame for posterity that Kingi does not clarify what he thinks the Queen Charlotte Sound Deed meant, what his signature at the top of that deed meant, or what the pile of trade goods that changed hands was for.

Kingi tugs at Fitzroy's heartstrings by comparing his (Kingi's) desire to retain his land at Waitara to Fitzroy's love of his own country. Touching as this is, and compelling as this might be to a Maori audience it is also naïve

[175] See Appendix 2 for the complete letter.

and totally missing the point – if – to use an analogy to the Ati Awa's situation with the Waikatos – England had been invaded by France and its entire population had fled to safety in America, it is absurd to think these evacuees would expect to see any of their former property, personal or real, ever again. While they may have indeed yearned nostalgically for their old home their lives had changed forever and they would just get on with building another one. That's life.

Kingi's letter does, however, clarify one important aspect. He claims that the people who sold the New Zealand Company land via the Taranaki Deed – the Group 3 Diehards – had only sold *their own* lands. In doing so Kingi is confirming that those few people huddled around Ngamotu were *not* in fact "fire burners" for the entire area of Ati Awa territory but only for the tiny Ngamotu area, which in turn means that for a full eight years the entire remainder of the Ati Awa territory had no "fires burning".

We also note that Kingi's letter refers to "Waitara" and Waitara only, in other words a relatively small part of the total Ati Awa area. It seems he has – at least at this stage – no objection to anyone else, the Ngamotu or the Puketapu *hapu* for instance, selling *their* land.

Clearly, in 1844 Kingi neither considers himself "paramount chief" of Ati Awa nor that he can claim right of veto over anyone else's decisions to dispose of *their* land. Indeed, confusingly, he does not even consider that those he agrees *did* sell their land – the Diehards of Ngamotu – to be part of what he calls "Ngatiawa". All in all there is considerable confusion as to precisely what "Ngatiawa" and "Waitara" are and who is "paramount chief", if indeed such a person actually existed. Both in Kingi's letter and in Spain's report "Waitara" seems to be the name given to "anywhere that isn't Ngamotu". The various *hapu*, the extents of their lands and the hierarchy of their chiefs, are never mentioned.

As we have seen earlier, Spain's New Plymouth judgement was indeed overturned by Fitzroy, although whether this had anything to do with Kingi's letter, whether Kingi had any reaction to Fitzroy's reversal, or whether Fitzroy got any thanks from Kingi for this huge and illogical favour, is not recorded.

Chapter 1-13

Grey lays down the law.

It is another two years, in 1846, before we meet Wiremu Kingi again.

By then the luckless Governor Fitzroy had been recalled and replaced by George Grey. Like Fitzroy and Hobson before him Grey was a yet another Captain, albeit of the army rather than the Navy. However he arrived in New Zealand with one thing Hobson and Fitzroy never had – prior experience as a Governor – and more importantly not just experience but *good* experience with success as an outcome. Even at the ridiculously young age of 34 he arrived as the man who had single-handedly turned around the fortunes of the very first Wakefield colony, that of Adelaide in Australia. As is par for the course for any Governor, or indeed for any political leader before or since, he had achieved this spectacular turnaround with tough decisions that had left him unpopular with the masses but nevertheless made him a star in the eyes of his bosses in the Colonial Office back in England. He arrived in New Zealand as a rising star, a trouble shooter, the man of the moment, a gubernatorial wunderkind.

While every New Zealand Governor was hated and vilified by the colonists of their time Grey stands unique as being the only one universally hated and vilified, or indeed remembered in any form or fashion, by today's brow-furrowing historians. In the great New Zealand history paradigm of black hats and white hats, George Grey will forever wear the biggest and blackest hat of them all.

Grey was paradoxically both very similar and completely different from his predecessor Fitzroy. Like Fitzroy, and like every Englishman of his time and social standing, he was a devoted Christian and his Bible was his best friend. But unlike Fitzroy he had little time for missionaries and their pharisaic thinking that saw future New Zealand in their blinkered image. Although Grey would form a strong relationship with the Anglican Church in New Zealand, most particularly with its head, Bishop Selwyn, he would not only attack the missionaries themselves but disestablish the "Trojan Horse" missionary conclave in government known as the Aboriginal Protectorate. Grey's arrival essentially marked the end of missionary influence, at least at a governance level.

Grey's first action on arrival was to address that chronic nemesis of flag poles, Hone Heke, whose axe-wielding days came to an end with the battle at Ruapekapeka on 11 January, 1846. Grey barely had time to catch his breath before he charged down to the other end of the island to address escalating disturbances around Wellington and the Hutt Valley. He arrived in Wellington on 12 February, 1846, to defuse a messy stand-off between settlers trying to occupy what they considered to be legally purchased land and Maori who either remained unconvinced or had suddenly decided they could have got more money for it.

It is perhaps not surprising to learn that the lynchpin behind the push-back against European settlement was Te Rauparaha's nephew and partner in crime, the famously aggressive Rangihaeata and in this he was aided by Ngati Tama chief Taringa Kuri and allies as far north as Wanganui. This set of skirmishes is important to the subject of this book only in what it tells us about Wiremu Kingi, his relationship with European authorities and his future aspirations.

Not long after Grey's arrival in Wellington Kingi wrote to him as follows:

> "Kaiwarawara, Port Nicholson, 21 February 1846.
>
> The Governor – This is our deliberation. We have decided that the natives of the faith should hearken fully to the laws of the Queen,

which proceed from your mouth, from the Governor. Leave us below under the wings of the regulations of the Queen and yourself. Let a good regulation be commenced, that the faith may grow among us; that we may not profess faith in God, while we are reverting to error, because there is no one to use the scourge; that our race, the native people, may grow; and that we may forsake our evil customs, great quarrels and little quarrels, such as taking away land, removing land-marks, robbery, murder, and very many other of our customs among ourselves. Now this is our consideration; it is for your good customs to beat down our evil customs, with the help of God, that the work left for us may be the cultivation of provisions for the life of the body, and the faith of Christ for the life of the soul. It is for you, and for the ministers of God, to make these evil people grow (in good), that they may grow; then they will hearken to the truth, to the Queen, to the Governor, and to the minister. It is for you to observe these considerations; it ends here.

From the people of your tribe, the Ngatiawa.

(Signed) William King Witi, Levi Te Ahu"[176]

Clearly Kingi was eager, at least on paper, to work in harmony with the new European order, or more accurately, to heed the words of the European God. A few months later, on 15 July, 1846, Kingi wrote again to Governor Grey:

"Friend the Governor, health to you. Our regard is great for you. We have a word to say to you. We have heard by a white person who has come from Auckland that a hostile party is on their way from Wanganui; they left them at Rangitikei (100 persons). It is on this account that we write this letter to you, to ask you to give us some guns and powder, some ball and flints, and cartouche-boxes. If you approve of this our request for guns, send us twenty cases, that there

---

[176] *New Zealand Spectator and Cook's Strait Guardian*, 10 February 1847, p3, quoting British Parliamentary Papers.

may be sufficient, as we are many. Our friend, make haste. The coming down of hostile parties has now commenced. This is the first party – presently there will be a second, a third, and fourth party to join Rangihaeata for the purpose of killing the white people; but not for the white people only – no, for us also, as you will consider we have been united by the Christian belief. It is on this account we have regard for you, as you regard us. If we were at Wellington we should stand up with you, as E Puni and his party have joined the white people. Don't think for a moment we are wavering as to what step we should take. No, we are looking to you. The consent (or allegiance) we made to you is sure, and remains for ever. Don't think that this hostility is for the white people only – it is for us both – to overturn the Christian belief. As we have heard that Rangihaeata has made sacred the road, to prevent the quiet and well-disposed from bringing down their pigs to Wellington, the road between Pukerua and Kaurarawara is the part to be set aside for Rangihaeata – for the man who has not yet believed or become a Christian. Now the Ngatitoa are aiding or strengthening Rangihaeata. Listen to the reason of our regard for you: it is because the white people are free from any charge of oppressing or first injuring the natives: hence the greatness of our love for you. The guns we ask are not for the purpose of assaulting Rangihaeata's pa. No: we want them here to lay in wait for those hostile natives who may come down upon us. Should you approve of this request, send to us on the 20th day of this month.

From your sincere friends.

Wiremu Kingi Witi, Te Here, Tuarane Hingarere"[177]

For a man who emerges from history as an inscrutable, enigmatic figure Kingi's letters provide a rare opportunity to try to unravel the mysteries of his mind. While we need to be cautious in assigning European meanings to written 1800's Maori documents it seems that while superficially Kingi

---

[177] *New Zealand Spectator and Cook's Strait Guardian*, 4 August 1847, p3, quoting British Parliamentary Papers.

appears to be reiterating his "love" of Europeans, if we read the fine print there is a strong implication that this "love" is not actually for "Europeans" *per se* but rather for anyone who worships the same European God as he does – in other words the key mechanism that "binds" him with Europeans is that of a shared religion.[178] While heeding the words of the European God is a deal breaker for Kingi, time will prove him to be not so particular about heeding the words of the European Governor.

The thrust of Kingi's argument seems to be that, because he has accepted the European God, he needs protecting from the still-heathen Rangihaeata as much as the Europeans do – his request for arms is not for the altruistic purpose of protecting Europeans but for the purely selfish one of protecting *himself*. He is not so much *offering* help to Grey as *requesting* it for himself. Interestingly he also suggests that in spite of all the complicated and ongoing wrangles over land sales he considers that as at July, 1846, Europeans "are free from any charge of oppressing or first injuring the natives".

It will later be argued that Grey's docile acquiescence to Kingi's return from Waikanae to Taranaki – which we shall cover in detail later in this book – was at least in part an example of European *utu*, a *quid pro quo* granted by Grey as payment for Kingi's loyalty and assistance in the defence of Wellington during this time. In practice, however, the jury seems to be out on what, if any, practical assistance Kingi did in fact provide. To be honest, if we are to believe the admittedly sometimes biased newspaper reports of the time Kingi's "assistance" during the 1846 Wellington disturbances comes off as being somewhat questionable:

> "In order to induce William King and his tribe to engage more eagerly in the pursuit of Rangihaeata and his fugitives, Captain

---

[178] Kingi, or indeed any Maori of this time, did not yet know enough about the "European God", and its 1800 year history, to understand that the "religion" he received from his local missionary Octavius Hadfield in no way resembled the "religion" as it was understood and practised by the average European colonist. He had both the extreme zeal and extreme ignorance of a neophyte.

Stanley despatched Mr Strode and twenty of the armed Police to Waikanae for the protection of the women and children that were left in the pa: In a few hours, however, William King and his natives returned from the pursuit, which they had continued only to the extent of their cultivated grounds. They alleged as their reason for abandoning the pursuit, that they had done all that had been required of them by the Governor ; that they had taken up the position at Wainui, where they had captured eight prisoners ; that they had prevented the rebels from coming down to the coast, and had chased them through their own district."[179]

"Our supposed ally at Waikanae, (commonly called William King) completely disgusted the Port Nicholson and Porirua tribes, by refusing to take the bush."[180]

"William King has returned to Waikanae to strengthen his pa, but we are going to persuade him to-morrow, if possible, to take the field."[181]

"On the Thursday we anxiously awaited, the arrival of William King, with the above mentioned party; but finding that there were no signs of his approach..."[182]

"We hear that Rangihaeata, in company with the soi-disant ["so-called"] friendly chief William King, paid a visit to Kapiti a few days back, and that he crossed over to the main land, in a canoe, at the time H. M. war steamer *Inflexible*, Captain Hoseason, passed Kapiti, on her return to this port, from Wanganui. We greatly regret that the known rebel [Rangihaeata] and the false friend [Kingi] were not captured together, for there would then have been some probability of the disturbances being suppressed, and that too at an early date.

---

[179] *New Zealand Spectator and Cook's Strait Guardian,* 29 August 1846, p2.

[180] *New Zealander*, 12 September, 1846, p2.

[181] *New Zealand Spectator and Cook's Strait Guardian,* 12 September, 1846, p3.

[182] *Wellington Independent*, 12 September, p3.

> As it is, Rangihaeata keeps up a correspondence with chiefs professedly favorable to Government, from whom he receives supplies and every requisite information as to the movements of the troops."[183]

With the debatable assistance of a number of native allies, including not just Kingi's Waikanae Ati Awa but the Wellington Ati Awa and a portion of Ngati Toa, the brief and messy "Battle for Wellington" reached an equally ill-defined "conclusion" with Rangihaeata retreating in September, 1847, to the Porou-ta-whao swamp near the coast south of the Manawatu River[184]. Rangihaeata remained a discontented, sulking presence, lurking in the background, but causing no more trouble, until his death in 1855.

With that crisis over this temporary "alliance of convenience" between Kingi and Grey evaporated and their attention turned back to their own individual agendas. As it happened the top of the agenda for both parties was land, and in this their agendas were anything but harmonious. Kingi, it seems, was harbouring a desire to return to "his" ancestral lands in Taranaki. Grey, on the other hand, was adamant that that land now belonged to the Europeans by virtue of the various sales we have already described. Indeed Grey had been specifically charged by his boss back in London, Colonial Secretary William Gladstone, to overturn Fitzroy's overruling of Spain's original judgement:

> "I cannot but express my great surprise and regret at not having been placed by Captain Fitzroy in possession of a full report of the course which he pursued in this case [Fitzroy's overturning of Spain's judgement], and of his reason for that course. I, however, indulge the hope that you may have found yourself in a condition to give effect to the award of Mr. Spain in the case of the Company's claims at New Plymouth; and, in any case, I rely on your endeavours to gain that end, so far as you may have found it practicable, unless, indeed, which I can

---

[183] *Wellington Independent*, 23 June, 1847, p2.

[184] Dictionary of New Zealand Biography - Vol 1, Angela Ballara, p491.

hardly think probable, you may have seen reason to believe that the reversal of the Commissioner's judgment was a wise and just measure.

I have, &c., W. E. Gladstone."[185]

If 1846 was a year of theoretical alliance between Grey and Kingi then 1847 was shaping up to be a year of conflict.

Things came to a head in early 1847 when Grey made his first visit to New Plymouth. In February, 1847, Grey was arguably at the height of his powers. He had swept through New Zealand like a whirlwind. He was everywhere, he was always there on the front line and his fingerprint was on everything. In the previous year he had dealt to both Hone Heke and Rangihaeata and perhaps most impressively he had gained the awe of Maori all over the country by his audacious – some would say illegal – kidnapping of Te Rauparaha. While his methods might be dubious to Europeans it is clear he spoke to Maori in a language they could understand. Unlike Fitzroy he was not a man to be trifled with. At last, it seemed, here was a man with a backbone, who could command respect and understood the same rules.

The object of Grey's visit to New Plymouth was clearly both to make a good first impression with the colonists and to demonstrate absolute authority and resoluteness to Maori. In his own words his strategy was to "assume a high tone"[186]. That land was the number-one topic on his agenda was signalled by his stopping off in Waikanae en-route from Wellington to New Plymouth to pick up any influential Maori who might have land interests in Taranaki. Among this number was Wiremu Kingi.

Any meeting with land on its agenda was bound to be stormy one and so it proved:

---

[185] Despatch Gladstone to Grey, 2 July 1846 (AJHR 1861, C1, p181).

[186] BPP, December 1847, New Zealand. Papers relative to the affairs of New Zealand: Correspondence with Governor Grey in continuation of the papers presented by Command in January and June 1847, p3.

"His Excellency Governor Grey, accompanied by Mr Thatcher, his secretary, Colonel Wakefield, Mr. Domett, M.C., and Mr. Crawford, arrived at this settlement [New Plymouth] on the 26th of February [1847] in H.M. war-steamer *Inflexible*.

The Governor stated that the title to land was the great question, and that everything else was based on it. In no other part of the colony had he found it so encircled by difficulties. On the one hand, Mr. Spain had awarded in favour of the Company, and had always since relied on the justice of that decision – Captain Fitzroy had exercised an undoubted right to revise the award, but he had given the Home Government no reason whatever for so doing, and his Excellency could find amongst his predecessor's documents no record of his motives. The [British] Government had therefore referred to him (Captain Grey) for information, and it was with a view to save the twelve months that must be lost by communication and to set the question at rest for the sake of the settlers, that he had come to carry out an arrangement of his own. He intended to adopt so much of Mr. Spain's award as to consider that the natives had alienated their lands, and so much of Captain Fitzroy's revisal of it as to pay for what he should take in extension of the present block of 3,800 acres; at the same time he guarded himself by treating as doubtful any right of the natives to compensation. He should acquire not merely the 63,000 acres claimed by the Company under the award, but 20,000 or 30,000 acres in addition for the Government, making in all 80,000 or 90,000 acres, and he would select that further extent of land around the Company's block. The Government land would be disposed of by public auction in the settlement, and one-half of the proceeds applied in the construction and repair of roads and bridges. He did not contemplate any interference with the natives in their pas and present cultivations, but he would reject the reserves made for them, and set apart blocks of land for the different tribes that they might live by themselves. His plan of payment would extend over four or five years. The Governor intended to communicate his resolution to the different tribes that there might be no mistake, and, if they offered any obstacle, he would inquire into their very doubtful titles and dispose of them accordingly.

He was resolved to have the land, and trusted that the natives would see the advantageous nature of his terms.

...The Governor then received the natives from Ngamotu, Huatoki, and Waiwaikaiho [Waiwhakaiho], as well as those from Wellington and Waikanae, who were brought up in the steamer. Amongst the latter were Te Puni, Wiremu Taku [Wi Tako], William King, &c. The subject of their speeches may be expressed in a few words. The natives wished to abide by Captain Fitzroy's decision and retain their land. The Governor explained the arrangement he intended to carry out, and, as they had thought proper to show a disinclination to accept his offer, which was made with a sincere wish for their welfare, he would institute a rigid inquiry into their claims, and they would lose the benefit of his kindness. He also stated his opinion that they had no claim to the land, and that his offer of compensation was an act of grace, not a matter of right.

... On the following morning the Pukatapu [Puketapu] natives, to the number of 200, met his Excellency. This tribe has always been conspicuous for its aggressions on the settlers; and from the time that Captain Fitzroy unfortunately meddled with the land question, there was little reason to anticipate that anything short of coercive measures would ever bend these lawless people to our rule. Few natives spoke, but they represented the tribe, and refused to part with their land or allow the few remaining settlers to remain outside Captain Fitzroy's block, unless compensation was given. To Mr. Cooke's land there were forty claimants, and to Mr. Flight's 200! The Governor treated these natives in a becoming manner; said he would not allow an out-settler to be molested whether he had a title or not, until the native claims had been investigated; and threw out the greatest doubts on their justice. His opinion was, and it was several times repeated to them, that they had no claim, and the Governor more than once twitted [teased or taunted] them on the conquest of the district some years since by the Waikatos, whose claim on that ground had been purchased by the Government. This allusion was very disagreeable to them, and they left his Excellency without any alteration in their minds. The Governor's firmness and admirable manner took them by surprise, and may have a beneficial result but these natives are almost too bad for hope.

On Wednesday the Ngamotu, Huatoki, and Waiwaikaiho natives again waited on his Excellency by their own desire. The firm policy of the Governor was evinced by their altered tone since the previous Monday ; for this morning, after many inquiries, they came over to the Governor's views, and surrendered all their land between the Sugar Loaves and Waiwaikaiho; within these boundaries is also, the small block of 3,800 acres. The only dissentient native was William King, who had been brought up in the steamer from Waikanae to assist in the purchase of Waitara, but has been using his exertions to prevent an arrangement of the land question throughout the district. He said he should return to Waitara, and so should the natives of Waikanae and Arapawa (Queen Charlotte's Sound). The Governor reprimanded him for his deceitful conduct, and promised him that if he did return with his followers to Waitara, he would find a strong party of soldiers ready to escort them back again, and that he would not allow the natives of the Sound to cross the Straits. This chief seemed much discontented, and, as he is an obstinate fellow, it is not improbable he will abide by his resolution"[187]

Grey's personal summary of this meeting, sent to his superiors in London, ended on an ominous note:

"But very few of the natives seemed disposed to assent to this arrangement; but they distinctly understood that it was my intention to enforce it. I trust that it may meet with your Lordship's approval, as the best which could, under circumstances of such difficulty, be made, and as one which, whilst it ensures the interests of Her Majesty's European subjects, inflicts no injury on Her Majesty's subjects of the native race; although I fear that these latter, now that their cupidity

[187] *Nelson Examiner and New Zealand Chronicle*, 5 March, 1847, p7.

has been so strongly excited, may, if they think they are strong enough, endeavour to resist it by force of arms."[188]

Is this one of Grey's famous "bait and switch" routines in which he appears to vigorously promote one course of action while laying the groundwork to shoot off in the opposite direction? But to be fair to Grey he would be an idiot if he did not recognise and communicate the difficulty, and probable impossibility, of his being able to achieve the task he had been set of overturning Fitzroy's overturning of Spain's findings.

Thus the meeting ended with an unresolved show-down, a battle of wills between an obstinate Grey and an equally obstinate Kingi.

In 1847 Wiremu Kingi and the Group 2 contingent of Ati Awa had been living in Waikanae since they left Taranaki with Te Rauparaha in 1820 – a period of almost 30 years. After building a new life in Waikanae we might reasonably ask not only why after all this time Kingi now suddenly felt so strongly about returning "home" to Taranaki but why he thought he had a right to do so.

There are various schools of thought as to when Kingi made the decision to return "home" to Taranaki – early historian George Rusden suggests Kingi pronounced this objective as early as 1839[189] while a more recent assessment by Keith Sinclair suggests as late as 1845."[190]

Sinclair probably hit the nail on the head in linking Kingi's decision to return to Taranaki to the death of his father and that the primary – and

---

188 BPP, Dec 1847, Papers relative to the affairs of New Zealand – Correspondence with Governor Grey, pp4-5.

189 *History of New Zealand - Vol 1,* George Rusden, p206. Rusden's work is famously partisan to the point that it is rarely cited and should be read with caution – for instance, Rusden does not mention the existence of Kingi's father other than to note his death and suggests Kingi himself as the leader of the migration south in 1819.

190 *Some Historical Notes on an Atiawa Genealogy*, Keith Sinclair, JPS, 1951, Volume 60, No.1.

possibly only – reason for Kingi's desire to return was to honour his father's dying wish that he should do so. Contemporary Waikanae teacher Riwai Te Ahu's comments tend to confirm that Kingi's motives were linked to promises made to his dying father rather than to some long-standing sentimental desire related to "ancestral lands":

> "I myself," says Riwai Te Ahu, "formerly heard the private language of Reretawhangawhanga, William King's father, in the pa at Waikanae, in 1840, in reference to Waitara, not to sell it to the Pakehas. And he continued to express the same determination until his death in 1844. And he left a strict injunction to William King to carry out his wishes after his death."[191]

Certainly a desire to honour his father's wishes is an understandable motivation to return and indeed it is the only one that makes any sense. But it is also impossible not to note that his father's wish, and his own natural desire to honour that wish, came at a time when the European presence at Taranaki, and the Pax Britannica brought to the country in general, had made that wish actually possible to achieve. Prior to 1839 and the arrival of Europeans any attempt by Kingi to honour his father's "strict injunction" would have been absurd and tantamount to a death-wish.[192]

But interesting as this debate is it is also irrelevant. The reality is that it makes no difference when Kingi may or may not have "pronounced" his intention to return to Taranaki, or why. His wish – whenever it was expressed – was just that – a wish. It is a bit like a small boy saying that when he grows up he wants to be an All Black – it is all very well to have

---

[191] From "The Maori King Movement, and the Queen's Supremacy" which may be found in *The Pamphlet Collection of Sir Robert Stout: Rare Volume*, p37 (https://nzetc.victoria.ac.nz/tm/scholarly/tei-StoutNewZ-t14-back-d4.html)

[192] Keith Sinclair (*The Origins of the Maori Wars*, p117) suggests that this "strict injunction" was "in effect, a will" and cites Peter Buck as to the importance of this in Maori culture. Be that as it may, it is surely unreasonable to suggest that for any and every dying Maori who leaves such a dying wish the world will stop spinning in its axis in order that it *must* happen.

wishes but the existence of a wish is not a guarantee that it will automatically come true.

In the 30 or so years since Kingi left Taranaki in 1820 there had been a cataclysmic upheaval in every aspect of Maori life. Entire tribes had disappeared or were at best a very faint shadow of their former selves. The ownership of much of the west coast of the North Island and the top of the South Island had changed hands in the complex way we have described. Europeans had arrived bringing treaties, literacy, a new religion and peace – not to mention shiploads of land-hungry colonists. Taranaki had been bought, sold and disputed multiple times. In 1847 Maori were an entirely different people living in an entirely different world. Surely Kingi was being delusional in thinking that after 25 years absence he could just waltz back to Taranaki as if he has returned from a two week vacation in Fiji, pick up his mail and the cat from the neighbours and carry on as if nothing had happened?

On the other hand, at the time of Grey's meeting in Taranaki Fitzroy's reversal of Spain's decision returning land to the original owners had been in place for a full two and a half years. In that time many of the Puketapu *hapu* had returned to their original territory, sandwiched between the now tiny township of New Plymouth constrained within the 3500 acre block bought by Fitzroy and the traditional Waitara area to the North. Fitzroy opened the stable gates and the horse had well and truly bolted and was missing in action. Kingi could therefore possibly be forgiven for thinking that for all Grey's bravura and threats Grey would never get that horse back in again.

A few weeks after Grey and Kingi's verbal spar at the Taranaki meeting Grey delegated the possibly impossible mission to belatedly implement Spain's original judgement to his trusty sidekick Donald McLean in a 14 point set of instructions, the most important of which are:[193]

---

193 BPP, December 1847, Papers relative to the affairs of New Zealand – Correspondence with Governor Grey, pp13-14. Enclosure No.11, Memorandum Grey to McLean, dated March 5, 1847.

> "5. Every effort should be made to acquire for the European population those tracts of land which were awarded to the New Zealand Company by Mr. Spain...
>
> 6. If possible, the total amount of land resumed for the Europeans should be from 60,000 to 70,000 acres; a grant of this tract of land will then be offered by the Government to the [New Zealand] Company.
>
> 7. The price paid for any portion of land should not, under any circumstances, exceed 1s. 6d. per acre, and the average price should be below this amount.
>
> 8. No time should be lost in completing these arrangements.
>
> 12. Those natives who refuse to assent to this arrangement must distinctly understand that the Government do not admit that they are the true owners of the land they have recently thought proper to occupy."

Although Kingi was not specifically mentioned in these instructions we can probably assume that Grey was still as adamant as ever in preventing his return. However Grey's sense of urgency seems to imply a recognition that he had no power to actually prevent Kingi returning other than by buying up the land before Kingi could settle on it. It was now, literally, a race for the land.

A report by Grey in late April, 1847 suggested that Kingi had taken up the challenge with enthusiasm:

> "I received last night a letter from Major Richmond[194] informing me that the Natives at Petoni Pah were engaged in putting together nine large canoes capable of holding for a long passage, about sixty persons each. I consider it to be a matter of the utmost importance for the protection of the isolated settlement of Taranaki and its undefended

[194] Superintendent of the Southern region, Mathew Richmond

> settlers, that the Ngatiawa tribe should not be allowed to proceed for the present to that place...
>
> My own opinion also is that these canoes are not intended solely for the conveyance of E. Puni's own tribe [the Group 2 Ati Awa at Wellington rather than Kingi's Group 1 Ati Awa at Waikanae] : they are capable of conveying about 540 persons, whereas E Puni's tribe consists of but 200 souls, including men, women, and children. I believe that they will be moved out of the harbour one by one, as opportunity may offer, to other places inhabited by the Ngatiawa tribe [eg, to Kingi at Waikane]...
>
> I should therefore feel much obliged to you if you, in conjunction with Major Richmond, would require E Puni to dismantle these canoes in such a manner that they may be rendered unfit for the voyage to Taranaki; at the same time, injuring the canoes themselves as little as possible: in fact the best plan would perhaps be to require him to take them to pieces again. If E Puni should refuse to comply with the wishes of the Government in this respect, my opinion is that if his conduct is such as to afford reasonable grounds of suspicion, the canoes should be seized by the Government, and either be retained in their possession until the land question at Taranaki is settled, or that they should be destroyed, as may be thought most advisable; and E Puni should be distinctly warned that these consequences will follow from his refusing to comply with the request of the Government."[195]

A day later Grey received a letter from Superintendent Richmond outlining all the conceivable overland tracks from Waikanae to Taranaki. Thus it seems that in late April, 1847, Grey was still undeterred in his goal of preventing Kingi's return, by land or by sea.

Then out of left field things suddenly took a very strange turn when Grey issued McLean the following "further instructions":

---

[195] Despatch Grey to McCleverty, 27 April 1847 (AJHR 1861, E-01, p29).

> "It is proposed that the whole of the Natives having claims to land lying between Ngamotu and the Waitara (with the exception of the Puketapu Natives now resident within this block) should, if possible, be induced to abandon their claims without further enquiry, and to locate themselves on the North bank of the Waitara [River].
>
> These Natives may be divided into two classes: those now resident on the north bank of the Waitara: those who are shortly expected to arrive here from the Southward [Wiremu Kingi's people in Waikanae.]
>
> It is proposed that the first of the above classes should be induced to agree to abandon their present cultivations within a period of three years, and then to remove to the north bank of the Waitara, if they remain within this district. The second class should be induced to proceed at once to the North bank of the Waitara, there to locate themselves on such sites as they may select – relinquishing all pretensions to any lands to the south of that river..."[196]

Thus in the space of a few months Grey has inexplicably and suddenly abandoned what seemed a very clear and resolute plan to prevent Kingi returning and is now reverting to Plan B – Grey will now let Kingi return *but* he must settle where Grey tells him to – specifically on the north bank of the Waitara River, leaving the "Waitara" area on the south side clear for settlers.

---

[196] Memorandum of an arrangement proposed to be entered into with the Native Land Claimants in the Taranaki District. Grey to McLean, undated but in 1847 (AJHR 1860, Session 1, E-04, p16, and can also be found in the context of the famous debates of Octavius Hadfield and Donald McLean on 14 August 1860 "to give evidence as to the cause of the Taranaki War"(These debates may be found in the Parliamentary Debates of 1858 to 1860, pp284-306. The quoted excerpt may be found on p298 and is unhelpfully "dated" by its presenter, Donald McLean, as being received by him "from Sir George Grey sometime in 1847").

In June 1847 Kingi was reported as consorting with the "rebel" Rangihaeata and that he already has 25 canoes standing by at Waikanae to take his people home to Taranaki.[197]

In July 1847 Grey received an update from Superintendent Richmond:

> "Wellington, July 26, 1847. When I was up the coast last week, I was met at Waikanae by a large concourse of the Ngatiawa tribe, including "William King", and many of the most influential Chiefs, to whom I made known your Excellency's views relative to their meditated move to Taranaki, and was much gratified to find that no disposition existed, on their part, to act in opposition to them; their demeanour was quiet, respectful, and exhibited no symptom of annoyance with, or resistance to, the Government. "William King" stated, that although they were still bent upon going to that district, yet they repudiated the idea of doing so by stealth, or before consulting with the Governor, and learning the time he would permit of their removal; adding, that the Ngatiawa tribe had always been friendly to the Europeans, and it was their desire to continue on the same amicable terms they have hitherto been. I, however, much incline to the opinion, that the migration, if it ever takes place, will be very partial, probably merely "William King", and his followers, as I found many indifferent, and some altogether averse, to leaving Waikanae. At Queen Charlotte's Sound, also, it appears the principal Chief, "Robert", has not yet given his consent, and, in this neighbourhood, the Ngatiawas are cultivating as usual, and now show no symptom of moving. "William King", on behalf of those at Waikanae, urged strongly the purchase by Government of the district, and when I mentioned that I did not think your Excellency contemplated making further purchases of land at present, they evinced the utmost anxiety (engendered no doubt by the scarcely concealed intention of the Ngatitoa tribe to take possession of the land when they leave it) that a promise should be given, if the

---

[197] *The New Zealander*, 30 June, 1847, p2.

> Government did not wish to obtain the district when the time was decided upon for their departure, that they should be the parties negotiated with, and to whom the purchase money should be paid, whenever it was considered expedient to require the land."[198]

Although this communication does not elucidate precisely what Richmond's understanding of his "Excellency's views" was, and whether or not this included the recent concession to return being conditional on settling on the north bank, it is clear that not only is Kingi "bent on" returning but that Grey has sanctioned it. More than that, somewhat incredibly, Kingi also expects Grey to buy "his" vacated land at Waikanae when he does so – it is certainly hard not to admire Kingi's chutzpah.

By February, 1848, Kingi's plans to return are well in progress. Amazingly, as will be elaborated on later, the business of Kingi's return is not the hotly debated *cause célèbre* one would expect from the usually vociferous New Plymouth colonists that it will greatly affect. His imminent return largely flies under the public radar, with a few exceptions noted in the press:

> "For some time past the natives at Waikanae have been making preparations for their return to Taranaki. They intend to go by sea, and will embark in a fleet of 40 canoes, the number of those returning amounting to about three hundred persons. The emigration will be so general that it is expected not more than from thirty to forty persons will remain behind [at Waikanae]. Their horses, to the number of forty, will be sent overland to Taranaki. The Government have entered into negotiations for the purchase of the Waikanae district, and though the arrangements are still in progress there is every reason to believe they will shortly arrive at a satisfactory termination."[199]

> "And what is the ready course adopted by Captain Grey? The fulfilment of his deliberate threat to the natives, and of his word to us

---

[198] Extract from letter of the Superintendent of the Southern Division to Governor Sir George Grey, date 26th July, 1847 (AJHR 1860, E-02, p23).

[199] *New Zealand Spectator and Cook's Strait Guardian*, 16 February, 1848, p2.

> as a Governor? Just the reverse. He now foresees immense advantages to us in increased trade from the residence of William King and his people at Waitara; they are highly civilized, and will exercise the arts of peace, at least so long as inducement offers; and his Excellency really could not say No to his faithful allies in the South, because they will come with or without it. What can be more miserable than the reasons advanced by the Governor for his change? Six or seven hundred natives will increase trade, and he trusts to confine them to the North side!"[200]

It is now a full year since Governor Grey laid down the law, as he thought, to Kingi at the meeting in New Plymouth, absolutely forbidding the return of the Waikanae Ati Awa to Taranaki and threatening to have soldiers waiting to turn Kingi back if he tries. Just what has happened to cause this hundred and eighty degree U-turn in Grey's thinking? This is what we will try to clarify in the next chapter.

---

[200] Letter to the Editor, *New Zealand Spectator and Cook's Strait Guardian*, 22 March, 1848, p3.

Chapter 1-14

The return of the prodigal son.

What indeed has Grey been up to in the interim as Kingi forges ahead with his plan to return to Waitara? Unlike his first hectic year putting out the fires of Hone Heke and Rangihaeata, 1847 and 1848 are years of relative peace, a *Pax Britannica*, which as we have noted, is the only reason Kingi can even contemplate his return to Taranaki. Ironically war is a relatively easy business to manage – in wartime the priorities, national focus, goals and the means to achieve them are generally abundantly clear. The management of peace, however, is an entirely different animal – there are a thousand things of equal priority to handle simultaneously, most of them interdependent. In such circumstances Grey, and anyone, could possibly be forgiven for being too overwhelmed in 1848 by the unrelenting pressures of peace to give much thought to a veiled threat he made to an individual a year before.

By 1848 the administration of New Zealand was considerably more complicated than it was when Grey had his encounter with Kingi in 1847. The country had now been divided into two provinces – New Ulster, being all country north of a line drawn east from the mouth of the Patea River, and New Munster, being the rest of the country south. Grey was no longer simply "Governor" but "Governor in Chief", in charge of two "Lieutenant Governors" directly responsible for the two provinces. However by virtue of Grey living in Auckland, the most populous European centre in New

Ulster, he was in practice also *de facto* Lieutenant-Governor for New Ulster. Edward John Eyre was appointed from England as Lieutenant-Governor for New Munster. As fate would have it Grey had an implacable hatred of Eyre and made his life a continuous hell, but that is another story.

By early 1848, then, it was nominally Grey as *de facto* "Lieutenant-Governor" of New Ulster who was responsible for Taranaki, the end point of Kingi's proposed journey, while Eyre was responsible for Waikanae, the starting point for Kingi's journey which was in New Munster. Increasing Government bureaucracy and resulting layers of delegation were perhaps a contributor to the ball being dropped on the Kingi issue but ultimately it was still Grey's responsibility, especially since it was he who made the original ultimatum to Kingi.

This is a good time to introduce a man who was probably the most remarkable, or at least influential, civil servant New Zealand has ever seen.[201] His name is Donald McLean and he was the loyal pillar, guiding mentor and power behind the throne of a succession of Governors and Government Ministries from 1844 until his death in 1877. Although he had many roles during this time he is especially associated with land purchases and indeed there are few North Island land purchases that do not have his fingerprints on them to a greater or lesser extent. It is a great tribute to him that, despite having the most thankless and potentially animosity-generating job in the world, he was highly and universally respected by Maori, if not always respected by all his European colleagues. Perhaps even more astoundingly, despite his role in masterminding the alienation of millions of acres of Maori land he has somehow managed to escape the mountains of abuse we might expect to be heaped upon him by present day apologists.

Since his arrival in New Zealand in late 1841 McLean's first "real" job came in 1844 as a Sub-Protector of Aborigines in which role he assisted Fitzroy in assessing ownership claims in Taranaki prior to Fitzroy's

---

[201] His most recent biographer, Ray Fargher, titles his book *The best man who served the Crown?*, albeit with a question mark.

overturning of Spain's judgement. With the abolition in April, 1846 of the Protectorate Office by incoming Governor Grey he was appointed as Inspector of Police in Taranaki, a role which was soon supplemented by assisting Grey with land purchase related activities. Grey and McLean made a good team. Both men were genuinely interested in Maori, their culture, their language, their welfare and their future. Both men were deeply religious. Grey was a blusterer, a good front man, good at raising hackles. McLean was silver tongued but in a good way, trusted, infinitely patient, difficult to dislike, good at smoothing hackles.

At the end of the previous chapter we left Kingi in February, 1848, attending to the final preparations prior to his migration from Waikanae to Taranaki. Notwithstanding Grey's earlier orders to have his canoes dismantled or "blown up" Kingi had, by hook or by crook, amassed a fleet of "40 canoes" for the purpose. In late April, 1848, Grey's perennially unlucky underling, Lieutenant-Governor Eyre, reported to Grey:

> "I have the honor to report for the information of your Excellency, that a large majority of the Ngatiawa Natives emigrated from Waikanae on Monday, the 17th of April, on their route to Taranaki.
>
> This intelligence was conveyed to me in a letter from the Resident Magistrate of Waikanae, from which I enclose an extract stating the number of canoes and boats and probable amount of ammunition which they took with them. With respect to the latter, I may observe that I had previously been made aware that there was a probability of this ammunition being taken, and I had in consequence summoned my Executive Council, to consult with them as to the policy of adopting any measures for taking possession of, or at least preventing the exportation of so large a quantity of gunpowder...
>
> ...In connection with the departure of the Ngatiawa Natives, and in reference to your Excellency's instructions to me, to endeavour to come to an understanding with them that upon reaching the Taranaki district they should consent to settle on the North side of the Waitara, instead of occupying both banks of that river, I have the honor to state, that prior to Mr. McLean's arrival, I had two or three interviews with William King, and endeavoured, but unsuccessfully, to

accomplish this object. That Chief expressed strongly his desire to be on friendly terms with the Government, but at the same time stated that he would not bind his followers to any particular course, and would not decide anything until after his arrival at Taranaki. Upon Mr. McLean's arrival, I sent that officer up to Waikanae to see W. King again on the same subject, and to point out strongly to him that unless he came to some understanding with the Government on the subject of his contemplated emigration, they would not in any way acknowledge or recognise his rights in, or his claims to a district from which he had been so many years absent. Upon returning to Wellington, Mr. McLean informed me that he thought William King had considerably altered his views, and that he now stated that he was disposed to use his influence to bring about the arrangement proposed by the Government, but that he was still anxious that nothing further should be done until he reached Taranaki, or, to use his own expression, that he should not be pressed too closely. Finding therefore that nothing could be gained by urging the matter immediately, I have requested Mr. McLean to follow W. King to Taranaki, so as not to be in the way, to endeavour to effect the required arrangements when the Natives are actually on the ground.

As no definite understanding could be come to with regard to Taranaki, I did not consider it advisable to enter upon the purchase of Waikanae, and especially as, until the departure of that portion of the tribe which intended to emigrate had taken place, it could not be ascertained how many Natives would remain, or what reserves it would be necessary to set apart for their use.

I have, &c, E. Eyre."[202]

And so, it seems, Kingi has won round one, he is on his way home – it is all over bar the shouting. The next round for contention is where he will settle when he gets there. In theory it should be a no-brainer. Richmond's

---

[202] Despatch from Eyre to Sir George Grey, 25th April, 1848 (from AJHR 1863, Session 1, E-17).

memo of July, 1847, is adamant that Kingi will do as Grey asks. Kingi is – according to Richmond – as meek and obedient as a lamb. Eyre's April, 1848, update is, however, worryingly vague and non-committal. Kingi's commitment to be "disposed to use his influence to bring about the arrangement proposed by the Government", loosely translated, means he has absolutely no intention of doing what Grey wants.

Grey's reply to Eyre's memo is astounding:

> "I have the honor to acknowledge the receipt of your Despatch, No. 41, of the 25th of April last, reporting the emigration of the Ngatiawa from Cook's Straits to Taranaki, their refusal to meet the wishes of the Government in reference to the proposed settlement of the land question at Taranaki, and the fact of their having been permitted to carry with them about half a ton of gunpowder.
>
> The first of these points does not appear to require any comment from me. The second I can only regret, as it is clear that yourself and Mr. McLean made every exertion to induce the Ngatiawa to accede to the proposed arrangement. The third point alluded to by you has, however, caused me a great deal of concern..."[203]

Grey then proceeds to spend the majority of his despatch on the subject of the transporting of gunpowder.[204]

Just what is going on here? We need to take a step back and try to join the dots between the blustering, sabre-rattling George Grey who laid down the law to the chiefs at the Taranaki meeting in February, 1847, and the George Grey who submissively rolled over and let Kingi trample all over him a year later. Where did he go? And how has this come about?

Has Grey, or his masters back in London, had a "road to Damascus" epiphany and seen the error of their ways and decided Fitzroy was right

---

[203] Despatch from Sir George Grey to Eyre, June 5th, 1848 (from AJHR 1863, Session 1, E-17).

[204] A later report suggests this as two and a half tons!

after all? Or was Grey conveniently making the best of the recent replacement back in London of Colonial Secretary, William Gladstone, who gave him the mission to overturn Fitzroy's decision, by the confusingly named *Earl* Grey, who might not feel as strongly on the subject of Fitzroy's decision, or not at all?

Has Governor George Grey and/or Earl Grey dropped this particular goal to the bottom of the priority list in order to concentrate on more important things, such as the abortive 1846 charter to introduce representative Government to New Zealand? Or is George Grey just fed up with the perpetually moaning and mercilessly vituperative colonists and walked away from their corner? His macho performance of February, 1847, at the Taranaki meeting was, after all, intended as much as for the good citizens of New Plymouth as it was for Maori. Have the settlers already seen through him and he no longer needs to maintain that façade? Did Grey think that Kingi's debatable "loyalty" during the 1846 crisis around Wellington called for some sort of concession, a balancing of *utu*? Has Grey seen the wisdom of McLean's more diplomatic and pragmatic approach and now understands the impossibility of preventing Kingi's return without warfare? Or has he simply been out-blustered, out sabre-rattled, out manoeuvred – out-Kingi'ed – and finally met his match?

Frustratingly the answer is unclear. On this pivotal point the records are amazingly silent, or at best elusive.[205] While we can find plenty of retrospective references to Grey instructing Kingi to settle on the north side of the Waitara none indicate why he suddenly changed his mind and allowed Kingi to return at all. It is as if someone has removed this particular folder from the great filing cabinet of New Zealand history.

---

[205] There are some clues in Donald McLean's records, some of which we shall cover later.

James Cowan would later opine:

> "Wiremu Kingi te Rangitaake, the head chief of the Waikanae people, had given valuable protection to the Wellington Settlement at a very critical period. The Governor could not very well ignore this."[206]

Much as Cowan's work is rightly seen as seminal on the subject of the New Zealand Wars this view seems unsupportable by evidence.

Europeans of the time were evidently equally dumbfounded by the lack of communication on the subject, as this contemporary newspaper article suggests:

> "It is now nearly three months since the Governor-in-Chief communicated to the Resident Land Purchasers in this settlement his intention of effecting, if possible, an arrangement with those natives at the southward [Kingi and the Ati Awa of Waikanae] who had expressed their intention of coming up, respecting Waitara; limiting their occupation of that district to the land between the Taniwa (our northern boundary) and the north bank of Waitara...Yet beyond a private account received from a gentlemen at Wanganui, and vague statements derived from native sources, we the land claimants, deeply interested in the success or failure of the mission, are kept most completely in the dark... In the absence then of official explanation of any kind, it appears, according to the private account adverted to, that at the time it was written 587 native men, women, and children had reached Rangatiki [on their way up] from Waikanae."[207]

Only one thing seems clear. Wiremu Kingi has walked all over Grey, walked all over Eyre, walked all over Donald McLean and walked all over Superintendent Richmond. He has walked all over the entire Government

---

[206] *The New Zealand Wars: A History of the Maori Campaigns and the Pioneering Period – Vol 1*, James Cowan, p146.

[207] *New Zealand Spectator and Cook's Strait Guardian*, 20 May, 1848, p3.

administration from the cleaner to the Governor. The Government, and Grey in particular, has been proven to be a toothless, paper tiger, from top to bottom. Things are officially out of control and anarchy rules supreme, at least as far as New Zealand's native constituents go.

One of McLean's biographers wryly and perceptively notes:

> "Grey's negotiating stance was to take an extreme position at the initial discussions. If he found resistance, he devised a line of retreat, which he would present in his despatch to the Colonial Office as a masterly change in tactic".[208]

That is perhaps a little harsh – would we not all be tempted to make a virtue out of necessity in that situation? But there is no doubt that Grey was a very different animal from his predecessors. Fitzroy and Hobson were lambs in a country of wolves. Grey was a chameleon in a country full of wolves – he shape-shifted, adapted and rolled with the punches. In a nutshell while Grey, Fitzroy and Hobson may all have been captains Grey was the only politician among them. Fitzroy had the backbone to stand up for what he believed in and paid the price for it. Grey's backbone was flexible enough to do a backflip at will.

Moving from the unknown back to the known, in the month of April, 1848, Kingi and his contingent began to wend their way leisurely up the coast from Waikanae to Taranaki. After 28 years absence Kingi was still in no hurry and the migration party took at least six months to reach its destination of Waitara.[209] Perhaps they were hoping that by the time they got there Grey would have forgotten about them, been side-tracked by more pressing business, or even – that most probable of fates for early Governors – been recalled. Perhaps they were just rubbing the salt in, enjoying seeing Grey fuming and helpless over a longer period of time.

---

[208] *The best man who ever served the Crown?,* Ray Fargher, p65.

[209] Letter McLean to Resident Magistrate, New Plymouth, 28 November, 1848 (AJHR 1861, Session 1, C-01, p189).

According to McLean's records 578 persons of various *hapu* set out for Taranaki by means of a small armada comprising one "vessel", four boats and forty-four canoes, supplemented by some who travelled overland by horse.[210] Kingi himself is noted as being the "principal man" of a canoe named Kaupahanui, carrying 14 people. The "principal man" of an unnamed "boat" carrying 7 people is recorded as being a "Te Teira", someone we shall hear a lot more of later.

It is interesting to note the disparate range of *hapu* represented in this migration – listed as Ngati Tama, Ngati Mutunga, Puketapu, Ngati Rahiri, Manukorihi, Taranaki and Ngati Ruanui – indicating that the "Waikanae" contingent was not a homogeneous group but a mixed bag over half of whom did not belong to Kingi's *hapu* and including tribes which had nothing to do with Ati Awa.

And so in the closing weeks of 1848, after an absence of between 16 and 29 years[211], this varied contingent arrived back in Taranaki, no doubt overjoyed to be back in their ancestral lands. For those younger than 29 it would be the first time they have been there.

Historian Lyndsay Head gives an interesting aside to Kingi's return to Taranaki:

> "Rakorako of Ngati Maru had built canoes and provided food for the Ngati Awa homeward migration to Waitara, and had been paid in land called Tipapa."[212]

Head's reason for including this snippet was to demonstrate aspects of land transfer. Its inclusion here is a demonstration of what we have

---

[210] See for example, Wells, p145, NZHR 1860, Session 1, E-02, p24, etc. This figure seems quite low given that Octavius Hadfield records that his Waikanae services numbered 2,000.

[211] 29 years for those who joined Te Rauparaha in 1820, 16 years for those who left in the aftermath of Pukerangiora in 1832.

[212] *Land, authority and the forgetting of being in early colonial Maori history*, Lyndsay Head, p181.

alluded to before – the seemingly selective nature of the universal notion of reciprocity, the notion described in Maori culture by the word *utu*. In this example we see Kingi clearly understanding – and honouring – the concept of *utu* in a Maori to Maori transaction – Rakorako has supplied canoes and food for which Kingi has repaid in land. Thus you would think – would it not be unreasonable to expect similar recognition by Kingi of the European contribution to his returning home, which, being the pacifying of the Waikatos – either by European presence or European money – is everything? It is a point not just worth factoring into the equation but is surely fundamental to everything that follows.

So far in this little game of wills the score is: Wiremu Kingi - 2, Sir George Grey - 0.

But the game is not over yet for there is one more round to play – who will win the round of deciding where Kingi and his people will settle? We wait with bated breath to see if Grey will make a last minute comeback and score the winning goal or at least save a small amount of face by achieving a draw.

Chapter 1-15

The wrong side of the tracks.

At the 1860 Kohimarama conference Donald McLean shed a certain amount of light on the murky events of the year prior to the migration:

> "In the year 1847 Waitara was offered for sale. Claims were duly investigated. This was before the return of the people from Kapiti [Waikanae]. The Natives residing on the land [Group 3 Diehards] said, "It will not be right to entertain the claims of those absentees who forsook the land [Ati Awa Groups 1 and 2], and took no part in defending it against the Waikatos: let the whole payment be given to us". The Government did not, however, accept this view, and when any payment was made, it was divided, and a portion was sent to Kapiti. The purchase of the Waitara was kept in abeyance until the claims should be clearly ascertained. In 1848 I went to Kapiti, and there was a large gathering at Waikanae, at which William King Te Rangitake proposed to return to Waitara. When he was informed that the Waitara was under offer to the Government he said, "Let me return thither, and I will then consider the matter. When I get there one side of the river shall be yours and the North side mine, whence I can look out for the Waikatos, in case that tribe should meditate an attack upon us". That was his word, which is retained in the memories of myself and of others here present, who heard what passed between us. William King was allowed to locate himself at

> Waitara, and nothing was said by the Europeans about the land: there was no attempt to press the matter hastily. William King returned with his people; the sanction of the Governor to his doing so had been given, though the act was on his part intended as one of defiance."[213]

Evidently Maori were already living on "Kingi's" Waitara land in 1847 and had no compunction in denying Kingi's right to it, although we might speculate that selfish reasons might be partly to blame for this attitude. But what is most relevant is that McLean, presumably with Grey's blessing, has at some unspecified point in 1847 entirely abandoned Grey's strongly worded position of February that same year, that Maori had no right to the land whatsoever. Kingi is in complete control and calling all the shots – he has effectively usurped Grey's position and is McLean's *de facto* boss, dictating his terms to him. We also note that apparently Kingi is apparently still living in fear of the Waikatos, although this may simply be a ruse to justify his subsequent actions:[214]

> "...In 1847, the exiled William King, not daring to return sooner, resolved to leave Cook's Straits [Waikanae], where he had resided about 14 or 15 years, and return to Taranaki. He had come to the conclusion, as he expressed it, that "the English dog would bark, but not bite", and the Waikato Chiefs would not now molest him. So he sold his lands in Cook's Straits which he had conquered from the aboriginal owners, and came back with about 20 large canoes".[215]

Earlier we briefly introduced another of the Waikanae migrators, Te Teira ("Taylor"). Here is his rather long-winded account of the process by which Kingi and his followers came to be positioned in Waitara:

---

213 AJHR 1860, Session 1, p13.

214 Some accounts (eg, Wells, p145) suggest that Kingi had specifically got permission from the Waikatos to return peacefully.

215 Ex-Missionary Samuel Ironside, Letter to the Editor, South Australian Register, 26 September 1864, p6.

"When, in migrating from Waikanae [back to Waitara], we arrived at Tangahoe, Hone Hira stood up in the evening and said "When we arrive at Waitara we will give one side of it to the Governor in accordance with the understanding he came to with William King at Waikanae." But Tamati Tarepa [Teira's father] said – "It will not do to do this while we are still in the water [on the journey]; when we have got to the bank, and our legs are dry, then we will settle it."

William King repudiated his agreement with Governor Grey. We arrived at Waitara in November, 1849 [1848], and the heads of our migration consulted together – Huriwhenua, Rangikatahi, Nikorima, Ngahaupakeke, Hohepa, Huriwhare, Kamukingi, Takaratai, Parata Ngeru, Putuiwi, Ihakara, Herewaka, Te Punga te Raho, Katene Kiha, Tamati Tarepa, Wi Ropeta Kaupane, Wi Ngawaka Manuwhirituarangi, these chiefs consulted together about a place of safety for the women and children lest they should be killed by Waikato or Ngatimaniapoto. William King said it would be better to build the pah for them on the other [north] side of Waitara, but Iharaira te Tuki and Patara te Huia said let them remain at Te Kuhikuhi, Te Hurirapa and Werohia, that [we] may be near Puketapu, in case the enemy should appear.

William King stood and spoke inquiringly to the chiefs and all the people. Listen, O people! The decision concerning [the occupation of] this land is not with me, but with the men to whom the land belongs. It is not intended to make a permanent dwelling-place, but only a temporary residence until we shall have heard that the fire is reduced to ashes [i.e., till the anger of Waikato has died out]. For we are now living in one body: do not let us be separated; so that if the enemy should come, we may be altogether. When we are safe, we will disperse each to his own Kainga.

Upon this, Tamati Tarepa, and Ihakara Herewaka, consented that they should live for three years, and then go to their own places. The land was by no means given them to live on always, but temporarily, from fear of Waikato. At the end of the three years, they went away to Pukearuhe, te Mimi, Onaero, Urenui, Turangi, Pukerangiora, and [the places of] Mgatimaru. In the third year, 1852 [1851], they all went to their own places, William King alone remaining on that piece [Teira's block]."[216]

In this way – at least according to Teira – Kingi inflicts his final indignity on Grey – he settles on the precise spot that Grey has told him not to.

Kingi has attained a perfect score: Kingi - 3, Grey - 0.

Kingi's disdain for Grey and his thumbing of the nose at the basic principles of sovereignty do not go unnoticed by the press:

> "So we have here three distinct refusals by the Waikanae natives to be in any way influenced by the Government, and all arising out of the original question of whether they should be permitted to come up at all to this place – the migration of 587 of their number against orders – their refusal afterwards to confine their residence at Waitara within the limits, proposed by his Excellency – and the retention of Waikanae by the remainder of the tribe."[217]

And so William Kingi is finally home, settled precisely where he always intended. He has done well, proven himself a force to be reckoned with and is able to claim what few others can claim – that he has not just out-Greyed Grey but done so in style. The English dog put on a good show at first and barked impressively, but, as Kingi predicted, was well and truly muzzled.

Much as it is customary in the present to cast aspersions on Grey at any and every opportunity we need to cut him some slack. The return of Kingi to Taranaki, being one continuous stream of laughing in the face of the supposed head of the nation, was just another example of the façade that New Zealand was a sovereign nation and that any Governor actually had any power to make a decision that Maori did not want him to make. Grey had tried his hardest, indeed put on such a good front that even the colonists believed him, which of course only made him even more of a

---

[216] *Taranaki Herald*, 15 August, 1863, p2.

[217] *New Zealand Spectator and Cook's Strait Guardian*, 20 May, 1848, p3.

villain when he failed. He had in his desperation been forced to reduce his demands on Kingi but even in this he had absolutely no power, moral or otherwise. In his first two years he had quelled two Maori initiated rebellions, those of Heke and Rangihaeata, with aplomb and efficiency. He can perhaps be forgiven for not wanting to create a British initiated rebellion by forcing the issue with Kingi.

Returning to our central narrative of Wiremu Kingi and his followers in Taranaki let us look at how things fared for him after his return in late 1848.

After the violence and extreme turbulence of the previous three decades the years 1848 to 1853 must have been somewhat of an anti-climax for Kingi and indeed for Maori in general. He was now "home" and thanks to the new European order for which he is so ungrateful he is about to make a killing – not in the traditional sense but in the metaphorical financial sense.

Even in his Waikanae abode Kingi was living in relative opulence, reaping the benefits of European technology. During that time it seems that despite his animosity to Grey he was happy enough to accept his gifts:

> "At Waikanae there are about 250 acres, at Otaki about 200 acres under wheat this year. Last year there were about 9 acres of wheat at Otaki, and the quantity at Waikanae also was inconsiderable. Next year the natives say they shall have more than twice the present breadth of land under wheat, as about the sowing time last season their labours were interrupted by the disturbances caused by the rebels under Rangihaeata:
>
> The whole of the ground was prepared by spade husbandry, the previous crop having been potatoes, and next year these natives, who have been informed, and have become sensible, of the advantages of a rotation of crops, intend bringing their deserted potato grounds under cultivation with wheat...
>
> They thrash and grind their own corn themselves, using for the latter purpose some steel corn mills given them by his Excellency Capt. Grey, and some which they had purchased ...

> They find the grinding of corn by means of steel mills a tedious and laborious operation, and are determined to imitate their more civilized neighbours by having a flour mill erected which shall be adequate to the growing wants of their districts...
>
> The machinery will be chiefly constructed by engineers belonging to this settlement. It is estimated that, exclusive of the labour for sawing the timber, forming the dam and executing other works which may be performed by natives under the superintendence of an European, the sum of £300 will be required for its erection. This sum it is proposed to raise by means of a company, the amount being divided into thirty shares of ten pounds each. At Waikanae the natives have sixteen horses and one cow, at Otaki they have nine horses, two cows, and ten goats; besides these there are several cattle at the latter place belonging to settlers. At both places there is a great desire among them to increase the amount of their stock..."[218]

The enormous growth in agricultural production, described in detail in a subsequent chapter, was by no means limited to the Waikanae, another winner being Taranaki itself which, because of the richness of its soil, had long been referred to by Europeans as the "Garden of New Zealand". This was particularly true in the Waitara area which is, of course, why it was so coveted by the New Plymouth settlers.

We do not know much about Kingi in the years following his return to Taranaki. Although whatever he did was not dramatic enough for it to be recorded for posterity it is clear that Kingi and his followers were certainly not idle for by 1854 he was apparently King of a veritable agricultural empire:

> "...in 1854 he [Kingi] possessed 150 horses, 300 head of cattle, 40 carts, 35 ploughs, 20 pairs of harrows, 3 winnowing-machines, and 10 wooden houses."[219]

---

[218] *New Zealand Spectator and Cook's Strait Guardian*, 17 February, 1847, p2.

[219] *The story of New Zealand – Vol 2*, Arthur Thomson, p298.

"In 1856 they sent to market about £8,000 worth of produce, and spent the proceeds on goods in New Plymouth."[220]

Unlike Waikato Maori neither Kingi, nor Ati Awa in general, succumbed to the temptation of erecting flour mills. It has been speculated that this was because their target market was the "English [that is, local European] market" (rather than Australia) and because their coastal location made shipping the heavier raw material of wheat a better economic proposition than shipping the lighter finished product of flour.[221]

Adding variety and humour to his agricultural pursuits Kingi was from time to time treated to a visit by his would-be nemesis Sir George Grey, ostensibly the most powerful man in the land:

"...it appears that during his late visit to that settlement [New Plymouth] Sir George Grey... was proceeding on horseback to the Waitara district, which was awarded by Mr. Spain to the [New Zealand] Company, but which the natives were allowed by Captain Fitzroy to occupy in spite of the Commissioner's [Spain's] award:

At a short distance from the town his Excellency was waylaid by about 20 natives armed with spears and tomahawks, who forbade him to proceed. Losing sight altogether of the position he ought to have assumed, Sir George told his assailants that he was only out on pleasure and not about the lands, and requested that they would allow him to go on. They refused and rudely turned him back, one of them seizing his bridle and flourishing a tomahawk. The Governor yielded and went to a friendly pah, whither he was dogged by the hostile natives.

---

[220] *The New Zealand War... – Vol 1,* James Cowan, p146.

[221] *Chiefs of Industry,* Hazel Petrie, Chapter 7, Reference 48, suggests that at an unspecified "Taranaki South", Maori had come to a different economic decision, which at the early stage of 1849 had yet to break even – "At Taranaki South the crops of wheat, potatoes, and other food are abundant. The natives have two large flour mills, driven by water, at work. Hundreds of pigs have been sent to New Plymouth in payment of those mills, but they are still in arrear" (*The New Zealander,* 10 March, 1849, p2).

...what shall we expect from Sir George Grey, when in his own person, the living representative of the British nation is thus bearded[222] and insulted? The least will be the summary arraignment of the offenders, and the infliction by military force if necessary of a punishment commensurate to the insult. He sent for the tomahawk, and on its being laid at his feet, (without we believe any apology from the transgressors), he quietly dropped the matter..."[223]

[222] "Taken by the beard; opposed to the face" (Webster's 1828 dictionary).

[223] *Wellington Independent*, 3 April 1850, p2.

Chapter 1-16

The paths begin to split.

The years 1852 to 1856 were pivotal ones for New Zealand in which the nationalistic tendencies of both races were simultaneously and independently forged and inevitably began to part company.

In 1852 Maori had – for the first time in at least 30 years and probably for a lot longer – experienced not only peace but unprecedented prosperity. It was, quite literally, a brand new and hitherto unknown era in which former enemies could actually exchange words rather than bullets. Everyone was united in the common and enjoyable cause of making money. It would be incredible if this unprecedented prosperous and harmonious environment led to anything other than a sense of belonging as a wider, ethnic group bigger than one's own *hapu*. It was, in short, a recipe for nationalism.

On the European front in 1852 the British Government granted New Zealand a much requested and somewhat delayed Constitution. This marked the beginning of the end for New Zealand as a "British" colony – the country would no longer be autocratically ruled by a British appointed, Governor but governed largely by an elected representative Government. Much to the Colonial Office's annoyance Governor Grey unilaterally ended his first Governorship and departed New Zealand on New Year's Day 1854 prior to seeing this new Government put in place.

While we might in modern times frown on the perceived inadequacies of the 1852 Constitution Act we would be wise to remember that in its day it was the last word in liberality and progressiveness – we too easily forget that representative government and the universal franchise are *very* new concepts. While the governing system specified by the 1852 Constitution was, for its day, staggeringly progressive, fair and equitable to all races, the machinery of its practical implementation made it less than perfect in practice, especially as viewed when sitting in the wonderful and comfortable chair of hindsight.

The prevailing philosophy at that time was that control of anything was given to those who had most to lose if the job was not done properly – in other words to those who had "skin in the game". For this reason the British armed forces were run not by experts in their field appointed on merit but by the wealthy and landed[224] and for exactly the same reason the qualification required to vote for any Government of the time was the ability to prove wealth and/or land ownership.[225]

With the impossibly complex system of Maori land ownership and the consequent non-existence of written land titles for Maori-owned land, this requirement immediately eliminated the great majority of Maori from the electoral roll. Although it was not intended that way the theoretically equitable Government defined by the 1852 Constitution Act could thus easily be perceived by Maori to be practically a vehicle for European domination. While it could be, and has been, theoretically argued that the budding Maori nationalist tendency mentioned above was accentuated and accelerated by what might have been seen by Maori as a wholesale rejection of giving them a voice in Government, this theory is not

---

[224] Often with disastrous results, although in an age in which Governments were petrified by the thought of revolution of the masses one can see the reasoning behind why this was done.

[225] The franchise conditions associated with the 1852 NZ Constitution Act were "...to include all British subjects twenty-one years of age, having £50 freehold estate. £10 household in town, or £5 household in the country." (Wells, p151)

supported by Maori comment at the time. In fact the distinguishing feature of Maori sentiment regarding the new Government, and what may or may not have been its downfalls, seems to have been complete indifference.

All causes must have at least one banner to rally around and it does not take too much imagination to surmise that for Maori in the 1850's this banner would be land. A common starting point for discussion on this point is the so-called, much debated and possibly even mythical "Maori Land League"[226], which is generally said to have its genesis in a visit by Matene te Whiwhi to central North Island tribes in early 1853 and to reach maturity with a large inter-tribal meeting at Manawapou in the lower part of Ngati Ruanui territory, a little north of Patea.

Depending on whose account you read, between 500-1,000 Maori attended this later event, which was deemed important enough to warrant building not just a new meeting hall but the largest one of its kind in the country – a significant achievement for the Ngati Ruanui hosts. Wanganui missionary Richard Taylor says of this meeting:

> "Taiporohenui, a name for the West Coast, and also a word used in a Karakia Kumara, signifying – the ending of the matter. This was applied as a name for the building in which a great council was held at

[226] This theory is mooted, for instance, by James Cowan who says of the Maori Land League - "This powerful movement, to which was conjoined an effort to found a Maori kingdom, was initiated shortly after New Zealand received its Constitution Act bestowing representative government upon the colony. The connection between these most important political developments may be rather difficult to trace exactly, but the coincidence is certainly remarkable. The Maori was not to be behind the white in his struggle for national power, and while the settlers had been successful in their agitation for self-determination, he was determined that the newcomers should be restrained in their race for Maori land." (*The New Zealand Wars – Vol 1*, James Cowan, pp146-147).

> Manawapou, in May 1854[227], to pupuru, or retain the land, and form a confederacy of the tribes, so that the European should not obtain any further hold of the country than he then possessed:
>
> The land thus made sacred was to extend from Kaiiwi to Kurukuru, and anyone who attempted to sell a portion within these lines was to be tomahawked.[228] The spirit then manifested was anything but friendly to the British Government. A hatchet was passed round as a bond of union, to show that whosoever infringed upon the law then established, and sold land to the Government, should be put to death; the handle of the hatchet was beautifully carved. Some years later this was purchased of its owner, Rio, who was shortly afterwards murdered.
>
> It is right to say that the hatchet was only received by the Ngati Ruanui and Taranaki natives. There were Wanganui and Ngati Raukawa chiefs present, but they would not touch it..."[229]

Much has been made of this meeting and the alleged "Land League" which was said to have been either created or validated by it. In more recent times there have been various views on the

---

[227] There seems to be some confusion as to the date of this event. Keith Sinclair gives an alternative date of "April 1854" which may simply indicate the meeting took place over a period of two months.
Alternatively https://teara.govt.nz/en/taranaki-places/page-7 suggests the meeting hall itself was not erected until 1855. Octavius Hadfield quotes Donald McLean as giving in 1860 the vague date of "about seven years ago" (*The Second Year of one of England's little Wars*, Hadfield, p45)

[228] An alternative account suggests that "A New Testament was buried and a heap of stones raised in witness of the covenant entered into. To give permanency to this determination a "beating the bounds" has taken place at certain periods."(*Marlborough Press*, 8 September, 1860, p3).

[229] *The Past and Present of New Zealand with Prospects for the Future*, Richard Taylor, pp299-300.

existence of such an entity, the most persuasive of which is that it did not exist.[230]

But, as the saying goes, "perception is reality". Real or fictional the term "Land League" provided European settlers with a convenient catch-all term for a "bogey man" which enabled them to put a name to something they could direct their anger and frustration at. Ridiculous or not that was the reality settlers lived in and in the present we could give plenty of examples of similar fictitious "bogey men" to which, real or not, we are all in thrall to.

And in their defence the settlers were correct to a degree for one thing was both very clear and very understandable. Call it what you want – a league, a federation, a confederation, a general feeling – Maori *were* converging – albeit at different rates and with varying levels of animosity – towards limiting land sales, for a complicated mix of reasons, some of which paradoxically had little or nothing to do with land. It was not so much that *selling* land was the real problem for Maori as that *not* selling land was the *solution* to *other*, more important problems such as maintaining tribal independence and sovereignty. Withholding things is, after all, *the* classic tactic used to gain or maintain control in any relationship because it gives you power. *Not* selling land was the only and most powerful card in the Maori hand, the only and biggest wrench in their toolbox, the biggest and only stick they had to keep the Europeans at bay.

Perhaps the most interesting thing about the Manawapou meeting was who was, and who was not, present.

---

[230] In 1950 Keith Sinclair wrote the bulletin *The Maori Land League – An Examination into the Source of a New Zealand Myth* on this subject. This was subsequently challenged by Edward Hill's – *There Was a Taranaki Land League*, in 1969.

According to an alternative account by Richard Taylor:

> "... all the head Chiefs from Wellington to the Waitara, a distance of near three hundred miles, assembled at this meeting."[231]

Given that Kingi considered himself King of Waitara, together with his very publicly aired antagonism towards land selling and the example of his incredible and successful defiance of the nominally highest person in the land, Governor Grey, on this subject, it would surely be unthinkable were he not invited. But incredibly, for whatever reason, he is not noted as being not an attendee of this surely pivotal meeting.[232]

Buddle's account of this meeting clarifies the boundaries of the supposedly land league as:

> "...Kai Iwi on the South side, and a place within a short distance of New Plymouth on the North."[233]

If this is so then the league's jurisdiction did not include Waitara or indeed any Ati Awa territory, although that is perhaps a moot point given that Kingi is his own one-man land-league anyway.

The second point of interest is where the meeting took place – in Ngati Ruanui territory. Up until now the Ngati Ruanui have not featured in our story other than to note their existence in passing. Although theoretically the New Zealand Company purchased their territory, and that of the neighbouring Taranaki tribe, as part of their various purchases in early 1840, William Wakefield elected to drop claims to these areas:

> "...in consequence of its having become thickly inhabited by its former owners, who have returned to it since the European settlement was established between it and their enemies..."[234]

---

[231] *Te Ika a Maui*, Richard Taylor, p278.

[232] PDNZ, Volume B, p221.

[233] The King Movement in New Zealand, Thomas Buddle, p5.

Consequently neither the Ngati Ruanui nor the Taranaki tribes had ever had any issues with Europeans or claims to their land, that pleasure being reserved for the Ati Awa. Logically, *utu* being what it is, given that, like Ati Awa, the Ngati Ruanui and Taranaki tribes had only been able to return to their ancestral lands thanks to the presence of Europeans, you would think there would be a degree of gratitude or at least an understanding of *utu* being owed to the Europeans. Therefore it comes as some surprise that from the Manawapou meeting onwards, both tribes, and Ngati Ruanui in particular, would become increasingly vocal and violent on the subject of land sales which they had yet to suffer.

---

[234] Letter Wicksteed to Colonel Wakefield, 23 November, 1844 (Wells, p116).

Chapter 1-17

The Buying of Taranaki – Take 3.

In 1839/40 the New Zealand Company had a crack at buying Taranaki and either succeeded or failed depending on your narrative of choice. In 1841 Hobson had a second go buying it from the Waikatos. In 1848 it was Grey's turn.

For while Grey had failed either by threat or diplomacy in preventing Kingi's return to Taranaki he could perhaps salvage some of his battered reputation by doing better in his pledge "to acquire for the European population those tracts of land which were awarded to the New Zealand Company by Mr. Spain", preferably before Kingi finally arrived back in Waitara after his leisurely migration home from Waikanae.

Accordingly Grey's 14 point instructions to his trusty, land-buying agent, Donald McLean, unleashed a veritable flurry of land purchasing activity leading to a series of patchwork-like land purchases and by 1849 30,000 of the 60,000 acres promised by Spain's award had been purchased, albeit in the face of considerable hostility.[235] While Grey may have lost kudos for failing to prevent Kingi from returning he and McLean could at least be

[235] Some of these "patches" of purchased European land are shown in green in the map shown on the cover of this book.

congratulated, by the settlers if not by local Maori, for being 50% of the way towards keeping his promise of honouring Spain's award.

Impressive as that result may sound what looks good on paper does not necessarily look so good on the ground. We have commented before that while New Zealand may indeed cover 65 million acres most of it was – for European purposes at least – totally useless land. It was not so much that early surveyors such as Frederick Carrington made *bad* choices for the location of settlements as they made the *only* choices, selections of desperation and necessity. Consequently many of these settlements were doomed before the first settlers set foot in them. Nowhere is this better demonstrated than in the European settlement of New Plymouth.

If we were to look at an aerial view of modern Taranaki we would find, with the exception of Mount Taranaki itself, a well ordered expanse of open, if deeply rutted, land. This, however, is the result of 180 years of toil, sweat and tears and millions of axe blows by the pioneering settlers and their descendants. In the 1850s Taranaki was a completely different world with its only usable part confined to a coastal strip, a ribbon of land perhaps two or three miles deep, which ran north around the coast from Nga Motu up to and past the Waitara River. The rest of the land inland of this coastal strip was covered in bush and vegetation back to and up the mountain, of no use to anyone until said toil, sweat and tears were, over many decades, applied. The uselessness of most of the Taranaki land was why Spain's award was for the relatively trivial amount of 60,000 acres of actual usable land, an amount which is a mere peccadillo when compared to other Government land purchases which were in the order of hundreds of thousands, or even millions of acres.

In short, much of McLean's newly purchased theoretical land was in practice completely useless – swamp, bush covered or carved up by the numberless ravines formed by the run-off from Mount Taranaki, or the useless sides of the mountain itself. Half of the land purchased by McLean was from outside the area of Spain's original award[236] and all of it was

[236] For example the Omata and Tataraimaka Blocks, which were bought from the Taranaki tribe.

bought with such difficulty and hostility that some of it would not actually become inhabitable by its new owners until many years after its supposed purchase.

Whilst there was never any land in Taranaki that could be described as "low hanging fruit" the lowest of the high hanging fruit had now been picked. Any remaining fruit was hanging tantalisingly out of reach at two very much higher levels of branches. Level 1, the lower of the two, was the remaining Puketapu land directly north of the European owned land on which the settlement of New Plymouth was sited. The picking of this fruit began in 1854 and in the process caused a five year inter-*hapu* war. Level 2 of the remaining fruit was the land north of that, the area known as Waitara, and the picking of this fruit would eventually create the spark that ignited the ten years of the New Zealand Wars.

Since Waitara was occupied by a number of returned *hapu,* including the Manukoriki *hapu* with its intractable chief Wiremu Kingi, the level of this hanging fruit was so high as to be almost invisible. And, as Murphy's Law would have it, this very highest of fruit was also frustratingly the most coveted one. If we return to our aerial map of Taranaki we will see that while the great majority of it is carved up in numberless gorge-lets Waitara is by comparison flat and rut free – perfect land for cultivation. Waitara was renowned for its fertility and was a key reason why Carrington chose Taranaki as the "best of a bad lot" choice for the site of New Plymouth.

Waitara was an area European settlers had previously been in possession of but had been forced to give up by Fitzroy's repudiation of Spain's award. Waitara had the alluring attraction of the proverbial forbidden fruit and ironically the settlers may have been feeling precisely as Kingi did in his vow to return to his previous home. Donald McLean had tried valiantly to pick that fruit but in 1854 the forbidden fruit of Waitara was still well beyond the reach of mortal man.

Chapter 1-18

The "Taranaki Civil War"?

1854 was a pivotal year for Taranaki. It was the year Maori anti-land selling sentiment reached a critical mass and manifested itself in the pan-Maori meeting of Manawapou of May, 1854, which we have already mentioned. And it was also the year in which this "sentiment" manifested itself in *actual* violence in Taranaki.

We need to be quite clear that this violence was not between Maori and European but between Maori and Maori. We have already mentioned that the various land-purchases made by McLean in 1847-48 were made with great difficulty, the reason being that Maori themselves fell into two categories – those who wanted to sell land and those who did not. When each block of land had literally hundreds of individual Maori owners the chances of getting all claimants to agree to a sale was about nil. Consequently potential land-purchases pitted Maori against Maori, *hapu* against *hapu*, brother against brother.

Add to this the interference of individuals and groups who did not have claims to the land in question but objected on principle to the sale of *any* land to Europeans – as codified in the Manawapou meeting – and we have a sure recipe for inter-Maori mayhem. And if that were not enough, throw in the ever-present, long-standing personal animosities and grudges between the individuals involved, in which selling land which partially belonged to your enemies provided a perfect way to exact vengeance, and you have mayhem multiplied by mayhem.

Given this tinderbox of untangleable conflict all McLean could do was to let the various parties sort it out among themselves. Sometimes, as in the case of the Grey, Omata and Tataraimaka blocks, differences were able to be resolved satisfactorily. In the case of the Bell Block purchase however things very nearly came to blows when the "leading Puketapu Chief"[237], Rawiri Waiaua[238] pushed through the sale in the face of vehement opposition from Waitere Katatore[239].

From 1848 to 1854 things were quiet land sales wise but this situation was too good to last.

In August, 1854, six years after the problematical Bell Block sale, Rawiri Waiaua decided to sell more land. He and his party were in the process of marking out this land when they were attacked by his old foe Katatore's party, resulting in the death of Waiaua and five of his followers.[240] So marked the beginnings of a complex and tangled conflict which hung over

---

[237] *War and politics in New Zealand, 1855-1870*, B. J. Dalton, p26.

[238] "The most notable friendly Puketapu Chief was Rawiri Waiaua, *i.e.,* David the Porpoise, a well-proportioned man, mild of disposition, profusely tattooed, who was in the habit of paying visits to the town on a grey horse, wearing a white hat and green spectacles." (Wells, p158).

[239] "Katatore belonged to the small Puketapu *hapu* Ngati Tanewai. He seems not to have been of high birth. Slight in build, with an immense bush of hair which stood a foot above his head, he was a person of impressive character, an orator, and a shrewd leader of men. In a community composed very largely of returned *taurekareka* [slave], deprived by war, epidemic and migration of its natural leaders, Katatore had seized his opportunity, and he soon emerged as the Puketapu spokesman." (*He Whenua tau Utu*, Ann Parsonson, p158). As his baptismal name of "Waitere" suggests he is at this stage a Wesleyan, being named after the Wesleyan missionary John Whiteley.

[240] See for instance Wells, pp158-9.

Taranaki and blighted its progress for the next five years and which is referred to by historians as the "Puketapu Feuds".

A few months after Waiaua's death, this feud, which was at that stage a purely inter-Puketapu affair between the Katatore faction and the Waiaua faction, was spread further afield and escalated by the actions of a certain Rimene, a member of the Ngati Ruanui tribe and who also had relations in the Taranaki tribe. Rimene had unwisely committed adultery with the wife of Ihaia Kirikumara, chief of the Mamaku *pa* and part of the Otawaura *hapu* of Waitara, and was subsequently shot for his troubles on orders from Ihaia. Ihaia was a good friend to the Europeans, a friendship which was reciprocated with enthusiasm since Ihaia had offered to sell land at Waitara on at least three occasions.[241]

Here, after an absence in our story of six years, our old friend Wiremu Kingi made a reappearance. It is said that in order to get back at the land-selling Ihaia, Wiremu Kingi twisted the reasoning for Ihaia's killing of Rimene from being the result of adultery to the result of Rimene being a follower of the anti-land seller Katatore. In this way Rimene's death was converted from the consequence of lust to martyrdom for the anti-land selling cause. Not that that really mattered, for no matter what the cause, Ngati Ruanui *must* seek revenge for Rimene's death and consequently before you can say "*utu*" Ihaia found himself ensconced in Mamaku *pa* surrounded by 300 angry Ngati Ruanui warriors.

In this banal and lust-driven way, what started as a small localised "Puketapu" feud now became a full-blown "Puketapu-Ngati Ruanui-Taranaki-Manukorihi" feud raging across the territories of three tribes encompassing a good portion of Taranaki. This feud would grind on in a complicated, sporadic way for another five years, virtually to the start of

---

[241] The offers were made in 1844, 1847 and 1850 but not accepted because of objections from Wiremu Kingi. Ihaia was one of the reputed "diehards" taken prisoner at the Mikotahi siege mentioned previously. He returned to Waitara as a returned slave at least 6 years prior to Kingi's return in 1848 (DNZB, Steven Oliver, pp461-2).

the actual "Taranaki War" generally regarded as the beginning of the New Zealand Wars towards which this story is moving.

It is a long, complicated story, and like many feuds, largely illogical to anyone but its participants. Different players came and went and changed their minds. The dead Rawiri Waiaua's place was filled by Arama Karaka (Adam Clark). Katatore inexplicably suddenly changed from being an anti-land seller to a pro-land seller and eventually met the same fate he bestowed on Rawiri Waiaua. Although Arama Karaka and Ihaia were nominally both on the same land-selling "side" Ihaia would only come to Karaka's aid if Karaka gave him some land, a remarkable demonstration of either *utu* or of blackmail, as well as of the ease with which Maori land can easily change hands under the strangest and "right" circumstances. This increasingly bewildering situation climaxed in early 1858 with the besieging of Ihaia and his followers in the Karaka *pa* by Wiremu Kingi and his followers who were seemingly intent on wreaking indiscriminate death and destruction on its inhabitants.

The details of this sordid business are interesting in a voyeuristic way and if nothing else tell us about the day to day interaction and customs of Maori at that time. Other than that they are largely irrelevant[242]. They are merely symptoms and just like a doctor our job is to use symptoms to help us find the problem.

Standing back and looking at forests instead of trees can shed great swathes of light that illuminate the road to the New Zealand Wars. In particular examining these "feuds" helps us answer important questions such as – what exactly was the structure and hierarchy of "Ati Awa"? What was the role and authority of certain individuals and in particular of Wiremu Kingi? While at this point these questions may seem rather random and "off-topic" it will soon become apparent that their answers are pivotal to our understanding of the road to war.

---

[242] For those interested Johan Riemenschneider's account in *AJHR 1861, Session 1, E-03*, pp3-8 gives a good account of the thought processes and motivations of the Ngati Ruanui and Taranaki tribes as at 1855.

Stepping back and analysing the "symptoms" of the Puketapu Feuds suggests the following conclusions:

• That the term "Ati Awa" at this time had virtually no meaning.

We have struggled from page one of this book to clearly define exactly what, or who, "Ati Awa" was during this period. This has been a problem for anyone who has written on the subject since 1840.[243] Up until this

---

[243] Just a few random, but hopefully sufficient, examples demonstrating the confusion in this area, at least among Europeans of the time, include:

1) "...Mr Heaphy must include the Puketapus and Huirangi natives, who, we are informed, properly speaking, are not Ngatiawas." (*The War in Taranaki during the Years 1860-61*, Grayling, p106).

2) "The AtiAwa now [1848] in Taranaki now formed two main tribes [Manukorihi and Puketapu]" (*War and politics in New Zealand*, B.J. Dalton, p26). Dalton also tells us (p25) that George Grey regarded Puketapu as a "family", a subtle but important distinction from a *hapu*.

3) "Katatore belonged to the small Puketapu hapu Ngati Tanewai" (*He Whenua hua Utu*, Ann Parsonson, p234), indicating the existence of *hapu* of Puketapu (which S. P. Smith does not, see below), suggesting that "Puketapu" was not simply a "*hapu*" of "Ati Awa" but a complete "Iwi" structure in its own right.

4) Ballara (*Taua*, p322) defines Ati Awa, at least for the purposes of her book, as "the people originally from Waitara to New Plymouth, including 'Nga Motu' hapu, which were Ngati Rahiri, Ngati Te Whiti, Ngati Tiwhirikura and Ngati Tupparikino", indicating that, like Puketapu, Ngamotu are also best considered as an independent "family", or "Iwi" structure, in its own right.

5) "The Manu-korihi hapu, as such, was not in existence at that time, nor were the ancestors of W. Kingi, of any note then" (*JPS, Vol 19, No.1, S. P. Smith*, p28) – speaking of circa 1820, with Smith somewhat contradicting what he says elsewhere.

6) The usually reliable James Cowan not only speaks of Ati Awa as a homogeneous unit but maintains that Kingi is its "paramount chief" (*The New Zealand Wars - Vol 1*, p155).

7) "He there declares that not a single man of the Ngatiawa tribe received payment from the New Zealand Company, but only men of the Puketapu and Ngamotu tribes. This would be false, even if there were any foundation for the

point in our story this vagueness has not hindered us greatly and we have been able to skirt around the issue. But we have now reached a point where that vagueness can no longer be tolerated and the so-called "Puketapu Feuds" provide clues that can help us clarify what by 1860 would be an absolutely key point.

In the preceding chapters we have described how whatever the "Ati Awa" are hypothesised to have been in 1820 when Te Rauparaha made his way south, that over the next 30 years they split up into many entities living in many disparate locations. Some of these groups, such as Te Puni's Wellington group, and those in Queen Charlotte Sound, chose to never return to Taranaki *at all*.

Those Ati Awa groups that *did* return arrived back in Taranaki not only at different times but with very different statuses and religions. The ex-slaves of Waikato returned in the early 1840s as Wesleyans with massive chips on their shoulders trying desperately to puff themselves back up to their former pre-slave levels of *mana*. Wiremu Kingi's contingent, the returnees from Waikanae, were, by comparison Johnny-come-latelies – they did not return to Taranaki for about another six or so years after the returned slaves and when they did they did so as Anglicans. And even then a good proportion of Kingi's "flock" chose to remain behind in Waikanae.

If Ati Awa had a known hierarchy at an "iwi" level in 1820, then by 1840 their unity and leadership structure was well and truly shot. This is clearly evident if we compare them to other Maori groups. The "Waikatos", for instance, who have over all this time remained in one spot with some minor movement around the edges, still had a defined degree of hierarchy. If Hobson, Fitzroy or Grey wanted to talk turkey with the Waikatos they called Te Wherowhero. Likewise, if they wanted to do

---

distinction attempted to be drawn between the Ngatiawa and the Puketapu and Ngamotu people; but there is no manner of doubt that these were hapus or families of the Ngatiawa equally with the Manukorihi branch to which Kingi himself belongs." (Governor Browne quoting Wiremu Kingi's letter to Fitzroy discussed earlier, *AJHR 1861, E-01*, p12).

business with Nga Puhi, their go-to guy was Tamati Waka Nene. But if anyone wanted to do business with the "Ati Awa" they had to deal with a raggle-taggle bunch of individuals of no particular status, something we see time and time again in the string of attempted and actual land sales between 1844 and 1854.

It seems clear that at that time there was no paramount chief at the *iwi*, "Ati Awa" level, whatever we may assume "Ati Awa" was. Neither was there a "paramount chief" at the *hapu* level, nor even a "paramount chief" at a sub-*hapu* level. It was a free-for-all between individuals who often belonged to the same *hapu*, or sub-*hapu*, and who felt no obligation to anyone but themselves.

The word "feud" in "Puketapu Feud" says it all – feud is a word used to describe conflict between two bunches of rabbles. Nations do not have feuds, and neither do *iwi*. At that time the land was inhabited not by a united Ati Awa *iwi* under a single paramount chief but by a disparate bunch of *hapu* and sub-*hapu* whose boundaries just happened to meet. The "Puketapu feuds" were five years of shambles that could only happen within an anarchy – there *was* no "paramount chief" because, if there was, these feuds would never have happened.

If these conclusions drawn solely from observations of the Puketapu feuds are not sufficiently conclusive it is encouraging to have historian Keith Sinclair concur:

> "During the Puketapu feuds of the eighteen-fifties Wiremu Kingi usually assisted whichever party was opposed to land sales, but he was not universally respected. Such chiefs as Katatore, whom McLean in 1844 said had "assumed chieftainship" over the Puketapu, or Ihaia, a chief of the Otaraua hapu, were virtually independent, with their own followers. The division of opinion in the tribe about land sales had further weakened the old powers of

the chiefs, and Wiremu Kingi's authority was effective mainly in the close vicinity of the Waitara."[244]

- **The days of "the chief" were over.**

This is very much inseparable from the subject of the previous paragraph and could be seen as the same thing viewed from a different angle. We have said it before but it is worth repeating in this particular context; thanks to the introduction of Christianity and exposure to European modes of social hierarchy the power of "the chief" had taken a plummeting nosedive and the voice of the individual was now in the ascendant. The days of "paramount chiefs" with actual power were over and it was every man for himself.

The details of the various land sales around New Plymouth make it quite clear that these sales had nothing to do with chiefs but were made between groups of like-minded individuals and the Crown. The days when "the chiefs" had the power to keep a group in lock-step were over. This was true in general throughout 1840s Maoridom but especially so in Taranaki for the reasons of dispersal already mentioned.

So whatever may or may not have been codified, and by whom, at the meeting at Manawapou in 1854 the "Puketapu feuds" demonstrate that it was largely irrelevant to those on the ground in Taranaki. With the new multiplicity of voices, and everyone free to rally around the person of their choice, the logical outcome was that some people would want to sell land while others would not. This is democracy in action, which is a fine thing if it can be controlled and if everyone has signed that social contract.

- **Wiremu Kingi was not "paramount chief" of Ati Awa.**

If, as we have suggested, "Ati Awa" was not a homogeneous body under the control of *any* paramount chief then it follows that neither Wiremu Kingi, nor *anybody*, was its paramount chief.

---

[244] *Some Historical notes on AtiAwa Genealogy*, Keith Sinclair (JPS, Vol 60, No.1, p59).

The "Puketapu Feuds" make it quite clear that Kingi not only had no authority over Puketapu but that he had even less interest. Puketapu could squabble amongst themselves until the cows came home. They could choose to sell land or not sell land.

The "non-Puketapu feuds", in which Kingi, supposed head of the Manukoriki *hapu*, chose to do battle with Ihaia, supposed head of the related Otaraua *hapu*, suggests either that there was no "paramount chief" or, that if there was, others in the organisation were challenging it. A reasonable conclusion is that Kingi was "chief" only of the Manukorihi *hapu*, which is in turn consistent with everything we know about his father.

Again Keith Sinclair makes the definitive statement:

> "But for all practical purposes there was no single chief of the Atiawa."[245]

- **A more useful expression for these "feuds" may be the "Taranaki Civil War".**

"Feud" is a useful word in that it accurately captures the feeling of low-level, small-scale anarchy totally beyond the control not only of the hypothetically ruling Government but of any equally hypothesised over-arching "Ati Awa paramount chief".

But although the "feud" may have *begun* among the Puketapu the greater part of it involved *most tribes* of southern and central Taranaki. For reasons which are difficult to explain beyond kinship and natural belligerency, the Ngati Ruanui, who had never been troubled either by land sales or proximity to Europeans, and the Taranaki tribe, who had previously happily sold land to Europeans, were also moved to become involved. Given the geographical scope of the parties involved a more

---

[245] *Some Historical notes on AtiAwa Genealogy*, Keith Sinclair (JPS, Vol 60, No.1, p59).

accurate term for this period of conflict might therefore be the "Taranaki Civil War".[246]

Further reasons for preferring this term over "Puketapu Feuds" is that it emphasises that violence in colonial New Zealand was not always with Europeans, that Maori did have agency and held a wide range of opinions regarding land sales and attitudes to Europeans in general, and that Maori were quite capable of creating their own violence, for many reasons including the time-honoured ones of settling personal vendettas and point scoring.

- **"Waitara" was not the sole preserve of Wiremu Kingi.**

The term "Waitara" is bandied about in history books as a single homogenous area without defining geographically what it is or what its ownership options may be.

The "Puketapu Feuds" tell us that "Waitara", whatever the geographical extent of that may be, is either not the sole property of the Manukorihi *hapu,* or that at the very least its ownership is disputed – Ihaia of the Otaraua *hapu* considers himself able to sell to the Europeans what they consider to be "Waitara".

In summary, not only is Wiremu Kingi not "paramount chief" of Ati Awa, he is not "paramount chief" of Waitara. He is, one presumes, paramount chief of his own *hapu*, the Manukorihi, but as we have said elsewhere, because of the rapidly changing social order, a "paramount chief" in 1855 was by no means the same thing as a "paramount chief" in 1835.

- **The feuds tell us something about the character and motives of Wiremu Kingi.**

The most obvious observation is that the feuds reveal Kingi to be anti-land selling, at least of his own land, very probably of any land that is not his but which might come under the name "Waitara", and possibly of any land full-stop. The latter two categories are hard to define because the

[246] Indeed Buddle refers to the feuds as the "Native War at Taranaki". *The Maori King Movement in New Zealand*, Buddle, p6

feuds seem to be as much nurtured by personal grudges as they do by conflicting opinions regarding land sales.

Yet for all that, Kingi reveals himself to be somewhat selective in his anti-land selling stance, for in the eleven years since he migrated from Waikanae he has repeatedly tried to sell "his" vacated land in Waikanae to the Government, who declined to do so because it would cause its de-landed inhabitants to migrate to Taranaki.

To further confuse the issue Kingi was as late as February, 1860, declaring:

> "I will not consent to divide the land, because my father's dying words and instructions were to hold it"[247]

Coming a full ten years after using similar words to justify his return from Waikanae this does tend to confirm that his over-arching consideration in the sale or non-sale of at least what he considered his own lands was not that of "anti-land selling" but of his continuing respect for his father, which, as has been remarked previously, is both understandable and noble but not something pre-ordained by the Gods to the exclusion of all else.

In the course of these feuds, in March, 1858, we find Kingi and 800 of his followers besieging Ihaia with his 80 followers in his Karaka Pa. We are told that Kingi:

> "...had cut a great quantity of fern, which was to be tied up in order to set fire to the Karaka Pah, and drive the inhabitants out of it, that Wm. King and his people might fall upon them."[248]

This is not to say that Kingi's actions are any different, or any worse, than anybody else's at that time.[249] But it does demonstrate the strength of his

---

[247] AJHR 1861, F3, p34.

[248] *Ibid.*

[249] Indeed, on Kingi agreeing to let Ihaia and his followers escape in order that Kingi could take his frustrations out on Ihaia's pa in lieu of Ihaia's people, Ihaia's team instead faked leaving but actually remained behind to ambush Kingi as he came in.

feeling, and the extent he will go to, to challenge an opponent's attempt at land-selling.

A contemporary newspaper report quotes this speech of Kingi's to "the Taranaki natives":

> "Men of Taranaki! Be strong! Be brave, and capture Ihaia, Nikorima, and Pukere as payment for the tapu of Taranaki and the Umuroa. Then we will stretch out their arms and burn them with fire. To prolong their torture let them be suspended over a slow fire for a week, and let the fire consume them. Like the three men of old whom Nebuchadnezzar commanded to be cast into the fiery furnace, even as Shadrach, Meshach, and Abednego, shall it be with Ihaia."[250]

Kingi is clearly an Old Testament, "eye for an eye" sort of guy rather than a proponent of peace and love as espoused in the New Testament. Metaphorical though his speech may be he is clearly not a man to be messed with and open warfare *is* an option.

- **It shows the state of progress – or lack of it – in New Zealand becoming a sovereign nation.**

We might well ask – over this five year period of sporadic warfare in Taranaki, just what was Britain, or the nascent New Zealand government, doing about it? Surely they did not just sit back and watch while the Taranaki Maori destroyed each other?

Well actually that is precisely what they did do. The acting Governor of the time, Robert Wynyard, elected not to intervene, for precisely the same reasons every previous Governor had refused to intervene in similar situations – they knew that intervention would precipitate an all-out, possibly nation-wide, race war. It was a "damned if you do and damned if you don't" situation.

What can we say about an inter-tribal feud in which an alleged "sovereign power" – Britain – refused to intervene for fear of starting an all-out

---

[250] *Taranaki Herald*, 10 April 1858, p2.

interracial war? Quite clearly this is an acknowledgement that there *was no sovereign power*. This however was nothing new – everyone in the colony had known that for the best part of 20 years.

- **The feuds demonstrate not just the lack of "sovereign power" in Taranaki but that this lack was actively pushing the two races further apart.**

In history – and in life in general – it is the squeaky wheels that get all the attention and press. Consequently while in the historical records we hear a lot about the Katatores and Wiremu Kingis of the world we hear very little of the many Maori who were actually committed to British sovereignty and the law and order that it implied.

The relatives and followers of the dead Rawiri, and of the besieged Ihaia, therefore expected the European sovereign they had put their faith in to behave like one and protect them against enemies such as Katatore and Wiremu Kingi. They expected law and order to be applied equally and consistently, not just to Europeans but to Maori – that is what a sovereign government is supposed to do in such situations. Consequently the lack of Government intervention and protection during the course of the Puketapu Feuds felt like a cutting betrayal of their loyalty.

British non-intervention in the feuds had two effects – first it turned the not inconsiderable portion of Maori who were formerly pro-European against them and secondly it created a realisation that if the theoretical British sovereignty would not protect them then Maori needed to come up with their own system of governance. By not intervening in the "Puketapu Feuds" the Government forced Maori to consider other options, the most logical of which was to form their own government which *would* take charge in such situations and which *would* work for them.

This was a situation that demanded instant Government action to prevent the two races veering off along two separate paths. The presumed British "sovereign power" needed to do something – and fast.

Chapter 1-19

The vexed issue of Sovereignty.

Thus far in our story we have been following the journey of a very particular part of Maoridom – the relatively small Ati Awa tribe, and in particular, its issues related to land. We now temporarily leave this very specific narrative and widen our focus to take in the *whole* of Maoridom to discuss a more generic issue that is far more important than land – that of *sovereignty*.

"Sovereignty" is a word we have already used frequently, so far without elaboration in order not to divert the reader from the historical flow of our journey. Since we will be using this word constantly from now on it may be helpful to take a slight pause in our journey to ensure we truly understand what this pivotal word means, for when we return to our journey we will find that sovereignty is front and centre of our story. We will find that The New Zealand Wars were not a battle for land but for *the determination of sovereignty.*[251] It is a battle that continues to this day, albeit as a political battle rather than a military one.

"Sovereignty" and "sovereign" are not words we commonly use in daily life and if we were to ask the man in the street to summarise their

---

[251] And for this reason the term "Land Wars", sometimes applied to the "New Zealand Wars", is incorrect.

meaning he would probably be hard pressed. In the modern political world the words we hear most often instead of sovereignty are "independence" and "self-determination", which are similar but different.

"Sovereignty" and "sovereign" are words traditionally reserved for diplomatic purposes, generally to define relationships between countries. But as far as our story is concerned the crux of "sovereignty" and a "sovereign power" or "sovereign nation" is simple – a "sovereign nation" is a unified body of people governed by a recognised head, be that "head" an individual or a body of people. All individuals within that sovereign power have a social contract with that "head" to give up a portion of their personal freedom as the price to pay for the freedom from the anarchy which must otherwise result.

Sovereignty is a national and unanimous recognition that some known entity is in control which has ultimate right of veto on all things for all subjects of all creeds and races within that sovereign nation. The *sine qua non* of a "sovereign nation" is that there is a non-negotiable infrastructure that is recognised and honoured not only by all its citizens but by all other sovereign nations who may wish to interact with it.

Being a "sovereign nation" does not mean there is no room for dissent[252], just that there is an infrastructure to manage dissent and that the decision of that infrastructure is binding. We can march in the streets, wave placards, present petitions and resort to a succession of Courts, High Courts and Supreme Courts. In theory, at least, we can live peacefully and orderly, if perhaps on the cusp of benign instability, in an environment in which 51% of the population believe fiercely in something while 49% just as fiercely oppose it. In modern times we have the opportunity to "overthrow" the ruling regime every electoral cycle.

Moving from philosophical generalities let us look at the specifics of the sovereignty situation in 1840's New Zealand. We have already seen that in 1835 Britain officially accorded "New Zealand" the status of a sovereign state under the domain of a mythical entity called "The United Chiefs of

---

[252] At least in a democracy.

New Zealand" and noted that decision as being kind but supremely flawed.

The buying of land is a good demonstration of the lack of a Maori "sovereignty" in pre-Treaty times. When William Wakefield arrived in the *Tory* in late 1839 there was no single body he could go to to discuss the business of buying land. Consequently he found himself shuttling backwards and forwards between Whanganui a Tara, Kapiti, Taranaki and Queen Charlotte Sound trying to track down owners. Te Rauparaha had a different view from Te Puni who had a different view from the signatories at Queen Charlotte Sound who had a different view from the signatories at Moturoa who had a different view from Te Wherowhero and the Waikatos. They were all wheeling and dealing, looking out for number one, not for what was best for a united nation or some vague concept of shared ethnicity.

Wakefield obtained so many signatures – of men, women and children – because *every* Maori individual had a claim while nobody had authority. There were major chiefs, minor chiefs, principal chiefs, inferior chiefs, second rate chiefs, important chiefs – every second person seemed to be a "chief" on some mysterious, infinitely graduated scale, no doubt crystal clear to Maori but impenetrable to Europeans. The best Wakefield could do was to get as many signatures as he could and pray that some of them meant something. Wakefield could have made a thousand treaties in a thousand places with a thousand signatures and ultimately they would still all be worthless. The situation is symptomatic of a group of people who, while they may have their own methods of land management which worked for them, were clearly not a united people who could be collectively considered as a "sovereign nation".

In theory New Zealand became the sovereign nation of "New Zealand" in 1840 by virtue of Article 1 of the Treaty of Waitangi, which made "Britain" *the* sovereign power, meaning in turn that *all* its subjects – of *all* races – came under the sole authority of Britain's representative, the Governor for the time being.

According to this theory the inviolable rule for any Governor of New Zealand from Hobson onwards was quite clear – *they* were the singular, all powerful, boss. They might – and did – consult others, and they were in turn responsible to their bosses back in England, but on a day to day basis *they* made the decisions and *everyone else did what they said.* While there were well organised and defined checks and balances to their power the buck stopped with them. That was the theory anyway, which may or may not have always translated to reality.

Far be it for this book to add to the millions of unread words already written on this subject but whatever anyone thinks about the Treaty in the present and recent past is irrelevant – the only thing that matters is what people thought of it *at the time*, because that explains why they did what they did. For this reason it is as well to summarise very briefly how the Treaty was viewed by European and Maori at the time under discussion – between 1845 and 1855.

First the "British" view. If we have no idea what the Treaty means in the present at least the British had a very clear idea of what it meant in 1840. As far as the British Government and the New Zealand Governors were concerned, it was the "Bible" for the humanitarian colonisation of New Zealand, the key document used to justify reasons for doing things and for not doing things. It was quoted and relied on by missionaries, Governors, British politicians and protection societies and equally vilified by colonists who claimed it as impeding their progress. The Treaty was to the British a genuinely useful document and it is not too extreme to equate the Treaty with a "founding document" at that time. It served its purpose well at that time.

The concept of sovereignty was, of course, in the DNA of the newly arrived British subjects of New Zealand – they had lived under this social contract all their lives. Fitzroy's repudiation of Spain's Taranaki judgment is a perfect example both of how sovereignty is supposed to work and of the British settlers' unconditional subjugation to the Governor. Although the settlers of New Plymouth did not get the decision they wanted they none the less obeyed the social contract of sovereign power to the letter. They did not revolt and overthrow the Government and they did not slaughter the "winners" or burn their dwellings. No doubt they muttered under their collective breath. No doubt they had heated meetings and sent scurrilous petitions to the Queen to recall Fitzroy. But for all that, they played the game, packed up their belongings and moved into Fitzroy's little 3,500 acre domain. It is an example of sovereign power in action, of how that particular social contract is supposed to work in practice.

So much for the Europeans, who in the early 1840s represented a tiny proportion of the total population. What about the great majority of the population – the Maori – now presumed "British subjects" courtesy of the Treaty of Waitangi? What was their view of sovereignty? Did they understand the concept of sovereignty and, if so, did they agree to abide by it?

There is less written information on what Maori thought of the Treaty at this time but their actions, and more particularly their *lack* of actions, speak for themselves.

If the word "sovereignty" was both unknown to and unpronounceable by the Bay of Island chiefs who signed the Treaty at Waitangi they seem to be clear of the *concept* of sovereignty and knew precisely what they agreeing to in signing. Colenso tells us, for instance, of Te Kemara's words:

> "Were all to be on an equality, then, perhaps, Te Kemara would say, "Yes;" but for the Governor to be up and Te Kemara down – Governor high up, up, up, and Te Kemara down low, small, a worm, a crawler – No, no, no. O Governor!"[253]

Te Kemara's words may be metaphoric but he hit the nail firmly on the head – sovereignty is, after all, not a difficult concept – it is all about entering into a social contract giving up your rights of equality and subjecting yourself to someone, or something, "bigger than" the individual – the Governor "high" and the individual "low". That is, by definition, what being a "subject" is – you are subject to an ultimate power.

These particular Treaty signatories subsequently proved by their actions not just their *understanding* of sovereignty but their determination to

---

[253] *The Authentic and Genuine History of the Signing of the Treaty of Waitangi, February 5 and 6, 1840*, William Colenso, p17.

abide by it. They regarded the Governor as the sovereign power to the point that to all intents and purposes, with one notable exception, the tribes of Northland "disappeared" from New Zealand history.[254] The "one notable exception" was, of course, Hone Heke, who understood the Treaty he was the first to sign in 1840 but who subsequently changed his mind and reneged on it in 1845. Heke would find that his greatest opponents in his rebellion were not the British but his own countrymen, proving in the process that they not only understood the theory of British sovereignty as espoused by the Treaty but were prepared to honour and protect it in practice, even to the extent of fighting their own people.

While it is impossible and dangerous to generalise the thoughts of hundreds of tribes scattered the length and breadth of two large islands it seems that in the period 1847 to 1855 the Treaty, and its associated sovereignty issues, were largely non-controversial in the greater Maori world. The interaction between European and Maori proceeded as it did largely on the basis of the many mutual benefits and prosperity it brought to both parties, not because of what was, or was not, written on a piece of parchment in 1840. This was the honeymoon period, in which Maori were either actively prospering from the relationship or were as yet so far removed from or affected by it as to be aware that there even *was* a relationship.

On the few occasions the Treaty was mentioned in early written Maori communication of that period it was referred to simply as "The Treaty", a monolithic underpinning document, its content and intent unquestioned in meaning. It would be many decades before the Treaty would be questioned at all and 130 years before the "angels dancing on heads of pins" debates regarding different Treaty versions and creative modern interpretations of what particular Maori words may or may not have

---

[254] That is, they disappeared from history in a positive way. Since history generally only records wars and disasters, *not* being recorded in history is the highest accolade that can be accorded, in this case demonstrating precisely the positive effects that followed from a system of sovereignty – the bringing of peace and order.

meant to whom in 1840 would appear[255]. It would be 150 years before New Zealand finally decided it hadn't a clue what it meant, abandoned it, and replaced it with random "principles". It would be 170 years before Sir Robin Cooke would opine in a *dictum,* subsequently seized upon and incorrectly interpreted as a *ruling*, that the Treaty is "akin to a partnership", whatever that might mean and to whom.

Returning to simpler times in 1840s New Zealand, the great majority of Maoridom – Maori of the entire South Island, the entire East Coast of the North Island and Northland – seem to have committed themselves to British sovereignty. This does not mean Maori in these areas were always happy[256] – sovereignty is a tool for order and trade-offs not for universal utopia – but that they accepted the tenet of subjugation and the power of ultimate authority that sovereignty requires.

But as with most things in life it only takes one dissenter to render a system unworkable and knowing what we already know there are no prizes for guessing that the portion of Maoridom that most openly pushed against the concept of sovereignty was that of the lower West Coast of the North Island – the various Taranaki tribes and Ngati Toa whose paths we have been following for twenty or so years.[257]

In Taranaki – and in Taranaki only – as we have seen, Governor after Governor were continually treading on eggshells to prevent a race war, kowtowing submissively at the feet of their own so-called Taranaki "subjects". We have seen Fitzroy cave regarding Wairau, and again in

---

[255] It is reasonable to say that the presentist linguistic dissection of the Treaty on a sub-atomic level began with Ruth Ross's famous article of 1972 which we have mentioned previously.

[256] The European colonists, for instance, for all that they might both understand and abide by the principles of sovereignty, were *never* happy about anything.

[257] We are speaking here of the late-1840s up to the mid-1850s. In due course the Waikatos would do a U-turn on their acceptance of sovereignty, as we shall see in Part 2 of this book.

overturning Spain's decision. We have seen Grey walked all over by Kingi. We have seen Wynyard helpless in the Puketapu feuds. Taranaki Maori did precisely what Taranaki Maori wanted with impunity.

There are only two possible outcomes in such a situation. Option one is that the presumed "sovereign power" clearly demonstrates its supremacy by negotiation, moral suasion or, as a last resort, force. Option two is that the hypothesised "sovereign power" does nothing, thereby perpetuating and confirming that it is not, in fact, the sovereign power.

We can summarise all this in two key points.

Point one is that during this period Taranaki is the odd man out in a general Maori acceptance of British sovereignty. The chances are high that whatever Hell breaks loose in the future all comes back to Taranaki.

Point two is that in late 1850 almost twenty years of Governors – from Hobson to Grey – had tip-toed around the issue of British sovereignty in Taranaki. The theory was, presumably, that time would solve everything, but that was a cop-out and problems that are left to fester only get worse with time, not better. Eventually a Governor would come who would have the backbone to face the sovereignty issue head-on and inevitably, when that happened, there *must* be conflict and tears.

Chapter 1-20

The arrival of the "steel".

The period 1854 -1858 was a pivotal one in the history of New Zealand, a period where the planets of war began to align. Some of these planets included:

- It was a period of instability of Governors. Grey left the colony in the lurch on New Year's Eve 1853, leaving an interim Governor in his place whose role was simply one of maintaining the status quo until the replacement Governor arrived in late 1855. Pro-active governance of New Zealand effectively ground to a halt for 19 months.
- In 1856 there was a gigantic shift in the tectonic plates of New Zealand governance as New Zealand ceased to be a Crown Colony and governance was passed from Britain and its appointed Governor to an elected New Zealand Government, better known as the "General Assembly", along the Westminster system.
- Taranaki was a powder keg just waiting for a match. As early as 1855 the feeling of imminent war was in fact so strong that the colonists

deliberately postponed their long-held wish for responsible Government so that Britain would foot the bill for it.[258]

- There had been an economic boom and bust cycle associated with the Victorian gold rush which had left Maori, particularly in the Waikato, disillusioned.
- There was a rapidly growing and militant spirit of Maori nationalism in the central North Island which was given form, focus, organisation and identity by the "King Movement".[259] This was a direct challenge to the presumed European sovereignty which demanded that the Governor up his game and make his authority, and real sovereignty, over *both* races, unquestionable.

Taken collectively the situation had the look and feel of what is known these days as a "perfect storm". It did not take a Nostradamus to predict that it was not a matter of "if" but *when* the day of reckoning would come – the only unknown was what form it would take. It was a very complex situation which we can only begin to skim the surface of here.

The New Zealand Constitution Act passed by the British Government in 1852 granted New Zealand a *representative*[260] Government, with an

---

[258] See for example *War and Politics in New Zealand, 1855-1870*, B.J. Dalton, which gives an excellent summary of this complex period in New Zealand history and is highly recommended.

[259] This is discussed in detail in Part 2 of this book.

[260] "*Representative* Government" in this context simply means that one of the Governor's two advisory bodies was made up of members who had been elected and therefore represented the views of their electorates. It was a minor change to the governance system already in place. Under this new system New Zealand was *still* a Crown Colony with all decisions still ultimately made by the Crown's representative, the appointed Governor. In making his decisions he called upon the advice of two groups of advisors – a group of members *nominated by the Governor* (the "Legislative Council") and a second group of members *elected by the people* (the "House of Representatives").

infrastructure based on Provincial Councils to manage local governance in their provinces overseen by a General Assembly to provide holistic governance over the whole country. When Governor Grey departed on 31 December, 1853, the Provincial Councils were in place but much to the British Colonial Office's chagrin the General Assembly was not yet in operation.

Until Grey's official replacement arrived the short straw of Governorship was temporarily passed to Colonel Robert Wynyard. In 1854 the first session of the new General Assembly was held, the major outcome of which was that the newly elected House of Representatives realised – if it did not already know – that representative government on its own left them as powerless as before. They duly demanded not just representative Government but *responsible*[261] Government, a request which was readily granted by Britain in 1855 without contest. Thus in April, 1856, the General Assembly met for the first time not as an advisory body to the Governor but as an independent governing body in its own right. It was one of those "be careful what you wish for" outcomes.

During Wynyard's 18 month reign as interregnum Governor he did what anyone in that position would do – tread water while praying there would be no crises before he could pass the baby to someone above his pay grade. On the subject of the "Puketapu feuds" he took the only course possible in his awkward position – he stayed out of it.

As already noted, sovereignty – or, in practical terms, a unanimous acceptance to be governed and accept authority – could not be said to exist in Taranaki. If Wynyard *did* intervene in an attempt to solve the Puketapu problem it could escalate the localised "Taranaki Civil War"

---

[261] "*Responsible* Government" is a system of government in which an executive group (the "Government" or "Ministry") is chosen from amongst the elected members of the House of Representatives. The Government's job is, as the name suggests, to govern the country by doing what the majority of the House of Representatives allows it to do. In such a system the Government is *responsible* for the running of the country with the Governor's role greatly diminished.

between rival Maori factions into a racial war between Maori and Europeans, possibly involving the entire country. On the other hand, if Wynyard did *not* intervene it would totally undermine the faith many Maori had put in the European government and in the precepts of unity and the rule of law promised by the Treaty – it would be tantamount to the European Government saying "you're on your own" and therefore a major incentive for Maori to do precisely that – to reject European rule, break away, form their own Government and provide the justice that Europeans had promised but had seemingly reneged on. It was all a dress rehearsal for what would happen in the Waikato in just a few years.

Wynyard's dilemma regarding the Puketapu feuds was solved by the arrival in September 1855 of the new Governor, Thomas Gore Browne.

Thomas Gore Browne is not a name well-known to the modern public. Since some would say he was personally responsible for the New Zealand Wars this is somewhat surprising and yet somehow he has escaped the disapproval and vilification that might be expected to be heaped upon a person with such a legacy. Perhaps this is just a quirk of history or perhaps it is for the simpler reason, that no matter what he may have initiated, no matter how far, wide or deep you dig, you will not find anything but the very best of intentions and logic in what he did.

Browne's despatches are models of clarity, unarguable logic, absolute commitment to justice and equality for New Zealanders of both races and absolute respect for Maori welfare and custom – all phrased with a selflessness and lack of guile that cannot be said of all New Zealand Governors. If you are looking for evidence of a man who has utterly subsumed himself for the benefit of his people you need look no further than Governor Browne. Historians will not find fault or intrigue in every second word of his despatches as they will with Grey's, nor will they for a second doubt his motives, his integrity, his honesty and his absolute desire to do good. The very worst you can say about him is that he was naïve, imprudent and stubborn and even that is debatable.

A point that is rarely noted is the influence of his wife Harriet, for in truth Browne and his wife came as a matched and complementary set. Hobson's wife was a great social mixer, Fitzroy's may as well not have existed and

Grey's was a long-suffering cipher. Harriet Browne however was, in her quiet way, the rock behind her husband's Governorship, his chief adviser and provider of "checks and balances", especially on questions of ethics. While Browne's governorship was notable for his willingness to seek out and value the opinions of others his ultimate advisor and joint moral compass was his wife.

The Constitution Act of 1852 has been described by one historian as "surely the most liberal and elaborate ever devised for 26,000 colonists".[262] This is a courteous understatement, for even with the hindsight of 160 years of retrospective analysis to assist us, the complexity of the political machine this Act created is still mind-bogglingly complex to the point it is difficult to know where to start.

The Constitution Act created a three[263] tier Governmental/Political structure – at the top was still the Governor, under him was the "Government"[264] and under that were six[265] Provincial Councils. The theory was that the great majority of governance on a day to day basis would be done at a local level by the Provincial Councils, the Government met very intermittently to discuss and act on matters of a national interest, while the Governor sat at the top keeping an eye on things, acting as a backstop, ensuring that Britain's obligations to "its" subjects – both European and in particular unrepresented Maori – were met and that nothing was done which reflected badly on "the honour of the Crown".

So far so good, but the practical situation was somewhat more complicated than this "simple" structure suggests on paper. It was a

---

[262] *War and Politics in New Zealand 1855-1870*, B. J. Dalton, p9.

[263] Arguably we could add a forth tier – the British Colonial Office – above the Governor. However in practice during this particular period the Colonial Office was hands-off in all but top-level guidance, placing their trust in the Governor's wisdom and superior local knowledge.

[264] Usually referred to at that time as the "Ministry", selected from within the ranks of the "General Assembly"

[265] Later increased to nine.

system which might be pictured as having a rope between the Governor and the Government and six ropes connecting each of the Provincial Councils to the Government, the whole system at any time a balance of constantly changing tensions on constantly changing lengths of rope.

Further complicating the matter was that at that time the South Island was to all intents and purposes a different country from the North Island. The South Island was where most of the revenue came from and with its very small and peaceful Maori population it shared none of the issues and associated possible expenses of war and defence that the North Island did. Consequently, in addition to the normal jealousies between Provincial Councils, there were North Island and South Island rivalries. And just to cap things off most of the Provincial Superintendents were simultaneously members of the House of Representatives, meaning that when they were in the General Assembly they were also pushing their own provincial barrows.

As already noted, the Government itself consisted of two chambers – a Lower "House of Representatives" comprising elected members and an Upper House called the "Legislative Council" made up of members nominated by the Governor. As in most bi-cameral systems the Lower House made the laws while the Upper House acted as a reviewing panel.

We should also add that, structure aside, the early Governments were totally unlike those of today. Since at that time there were no political parties the House of Representatives was a band of individuals with no party-lines to toe or restrict them. The corollary of this was that, unlike today, an election did not automatically identify a Prime Minister or – as the position was termed then – "Premier". The Premier was generally selected by the Governor from the talent available in the House and a "Ministry" [266] was built around him. A further corollary is that with every individual acting for himself rather than along party lines every decision in the House could result in a vote of no-confidence, which, if successful,

---

[266] Unlike modern Governments, in which there is seemingly a ministry for everything, there were only three ministerial positions at this time.

resulted in the resignation of the incumbent Ministry followed by a frantic search to find a replacement group. For this reason the lifetime of some of these early "ministries" was extremely short.

It was into this system that Governor Thomas Gore Browne arrived in New Zealand in September, 1855, and as such he arrived as the first "Governor who wasn't really a Governor"[267]. Hobson, Fitzroy and Grey before him all had, in theory at least, total authority, checked only by the approval of their bosses back in London above them and the tolerance of their "subjects" below them. Under the system of responsible Government just described, Britain was *still* the supreme "sovereign" ruler of New Zealand but had delegated day to day government of the country to the colonists. Britain, and Gore Browne as Britain's representative, could not simply throw the keys to the car to colonists who did not even have a learner's licence, wipe their hands of New Zealand and disappear forever into the sunset. The transition of power had to be done in an orderly manner and for that reason Gore Browne's new job was something like that of a dog trainer – he needed to keep the colonial Government on a short leash until it had been trained and tested. The colonial Government was still on probation and Gore Browne would lengthen the leash bit by bit until Britain had confidence that it was safe to let the hound off the lead.

One of the mechanisms by which Britain could apply this short leash was to require all legislation passed by the Colonial Government to be vetted by Gore Browne and his British masters before it could become law.

Another mechanism to manage the transition of power was for Britain to drip-feed transfer of power to the colonists by maintaining control of selected portfolios until the colonists proved they were ready to handle them.

This brings us to the clichéd "elephant in the room". This is easily identified by examining the earlier observation that the Constitution Act

---

[267] Strictly speaking Browne was a *real* Governor for the short period between his arrival in September 1855 and the implementation of responsible Government in July 1856.

was "surely the most liberal and elaborate ever devised for 26,000 *colonists*", which begs the question – just how did this shiny new European oriented governmental architecture work for the majority of New Zealanders at that time, its 60,000 or so *Maori* subjects?

This single question can be subdivided into a whole raft of sub-questions and considerations:

- At this time there was no standing "New Zealand Army". The colonists expected that any military assistance they might require, either to manage internal threats – most likely related to Maori uprisings – or aggression from foreign nations – would be provided by Britain and therefore potentially a very considerable drain on the British taxpayer which – unsurprisingly – Britain was keen to minimise. While the colonists were adamant that they *must* have complete self-Government, when it came to the crunch they were mysteriously hesitant to take responsibility for the expenses that came with it. So began a little game between the new New Zealand Government and Britain in which the colonists devised all manner of creative dodges to shirk their financial responsibilities and pass the bills back to Britain. It was a game that did them no credit and which unsurprisingly rather blunted any sympathy Britain had for them in times of trouble.[268]
- Given that in the event of war in New Zealand Britain was morally obliged to provide the soldiers and foot the bill for waging it, it was only fair Britain should have control over the likely cause of such a war – Maori related issues – by having control of "Native" affairs. The alternative – of letting the colonists stir up trouble which Britain had to resolve at their expense – was never going to be an option.

---

[268] We have already noted two "R words" which feature prominently in describing Governments of this era – "representative" and "responsible". This issue of who pays for defence introduces the third "R word" – reliance – often expressed as "self-reliant", meaning a Government that relies on itself to protect/fund itself. The business of the colonists going to great and devious means to avoid paying the defence costs related to events caused by their own actions and passing the literal buck back to Britain was an on-going festering sore which sapped the British Colonial Office of much pro-colonist sympathy.

- In ethical terms the arguments for Britain/Governor Browne maintaining control of Native Affairs were even more compelling. The Treaty of Waitangi was one between Britain and the collective Maori people. The 1852 New Zealand Constitution Act did not change this and simply put in place a European form of Government, designed by Europeans with no input from Maori. This did not mean that the Constitution Act wilfully ignored Maori needs, rather that the English framers of the Act did not understand the New Zealand situation sufficiently. The Act provided for the creation of what might be called Native provinces in which their own laws would prevail but which would still be ultimately under the umbrella of the Government. And while it theoretically gave Maori the same conditions of franchise as Europeans these conditions essentially eliminated Maori from participating in the electoral process. Under these conditions, for Britain, in the form of the Governor, not to take Maori under its wing would be both unilaterally tearing up the Treaty and throwing Maori to the wolves, something that most definitely did not fall into the category of "maintaining the honour of the Queen".

For these reasons it was agreed that management of "Native Affairs" would be excluded from the colonial Government's responsibility and instead be managed directly by the Governor on behalf of Britain.

In this way the governance of New Zealand temporarily – and in its most critical period – entered into a rather messy system of "dual Government" in which Governor Browne managed "Native Affairs" while the General Assembly of the Colonial Government managed everything else.

While we might understand the theoretical advantages of such a system the practical realities of implementing it and making it work in practice were quite another story, as anyone who has ever worked for two bosses with two different agendas will appreciate. Such a shared system of Government – with the "actual" elected Government handling 80% of the portfolios while the unelected, British appointed Governor Browne handled the remaining 20% – was bound to be problematical, not just because of its inherent systemic faults but because the elected Government held the purse-strings to implement any initiatives or decisions made by the Governor, essentially hobbling him from day one, and rendering any positive effects this dual-governance system might have had, nugatory. This complicated method of managing Native Affairs would be continually challenged by the Government with the result that it was not always clear who was in charge of what and with what rights of veto.

If this situation seems confusing to European eyes somewhat used to such systems of government we can only imagine what the Maori subjects of New Zealand must have made of it. For twenty years Maori had been used to dealing directly with the Governors, treating them as "fathers", and through them as a direct link to the Queen. Under the new system they had no idea what to do and who to talk to, and whoever it was, was a stranger and a minor bureaucratic official.

In his management of Native Affairs Governor Browne assembled a small department which reported directly to him for the purpose of managing the Maori subjects of New Zealand. Over the next year or so this department became known as "Native Affairs" and was led by our ubiquitous friend Donald McLean, who also dealt with more mundane issues such as land purchases.

With Gore Browne now in the privileged and unprecedented position of not having to deal to European issues he could now turn the entirety of his attention to the "Native Question".

So what exactly was "the Native Question"? This was of course a "British" question from a "British" perspective – Maori would probably be surprised to learn that there *was* a "Native Question". There were in fact quite a few "native questions" but they can all be encapsulated by a single word that is so important we have already dedicated an entire chapter to it – sovereignty.

In the eyes of successive Governors the "native question" was how to make Hobson's famous words – "we are all one people" – come true.[269]

So how was that fanciful premise working out when Gore Browne arrived in late 1855? If actual "assimilation" may have been a naïve pipe-dream, peaceful co-existence between Maori and European, and a respect for the Government, did in fact exist in many, if not most, areas of New Zealand. It may have been a delicate balance that could collapse at any second but in those early days it was probably as much as anyone could reasonably expect. In this respect it might be said that, with one notable exception, Treaty Article's 1's claim to British sovereignty had been accepted, or at least, not rejected, by the great majority of Maori.

That one notable exception was, of course, Taranaki, and the extension of sovereign control to that area was Browne's major challenge on his arrival.

Starting from around 1857 the emergence of the "King Movement" compounded Gore Browne's woes, adding as it did a further challenge to British sovereignty, at least in and around the Waikato area and with the potential to sweep through the entire country. This was a scenario that Hobson, Fitzroy and Grey had never had to face and it was Governor Browne's eternal misfortune that it had to happen on his watch. Unlike his predecessors he could no longer temporise on the issue of asserting British sovereignty – if British sovereignty was to prevail then it needed to get its act together and start acting as if it actually existed. The days of hand-wringing over situations such as the response to the Wairau Affray and the Puketapu feuds were over. Browne had to take the bull by the horns and whack some sovereignty pegs in the ground. The time to make the fiction that New Zealand was a sovereign nation in which *everyone* was subject to a single, universally acknowledged master a reality, had come.

---

[269] There are a lot more "sub-questions", such as the issue of land, growing Maori nationalism and fighting in Taranaki, but these are all symptoms of a lack of sovereignty. If everyone agrees to abide by the law of a single entity most other issues will automatically resolve themselves.

Chapter 1-21

Teira lays down a mat.

On March 8, 1859, Gore Browne presided over a meeting that would within a year kick off the one and only thing for which he *is* remembered – the famous – or infamous – "Waitara Purchase", or, in the running analogy that forms the framework of this book "the spark that ignited the New Zealand Wars."

This meeting was in New Plymouth – Taranaki – the veritable "tinderbox of New Zealand" – for where else in New Zealand was a war going to start other than in this famously belligerent and fractious area that after five years was still in a state of smouldering civil war?

In the literature both the meeting, and its agenda, seem to appear out of nowhere.[270] We know that Browne received a missive from the Provincial Council of New Plymouth dated 19 May, 1858, bemoaning the state of that province in general terms and the lack of land in particular[271], subjects of

[270] Dalton (*War and Politics in New Zealand 1855-1870*, p93) states that in "...March 1859 Browne began a round of official visits which took him first to Taranaki", which gives the impression of a flag-waving exercise rather than a burning desire to announce major policy.

[271] *Taranaki Herald*, 22 May, 1858, p1. See also AJHR 1858, G03 for Browne and others' comments on this missive.

which the Governor was of course already more than well aware. Whether this meeting 10 months later was a direct result of that we do not know.

Taranaki newspapers of the time show no reference to its imminent occurrence, and astonishingly, apart from a brief report, scant reference to it after the event. Browne's proclamation at this meeting was clearly well prepared and, while correspondence both internally and with the Colonial Office was full of references to the "Native Question", there seems to be no specific pre-warning of what Browne was going to say and why.

It was very much a meeting of two halves and part one went something like this:

> "On Tuesday a meeting of the Moturoa, Town, Waiwakaiho, Puuketapu, and Waitara Natives was held in a paddock adjoining the residence of the Land Purchase Commissioner. It was less numerously attended than many former ones, the muster of the Waitara natives being particularly small.
>
> Shortly after 11 o'clock His Excellency the Governor, accompanied by his Private Secretary and the Chief Land Purchase Commissioner [Donald McLean], arrived on the ground and was welcomed by the assembled natives – the whole rising up to receive him, with the exception of William King and some few of his followers. The principal chiefs then paid their respects to the Governor...
>
> Mr. McLean, on behalf of his Excellency, spoke as follows:
>
> The Governor wished them to understand that the Queen regards equally all her subjects; that all her Governors have had and would have the same instructions, viz: - to do their utmost to promote the welfare of her subjects without distinction of race. The missionaries had imparted to them the blessings of Christianity and translated the Bible for their use. It was not in the power of man to confer any other gift which would bear comparison with that of the Bible; but, out of regard for the natives, his Excellency had caused an abstract of English law to be translated into Maori. He had no wish to enforce this law; on the contrary, it would only be put in force in those districts where the people are wise enough to desire it, and

prepared to carry it into effect themselves. Some tribes in the North had already desired to have English law; and a Magistrate had been appointed to instruct them how to put it into practice. They were now engaged in doing so, with every prospect of becoming a peaceful and prosperous people, and uniting themselves with the Pakeha. This tribe is the Ngapuhi.

The Governor had but two subjects on which he desired to speak, particularly, to the tribes living near Taranaki, and they were – first, in reference to criminal offences, second, in reference to land. He wished these subjects to be considered separately, and as having no sort of reference to each other. The tribes in the vicinity of Taranaki have greater advantages than most others, as they are much intermixed with the pakeha, and ought to profit by their intercourse with them. If they chose to live peaceably and cultivate their lands they would grow rich and multiply, instead of which they were constantly at war with each other and their numbers were decreasing. Their disputes were almost always about matters of little or no importance or about land which was not worth quarrelling for. Had the Governor been in New Zealand when Katatore slew Rawiri he would have had him arrested and brought before the Judge, and if the Judge had sentenced him to be hanged he would have caused him to be hanged; that he had not thought proper to arrest Ihaia because, though the murders to which he was a party were horrible and disgraceful, yet they admitted of some extenuation, in as much they were committed in retribution for the murder of Rawiri.

All this, however, now belongs to the past; but, for the future, he had determined that every man (whether he be Maori or Pakeha) who may commit any violence or outrage within the European boundaries shall be arrested and taken before the Judge, and the sentence of the Judge, whatever it may be, shall be carried into effect. He was determined that the peace of the settlers should no longer be disturbed by evil doers, and that those Maories who are not content to live in peace among the Pakehas had better go elsewhere.

> In reference to the second subject, the Governor thought that Maories would be wise to sell the land they cannot use themselves, as it would make what they could use more valuable than the whole, but he never would consent to buy land without an undisputed title. He would not permit anyone to interfere in the sale of land unless he owned part of it, and, on the other hand, he would buy no man's land without his consent.
>
> Tahana again addressed his tribe, approving of that portion of his Excellency's speech declaring that if murder were again committed that the murderer should be arrested and tried by British law. He then supposed a case of a native policeman or assessor (himself) shot whilst arresting a murderer, and inquired who would avenge him. He stated that if he were assured of the support of his Excellency, as he knew his Excellency would receive the support of the Queen, he could hereafter, single-handed, arrest offenders"[272]

While the specific word "sovereignty" rarely occurs in British Parliamentary and Colonial Office documentation, either before or after the Waitara event, it is quite clear that sovereignty is *the* issue on everyone's mind. While the sentiments may in practice be couched in terms of *desired outcomes* such as the ending of anarchy, a want of peace, a desire to bring Maori under the umbrella of a single authority, amalgamation, etc., all these outcomes are the natural consequence of the single word – sovereignty.

Thanks to the emergence of the King Movement[273] with its proposed alternative Maori sovereignty Browne now has no choice but to take the bull by the horns. The time to make the fiction that New Zealand is a sovereign nation in which everyone is subject to a single, universally

---

[272] *Taranaki Herald*, 12 March, 1859, p3. See also Appendix 3 for Teira's account of this meeting.

[273] To repeat, we are getting a little ahead of ourselves in referring to the King Movement – for the time being the reader will have to take this on trust until all is revealed in Part 2.

acknowledged master a reality, has come. And that sovereignty will be *his* sovereignty, not the King Movement's.

At the New Plymouth meeting Browne hammers two small "sovereignty pegs" in the ground. Peg 1 is that he will not just institute but *actively enforce* – and he uses the extreme example of hanging – sovereign rule "within European boundaries" – in other words there *will* be *one law for all* and we *will* get rid of the mixed messages that have in the past led to anarchy and confusion. On this point there will be no negotiation because that is the way sovereign Government works.

Although Browne does not specifically mention the Treaty his second peg is, in essence, confirming that henceforth he intends abiding by its Third Article – that "Her Majesty the Queen of England extends to the Natives of New Zealand Her royal protection and imparts to them all the Rights and Privileges of British Subjects."

When push comes to shove, Article 3 is not so much a separate Treaty Article as a footnote to Article 1 explaining one of the many benefits that the sovereignty of Article 1 confers in practice – that because the country will come under one law everyone will be treated equally under that law. When Browne says that he will not allow anyone to override the rights of others to sell land which can be shown to be their own he is effectively extending – at least in the specific case of land sales – the concept of sovereignty from areas "within European boundaries" to the entirety of the New Zealand, be it European or Maori owned.

Browne tells us that if he could turn back time he would have handled the murder of Rawiri Waiaua according to the single law that sovereignty implies and not watched helplessly from the side-lines – as Wynyard did – as the situation festered aimlessly into five years of violence covering a sizable portion of Taranaki.

Looking back we might ask ourselves – if acting Governor Wynyard had taken such a "sovereignty driven" approach on Day One of the Puketapu feuds, would this have led to instant, nationwide racial warfare or would it have immediately nipped the issue in the bud and prevented five years of internecine strife in Taranaki? We will never know but in 1859 Browne's point seems to be that *there is no choice* – either you have sovereignty or you don't. "Half sovereignty", or a sovereignty that changes from one day to the next, or depending on the colour of your skin, is not going to work.

If photographs of Browne might suggest him to be an avuncular and innocuous man this meeting reveals him to be a man of steel. The quiet, unassuming, cautious, largely forgotten Governor Browne emerges from this meeting as a man of mettle far greater than that of the blustering George Grey, or the less blustering Fitzroy or Hobson, who have successively led – or more accurately, allowed to happen through inaction – the country down two racial paths, the only possible result of which was the dissatisfaction of both races. But – to be clear – Browne is not suggesting subjugation of Maori by Europeans – and he gives the example of the Nga Puhi who are quietly going about their own business in their own way while still under the umbrella of the "sovereign" Government. While Browne does not specifically use the now reviled word "assimilation" he is hinting that it is actually possible to have unity of governance without losing one's identity and autonomy and that the resulting sum is greater than the sum of its parts.

Evidently Browne's leadership philosophy is based on what to him are inviolable personal principles and damn the torpedoes. When we speak of "principles" as they relate to us as individuals they are what make us who we are. Sometimes, if we care enough about our principles, we will stick to them despite the certain knowledge they will be our undoing. Principles are things that people will not infrequently choose to die for. People who do this are known as martyrs and while we may not always agree with their view, or their stand, we often admire them none the less. But what is the situation when the principles of an individual – such as Browne – potentially put *other people*, or even an entire nation, in jeopardy? Browne is playing a dangerous game. On one hand his view that the future of the nominal "country" as an actual "country" relies entirely on it having a single authority is absolutely right. But on the other hand it is possible that forcing the issue may cause all Hell to break loose.

Ultimately though, no matter who pulls the lever to switch the train from the tracks of anarchy to the tracks of order, it is all just a matter of timing – it is not a question of *if* it must be done but of *when* and by *whom* – and Browne has taken it upon himself to actively grasp the short straw, very probably knowing it will be his undoing, because that is how Browne works – duty always comes first. Either the country will continue to go down the slippery slope to complete chaos gradually of its own accord and reach a crisis point through inaction over a period of years, or the bandage must be actively ripped off through controlled and planned action. It is a gambler's dilemma to which there is no right or wrong answer but Browne has been forced into a corner by the King Movement and it is now or never.

So much for the proclamation of policy which seems to have been the nominal reason for the meeting. So far, so good – there seems to be no immediate dissent and indeed, to the contrary, Maori feedback on the day is reported to be cautiously supportive. There have been no outbursts or uproar in reaction and at this point we could be forgiven for thinking that Browne's moving of some small pegs in the direction of a united country has been an unalloyed success. Wiremu Kingi, the person who, given his history and recent narrowly averted wish to kill the occupants of the *pa* of his land-selling adversary, Ihaia, and therefore the man most likely to raise merry Hell at any initiative that seems to be relaxing the terms of land purchasing, says nothing. But knowing Kingi's history of saying nothing when he really should, his silence is perhaps more ominous than comforting.

Then, out of left field it seems, we enter into Part 2 of the meeting, the part that everyone remembers, in which Browne's bluff is immediately called:

> "Te Teira, a Waitara Native, then stated that he was anxious to sell land belonging to him, that he had heard with satisfaction the declaration of the Governor referring to individual claims, and the assurance of protection that would be afforded by his Excellency.
>
> He minutely defined the boundaries of his claim, repeated that he was anxious to sell, and that he was the owner of the land he offered for sale. He then repeatedly asked if the Governor would buy this land. Mr. McLean, on behalf of his Excellency, replied that he would. Te Teira then placed a parawai (bordered mat), at the Governor's feet, which his Excellency accepted. This ceremony, according to Native

custom, virtually places Teira's land at Waitara in the hands of the Governor.

Hemi Kuku then followed and stated his desire to dispose of land at Onairo, but in consequence of violent opposition his offer was not then entertained. Piripi, a relative of Ihaia's, then offered his land at Waitara – his right to sell was denied by Te Teira, Tei Waka (a town native) and several of the Waitara natives, who asserted that his land was forfeited as payment for the murder of Katatore by his relatives.

Paora then informed the Governor that Te Teira could not sell the land he had offered without the consent of Weteriki and himself, as they had a joint interest in a portion of it. Te Teira replied to him, and was immediately followed by William King, who, before addressing the Governor, said to his people "I will only say a few words and then we will depart," to which they assented. He then said "Listen, Governor. Notwithstanding Teira's offer I will not permit the sale of Waitara to the Pakeha. Waitara is in my hands, I will not give it up; e kore, e kore, e kore," (i.e., I will not, I will not, I will not. "I have spoken!") and turning to his tribe added "Arise, let us go", whereupon he and his followers abruptly withdrew..."[274]

There is some debate as to the possibility of Teira's offer being known beforehand to one or the other of Browne's party but it seems that the Governor himself was caught off-guard. There is, however, some history to the offer since District Land Purchase Commissioner Robert Parris had been involved in discussions on the possibility of Teira selling his land – which did not at that time culminate in an offer – since November 1857.[275]

Maori reaction to Teira's offer is interesting. Two Maori of unknown rank immediately also offer their land, indicating not only that they have understood Browne's message but are enthusiastically supportive of it.

[274] *Taranaki Herald*, 12 March, 1859, p3. The punctuation has been altered slightly to make it more readable to modern readers.

[275] AJHR 1861, F3, p34.

The alacrity with which they make their offers, as individuals and with no consultation with anyone else, let alone "chiefs", suggests that the voice and authority of the individual is in the ascendant, an observation which still stands even if their claims are quickly dismissed by other individuals. And once again we see the byzantine nature of land claims in the Maori world in the changing of hands of land as *utu* for the death of Rawiri Waiaua, a transaction which it seems is not widely known even in the local Maori world.

Browne's steely proclamation of the first part of the meeting informs us how we might expect him to react to the challenge laid down by Teira. Backtracking on a policy five minutes after he has announced it would be instant political death, both for him personally and for the sovereignty he has gone out on a very slender limb to proclaim. We might predict that Browne will be supremely fair but also ultimately supremely firm. The judge's decision will be final and no correspondence will be entered into. And that judge *will* be Browne, not Kingi, and definitely not the King Movement.

While the land offered by Teira is relatively small – just 600 acres – its sale would be a major coup for European settlers due to the precedence it would set for further, larger land sales and for "breaking" the resistance and influence of the anti-land selling faction, be that an actual "land league" or merely a group of individuals whose real interest is limited to retaining their *own* land rather than dictating what others do with theirs.

Certainly from the evidence of his son, Edward, Wiremu Kingi simultaneously recognises the threat of precedence and confirms himself as a "land leaguer" in his willingness to actively thwart others from selling their own land:

> "I had a long discussion with them, during which Edward (William King's son) said that they had determined the land should not be sold, for if they allowed Teira to sell, others would be wanting to sell also."[276]

---

[276] Letter Parris to McLean, 16 July, 1860 (AJHR 1860, Session 1, E-03a, p3).

And the icing on the cake for the settlers is that this small amount of land is in the fabled Waitara area and any sale that opens up that particular area is almost beyond value.

Consequently the tentative deal made with Teira, subject to investigation of his claim, is for the almost unheard of sum of £1 per acre.

Be that as it may Teira's offer is, in effect, a side show. What follows will not be a land related contest between Teira and Kingi but a sovereignty related contest between Kingi and Browne.

Chapter 1-22

Light the blue touch paper and stand well clear.

Browne and his trusty Land Purchasing team must now do their due diligence and check out the validity of Teira's claim to the land he is offering. In truth this step is both a fool's errand and unnecessary. It is a fool's errand, because as we have seen, the whole Maori land ownership issue is incredibly complex even in the best of times and 1859 Taranaki is most decidedly neither the best of times nor the best of places. We are now in the era and area of, if not an actual land league, such a strong anti-land selling sentiment that Taranaki Maori have been fighting each other for the last five years. Land sales that were once simply difficult are now under a microscope so powerful they are next to impossible.

And the investigation is unnecessary because every previous encounter with Kingi has shown him to be uniformly and entirely intractable. In his battles with Ihaia he has very clearly nailed his colours to the anti-land selling faction to the point of defending it with mass violence on an issue that does not even involve his own land. Browne can come up with the most watertight case known to man but, if Kingi is not going to acknowledge it, then what precisely is the point? It is a battle of sovereignty, or to put it in layman's terms, no more complicated than answering the question – "who's in charge here". Due diligence may make Browne and company feel good about their actions but it will not alter the outcome one iota – no matter if Teira's claim is good or bad there *will* be blood.

Be that as it may Browne's land purchasing team leaps into action. At its head is Donald McLean, who in 1859 is the Native Secretary with the dual roles of both attending to Maori issues in general and of buying Maori land in particular, roles which some would say have distinctly conflicting interests.[277] McLean's man on the ground is one of the District Commissioners on his team responsible for land purchases within each territory, in the case of Taranaki, local resident Robert Parris.

Unlike most previous land purchases, which Browne summarily delegated completely to McLean, Browne chose to take the lead on this one. McLean's involvement was largely restricted to investigation of claims by non-resident claimants in the upper South Island, a task he performed in the month following the meeting. Rather annoyingly he would spend most the rest of the time between then and the outbreak of war largely out of Governor Browne's orbit, including lengthy stints buying land in the Wairarapa and recovering from an unfortunately timed illness, studiously avoiding both the Governor's and Parris's pleas for help. The jury is out on

[277] McLean's position should not be confused with that of "Native Minister", a position held by Taranaki resident and MP, C.W (William) Richmond, who was at that time Native Minister in the Government Ministry then under Premier Stafford. By 1859 the system of "native" representation had become somewhat more complicated than the simple if flawed system previously described in which Gore Browne had sole responsibility for native affairs. In that system McLean reported directly and solely to the Governor. As was predictable, this arrangement created problems of a practical nature and jealousies of a personal nature regarding the virtual personal fiefdom that McLean's monopoly over Native affairs represented. In August 1858 Richmond was officially appointed Native Minister within the Stafford Ministry and a system of communications developed whereby McLean communicated to Richmond who in turn passed that communications to the Governor.

McLean's sudden and uncharacteristic retreat to obscurity but it has been suggested it may have been out of "pique" in having to share what had previously been his own private land-purchasing Kingdom with Browne. Whatever the reasons, to say his aloofness at this critical time on this most critical of all purchases was not helpful, would be an understatement.

McLean's absence left most of the heavy lifting on the case to Robert Parris, generally considered a good man except by those who have an ideological axe to grind. He goes about the thankless business of trying to unravel the competing claims to Teira's alleged land-holdings for the next nine months. No doubt this included large gaps of inactivity which must be inevitable in this situation but Parris has been familiar with Teira's land and claims for over a year and really, how long does it take to get the views of the various factions involved? That is the easy part – trying to figure out what it all means, if the knots can ever be untangled, is an entirely different matter. Parris's investigation of title to this land was later criticised for having been done in indecent haste. Gore Browne himself deemed that on the contrary:

> "This inquiry was prolonged till the close of the year 1859 not from any doubt that existed as to the title but in the hope that the opposing party might be brought to reason."[278]

The one exception to "getting the views of the various factions" is Wiremu Kingi himself. For nine months, given opportunity after opportunity, Kingi refuses to talk on the subject, which, considering he is the sole dissentient to the sale, is more than a little unhelpful. It is "*déjà vu* all over again" of his failure to articulate his concerns and his claims at the May, 1844, meeting with Spain. Since most Maori in that situation show themselves highly demonstrative we can only assume that this tendency

[278] Despatch from Governor T. Gore Browne to his Grace the Duke of Newcastle, March 22, 1860 (BPP, 1861, March 1861, Papers related to the Recent Disturbances in New Zealand, p20).

to withdraw into silence is a quirk of his personality, or a *modus operandi* of some sort.

Sometime before April 20, 1859 "The Councillors of Wiremu Kingi Whiti Rangitake" sent a letter to King Potatau to prevent the sale of Teira's land at Waitara.[279] While the precise wording of this letter is unknown, any appeal to the King Movement is somewhat surprising given Kingi's clear prior antagonism to it.

Perhaps a week later (April 25) Kingi sent a now oft-quoted letter to Gore Browne:

> "Sir: Salutations to you. Your letter has reached me about Te Teira and Te Retimana's thoughts. I do not agree to our bed-room being sold – I mean Waitara, for this bed belongs to the whole of us; and do not you be in haste to give the money. Do you hearken to my word. If you give the money secretly you will get no land for it; you may insist, but I will never agree to it. Do not suppose that this is nonsense on my part; no, it is true, for it is an old word; and now I have no proposal to make, either as regards selling or anything else. All I have to say to you, O, Governor, is that none of the land will be given to you, never, never, till I die. I have heard it said that I am to be imprisoned because of this land. I am very sad because of this word. Why is it? You should remember that the Maoris and Pakehas are living quietly upon their pieces of land, and therefore do not disturb them. Do not also say that there is no one so bad as myself. This is another word to you, O, Governor. The land will never, never, be given to you, not till death. Do not be anxious for men's thoughts. This is all I have to say to you.
>
> From your loving friend."[280]

---

[279] Letter Teira to Browne and T.H.Smith, AJHR 1861, C-01, p228. This is one of a string of letters from Teira and his co-sellers either to Browne himself or his delegated agents, defining his land boundaries, enumerating his claims, and increasingly, wanting to be paid. These letters reveal Teira to be an intelligent, respectful man with a touchingly allegorical turn of phrase.

[280] Letter from Wiremu Kingi to the Governor, 25th April, 1859

It is hard not to be moved by Kingi's passion and to be frustrated that he is his own worst enemy in not stating his case. But since his letter offers no justification for anything it can be of no use to Browne in his investigation. It reinforces that Parris's investigation into the land's title is of no practical use unless it proves Teira has no claim to the land he intends to sell. There is no way that Kingi, on being told that Teira's title is valid, is going to say "oh I *see*, very sorry, *my* mistake". On the other hand, if Kingi had presented his case more articulately, or even *at all*, there is no way Gore Browne would *not* have said "sorry, *my* mistake".

On 29 November Parris, acting on Gore Browne's instructions, paid Teira and his supporters the first installation of payment for their lands at Waitara:

> "On the preceding Friday Mr. Parris went to Waitara and informed Wi Kingi of his intentions, who on the 29th came into New Plymouth with a party of about thirty to oppose the payment. In the presence of a large number of Europeans Mr. Parris put the following questions to him and received the corresponding replies, calling the Rev. John Whiteley to be witness: –
>
> > Q. Does the land belong to Teira and his party?
> >
> > A. Yes, the land is theirs, but I will not let them sell it.
> >
> > Q. Why will you oppose the selling of that which is their own?
> >
> > A. Because I do not wish for the land to be disturbed, and although they have floated it, I will not let it go to sea.
> >
> > Q. Show me the justice or correctness of your opposition.
> >
> > A. It is enough, Parris, their bellies are full with the sight of the money you have promised them, but do not give it to them; if

---

(eg, Wells, pp183-184).

> you do, I will not let you have the land, but will take it and cultivate it myself."[281]

An alternative translation of this encounter adds to Kingi's answer to the first question the words "together with all of us".[282] Whatever the translation, Kingi's inability to explain his reasoning is not helpful either to his cause or to defusing the situation.

For Browne this whole Waitara business has never been about land but about the *sovereignty of New Zealand*, a fight for who is the boss, an answer to the question: "is New Zealand a sovereign nation or not?". Browne's "opponent" in this battle is not Kingi *per se*, whose sole motivation is personal rather than political, but it just so happens that Kingi's personal wants require defiance of the concept of British sovereignty, which Browne *must* object to to avoid being a laughing stock. Teira's land offer is simply one of thousands of similar sovereignty challenging confrontations – which might or might not involve land – that could bring this contest out in the open. While neither Kingi nor Gore Browne initiated this situation – that was Teira's doing – now that Teira has kindly erected a mast to nail colours to, the various sides must do just that.

It is now simply a battle of wills, of who will blink first.

"Who blinks first" is the oldest game in the book. But Kingi's version has a twist – in his version it does not matter who blinks first because Kingi will *always* win. Kingi himself will *never* blink, as he has so definitively proven with Grey back in 1848. If Browne blinks first then Kingi will win by default just as he did with Grey. And if Browne does *not* blink, Kingi will also win – but only if he plays his cards right. For Kingi to win if Browne refuses to blink requires Kingi to have the moral high ground.

Creating artificial moral high-grounds is as easy as falling off a log – all you have to do is make your opponent appear to be the aggressor. If that can be done – *voila* – you have created an instant moral high-ground and

---

[281] Wells, pp184-185.

[282] For a discussion see *The Origin of the Maori Wars*, Keith Sinclair, p171.

sympathy for your cause. And as a bonus, if you can increase the relative height of your own carefully constructed artificial moral high-ground by making it as difficult as possible for your opponent build *his* moral high-ground, so much the better. This is a game of blink and I win and don't blink and I also win. While Kingi no doubt would prefer there be no war, if it must be so – and given that neither Kingi nor Browne will ever back down there is no other possibility – Kingi's plan is to drag Browne into it and emerge as the wronged hero. His father may have been a great warrior who met his goals by brawn but the son is a master strategist who meets his goals by brain.[283]

To construct his moral high-ground Kingi prepares to implement what could be known as the "taunting two step", a tactic known to, and hated by, every parent from time immemorial. Step 1 is to taunt, gaud, prod or otherwise provoke by devious means the desired party into a response. Step 2 is for the taunter to proclaim indignantly and with feigned self-righteousness – "She/he hit me first". It is a time-honoured and guaranteed recipe for gaining instant, if faux, moral high ground.

The chain of events is therefore as predictable as if it has been planned and each party has synchronised watches. So begins the final, inevitable countdown to war.

25 January 1860 – Native Minister C.W. Richmond sends Robert Parris his instructions:

> "I have the honor, by the direction of His Excellency the Governor, to inform you that His Excellency with the advice of the Executive Council, has determined that the survey of Te Teira's land at Waitara shall be proceeded with without further delay.[284]

---

[283] Sinclair suggests Kingi was "unaware that if he could substantiate territorial claims the Governor meant to drop the purchase..." (*The Origins of the Maori Wars, Sinclair, p175)*. That is surely absurd and insulting to a man of Kingi's obvious intelligence.

[284] It should be noted that the purpose of this survey was simply to ascertain who owned what land so that Teira's land could be isolated and sold, leaving

The survey is to be commenced in the first instance without any display of force, by a surveyor attended only by an ordinary survey party – all being unarmed – you yourself being present on the ground, or not, as may seem expedient.

You are to take care that the intended commencement of the survey is publicly known; and in particular that Wiremu Kingi and his party are made fully aware of it, and of the firm determination of His Excellency to complete the purchase. You will, however, avoid any official or formal announcement which might wear the aspect of an irritating challenge to the opposing party.

Should resistance be made to the survey, the survey party will quietly retire; and you are then to intimate to Lieutenant-Colonel Murray that the assistance of a Military Force has become necessary.

Military possession of the Block will thereupon be taken and kept by the Forces under the command of Lieutenant-Colonel Murray, who has received instructions upon this subject, and the survey is to be prosecuted under the protection of the troops.

As regards the payment of Te Teira's purchase-money before commencing the survey, or at any subsequent time, you are to use your discretion. The Sub-Treasurer at New Plymouth has been instructed to make the necessary advances on your requisition.

The Governor relies upon your tact and firmness in the execution of the difficult service entrusted to you, hoping that matters may be so

---

the land of other claimants – such as Kingi's, if he actually had any – intact. There is no doubt that such a proposal would leave an awkward patchwork of land which would be annoying to neighbouring owners who could potentially be surrounded. This practice is, however, still commonly used by commercial concerns such as shopping complexes which expand by buying out adjoining residential neighbourhood properties house by house. Just a few blocks from where this book is being written a Government agency is currently building social housing by completely surrounding a number of very nice residential properties.

conducted as to obviate the necessity of resorting to force, but feeling at the same time that it is impossible for himself as Her Majesty's Representative to withdraw from the position which he had deliberately assumed in reference to this affair. – I have, &c,"[285]

From his wording Richmond clearly understands the game and that prevention of the gifting of moral high ground to Kingi by being seen to be the first to misplace a step is absolutely paramount.

19 February 1860 – a letter from Taranaki resident Charles Brown to Native Minister Richmond concisely and perceptively summarises the nub of the issue, that the issue is one of sovereignty, *not* land:

> "We seem to be fast approaching a settlement of the point, whether Her Fair Majesty or His Dark Majesty shall reign in New Zealand: I feel satisfied that the question of who shall have the sovereign power, now raised at the Waitara, cannot fail to draw the Maori King movement into it, or the Maori King movement will cease to be..."[286]

Charles Brown has a bird's-eye view of the situation and he is flying high above Waikato. In this big picture view he no longer sees the distractions of individuals such as Kingi and Teira but sees a very large movement called the King Movement – what he calls the "Dark Majesty". Brown goes on to say:

> "According to my information, the survey by Oct. Carrington tomorrow will be stopped by W. King's orders, but three men and one woman are specially appointed to deprive Oct. Carring. of his [surveying] chain &c, bring them into Town and bear the brunt of the act. If this is correct, it seems as if W. King purposes to try what remedy there is against him by our law. If the three men & the woman

---

[285] Letter Richmond to Parris, 25 January, 1860, see for instance, Wells, pp187-8.

[286] Letter C. Brown to Richmond, 19 February, 1860, *The Richmond - Atkinson Papers – Vol 1*, Guy Scholefield, p522.

> (his police as they may be termed) are punished, W. King will retaliate. If on the other hand his police are unnoticed, and the survey is supported by troops, W. King's object will be to make the troops appear the aggressors, in so far as shedding blood is concerned, and it is widely stated amongst the Natives that if W. King draws the first blood, we may cook his goose & welcome, but that if we draw the first blood, we shall not have them with us, that is, as I read it, we shall have them against us, and under any circumstances we must calculate on very few who will be heartily with us."

20 February 1860 – Richmond's instructions to survey the land are duly carried out. The two parties meet and go through their individually carefully choreographed routines:

> "On Monday, the 20th [February, 1860] Mr. Parris, with Mr. Octavius Carrington and Mr. W. Hursthouse, of the Survey Department, and one of the armed police force, proceeded to Waitara. They were met at various parts of the road by parties of natives, but no obstruction was offered to their progress. Arrived at the land to be surveyed, a large number of natives, men, women, and children, were found assembled, and a party, apparently appointed for the purpose, attempted to obstruct the unpacking of the instruments, without success, but when the chain was thrown out and taken by Messrs. Parris and Carrington they effectually prevented their making any use of it. The obstruction was managed in the least objectionable way possible; there was no noisy language, and no more violence was used than was necessary to prevent the extension of the chain. They laid hold of the middle of the chain, and so disturbed the measuring, and the surveying party, finding it vain to persist farther, forthwith returned to town."[287]

The performance has gone off like clockwork and the cast returns to their respective green rooms backstage. The critics however are not impressed:

> "Subsequently a communication from the authorities was made, giving the Waitara chief [Kingi] twenty-four hours to apologise for the

---

[287] Wells, pp188-189.

obstruction offered by his people, and to notify his relinquishment of his opposition to the survey. To this an answer was received to the purport that he, Wiremu Kingi, did not desire war, that he loved the white people very much, but that he would keep the land, and that he and the Government might be very good friends if the survey were relinquished."[288]

Kingi is presenting himself as the perfect, humble citizen touching his forelock. It will look good when things turn pear-shaped, as he surely knows they must.

22 February 1860 – a proclamation from Gore Browne instituting martial law in the province of Taranaki is published. Outlying settlers begin to move themselves and their portable belongings into the town of New Plymouth.

1 March 1860 – Governor Browne arrives in New Plymouth accompanied by 200 troops of the 65th Regiment. Browne invites Kingi to discuss the matter in person. Kingi, true to form, declines to accept.[289]

Browne attempts to convey his summary of the situation and clearly outlines what will happen next:

> "Thursday, March 1st, 1860, the *Airedale* arrived from Auckland with Governor Browne and suite, accompanied by Colonel Gold, an extensive military staff, and 200 rank and file of the 65th. The same day H. M. S. S. *Niger* dropped her anchor in the roadstead. The first step of the Governor was to issue the following proclamation in Maori, a translation of which is given in full, as it tends to explain both the origin and justness of the war: –
>
> 1. When the Pakehas first came to Taranaki there were no Natives at the Waitara. The Ngatiawa had been dispossessed by the Waikato.

---

[288] *Ibid*, p189.

[289] *Ibid*, p185.

2. The Waikato transferred their rights to the Government and received a payment for the land.

3. Afterwards the Ngatiawa returned and occupied the land: the Government acquiesced in this occupation.

4. In March, 1859, some of these occupants, Te Teira and others, openly offered to sell to the Government their claims to a portion of the land at the Waitara.

5. Wiremu Kingi opposed this offer, and said that no land at the Waitara should be sold. But the "mana" of the land was not with Wiremu Kingi, and he had no right to forbid the sale of any land which did not belong to him personally.

6. The Queen has said that all the natives shall be free to sell their lands to her, or to keep them – as they may think best. None may compel the Maori people to sell their lands, nor may any forbid their doing so.

7. Wiremu Kingi sets his word above the Queen's, and says, though the rightful owners of the land may wish to sell, he will not allow them to do so.

8. The Governor cannot allow Wiremu Kingi's word to set aside the words of the Queen.

9. The Governor has said that he will not allow land to be bought, the title to which is disputed. He has also said that he will not allow interference with the rightful owners in the sale of their lands. When land is offered, the title to which is clear, the Governor will use his own discretion in accepting or declining the offer.

10. The Governor accepted Te Teira's offer conditionally on its being shown that he had an indisputable title.

11. Te Teira's title has been carefully investigated and found to be good. It is not disputed by any one. The Governor cannot, therefore, allow Wiremu Kingi to interfere with Te Teira in the sale of his own land.

12. Payment for the land has been received by Te Teira. It now belongs to the Queen.

13. Wiremu Kingi has interfered to prevent the survey of the Queen's land by her own surveyors. This interference will not be permitted.

14. The Governor has given his word to Te Teira and he will not go back from it. The land has been bought and must be surveyed. The Queen's soldiers will protect the surveyors. If Wiremu Kingi interferes again and mischief follows, the evil will be of his own seeking.

15. The Governor desires peace. It depends upon Wiremu Kingi whether there shall be peace or not. If he ceases to interfere with what is not his own he will be treated as a friend, and there will be peace."[290]

3 March 1860 – 400 troops set off from the New Plymouth garrison north along the Devon Line to Waitara with orders to occupy Teira's land. They encamp on the coastal portion of it with the corvette *Niger* standing off out to sea.

5 March 1860 – a *pa* is found to have been built across the Devon Line[291]. On 6 March Browne sends troops bearing a letter to its occupants advising them that they have built on the Queen's land and that the building of the pa is "levying war against the Queen". They are given the choice of destroying the pa and being forgiven, or being fired at if they do not comply within 20 minutes.[292] As it happens the crisis is averted because on arrival the pa is found to be deserted. Browne's resolute state of mind, however, is clearly demonstrated.

16 March 1860 – A *pa* is reported to have been built on the land purchased from Teira.[293]

---

[290] *The War in Taranaki, during the years 1860-1861*, Grayling, p15.

[291] The main and only road from New Plymouth northward to Waitara.

[292] Wells, p191.

[293] Because of its shape this is commonly referred to as the "L pa".

17 March 1860 – Parris inspects the pa and confirms it to be within the boundary of Teira's land. A subsequent military inspection reports the *pa* as being very strong with double palisading, ditch and galleries. A letter is sent to the *pa*'s occupants ordering them to move off the Queen's land and warning them of the consequence of refusal. The occupants however refuse to receive this letter.[294]

It is the just the latest in a long string of taunts and provocations from Kingi and it is now crunch time. Why would anyone bother with further diplomacy to be rewarded with yet another rebuff? The time has come. Either people respect the Governor's/Government's authority or they do not

The *pa* is attacked with rockets and 24 pound howitzers.

There are a lot more details but they are irrelevant.

All that needs to be said is that Kingi has won the battle for the moral high-ground and he can now appeal righteously not only to every Maori in the country but to every so-called "philo-maori" European, of whom there are many in high-powered and influential positions.

As Charles Brown perceptively predicted:

> "At his first trial of strength W. King will not have more than 300 men, take off 100 for native exaggeration, leaves 200, until he appears as a champion of Maori prerogative in the eyes of the Natives, and then his party will increase like a rolling snowball..."[295]

Kingi with his shiny new moral high-ground is now that champion and the snowballs will not be long in coming.

The flint has finally hit the steel and the spark has officially been launched into the air. All it needs now is something to light.

---

[294] Wells, p191.

[295] Letter C. Brown to Richmond, 19 February, 1860.
The Richmond - Atkinson Papers – Vol 1, Guy Scholefield, p522.

Chapter 1-23

The experts emerge from the woodwork.

There is a well-known quip which says that the only certainties in life are death and taxes. To this we could add a third – that when things go pear-shaped there will within minutes appear out of the woodwork a small army of self-appointed experts to tell you what you have done wrong. These people will, of course, have been strangely silent and have had nothing to do with the decision making process and have absolutely no responsibility for anything either before or after the decision is made.

If ever evidence was needed to support this hypothesis we need look no further than the aftermath of the Waitara Purchase. Critics and experts are lining up and sounding off before the smoke from the first gunshot has cleared. There seem to be more of them than there are soldiers fighting the actual war. On the defence side we have the Governor/Government angle of Browne, Richmond and McLean. For the prosecution the ringleaders are the righteous Anglican triumvirate of Rev. Hadfield, Bishop Selwyn and Chief Justice William Martin.[296] More words will be written by contemporary authors of various colours than bullets will be fired. The bibliography at the back of this book listing just some of the

---

[296] Although Martin was not part of the official Anglican hierarchy he was in practice the next best thing.

more well-known and easily accessible commentaries written in 1860 and 1861 alone weighs in at over 1,000 pages.

While the Europeans were getting hot and bothered dissecting arcane Maori land law/lore to microscopic levels Maori themselves could hardly care less. As we have noted, Kingi himself went to extreme lengths *not* to justify *anything*, arcane or otherwise – his objections to the Waitara sale had absolutely nothing to do with what Europeans are arguing about. Likewise Teira made no claims to anything based on Maori lore and likewise the King Movement's decisions were based on entirely different matters. It is a very strange European obsession.

As far as I am aware no one in recent times has attempted a rigorous analysis of this vast outpouring of opinion. No one, for instance, has tried to do what Richmond did – write a sentence by sentence dissection of William Martin's critique. And no one has in turn done a sentence by sentence critique of Richmond's critique of Martin's critique. There is a very good reason for this – it would be a completely pointless exercise. At the end of the day every one of these hundreds of dissected points would only be someone's opinion. It is like trying to nail a jelly to the wall. Such an exercise would be interesting but ultimately prove precisely nothing. It would only add more meaningless words to the already existing mountain of meaningless words.

Would it be possible for a modern author to set aside everything that has been written on the subject, start with a clean slate and produce a "definitive" case in Kingi's favour or in Gore Browne's favour? Yes of course it would but again it would still only be someone's opinion, and worse still it would the opinion of someone who is 160 years removed from the event and inevitably thinking in presentist terms.

Would it have been possible at the time, before the first shot was fired, to have passed the matter to a Tribunal or some mutually agreed upon arbitrator? Yes it would, but how likely is it that that course of action would have had any positive effect? The whole Waitara issue was one of debated sovereignty, of Browne putting a line in the sand and saying – "this is how the system works – there is one authority, and it is me. Sometimes you will agree with the decisions made by that authority and sometimes you will not, that is the contract". Under these circumstances how likely is it that the party who is denying this authority would suddenly abide by the decision made by that authority if it ruled against them?

For all these reasons, tempting as it may be, this book will not attempt to follow all the convoluted threads of the raging debates of the time.

After hundreds of pages grinding through forty years of the peregrinations of the Ati Awa up and down the west coast of the North Island this may seem like a scant reward for the reader's patience and appear that we are rushing through this pivotal moment with indecent haste. But that, in a nut shell, is the whole point. It is not so much that we will be "rushing through" the Waitara Purchase as we will be giving it the attention it *deserves* – which in this author's opinion – is very little. Others may of course disagree but here are some reasons for advancing this argument.

• The Waitara purchase was no more than a "spark"

The basic premise of this book is to suggest that it may be more helpful to view the New Zealand Wars as the inevitable end of a long path rather than as the result of a single "event" which can be analysed in excruciating detail to identify convenient heroes and villains to suit preferred narratives. This is not necessarily a novel viewpoint but it is a minority view which I believe deserves further discussion.

As suggested in this book's introduction sparks are a dime a dozen. The Waitara Purchase is just one of a thousand sparks which could have occurred at any time and been created in a thousand different ways with precisely the same outcome. We need to ask ourselves – is it logical that this Waitara event – no matter how it *might* have been handled – should be the "cause" of ten years of war, the confiscation of hundreds of thousands of acres of land, and the plunging of North Island Maoridom into despair and resentment that continues to this day? Logically the answer must be no – a spark flashes in the night and dies. No, the meat and potatoes of the "cause of the New Zealand Wars" will never be found in a *spark* of any kind – it is to be found in the "logs", which we shall discuss in detail in Part 2 of this book.

• **Even if the Waitara Purchase spark *was* important it is so highly disputed as to be meaningless.**

It has already been noted that the Waitara Purchase has been dissected at a sub-atomic level from 1860 until the present time, in the process generating a literature that is only surpassed in volume by the Treaty of Waitangi. Add to this 160 years of historical analysis, coloured as it must be by authors' agendas, presentism and ideologies of the day, and we are in a right pickle. It is true that since the legitimacy of the Waitara purchase turns on so few points much of this information is duplicated, triplicated, and quadruplicated – the same thing seen from different angles or motivated by different agendas – so that the actual volume of literature, once condensed, is of a more manageable size. While that may be so all such a process really reveals is that everyone is pushing a barrow of some sort and anyone's guess is as good as anyone else's. Most of the key issues are subjective or just plain conjecture and personal opinion. Chiefly lineages and competing views of Maori custom as seen by Europeans of different persuasions are lined up and used as ammunition – but there is *no* issue on which you can say unequivocally – *yes*, that is 100% correct, or even correct "beyond reasonable doubt".

• **The traditional "European" analysis of the "spark" is entirely missing the point.**

Even if the "Waitara Purchase" *was* relevant, the way it has traditionally been analysed by Europeans is entirely missing the point. The traditional arguments regarding the "Waitara Purchase" put forward by contemporary European commentators such as William Martin and Octavius Hadfield generally turn on these points:

1) Who really owned "Teira's" land? This simple question immediately takes us down a rabbit hole of Maori land law. Go down there at your peril. Many have and are still down there.

2) Irrespective of ownership, does a "chief" – whatever and whoever that may be – have the right of veto on land sales? Those who are interested can read eighty six pages summarising the opinions of

fifteen "experts" on this subject[297], the summary of which is "we have no idea".

3) Following from the above, what was the relative "chiefly" status of Teira and Kingi? Specifically, was Kingi "paramount " chief?

One historian has summarised the answers to these questions as follows:

> "Historians have difficulty in reaching firm conclusions or in apportioning responsibility over the Waitara purchase and the subsequent war in Taranaki".[298]

---

[297] On Seigniorial Rights (Despatch from Governor T. Gore Browne, C.B., to his Grace the Duke of Newcastle, Dec 4, 1860). BPP 1861, March 1861, Papers Related to the Recent Disturbances in New Zealand, pp169-255.

[298] *The best man who ever served the Crown*?, Ray Fargher, p218. For a view similar to Fargher's, taken from a review of the then recently-released book *England and the Maori Wars* by A.J. Harrop – "On the rights and wrongs of the war, complex as they are, no final verdict is possible; and the possession of new material does not tempt Dr. Harrop to pass judgment." (*The Press*, 12 February, 1938).

On the other hand, historian Keith Sinclair, in his excellent work *The Origin of the Maori Wars,* suggests Browne was ignorant of Maori Land lore. This seems highly unlikely – the complexity of "Maori land lore" lies not in its lores, *per se*, which are few and simple – its complexity lies in the infinite multiplicity of conflicting claims. The lore Sinclair claims Browne is ignorant of is very simple and explainable in just a few words – "chiefs have right of veto". We could probably assume that even Browne could comprehend these five words and no doubt he had heard them a hundred times before in his three-plus years in the country, as well as hearing them directly from McLean on the day of March 8, 1859.

The point is – Browne does not care about Maori lore. Not that he was actively trying to subvert Maori lore but his mission was to move towards universal European laws and equal rights in line with the Treaty and, that as the representative of the sovereign nation of New Zealand, he not only had a right but an obligation to do so. Given that a major goal of the King Movement was to transition from Maori lore to European law we would presume that Wiremu Tamihana and the King movement would heartily endorse Browne's actions.

Perhaps this is a not unreasonable summary if we were considering just these three questions related to land ownership in 1860.

But it is missing the point.

What does not seem to be comprehended – or perhaps it is avoided because it gives an unfashionable answer – is that these are *entirely the wrong questions* to ask to assess the rights and wrongs of the Waitara Purchase.

The question that needs to be answered is not which of Kingi or Teira owned the land but whether *either of them did.*

We have not spent the last two hundred pages plodding through the history of the south-west coast of the North Island for nothing. The whole point of this has been to show that the Waitara Purchase was simply the last in a forty year long line of dominoes, the most major of which were:

1. The abandonment by Ati Awa of their land in the face of attack by the Waikatos.
2. The buying of the land by the New Zealand Company by virtue of the Queen Charlotte Sound Deed.
3. The buying of the land by the New Zealand Company by virtue of the Nga Motu Deed.
4. Hobson's purchasing of the "mana" of Taranaki from the Waikatos.
5. Spain's award confirming the New Zealand Company's purchase of this land.
6. Retraction of Spain's award by Fitzroy.
7. The return of the Ati Awa slaves made possible only by the uptake of European Christianity, European presence and European created peace.

---

8. The return of the Waikanae Ati Awa made possible only by European presence and European created peace.
9. Kingi's settling on what even Maori (the Waikatos) agree is European land in a position specifically denied by Grey. In 1860 both Kingi and Teira have been squatting on this land for twelve years.
10. Five years of what amounts to civil war in Taranaki in which the customary Maori rights of land owners (whoever they may be thought to be) are challenged by external political factions of land sellers and non-land sellers.
11. Forty years of change in the social order in which the traditional rights and authorities of chiefs are broken down and diminished in favour of the right of the individual.
12. The Waitara purchase, in which Browne bought the land for a third time.

After perusing this summary it is difficult not to conclude that in 1860 both Kingi and Teira are living on land which by rights belongs to its European purchasers. In effect the war which occurred in 1860 was the war that should have happened in 1848 if Grey had done his job properly in preventing Kingi from returning from Waikanae. All Grey did was to delay the inevitable and leave someone else to fix the problems he would not.

In 1860 both Kingi and Teira were at Waitara only by the grace of Europeans who, by buying out the Waikatos, and by the peace that came with European presence, made it possible for them to do so. The same applies to the Ati Awa slaves, and indeed the entire Taranaki and Ngati Ruanui tribes. Without European presence and money Kingi and Teira would in 1860 still be living in Waikanae. It does not take a genius to conclude that in 1860 Taranaki Maori owed Europeans a huge, Taranaki sized, slice of *utu*. The one thing we know about *utu* is it always levels in the end and it looks like 1860 is the year that is about to happen.

We have noted a number of times that the current New Zealand historical paradigm is one of heroes and villains, of black-hats and white-hats, a patronising and demeaning paradigm which treats Maori as children and victims without agency. The summary above demonstrates the complete opposite – that between 1839 and 1860 Taranaki Maori were in complete and absolute control and did precisely what they wanted with impunity over a twenty year period.

We will conclude the "Spark" section of our story with an excerpt from an observation by Ihaia Kirikumara, who seems to be astute enough to understand the big picture issues that the likes of Hadfield, Selwyn, Martin, and many generations of historians agonising over useless details, did not:

> "Friends: - Formerly we, the Maoris, lived alone in New Zealand; we did wrong one to another, made war on one another, we ate one another, we exterminated one another. Some had deserted the land, some were enslaved, the remnant that was spared went to seek other lands.
>
> Now this was the arrangement of this Ngatiawa land. Mokau was the boundary on the north, Ngamotu the boundary on the south; beyond were Taranaki and Ngatiruanui. All was quite deserted; the land, the sea, the streams, the lakes, the forests, the rocks, were deserted; the food, the property, the work, was deserted; the dead and the sick were deserted; the landmarks were deserted.
>
> Then came the Pakeha hither by sea from other dwellings – they came to this land and the Maoris allowed them – they came by chance to this place – they came to a place whose inhabitants had left it. There were few men here – the men were a remnant, a handful returned from slavery.
>
> And the Pakeha asked, "Where are the men of this place?" and they answered, "They have been driven away by war; we few have come back from another land." And the Pakeha said, "Are you willing to sell us this land?" And they replied, "We are willing to sell it that it may not be merely barren; presently our enemies will come, and our places will be quite taken from us."
>
> So payment was made; it was not said, "let the place be simply taken", although the men were few; the Pakeha did not say "let it be taken" but the land was quietly paid for.

Now the Pakeha thoroughly occupied the purchase made with their money; and the Maoris living in the house of bondage, and those that had fled, heard of it; they heard that the land had been occupied, and they said, "Ah! ah! the land has revived, the men have revived, let us return to the land." So they returned. Their return was in a friendly manner. The thought of the Pakeha was, "Let us dwell together, let us work together."

The Maoris began to dispute with the Pakeha. When the Governor [Fitzroy] saw it he removed the Pakeha to one spot to dwell. Afterwards the Pakeha made a second payment for the land, and afterwards a third; then I said, "Ah! ah! very great indeed is the goodness of the Pakeha, he has not said that the payment ceases at the first time."

My friends the Pakeha, wholly through you this land and the men of this land have become independent..." [299]

[299] Letter from Ihaia Kirikumara to the New Plymouth settlers, 15 July, 1860. *The History of Taranaki*, Wells, pp163-4.

PART 2

THE LOGS

Chapter 2-1

Of logs and Kings.

"The thing we never had and must have is a king!" [300]

So what was the result of this little spark at Waitara? A flash in the night which if you blinked you would miss it? An unseen and unheard tree falling in the middle of a forest? Or were there some tinder-dry logs of discontent and despair just waiting for that little spark to ignite into a raging conflagration?

In 1860 most parts of Maoridom were either actively happy, or at least "not unhappy", with the current state of the country. If many Maori regarded the co-mingling of Maori and European as an imperfect work in progress they had seen a huge improvement in their standard of living and prosperity. It had been a compromise, an organic process of mutual accommodation, of give and take. Some things had been lost and others gained, carefully managed by both parties for their own mutual prosperity.

It is no more than anyone would expect, simply part of the universal, automatic, self-balancing effect which Maori call *utu*. Maori got peace and

---

[300] Part of a fable attributed to Aesop, a commonly rendered moral of which is "when you seek to change your condition, be sure that you can better it".

greatly increased material prosperity. European settlers got a new life in a new country and continued prosperity. We could say, then, that with the notable exception of Taranaki, the country was in an unprecedented state of peace and prosperity. With such a dearth of tinder-dry logs of discontent what damage could the little spark of Waitara possibly do?

Curiously the answer to this question is to be found in that part of Maoridom which had lost least and gained most from European contact – Waikato – and the mechanism by which it happened was something called the "King Movement".

All movements throughout history have a largely identical trajectory – the "big idea" mooted by an intellectual, its translation into some non-intellectual form to draw in the masses, dissension among the leaders, bickering about goals or implementation, the breaking up into factions or schisms, the falling outs, the rational peace parties versus fanatical war parties, the attraction of usurpers, subvertors and mal-contents of all persuasions, the fighting for leadership. We should therefore not be surprised to see most or all of these characteristics in the formation of the King Movement.

The aims of this "movement", and its connection to the wars, are by no means straight forward. In one sense its goals are blindingly obvious, in another it is difficult to disentangle goals from tactics, strategy from implementation, reactionary motivations versus revolutionary ones, rejection of Europeanism versus endorsement of Europeanism. As we shall see, the King Movement never clearly articulated its goals, which as is par for the course with any movement, were constantly changing as the influence of various individuals waxed and waned. It is this uncertainty – what the European colonists did *not* understand of the movement rather than what they *did* understand – which must be held accountable for most if not all of the problems that followed.

The King Movement left no handy bullet-pointed and numbered manifesto of its objectives or implementation plan. What follows is an attempt to give a broad-brush summary working backwards from what actually happened. It may not be perfect but at worst it is one way of looking at it.

The evidence suggests two diametrically opposed goals. "Goal 1" was in fact an "anti-movement" – for Maori to stay the same – to maintain their culture, their identity and their land, and, given the historical catastrophic results of European intersection with native peoples, to ensure their very survival as a people. Goal 1 was not so much a "movement" as the simple kicking in of a survival instinct – a reactionary response, not a revolutionary one. All entirely reasonable and utterly understandable.

This goal in turn spawned an implementation tactic – to not sell land to Europeans. This tactic was really the only thing that was consistently clear both to Maori and Europeans as to what the King Movement meant, not only in terms of land policy but in its extended interpretation as marking the movement as anti-European/assimilationist. But even here the details of this broad-brush, anti- land-selling tactic were never elaborated on, so in the final analysis confusion still remained supreme.

"Goal 2" is more confusing and can be considered in two ways – as a genuine separate goal in its own right or simply as a tactical means of achieving Goal number 1.

Goal 2 was the adoption and adaption of the European concepts of governance, law, unity and nationalism – a radical change in Maoridom which could indeed be called a "movement" in the classic European sense of that word – definitely a revolutionary goal rather than a reactionary one.[301] This component of the King Movement's objectives, far from being a rejection of European influence, is a wholesale endorsement of the positive benefits of European civilisation that had brought with it the peace, law, order and prosperity all Maori had come to expect and enjoy. There is no doubt that the prime mover of the Movement viewed it this way.

---

[301] The unification of "tribes", which in the limit might lead to the creation of a "nation" with an associated spirit of "nationality", was something that in 1860 was still very much a work in progress even in Europe. The King Movement's push towards "nationalism" was therefore cutting-edge stuff.

On the other hand there is a strong argument that many within the King Movement considered what we have called "Goal 2" simply as a tactical means of achieving Goal 1 – that what one person might consider the revolutionary building of a "nation" was simply a temporary necessary evil, an alliance of convenience to get the numbers and structure necessary to push back against another nation. It is difficult to imagine that after 500 years of tribes being fiercely independent to the point of fighting each other that they would spontaneously have an epiphany for a radical, permanent ripping up of their traditional way of living simply as an academic exercise.

So – conflicting goals then, one a reactionary goal of maintaining the *status quo*, the other a revolutionary goal of ripping up the *status quo*. One a pragmatic goal anyone can instantly understand the other an intellectual goal espousing a hypothetical untested outcome to which every individual will have to be personally converted. It does not take a genius to predict what is going to happen and which goal will ultimately dominate.

We might say that the movement viewed European civilisation as a smorgasbord from which it could pick the "good bits" while rejecting the "bad bits". Understandable and attractive as that goal may be life is rarely that kind – and even in a smorgasbord you have to pay for what you pick – it is not a freebie. Once again we would expect the concept of *utu* to apply but the King Movement seemed to want something – which included everything it wanted – for nothing.

So what were the "*bad bits*" of European colonisation perceived by the King Movement? Did they really exist? Absolutely, as this English interpretation of a poem by Wiremu Te Akeautangi suggests:

> "[Wiremu Te Akeautangi] feels shame that the sun of the Maori nation should have gone down. The present social condition of his countrymen is compared to fish once healthful swimming at ease in its native water, but now ruthlessly cast upon the stalls no longer to be admired, but simply looked upon as an article of food. He asks whether the New Zealanders [Maori] should be satisfied with the systems of foreign people which they have been called upon to adopt.

> He then censures the natives who were so credulous as to take for granted that the foreigner sought only the benefit of the New Zealanders by coming to this land and introducing other customs that came into collision with their own sacred usages; and concludes with a determination to maintain the national independence of the Maories."[302]

Thus the "logs" that fuelled the King Movement, and the New Zealand Wars in its turn, were simple emotional logs – logs of resentment and anger, fear and insecurity, powerlessness, hopelessness and despair – things we can all relate to.

A distinctive and peculiar component of the "King Movement" was – as its name suggests – the perceived need for a Maori King. Rightly or wrongly this unusual and unnecessary requirement would prove to be a major factor in European resistance to the movement.

In the 1850's European world, Kings, Queens and the concept of absolute monarchy, were rapidly approaching obsolescence. For thousands of years monarchs all over the world had two functions – to act as a figurehead and to personally manage their country at the top of a hierarchy in which their word was literally law. By the latter half of the 1800s that second function had in many countries been replaced by various forms of Governments rendering the role of monarchy largely ceremonial.

In the 1850's Maori world Kings and Queens were an ill-defined novelty. As can be seen from the preponderance of obscure Old Testament names chosen by Maori for their baptismal names the Old Testament was an endless source of fascination and inspiration. With its tales of lost tribes, oppressed peoples fighting for independence, angry Gods, heroic deeds, violence and miracles, myths and allegories – and Kings and Queens – it was an irresistible fount of very misleading and long out of date "knowledge".

---

[302] *Daily Southern Cross*, 6 August, 1858, p3.

Maori knowledge of "Kings" came from a combination of this archaic and mythical source and from what they knew of European monarchies, especially that of Queen Victoria.[303] The result seems to have been confusion or at least inconsistency. The not infrequent Maori letters and personal visits to the Queen suggest that Maori believed she was the next best thing to God and that she could magically cut through all the red tape created by mere minions such as her representative, the Governor. On the other hand the role, structure and operation of European style Governments, which actually *did* have the power, seemed to hold little or no interest to Maori.

Europeans of the time were troubled by the movement's insistence on a King, never quite knowing if the word meant the same thing to Maori as it did to them. To a British/European audience the seemingly innocuous four-letter word "King" was (and is) not a word but a symbol. There is a good reason why monarchs are often called "figure heads" – they represent, and are shorthand for, the actual "figure body" on which that figure head rests – that awesome body of power founded on things such as nationhood, unity, the principles and infrastructure of Governance, law and order, and – most importantly in the context of the King Movement, the big-daddy word of them all – sovereignty. Any movement that calls for an alternative "King" is therefore an automatic enemy of the state as well as a violator of Article 1 of the Treaty of Waitangi.

There is no doubt that Maori saw – and loved – the "figure head" part of the "King", a part which resonated perfectly with Maori concepts of *mana* and chiefly-ness and the love of uniforms and all the trappings that went with it. Whether they understood the massive "figure body" part that it represented, and what that meant in the European world, is harder to say.

But two things are very clear from the letters of the prime mover of the King movement – first, that he genuinely believed in the need for a King

---

[303] It is no coincidence that "Kingi" was a popular baptismal name and we can probably assume, for instance, that "Wiremu Kingi" alluded to Queen Victoria's predecessor, King William IV.

to meet his goals and – second – that he had no understanding of what the term "King" meant to the European component of New Zealand – that setting up a second King was virtually a declaration of war, and that things must end badly. The tragedy of it all is that it was so unnecessary.

Since we are now diving headfirst into the deep topic of sovereignty – the key subject of the planet-sized Gordian Knot we call "The Treaty"– it is appropriate to comment on the Treaty's usage by both the European and Maori parties during this period. In the 1850s the Treaty was a rarely discussed topic and while I have suggested that the Treaty was the "Bible" for European involvement it did so quietly in the background. Browne, Grey, Fitzroy, Hobson and the British Colonial office rarely referred to it by name and they rarely – if ever – referenced it to support any of their actions and policies, which were based simply on the humanitarian standards of the time, which – by definition – were state of the international art.

Browne did not invoke the Treaty in his pivotal March 8 1859 Waitara meeting. Kingi did not invoke it at any stage of his life. The small army of European critics of the future Waitara purchase did not invoke it. Few of the Maori participants in the rise of the King Movement and the subsequent war invoked it. Wiremu Tamihana, the "Kingmaker", who we shall meet shortly, did not invoke it in his creation of the King Movement – he simply denied that he had signed it, in the process admitting his acknowledgement that the Treaty ceded sovereignty of New Zealand to Britain. Whatever he did he did for the simple reason that, Treaty or no Treaty, and no matter who had or had not signed it, the situation in the mid-1850s was not working for him personally or for Maori in general. Fair enough.

One contemporary European observer interpreted the King Movement's goals and underlying motivations thus:

> "The two objects of the league [King Movement] may now be affirmed to be, first, the subversion of the Queen's sovereignty over the Northern Island of New Zealand, and, secondly, the prohibition of all further alienation of Territory to the Crown.

> As regards the first object, the more advanced partisans of the Maori king now distinctly declare that the Queen of England may, for aught they know, be a great sovereign in her own country, but that here, in New Zealand, she shall become subordinate to their Native monarch from whom the British Governor shall take his instructions: the utmost conceded to the Queen is an equal standing with King Potatau.
>
> The absolute prohibition of further land sales is a necessary part of the new policy. For it is plainly seen that unless the further colonisation of the country can be put a stop to the Europeans will shortly outnumber the Natives in the Northern Provinces.
>
> The general sentiment of the New Zealanders with respect to their territorial possessions entirely harmonizes with the views of the King makers. The Maori feels keenly the parting with his rights over the lands of his ancestors. The expressive words of the Deeds of Cession declare that, under the bright sun of the day of sale, he has wept over, and bidden adieu to, the territory which he cedes to the Queen. It is in vain to assure him that the land remains open to him upon the same terms as to the European settler. He cannot see the matter in this light. The soil , with all its memories, and the dignity conferred by its possession, have passed over to the stranger; and in its place he has acquired only perishable goods, or money which is speedily dissipated. The land-holding policy of the King party is popular, because it secures to every Native the occupation, in savage independence, of extensive tracts of wild land."[304]

This quote is interesting in many ways. First it seems to be not only a sympathetic, non-judgemental assessment of the state of Waikato Maoridom but one which more or less echoes that of the Maori view of Wiremu Te Akeautangi's quoted earlier. It is not as if Europeans of the

[304] Memorandum by C.W Richmond, Auckland, 27th April, 1860, AJHR 1861 E-01, p239. This is a late (1860) interpretation of how Europeans considered the movement after the movement's own goals reached some sort of stability over the previous 2 or 3 years.

day did not understand, and even empathise with, the movement's underlying motivations.

Second, this quote is from April 1860, a month after the Taranaki War began, over two years since the Maori King was ordained and after many key European actors, including the Governor, had attended many King Movement meetings. Yet for all this Europeans were *still* unclear as to the goals of the movement, what a "King" actually meant, especially as regards the thorny area of sovereignty. Some sort of gauntlet had been thrown down by the movement but what, precisely, was it? A harmless, fluffy, fingerless mitten or a 5 kg steel-scaled and chain-mailed gauntlet?

By 1860 Europeans seem to have concluded that the term "King", as understood by the King Movement, was indeed intended to mean a "head of sovereignty" rather than a simple salutation such as "Mister". But the author of this quote still, after 2 years, has no idea how this sovereign King sat relative to the British sovereign Queen. There is a very good reason for this and that is because the King Movement itself did not know either. While we do not have all the data we would like, judging from what remains of recordings of King Movement meetings it is total confusion both within the movement and, inevitably, even more so externally to Europeans. It is a communications disaster of epic proportions.

In the absence of facts imagination takes over. The monster in the wardrobe is always scarier than the reality. In such an environment it is easy to see why Europeans may have found the King Movement more threatening than it actually was (Or was it? Who would know). This mood of European uncertainty regarding sovereignty, then, was the backdrop against which Browne whacked his small pegs of sovereignty into the ground during the pivotal March 8 1859 meeting at Taranaki.

Those who promoted the idea of a Maori King insisted that it was possible for the English Queen and the Maori King to co-exist and that the adoption of a King did not mean the abandonment of the Queen. But that was simplistic or wishful thinking – a King or Queen is a sovereign of a country and therefore by definition you can have only one of them – to quote Governor Browne's oft-repeated response to the Waikato chiefs on this delicate subject:

> "Are there two suns in the heavens? Can there be two sovereigns in New Zealand?" [305]

Would it have been possible to achieve some sort of compromise that suited all parties? To have an autonomous, self-governed Waikato "nation" but still under the umbrella of the sovereignty of the Queen?

Absolutely.

New Zealand in the late 1850's was already set up as a type of federation in which six provinces essentially governed themselves with oversight from a central Government. Section 71 of the 1852 Constitution Act provided for the existence of Maori Districts/provinces and successive Governors would have been delighted had this happened.

This option would have been the perfect solution for everyone but it was an option with a built-in use-by date. Such an arrangement could only happen if these hypothesised Maori provinces remained totally homogeneous: you cannot have two different sets of laws – a Maori Law and a European Law – in one district. The option of the Waikato becoming an independent province under its own government was on offer to the Waikatos as late as 1878 but the then Maori King, Tawhiao, would not accept it.

With its fascination for Kings the King Party could only ever be an *illusion* of European governance achieved by plastering a veneer of past-its-used-by-date monarchy over the traditional Maori system of governance, a cosmetic change rather than a structural one, a rearranging of the traditional furniture. While the traditional Maori approach to authority may have been perfect for the traditional Maori way of life, if you are going to rip up the basic ways of Maori life and structure – as the King Movement certainly intended with its new-fangled ideas of nationality and monarchy – then you need to rip up the underlying support structure as well. To create a "sovereign nation" – as seemed to be the intent of the movement – it is axiomatic that the intended "subjects" of that potential

---

[305] *The Maori King*, J.E. Gorst, p48 (quoting from Colonial Office record C.O. 207, 141)

nation understand, and have signed up, for the social contract of obedience required to make that happen.

In 1860 Maori were not in that condition and therefore any attempt at sovereignty was, in the short term at least, doomed. Obviously, Maori *did* have a governance system and decision making process – they could not have survived 500 years in New Zealand alone without it. But the traditional framework in which Maori lived was a non-hierarchical, flat structure in which the glue holding any semblance of law and order together was the *mana* of the collective chiefs. While this structure theoretically gave everyone a voice it could not achieve the prerequisite for sovereignty, namely, an authoritative conclusion carried by a show of hands which *all* individuals – *especially* those who might personally disagree with it – agreed to honour.

John Gorst, sometime Resident Magistrate of Waikato and author of *The Maori King*, describes the Maori decision making process thus:

> "Amongst the members of a Maori tribe there is that absolute equality of condition, which is called democracy; and that want of organized government, which is known as anarchy. The traditional power of the chief is gone. It is true there are men like William Thompson and Rewi Maniapoto, who have the title of chief, and whose abilities have gained them respect and influence both in their own tribes and among strangers; but these men are the executors of the will of the people, not its guides. In all their plans, they have to consider what their tribes will think and say; and when their own opinion differs from that of the multitude, it is the former that has to give way. The democracy is too strong for them, and resistance would cost them their position. The supreme power in the tribes, legislative and judicial, resides in a promiscuous gathering of men, women, and children, held in the public sleeping house of the village at bed-time; in which certain individuals among the men – not always the wisest or the best – possess a prescriptive right to engross all the talk. This is called a rununga. The members do not

come to a vote; when there is a difference of opinion, one side out-talks the other."[306]

In short, in 1860 Maori were – at least in terms of social organisation – in a similar position to the British tribes when the Romans invaded Britain in 43AD. From there it had taken many hundreds of years of turmoil[307] for this rabble of tribes to become "Britain", for a motley collection of individuals to become "the British", and for the social contract that is the pre-requisite for sovereignty to become accepted and ingrained. It is this centuries-long process that the King Movement was attempting to achieve overnight, a task the magnitude of which they surely could not have realised.[308] While we can admire the intelligence it took to even consider attempting this audacious goal we should surely not be surprised if a few speed bumps would be encountered along the way.

A brief, chronological summary of the King Movement's formation based on contemporary quotes can simultaneously tell us a lot about the rapid changes in Maori mood between 1851 and 1860, demonstrate the vast polarisation of feeling amongst Maori and hence some of the limitations of the King Movement, and shed further light on the issues of the day which we have called "logs". Since the rise of the movement occurred principally in the undocumented Maori world we have only the sorry

---

[306] AJHR, 1862, E09, Sec III, p10.

[307] The nation that became "Britain" was formed over the course of four colonisations/invasions (the Roman invasion and Anglo-Saxon, Danish and Norman invasions/colonisations) not be mention countless incursions, civil wars, international wars and religious and social upheavals.

[308] Maori obviously *did* realise to some extent but it seems they were intent on reinventing the wheel all over again in their own time, see for instance – "When told that they are not acquainted with the art of government, they acknowledge it, and coolly ask, "How long were your ancestors in acquiring it? Did they understand it all at once? We also shall gain wisdom by experience: no doubt we shall make mistakes, but then we can correct them as we go along." *The Maori King Movement in New Zealand*, Thomas Buddle, p61.

scraps of data that come to us from the random intersection of Maori with Europeans such as missionaries. We will do our best.

January 1851

This 1851 letter from grateful Waikato Maori to Queen Victoria demonstrates what, if taken at face value, is an appreciation of European presence just prior to the agricultural boom created by the Victorian gold rush:

> "To Queen Victoria, England.
>
> THE QUEEN - Salutation to you. Here are we Hone Papita Kahawai, and myself feeling affection for you. Through Governor Grey we received your letter, and also the likenesses of yourself, Prince Albert, and your family, as a token of your love to us. O Queen! we give you our thanks on account of your remembrance of us.
>
> The kindness and love of Governor Grey to us natives, O Queen, is very great. He is quite a parent to us: he protects us, and gives us wise regulations; he is wishful that we should become as the Europeans (in our habits). The Governor has authorized Mr. Morgan to engage a European to instruct us in the art of ploughing; this is the second year of this European's stay amongst us, and, now some of us have learned to plough. Governor Grey gave us two horses, a plough, and a cart. After the European came to teach us ploughing, we saw the benefit of ploughs, and carts, and we purchased many for our use with flour ground at our mills. We have many ploughs and carts, and we will purchase many more, when our horses are trained to work.
>
> Our wheat fields are very extensive; we cannot grind all the produce of our fields at our mill; we are therefore about to have a new mill erected for the sum of four hundred pounds...
>
> From your friend, (Signed) Kingi Hori te Waru."[309]

---

[309] *Maori Messenger*, 2 January, 1851, p3.

On the basis of this letter we could be forgiven for thinking that in 1851 Waikato Maori were very happy with their lot and understood who they had to thank for their new prosperity.

1853

The idea of a Maori "King" was, apparently, first floated by Matene Te Whiwhi, who we have met previously:[310]

> "Gathering a few other chiefs around him who sympathised with the project, they formed a deputation, and went forth to visit Rotorua, Maketu, and Waikato, ostensibly for the purpose of exhorting the chiefs of the interior of the Island to submit to the authority of the Governor, but really on a mission of King-making.
>
> Their principal motto was "Whakakotahitanga," "Union." They proposed a confederacy of all the tribes, and that one chief should be appointed as King or Governor. It was commonly thought that Matini [sic] aspired to the kingdom. They returned from Rotorua and Maketu, having met with no sympathy from the chiefs of those districts..."[311]

It has been speculated that part of the push-back against Te Whiwhi at that time was the result of Te Heuheu not wanting to be eclipsed.[312] That may be so but it is difficult not to think that 1853 was not a good year for rocking too many European boats.

---

[310] Some accounts include the influence of Tamihana Te Rauparaha who spent over a year in England and was presented to Queen Victoria in June, 1852. He returned to New Zealand in late 1852 enthusiastic for the setting up of a Maori King but the actual message seems to have been spread by his good friend and relative Matene Te Whiwhi.

[311] *The Maori King Movement in New Zealand,* Thomas Buddle, p3. Even at this early stage we see the mixed messages as to whether the suggested "Kingly function" was sovereign "King" or administrative "Governor", two completely different roles with catastrophically different implications.

[312] The King Country, James Kerry-Nicholls, p5.

In 1853 the Waikatos were on a capitalistic high from their relationship with Europeans, basking in the prosperity of their agricultural pursuits. Not only was Waikato the "garden of New Zealand" supplying the domestic market but it had the bonus of an export market to Australia courtesy of the Victoria gold rush, complete with the inflated prices that such temporary phenomena bring. Moreover they did not share the land acquisition issues faced by their Taranaki brethren. In 1853 European co-existence at an arm's length was a golden goose right for the plucking, all pluses and no minuses. Any initiative that threatened that goose would be like shooting themselves in both feet and the head.

May 1854

In May 1854 (ono) the "Land League" meeting at Manawapou is held, as discussed previously. Although the meeting is not in Waikato, and although the issue of a Maori King is not recorded as being discussed, every other issue that will in future become a pillar of the King Movement is – unity, autonomy and vetoing land sales. Although, as we have noted, Wiremu Kingi is not reported as being present, Matene Te Whiwhi is – seemingly the common denominator in the "movement", wherever it is.

November 1856

In 1856, just 3 years since Te Whiwhi's visit, the Waikato is a different world, if not been upended, then knocked off its axis somewhat. The Victorian gold rush market is gone and in any event the Australian agricultural market is now being serviced from South Australia, Tasmania and Chile, among others. The New Zealand food market is still there but the prices Maori receive for their produce are now low. It is a national problem rather than specifically Waikato related, but since it is the Waikatos who gained most from the boom they have furthest to fall during the crash. Flour mills built at great tribal expense fell into disuse and/or were rendered obsolete by the emerging superior technology of steam mills in Auckland.

This seems fertile ground, and a captive audience for, a man with a plan – probably *any* man with *any* plan. If Te Whiwhi had arrived at this time instead of 3 years prior he would probably have hit the jackpot.

In 1856 the short-lived symbiotic relationship between Waikato Maori and Europeans that benefited both parties is gone, a flash in the pan. The honeymoon to a marriage of convenience is over. It is a common enough scenario when two worlds collide, a modern example of which we can see in the dilemma facing tourist hot-spots internationally. For decades, maybe centuries, these places have actively encouraged the "invaders" and ruthlessly milked them for profit. Now, somewhat late in the piece, they are realising the price they have paid. Negotiating the mutually beneficial "sweet spot" in such situations is a tricky business.

It is in this new, depressed environment that in November 1856 Te Heuheu Iwikau, chief of the Taupo based Ngati Tuwharetoa tribe, hosted a gathering of 1,600 attendees to celebrate the completion of a finely worked storehouse. Evidently Te Whiwhi's words of 1853 must had resonated and subsequently blossomed with somebody, for according to local missionary Thomas Grace:

> "Te Heuheu's subjects responded liberally to his call, and, when the store-house was filled, a great meeting was held for the purpose of eating the food so collected. The Waikato Maoris and other tribes evidently considered it a fine opportunity to discuss their project of making a King. Such was the origin of this great meeting...I have not been able to discover anything hostile to British rule in the minds of the Maoris who desire a King, but rather that, by having a King, they will be imitating us. They also appear to think that through the medium of a King they may be able to check the present lawless state of things and to promote peace. The idea of anything like a rebellion, so far as I have seen, does not seem to have entered their minds, and they are not able to understand why such a step should give offence to us [Europeans]."[313]

During this meeting Te Heuheu was offered the Kingship but declined that honour for himself and suggested premier Waikato chief Potatau in his place.

---

[313] *A Pioneer Missionary among the Maoris*, T. S. Grace, p76.

February 1857

In 1857 the man who history has dubbed "The Kingmaker" stepped into the limelight.

Most movements throughout history have been started and dominated by intellectuals and the King Movement was no exception. That key intellectual was Ngati Haua chief Wiremu Tamihana[314] and he was to the King Movement what Karl Marx was to the Communist movement. Without Wiremu Tamihana there would have been no King Movement and in practice he was, to all intents and purposes, the surrogate King. It has been said of him:

> "Thompson is about 40 years old: he has always borne a high character among the Missionaries and his other European acquaintances; though undoubtedly ambitious, he has uniformly evinced the desire to attain distinction by good rather than evil actions. At his conversion to Christianity he publicly declared that he would never fight again; since that time, though living in the midst of innumerable quarrels and bloodshed, he has never personally engaged in war, but has constantly and most successfully performed the part of a peace-maker. Thompson has been an active promoter of schools, having maintained at his own village, Matamata, a school of 60 children for more than two years, without any assistance from Government, and without even the advantage of a European teacher, for which he has always been most anxious: even during the past year he has been continuous in his efforts for this object, and has at length obtained a teacher who is to go to Matamata as soon as the present troubles are over. He has been a steady advocate for the establishment of law and order.

---

[314] The Maori transliteration for "William Thompson". He is also referred to as Wiremu Tamihana Tarapipipi and Wiremu Tamihana Te Waharoa after his father, the famous Ngati Haua chief and warrior Te Waharoa.

Page 303: The Treaty Makers – Architects of chaos.

Top Left: Captain Hobson, who inconsiderably fell ill at the crucial moment, leaving the final drafting of the Treaty to others.

Top Right: "British Resident" James Busby, an easy target much maligned by posterity, shown here in later life.

Bottom: The two luckless Williams' charged with translating the hastily drafted English Treaty into Maori.

At left: CMS Missionary Henry Williams, twenty years after the Treaty translation, in the 1860s (Credit: *Alexander Turnbull Library, PAColl-7578*).

At right: Henry Williams' son, Edward Marsh Williams, nineteen at the time of the Treaty translation but shown here in his 80s circa 1903 *(*Credit: *Alexander Turnbull Library, Ref: 1/2-111105-F*).

Page 304: The Inheritors of a dream.

Top Left: Robert Fitzroy, seen here circa 1860. A complex man, uncompromisingly "moral", "fair" and God fearing, often to a fault, Fitzroy detested and alienated his European subjects while simultaneously earning the disdain of those he tried his hardest to help – his Maori ones (Credit: *Alexander Turnbull Library, Ref: PAColl-6075-33).*

Top Right: Colonel Thomas Gore Browne, Governor from September 1855 to October 1861, essentially the meat in the sandwich between George Grey's two governorships *(Credit: Alexander Turnbull Library Ref: PA2-0740).*

Bottom Left: Fitztroy's successor Sir George Grey, looking somewhat care-worn and bedraggled, shown with Te Riwai Ropiha in 1862 *(Credit: Alexander Turnbull Library PA2-2510).*

Bottom Right: Grey's protégé and right-hand man Donald McLean, the power behind the "throne" and general fix-it man for a string of Governors (Credit: *Alexander Turnbull Library, Ref: 1/2-022090-F*).

Page 305: Kingi and his domain.

Top Left: A commonly used image of what is "possibly Wiremu Kingi Te Rangitaake", circa 1880. *(*Credit: *Alexander Turnbull Library, Ref: 1/2-0226688F).*

Bottom: The Waitara block, shown outlined in red on the southern head of the Waitara River. The L-Pa at which the first shots of war were fired on March 17, 1860, is marked by "L" in the top-right corner (Credit: *War in Taranaki, during the years 1860-61*, William Grayling, p79).

Pages 306 and 307: The building blocks of War.

A simplified schematic summarising the key factors contributing to the New Zealand Wars. The set of essential "dominoes" in the critical path to war are shown in black (Credit: The Author).

Page 308: The Logs and the Gasoline.

Top: Wiremu Tamihana with some of his family, this photo taken in 1865 after the disastrous Waikato War, which may explain why no-one looks very happy. Tamihana is often called the "King Maker" for his role in master-minding the "King" movement and installing Potatau as its first King (Credit: *Alexander Turnbull Library, Ref:PA1-q-177-30-4).*

Bottom: The "gasoline", Rewi Maniapoto, in a combination of European and Maori garb, looking inscrutable and with his thousand-yard stare a man not to be trifled with.

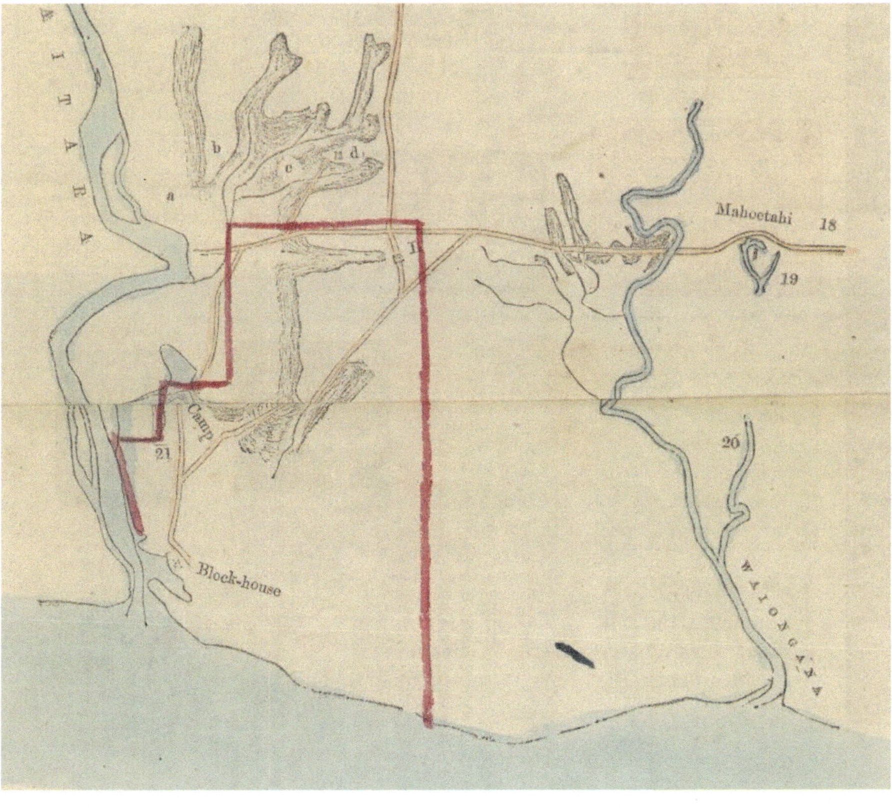
AITARA
a
b
c
d
Mahoetahi
18
19
1
Camp
21
Block-house
20
WAIONGANA

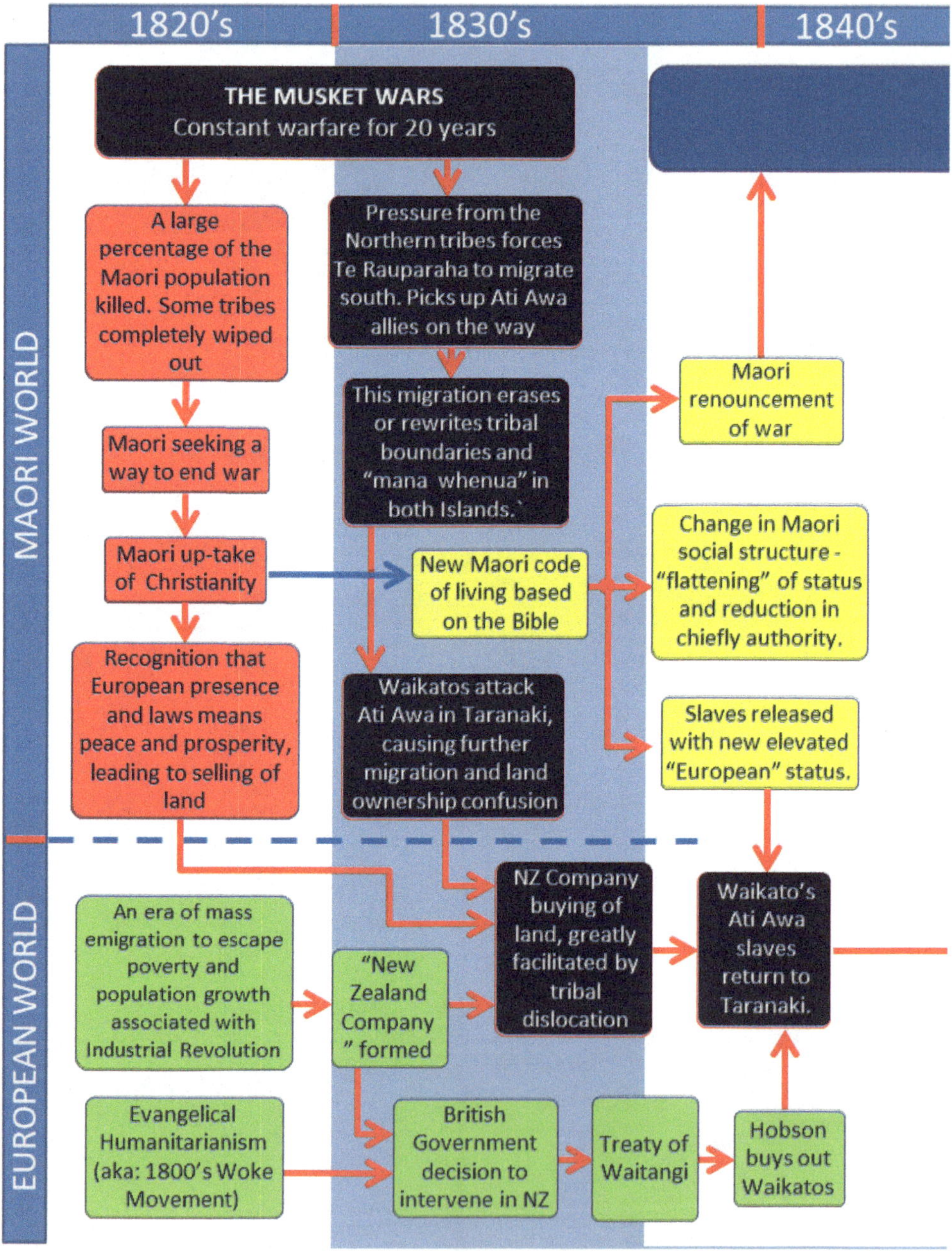
1820's
1830's
1840's
MAORI WORLD
EUROPEAN WORLD
THE MUSKET WARS
Constant warfare for 20 years
A large percentage of the Maori population killed. Some tribes completely wiped out
Pressure from the Northern tribes forces Te Rauparaha to migrate south. Picks up Ati Awa allies on the way
Maori seeking a way to end war
This migration erases or rewrites tribal boundaries and "mana whenua" in both Islands.`
Maori renouncement of war
Maori up-take of Christianity
New Maori code of living based on the Bible
Change in Maori social structure - "flattening" of status and reduction in chiefly authority.
Recognition that European presence and laws means peace and prosperity, leading to selling of land
Waikatos attack Ati Awa in Taranaki, causing further migration and land ownership confusion
Slaves released with new elevated "European" status.
NZ Company buying of land, greatly facilitated by tribal dislocation
Waikato's Ati Awa slaves return to Taranaki.
An era of mass emigration to escape poverty and population growth associated with Industrial Revolution
"New Zealand Company" formed
Evangelical Humanitarianism (aka: 1800's Woke Movement)
British Government decision to intervene in NZ
Treaty of Waitangi
Hobson buys out Waikatos

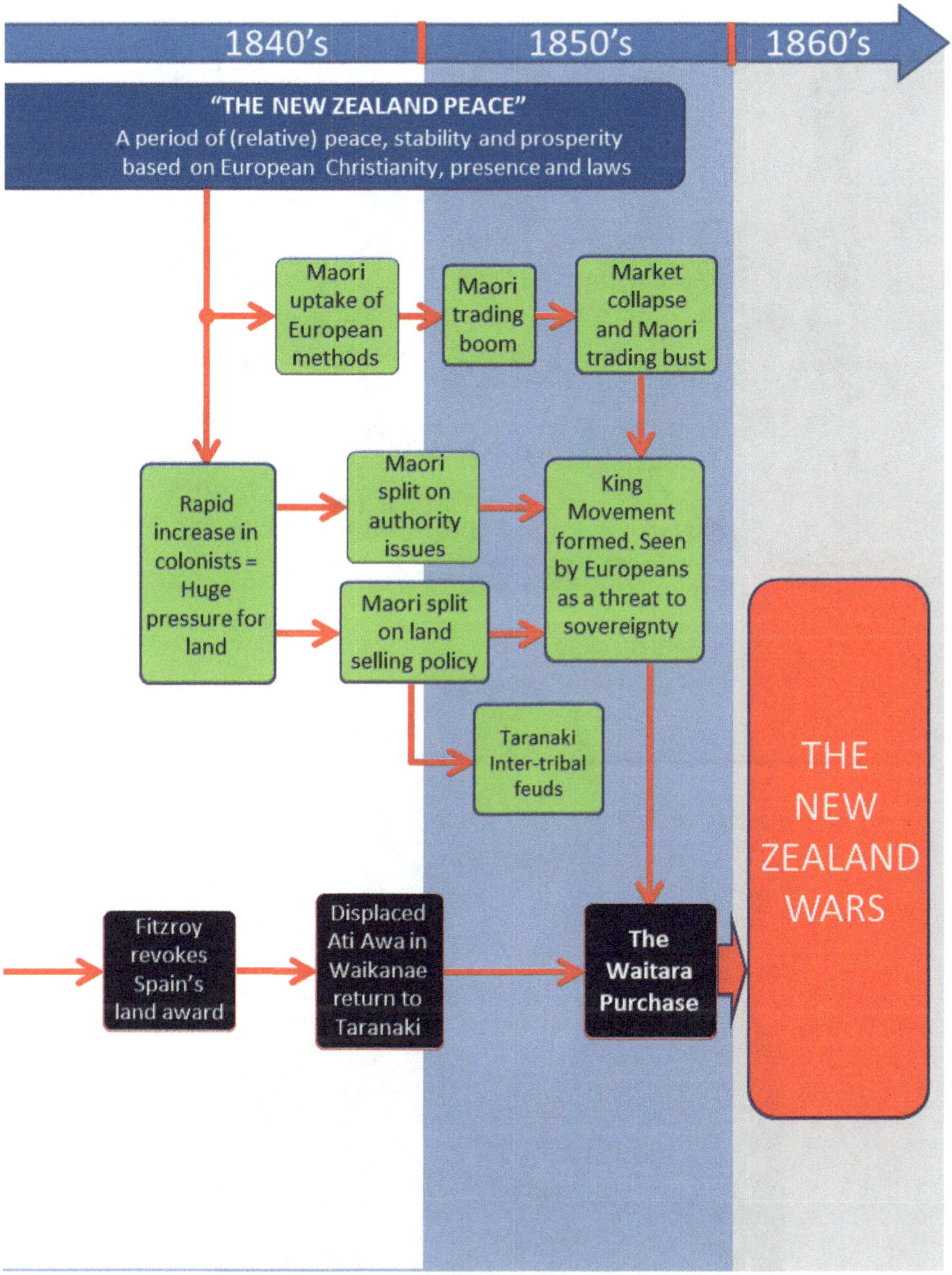
1840's
1850's
1860's
"THE NEW ZEALAND PEACE"
A period of (relative) peace, stability and prosperity based on European Christianity, presence and laws
Maori uptake of European methods
Maori trading boom
Market collapse and Maori trading bust
Rapid increase in colonists = Huge pressure for land
Maori split on authority issues
Maori split on land selling policy
King Movement formed. Seen by Europeans as a threat to sovereignty
Taranaki Inter-tribal feuds
Fitzroy revokes Spain's land award
Displaced Ati Awa in Waikanae return to Taranaki
The Waitara Purchase
THE NEW ZEALAND WARS

> Having embraced Christianity from conviction and not from hereditary custom, and being in the habit of reading the Scriptures as almost his only literature, his actions are governed by religious maxims, and his writings interspersed with Biblical quotation in an unusual degree: it would be a mistake to suppose this the result of cant or hypocrisy."[315]

John Gorst, who knew Tamihana well, gives us his ten cents worth as to how Tamihana's political epiphany occurred, in this famous anecdote:

> "At the beginning of 1857, while affairs were in this crisis in Waikato, Wiremu Tamihana paid his last (I believe his only) visit to Auckland. He has said that his chief object in going was to see the Governor, and lay before him the lawless condition of the country, in order that some plan might be arranged to cure the existing evils. He was also anxious to have a European magistrate stationed at his own village. He was, however, received coldly, and his requests were slighted, although nobody can now recollect how or why. He complains of some subordinate officer having treated him with great rudeness when he tried to obtain access to the Governor. It is quite certain that somebody took upon himself to refuse the Chief admission to the Governor's presence. He saw Mr. McLean, the Native Secretary and Chief Commissioner of the Land Purchasing Department, and asked him for a loan to erect a mill. He was refused. A notorious opponent of land-selling, he was not one to be looked on with any favour by a land-buying Government.
>
> Before leaving town he visited a friend and complained to him of the treatment he had received: his friend replied – "You see that your application has been thrown under the table; therefore, if you wish to erect a mill, or raise your own social condition, you must set about it yourself in earnest." Mortified and disappointed, he returned home to meditate on the advice he had received. It readily commended itself to a proud, self-reliant man. He determined to ask no more favours from

[315] *New Zealander*, 3 August, 1861, p3.

the English Government, but to work out what his countrymen wanted without that help which he had just been denied."[316]

The veracity of this encounter has been disputed[317], but be that as it may, as anyone in history who has ever tried to get anything out of any Government will attest, instant access to the big wheels of governance and instant gratification of your every whim are not noted characteristics of Government bureaucracies. And, if we are to be brutally, commercially honest, erecting yet another useless mill at that time was complete lunacy.

In any event, for whatever reason, in early 1857 Wiremu Tamihana wrote to the Waikato chiefs:

> "To all Waikato,
>
> This is the agreement of Ngatihaua, for Potatau to be king of New Zealand: -
>
> Friends - Our desire is great that Potatau should be set up in this very year. Do not delay. Hasten the assembling of the "rununga!" Hasten the establishment of the scheme, and when it is done the documents will be collected, and the day will be fixed for instituting him. Be speedy. You will write to the remote tribes that they may hear.
>
> From Wiremu (Tamihana) Tarapipipi, and all Ngatihaua, to Waikato, to Kereihi, Pukewau, Harapata, Toma, Ruihana, Waata Tengatete.
>
> Be speedy."[318]

So just who is this "Potatau" to whom Tamihana refers? He is, in fact, someone we have met before – that scourge of Taranakians – the former

---

[316] The Maori King, John Gorst, pp81-82.

[317] Tamihana's visit to Auckland, B.J. Dalton, Journal of the Polynesian Society, Vol. 72, No.3 (September, 1963), pp193-205

[318] Letter of Wiremu Tamihana, February 12th, 1857 (AJHR, 1860, E-1C, p3).

Te Wherowhero, now aged, harmless and renamed[319], his past sins conveniently forgotten and enjoying a peaceful retirement in Mangere courtesy of a Government pension. In today's world he would be called a sell-out, an Uncle Tom, but in those saner times his *mana* was still absolute.

Since Wiremu Tamihana was the key player in the King Movement it is helpful to understand where he was coming from in all this. The following letter, although written later, provides a good window into his mind:

> "When you [Governor Gore Browne] came the river of blood was still open, and I therefore sought for some thought to cause it to cease, as the ministers had long persevered. I considered therefore how this blood could be made to diminish in this island. I looked into your books, where Israel cried to have a king for themselves to be a judge over them, and I looked at the word of Moses in Deuteronomy xvii. 15; and in Revelations xxix, 4: and I kept these words in my memory through all the years; the land feuds continuing all the time, and blood still being spilt, I still meditating upon the matter. When we arrived at the year 1857, Te Heuheu called a meeting at Taupo. Twice 800 were assembled there. When the news of that meeting reached me, I said, I will consent to this to assist my work, that the religion of those tribes that had not yet united might have time to breathe. I commenced at those words in the Book of Samuel viii. 5, "Give us a King to judge us." This was why I set up Potatau in

[319] Hi name, according to Gorst, translates to "He that counteth by night". At this time he was an ancient warrior much venerated by Maori of that area and a good friend of successive Governors. Missionary Thomas Buddle summarised him as follows – "...They did not select him for his vigour and energy, mental or physical, or for his ability to give them new laws, and to administer the affairs of the proposed Maori Kingdom. His ideas and habits are all fixed and stereotyped in Maori. His day for improvement and progress is gone by. He is verging on the dotage of a second childhood, comparatively inert both in body and mind. It was the prestige of a name they wanted to give popularity to the project." (*The Maori King Movement in New Zealand*, Thomas Buddle, p11.)

> the year 1857. On his being set up the blood at once ceased, and has so remained up to the present year. The reason why I set up Potatau as a king for me was, he was a man of extended influence, and one who was respected by the tribes of this island. That, O friend, was why I set him up, to put down my troubles, to hold the land of the slave, and to judge the offences of the Chiefs. The King was set up, the Runangas were set up, the Kai-whakawas were set up, and religion was set up. The works of my ancestors have ceased, they are diminishing at the present time; what I say is, that the blood of the Maories has ceased (to flow)."[320]

Tamihana was an intelligent man – the "intellectual" with the "big idea" necessary to start a movement. He was a contradiction in that, while he was unanimously said to be a man of peace, his actions could only lead to war. He is liberally praised by posterity and New Zealand owes him its thanks.

But let us be brutally honest and judge him as we would any other man – he may indeed have been a "great man" but like every "great man" throughout history he was not without his flaws. The consequences of his actions suggest that his greatness in intelligence, integrity and vision did not in practice translate to excellence in implementation skills such as negotiation, real-politik, compromise and diplomacy, at least as they are recognised in the European world, which is the world he had to interface with. Consequently we shall see in due course that much of the praise subsequently heaped on Tamihana is equivalent to praising someone for their efforts in putting out a fire of their own making.

Although the germ of the idea for a Maori King may have been Matene Te Whiwhi's by 1857 it was officially Wiremu Tamihana's baby, the driving force who whipped it up from nothing and without whom it would never have existed. Whatever role the King Movement played in the New Zealand Wars Wiremu Tamihana is largely responsible for it.

---

[320] Letter from Wiremu Tamihana to Governor Browne, 7 June 1861. (AJHR, 1861, E-1B, p19).

We see from the letter above that like many Maori of his time Tamihana was an Old Testament enthusiast and this was possibly his biggest weakness.[321] His unbending reliance on his own personal understanding of the Bible, and his misunderstanding of the word "King" in that ancient context, misled him and many Maori of the time.

In recent times the term "the other" has burst into prominence and ubiquity – a foundation of the currently favoured "Oppressor/Oppressed", "Black Hat/white Hat" paradigm of history. While it could be a not un-useful term in emphasising that we all see things differently, in applying the term exclusively to the presumed "oppressed" party it becomes more than a little demeaning, a brutal put-down denying the agency and intelligence of the "oppressed" group and relegating them to idiots.

In reality we are, of course, *all* others to the other. In the New Zealand context, if Europeans did their best to understand Maori according to their own culture and sometimes failed then the same can also be said of Maori attempts to understand Europeans based on *their* own culture. It is a two-way street in which no one is guilty of anything other than just trying to do their best. Nowhere is this better demonstrated than in the mind of Tamihana who quite clearly failed to understand *his* "other".

Tamihana did not understand that the Old Testament writings were many-thousand-year-old apocryphal myths which in 1860 Western civilisation were thousands of years past their use-by date, referred to only allegorically and sparingly. And he did not understand that, while the Bible may indeed be the basis of Western civilisation, it did not contain all the fine print – you will not, for instance, find a discussion on the pros and cons of representative or responsible government, of democracy or a

---

[321] Gorst sums up the situation thus – "Most of the Maories are exceedingly fond of reading the books of the Old Testament, in which they find described a state of civilization not unlike their own; and though not possessed of the same critical powers as the Zulu Kafirs, they have sufficient intelligence to deduce maxims from both Old and New Testaments, which it is inconvenient to have to reconcile with the theories of our modern civilization." *The Maori King*, J. E. Gorst, p157.

thousand and one things in either the Old or New Testaments. And you will not find a thesis on the changing nature of monarchy over the thousands of years since the Old Testament was written, or an explanation of what British sentiment to their Queen meant.

And this, as we have discussed, was really the crux of the "problem" with the "King Movement"– its name with its implications of a sovereign leader – which for reasons Tamihana not only could not but would not see, was objectionable to Europeans.

Neither did Tamihana appear to understand the intricacies, problems, expense and myriad practical impediments to establishing control over a large, disparate population and area. Maori – or at least Tamihana – complained that the European Government had not immediately solved all their problems while failing to understand that everything deemed desirable in the European world took thousands of years to get to that state, a state which was, and is, still evolving. Like the prosperity transiently brought by the Victorian gold rush Tamihana seemed to think everything was easy, until – suddenly – it wasn't. The Bible held out a cargo-cult-like promise that, if you do *this,* then *that* will automatically happen, that life is easy. But life is not an equation and life is not easy, even for Europeans.

April-June 1857

A meeting to install Potatau in accordance with Tamihana's letter was duly held in Rangiriri. Governor Browne, Donald McLean and Major Richmond made the effort to attend but finding the meeting delayed, detoured to Rangiaowhia where, in a repeat performance of that given to Governor Grey six years earlier, Hori te Waru and Hoani Papita continued to lavish their praise on Europeans – or at least put on a good show of it:

> "The advantages we have received from the European can be no more concealed than the sun's light at noon. They are manifest to the eyes of the great and humble; the young and old appreciate them, for the heaviest burden is become light by the use of the cart; and, by the horse, the long and rough ways are made short and easy to the traveller. For all these benefits we are indebted to the Queen

> and her Governors. The plough has diminished the labor of our hands, in tilling the land and the spring of our riches is overflowing by the mill. These are the benefits we receive from you. It is said with reason, that God has given rulers to love and protect the people, which is proved by your presence amongst us."[322]

It is as if time had stood still in Rangiaowhia and everything was still sweetness and light, but given the nature of the impending King Movement meeting this moving speech can only be a façade.[323]

Browne's record of his reception here sheds further light on the many and varied possible permutations and combinations of Maori/European co-existence being bandied about depending on who you talked to:

> "...It was, however, clear that they did not understand the term "King" in the sense we use it; but though they constantly professed loyalty to the Queen, attachment to myself, and a desire for the amalgamation of the races, they did mean to maintain their separate nationality, and desired to have a Chief of their own election, who should protect them from any possible encroachment on their rights, and uphold such of their customs as they were disinclined to relinquish. This was impressed upon me everywhere; but only on one occasion, at Waipa, did any one presume to speak of their intended King as a Sovereign, having similar rank and power with Her Majesty; and this speaker I cut short, leaving him in the midst of his oration.
>
> ...I arrived at Rangiriri (where the meeting is to take place) simultaneously with Te Whero Whero, the intended King. I had two long interviews with him, and in a speech addressed to those of the Natives who had arrived (among whom were some Chiefs), he declared

---

[322] *Maori Messenger*, 30 April, 1857, p5.

[323] Hoani Papita ("John the Baptist") would, in fact, within a very short space of time become one of the leading lights in the King Movement.

> his intention to be guided entirely by my advice, and said that he was a dying man, and should bequeath his people to my care.[324]

The meeting was a huge event involving an estimated 2200 central North Island Maori. As noted by Browne, Potatau – a.k.a Te Wherowhero, the King-elect – was reluctantly present and a flag bearing his name, of great symbolic value, had been prepared. Over the course of many days a great many speeches were made, only a tiny fragment of which were recorded. Whether this fragment is truly representative of the general sentiment we can only speculate but the following samples give some idea of the polarised views regarding the idea of a Maori Kingship and all it implied:

> "**Paora:** God is good; Israel were his people; they had a king; I see no reason why any nation should not have a king if they wish for one. The Gospel does not say that we are not to have a king. It says "Honor the King – Love the brotherhood". Why should the Queen be angry? We shall be in alliance with her, and friendship will be preserved. The Governor does not stop murders and fights among us. A king will be able to do that. Let us have order, so that we may grow as the pakehas grow. Why should we disappear from the country? New Zealand is ours; I love it.
>
> **Takirei Te Rau:** The first Governor came and gave the word "friendship": so did the second – the third – and so does Governor Browne. The source of this word is God. It came in the Gospel; and now there is added the Law; what more do we want? I think this is the open road; the new one [King Movement] is overgrown and dark. I will not walk in it. Friendship to the Governor is the road to the Queen. Go on this road; it is the road to good. Let us go on this road.
>
> **Wiremu Te Awaitai:** I am a small man; and a fool. I am ignorant of these Scripture quotations. Ngatihaua, don't be dark. Waikato, listen. Taupo, attend. My name has been heard of in old day, and sometimes

[324] Copy of a despatch from Governor Gore Browne, C.B, to the Right Hon. H. Labouchere, 9th May, 1857 (AJHR 1860, F-03, p111).

it is still mentioned. I am going to speak mildly, like a father. My word is this: I promised the first Governor, when he came to see me, and I promised all the rest, that I would stick to him, and be a subject of the Queen. I intend to keep my promise, for they have kept theirs. They have taken no land. Mine was the desire to sell, and they gave me money. Why do you bring that new [King Movement] flag here? There is bother in it. I can't see my way clear. But I know that there is trouble in that flag. I am content with the old one [Union Jack]. It is seen all over the world, and it belongs to me. I get some of its honor! What honor can I get from your flag? It is like a fountain without water. Don't trouble me. You say we are slaves. If acknowledging that flag makes me a slave, I am a slave. Let me alone. Don't bring your bother here. Go back to the mountains. Let us alone in peace. I and the Governor will take our own course. That's all.

Wiremu Tamihana Tarapipipi: I love New Zealand. I want order and laws. The King could give us these better than the Governor; for the Governor has never done anything except when a pakeha is killed; he lets us kill each other and fight. A king would stop these evils. However, if you don't like the King, pull down the flag. Let Rewi[325] pull it down if you wish it."

In true, traditional, Maori oratorical style this was all top-level, allegory-based discussion, never addressing issues of practicality and implementation.

Tamihana's contribution confirms our earlier hypothesis – that far from rejecting Europeans and the wonders they bring, his burning desire is in fact to *emulate* European law and order. He seems to think that the law and order that took thousands of years to achieve in Europe can not only be achieved overnight amongst Maori but amongst Maori who do not even recognise European sovereignty and would likely object to an imposition of the European law he is craving.

---

[325] This refers to Rewi ("Levi") Maniapoto, one of the chiefs of the Ngati Maniapoto tribe and who we shall hear a lot more of later.

Amazingly he does not seem to understand that the reason European laws have not been extended to Maori regions is that the violent Maori response to European action makes it impossible – if Europeans try to intervene and apply European laws in Maori regions Maori will revolt, which is precisely why Europeans had specifically *not* intervened and applied European law in the Puketapu Feuds. And in two years' time that point will be made yet again, when Governor Browne's attempt to impose European authority in the case of Wiremu Kingi would cause a portion of the Waikatos – including Tamihana's own tribe – to rise in objection and begin the New Zealand Wars that will effectively mark the end of any possibility of peaceful co-existence of the two races.

What exactly was the nature and extent of what Tamihana perceived to be his "law and order" problems? His issues were, with few exceptions, not related to Europeans but to internal Maori issues of lawlessness amongst his own people. Unlike the pre-European Maori landscape of wholesale inter-tribal slaughter, thanks to the European peace Tamihana's issues were now limited to ones of an occasional dispute between Maori individuals.[326] His predictions about the relative efficacy of a Maori King versus a European Governor were unfounded and illogical. While Potatau, the King-elect, was once a mighty warrior and was still greatly revered, he was now in his dotage. He was there on sufferance, half blind and would rather be tucked up in bed. Perhaps Tamihana was speaking of a "king" as being symbolic of some sort of underlying infrastructure that *could* achieve his goals, but what this presumed infrastructure was and how it was to operate in practice he does not say.

Neither does Tamihana seem to understand what it actually takes to implement the "law and order" he desires. For five hundred years all Maori have had to manage is the extent of their own homogenous tribal territory, something that was achieved in a communistic and voluntary

---

[326] One report says that Tamihana "originally conceived the idea of a Maori King as a means of putting a stop to the bloody land feuds by which the Waikato district was being depopulated" but what these "bloody land feuds" are is not specified (quote is from *New Zealander*, 3 August, p3).

way under the guidance of chiefs. Now Tamihana wanted a "kingdom" presiding over a huge swathe of land – perhaps even the entire country – inhabited by numerous tribes who were often each other's former enemies, a system of law and order emulating European methodology requiring an actual infrastructure which in a capitalist society required people to be paid. And he wanted it to be accomplished immediately with the wave of a magic wand and preferably at Government expense.

The summary of these meetings is:

- Judging from the reported speeches the overall impression is one of division rather than unity, of confusion, of looking for a solution to an ill-defined and possibly non-existent problem.
- There were two groups – one which supported a King and one which did not.[327]
- Amongst those who *did* support a King there was no consensus on how this "Kingship" would work in practice, whether it would be an alliance with the "Queen", or Europeans, or a complete separation between the two races.
- Nothing of a practical nature was discussed.
- Given that the meetings involved between 2,000 and 3,000 people over a period of three months one wonders whether the gnomic and time-intensive traditional Maori approach, perfect for the traditional Maori way of life, could ever be adapted to the new European system of "law and order", which, depending on whom you asked, seemed to be the whole point of the "Kingship".
- Following from the above it is clear that Maori society was still a communistic organisation in which everyone must be involved, that

[327] Buddle's summary is that "...the Ngatihaua, Ngatimaniapoto, and Te Heuheu, being its principal supporters. The tribes of the lower Waikato and the Ngatimahanga, Wm. Naylor's tribe, opposing it." (*The Maori King Movement in New Zealand*, Thomas Buddle, p12.)

this "Kingship" process was exceedingly disruptive and would possibly cause more problems than it intended to solve, and that the disruption to productivity and huge drain on food resources caused by these meetings brought unnecessary hardship on top of that already caused by the depressed agricultural market at that time.

June 1858

It was another year before the next meeting, this time at Ngaruawahia, for the ostensible purpose of installing Potatau as the Maori King. While invitations were sent to all North Island tribes most were duly ignored and the attendees were all the usual suspects – the Waikato related tribes from Manukau in the north to the Waipa area in the south and to Kawhia areas in the west. It seems the Maori King was a Waikato fascination for which the rest of Maori New Zealand had little appetite.

The meeting was as divided as it was the year before. While there seemed to be unanimity that Potatau should be *something*, the debate centred around precisely *what* that something should be – whether he should be regarded simply as holding the "Maori *mana*" – however that might be defined – or if he was to have the "dignity and power of King".

It was Potatau himself who resolved this dilemma by stating his preference to be "King" rather than "father" and Wiremu Tamihana accordingly recorded the soon-to-be King Potatau's duties as follows:

> "The laws for the king are these. The power he is to exercise over men and land is the power of protecting them against quarrels, wars, and murders, – a power to extend to all the chiefs and councils of all the tribes.
>
> Second. Every man is to live upon his own land, and the king is to defend him against all aggressions against his land or person."[328]

---

[328] *The Maori King Movement in New Zealand*, Thomas Buddle, p14.

At this point "the great body of the Waikatos" – those who disagreed with this decision – abruptly left, while the remaining "Kingites" travelled to Rangiaowhia to "complete the installation of their sovereign".

Missionary Thomas Buddle does his best to clarify the situation:

> "...one party accepting Potatau as a Patriarch for the tribes, with what views and for what purpose did not transpire; the other vowing allegiance to him as a King, who is to protect their lands and their interests against all aggressors – not to give them laws, for they gave laws to him."[329]

A correspondent of Auckland's *New Zealander* newspaper added these insightful comments:

> "...Katipa's [speech] was perhaps the best. He insisted upon there being no divisions, but that Queen, King, Bishop, Ministers, and Laws, should all be held in one hand, and the bond of union be love. Potatau expressed himself in anything but rebellious strains. "Let the other Chiefs be kings," said he; "as for me, I am only a cook for the Pakehas; and the work for my children is to wash the plates of the Pakeha."
>
> ...On Tuesday the younger men had their turn at speaking; and as it had been intimated that this was to be the great day, our expectations were somewhat high. We were doomed, however, to disappointment. As you will see from the extract given below, the burden of their addresses was the constant repetition of the sentiment – 'The King on his piece; the Queen on her piece; God over both; and Love binding them to each other.'
>
> ...I had gone to the meeting expecting to hear some reasons assigned for transferring their allegiance from Victoria to Potatau, and to learn something about the form of government to be adopted by the new

---

[329] *Ibid*, p14. Presumably Buddle is alluding to some sort of demarcation between the King, who has accountability for land related issues, and an as-yet undefined form of "Maori Government", which takes care of the day to day issues of "law and order".

> monarch. Nothing of the kind was even hinted at, and it was only in private conversation with some of the leading men, that I could learn what "The King Movement" really means. The impression I received is that the King Movement is simply a great Land League formed to prevent the sale of any more land to the Pakehas. Of this league, Potatau has been chosen the head, and all who become members of the Union concede to him the veto upon the alienation of any portion of their estates.
>
> Not a disrespectful word was uttered against the British Government. The Natives simply think that to part with any more of their lands is the road to certain ruin, and to avert such a catastrophe, are adopting the expedient of a King or Land Protector. Every other question is of importance to them only as it affects this.
>
> We failed to perceive the slightest cause for alarm in the movement; and yet we are persuaded that it is of too much importance both to Natives and Europeans, to deserve being treated with pooh-poohing."[330]

So, if we are to believe the *New Zealander*, there was nothing to worry about. But that is the way all movements start and, as the saying goes, the road to Hell is paved with good intentions.

Thus, after a year and a half of intensive lobbying, Wiremu Tamihana's vision for a Maori King finally became a reality and because he had been the driving force behind the concept he is duly referred to by posterity as "The Kingmaker".

Potatau[331] was now officially recognised as being something to a territorially small proportion of North Island Maori, with a manifesto

---

[330] Letter from "Curiosus" dated 20 June, 1858, from *New Zealander*, 3 July, 1858, p3.

[331] Whatever the merits of a Maori King – and the King himself does not seem convinced – it has to be said that, if there had to be a King, then Potatau was the perfect choice – he was clearly a man of great dignity, humility, patience

consisting of two very general mission statements. However given Potatau's role as figurehead it is probably more accurate to say that Tamihana had established himself as proxy King, or at least the practical power behind the throne.[332]

While at this time there was considerable fuzziness and multiple disparate views of what the King Movement was, it was now clear that, if there was not an actual "land league" before the appointment of Potatau as King, there was certainly no question that there was one now – Tamihana's Mission Statement Number 2 expressly stated that the King was obliged to "defend all aggressions" against anyone's land. With these few words the fate of Maori New Zealand was unwittingly sealed and the door to the New Zealand Wars was flung open.

---

and pragmatism. One suspects that, if he actually had the power of the Kings of the Old Testament, things would have turned out very differently.

[332] Although the King Movement was in practice guided in traditional Maori style by an assembly or runanga of influential chiefs in some semblance of a "Ministry" Tamihana seems to have been the main point of communication between the King Movement and the European world and was the individual constantly mentioned in all matters of importance such as the signing of armistices.

Chapter 2-2

Kingi "does a Teira"

We now return to Taranaki to pick-up where we left off – with Wiremu Kingi being shot at in his L-shaped pa at Waitara.

We do not know much about Wiremu Kingi's involvement with the King Movement in its formative years. We are told that all the tribes of the island were invited to the various Kingite meetings and logically one would think that with Wiremu Kingi heavily involved as an anti-land seller in the Puketapu feuds raging at that time he would be high on the list as a key-note speaker. But whether or not he participated in these early debates his opinion on the subject of a Maori King just three months prior to the outbreak of war was very clear:

> "In December last [1859] a Native called Waitere, from Hangatiki, an active agent in the King movement, called at Waitara on his way to the South, and left secretly a King's flag with a Native called Erueti, the miscreant that proposed the plot to murder me [Robert Parris], who has done a great deal of mischief in this district. As soon as William King found out that this flag had been left there, he accused those who sanctioned it of acting treacherously by him, and finding some of his own people favourable to it, he threatened to leave the district. This matter caused a division among the party; William King left his Pa at Waitara, and went to live with Teito, near the

> Waiongona, while the other party still carried on the flag question, and commenced to prepare a flagstaff."[333]

It is an extraordinary situation that answers at least one question but raises many others. The question it answers is that regarding Kingi's authority over "his" tribe – clearly Kingi has authority over no-one and he is not "paramount chief" of anything. "His" tribe do precisely what they want in complete defiance of his wishes.

And how are we to reconcile his rejection of the King Movement with his letter written eight months earlier requesting the King Movement's assistance in the Waitara situation? Kingi is a smart man and he must know that the King Party with its anti-land selling manifesto is his only hope. Yet in December 1859, three months before war would break out, and nine months after Teira's initial offer of Waitara land, it seems that if Kingi has a master plan to prevent this sale it does not include the King Movement. Has he misread Browne and assumed that, like Grey before him, he will cave, that the bark will never become a bite and that he needs no-one's help?

If the outbreak of hostilities at Waitara on March 17, 1860 was a spark it was certainly not a surprise. Everyone, both European and Maori, had seen this clash coming since March, 1859, when Teira first laid down his mat. Since then it had been like watching a train wreck in a twelve month long slow-motion sequence. Europeans had assumed from Day One of the sale that the involvement of the King Party would be their greatest threat. It was as much a test case for the King Party as it was for Governor Browne, a test of whether the King Party really would enforce their manifesto for stopping land sales or whether it would trip at the first hurdle.

So why was Kingi so anti the Maori King, the very party that could be his saviour and whose anti-land selling sentiment aligned precisely with his own? Did he feel it beneath his dignity to ask for help from this quarter?

---

[333] Letter 16 July, 1860, from Robert Parris to Donald McLean (AJHR, 1860, E-3A, p3).

Was it simply a matter of personal pride? The Waikatos were, after all, his former, inveterate enemies and even in 1860 there was still little love lost between the Waikatos and the Taranakians, their former slaves and by extension a lower form of life. Or was it just the latest example of the obdurate nature that Kingi had demonstrated on previous occasions? We really do not know, except that whatever it was it was a personal reason which, it seems, his tribe did not share.

The mechanism by which the King Movement became embroiled in Kingi's local spat is somewhat hazy and raises some very fundamental questions as to precisely what the role of the movement's "land league" actually was. Was it supposed to stop the sale of land to Europeans by *anyone,* whether they were part of the King Movement or not? If, for instance, Teira had an undisputed clear right to sell his land, would that be a violation of the "land league" requiring intervention by the King Movement? And what if it was Kingi who wanted to sell land and had an undisputed right to do so – would that also require intervention by the King Movement resulting in them fighting him? If the answers to these questions are "no" then what precisely was the point of a land league/King Movement? If it did not matter if a sale was "right" or "wrong" but simply that a sale took place then why did Tamihana's decision to intervene in the Waitara sale turn on the rights and wrongs of that sale?

In April 1860 an extraordinary event occurred:

> "...in the Autumn of the present year [1860] a deputation from the Ngatiawa and Ngatiruanui tribes visited Waikato, entrusted with the important duty of presenting the allegiance of those tribes to the Maori King, and of handing over their lands to the league of which he is the recognised head.
>
> The deputation consisted of about sixty picked men, chiefly young men. They arrived at Ngaruawahia on the 10th of April, accompanied by Ngatimaniapoto from Kawhia, Rangiaohia and Upper Waipa. They marched up to the flag staff, three abreast, wearing favors to distinguish the respective tribes.
>
> On reaching the flagstaff one stepped forward, and with a clear distinct voice said, "Honour all men, love the brotherhood; Fear God;

> Honour the King;" then turning to the train he said "Honour the King:" all responded by uncovering and kneeling. The leader of the Ngatiruanui then read from a memorandum book an address beginning, "O King, live for ever: thou art bone of our bone, and flesh of our flesh; thou art a saviour for us, our wives, our children," &c., &c., and went on to pledge their allegiance. The leader of the Ngatiawa then read a similar address: "Honour the King" was again demanded, and a low salaam, and a general cry of hear, hear, hear, was the response."[334]

This party arrived at Ngaruawahia on April 10 1860, "apparently without Wiremu Kingi's consent"[335] and, seemingly and amazingly, unaware that war had broken out at Waitara three weeks previously.

The question this visitation raises is – what does Buddle mean when he refers to "Ngatiawa"? Is he suggesting these "Ngatiawa" were from Kingi's own *hapu*, as Gorst's comment regarding Kingi's lack of consent seems to imply? Kingi's "own" tribe had previously received the King's flag against Kingi's wishes – but would they really take things into their own hands – in effect mutiny against Kingi – and set out for Waikato against Kingi's wishes? And what would it mean if a tribe swore allegiance to the Maori King not only without the authority of but against the wishes of its supposed "chief"?

Another source[336] states that the "Ngatiawa party" included "Hori, Paori and Taimona, all of Kaipakopako" – which would mean they were of the

---

[334] *The Maori King Movement in New Zealand*, Thomas Buddle, p28.
Missionary John Whiteley's account differs slightly: "... about eighty men from the southern tribes of Taranaki and Ngatiruanui were at the king meeting at Waikato, on the 12th of April, giving in their allegiance, handing over their lands, and asking help for Wiremu Kingi" (*Nelson Examiner and New Zealand Chronicle*, 6 February, 1861, p3).

[335] *The Maori King*, J. E .Gorst, p140. How Gorst arrived at this conclusion is unclear and no other accounts allude to Kingi's involvement in any way.

[336] Wells, p204.

Puketapu arm of "Ngatiawa". It is quite possible that the entire "Ngatiawa" party were Puketapu and that Kingi's "own" *hapu*(s) was not involved at all. If so this would mean that only the Puketapu swore allegiance to the King and that the King Party's resulting obligations applied only to Puketapu land, not to that at Waitara. All things considered, this event surely cannot be said to have caused the land at Waitara to be put "under the *mana* of the King" and the evidence suggests that if Kingi actually did put the land under the *mana* of the King it happened at the *end* of the war, not before it.

Having made their allegiance, and "handed over their lands", to the King, this party of "Ngatiawa"– whoever they were – set out for home on May 23, 1860 accompanied by a contingent of Waikato.[337] One of these returnees, Wi Tako Ngatata, was charged with visiting Taranaki on his way home to investigate the Waitara issue and report back to the King Party.

In May 1860 there was yet another huge King Party meeting at Ngaruawahia to discuss the King Party's response to the outbreak of war at Waitara. In addition to the crowd of 3,000[338] Maori an influential body of Europeans, including Donald Mclean, Bishop Selwyn and five missionaries representing all three denominations, also attended.

As usual many words were spoken, only a handful of which were recorded, with an accuracy and representation we can only guess at. Much of what has been recorded is difficult for a non-1860s Maori to unravel and some speeches seem to suggest contradictory opinions within the same breath.

---

[337] *Daily Southern Cross*, 1 May, 1860, p2.

[338] Stated by Buddle as 1,600 males and 1,600 women and children (*The Maori King Movement in New Zealand*, Thomas Buddle, p28) although another account puts the number at 4,000. Since the population of Waikato at that time was estimated at about 10,000 (*Observations on the State of the Aboriginal Inhabitants of New Zealand*, F.D. Fenton) this represents a huge and socially disruptive event).

Wiremu Tamihana is recorded as saying:

> "I am disturbed by the letter received from Wm. King. I wish to understand the case, but do not see it. They (the Europeans) have forsaken the right way, they have become deranged like the King of Babylon who was turned into the forest. But let us not take up arms in an unrighteous cause. Ahab coveted Naboth's vineyard, and because Naboth would not give up the inheritance of his father's Ahab was greatly disturbed. Jezebel his wife saw his trouble and said, I will give it thee. She brought Naboth to death by falsehood, and took it, but God avenged the deed. I do not forget some of the Kings of Judah who engaged in unrighteous war, how they perished in their sin. Therefore I hesitate, and say let us see our way. Wm, King says the land is his; Taylor [Teira] says it his. I say let us find out the owner. Do not make haste lest we make a mistake. I do not condemn the Governor for I am not informed. As for the Queen she is the minister of God, and the minister of God is not supposed to do wrong. If wrong be done it is the fault of the Executive (te Kaihapai). I also remember the words of Paul, "Let every soul be subject unto the higher powers, for there is no power but of God; the powers that be are ordained of God." I do not say, let us find out that the Governor is right, that I may join him: nor am I idle or unwilling to go to war if necessary, but let me have a just cause. I have heard, but I have not seen. Do you ask what shall be done if my proposition be accepted to go and investigate? If the Governor says that this (the Maori King), is the cause of the war, I see through it. If he says that it is the land, I see through that also. But I do not speak it, that is a matter not to be spoken here, it is a hidden word that is to be kept in the heart. We intend to keep our land, and if the Governor comes to take another piece after this, then we shall have war."[339]

This would suggest that the King Movement was not making its decision based on Kingi having "passed the mana of his land to the King", because if he had then there would be no decision to make. Tamihana wants to

[339] *The Maori King Movement in New Zealand*, Thomas Buddle, p37.

judge the case simply on its rights and wrongs and land leagues do not enter into it.

It is a shame we do not have a copy of Wiremu Kingi's letter to which Tamihana refers but presumably the gist of it can be found in the final sentences of this speech from Kaperiera:

> "I accompanied Wi Tako on his return from Waikato. I wanted to have an explanation about the Parawai [the mat that Teira presented to the Governor]. We intended to see W. King, but on reaching Waitara we heard that war had commenced, that pakehas had been killed, so Tako would not visit King. We saw Ihaia and Teira. Teira asked – for what purpose have you come? We replied – to enquire about the mat and to take the truth back to Waikato. He said – the piece is small, the greater portion of Waitara is King's; mine is in the centre. Then came the news that Waikato was about to attack Auckland. I went to King and said – I have come to enquire about the mat. He replied – "The report is correct". I looked on in silence. I said – "That was your error, you ought to have taken it away". "I did not", he replied, "I simply threw a word at the Governor, and said to him "I will not give you my land"; I did not take up the mat, but I spake my word. The pakeha wants our land, but this war is about your Maori king. Don't listen to the pakeha, but bring your flag to Waitara. Go back and clear them out; send them all back to England."""[340]

Whatever the reason Kingi rebuffed the King Party in December 1859 his message six months later in May 1860 is clear – he is now asking for that King's flag he rejected and for the King Party's help. Is this equivalent to "putting his land under the *mana* of the King"? Issues of *mana* aside, the bottom line is that Kingi has passed his problem over to the King Party, essentially saying "put your money where your mouth is – you said you would not allow this to happen – now prove it".

---

[340] *The Maori King Movement in New Zealand*, Thomas Buddle, p38.

Kingi was a smart guy. His reference to "*your* Maori King" rather than "*the/our* Maori King" suggests he saw what Tamihana could not – that Waitara was not a battle for land but for sovereignty. Kingi was smart enough to understand that his trivial land spat was indeed just a spark and that the logs of war were to be found in the King Movement – he says: "this war is about your Maori king". He understood that Browne's proclamation during the meeting of 8 March, 1859, was a demonstration of "British" sovereign power necessary as a response to the threat of the King Movement's bid for sovereign power. Prior to the King Movement, Governor after Governor had walked a fine line between asserting true sovereignty and avoiding an inevitable Maori backlash leading to a race war. The King Movement's arrival on the scene had totally changed the rules – now that there was a competitor for sovereignty Browne had no choice but to up the ante and unequivocally demonstrate that *he* was in control. That is why he could never renege on his acceptance of Teira's offer, because if he did, his claim to have sovereign power would be in tatters. With the creation of the King Movement all bets were now off – the days of Governors treading on eggshells were over – even if the result was war. There *was* no other choice.

On a personal level, in saying "your Maori King" Kingi was admitting his remaining hostility to the King Party while simultaneously calling upon it for help. He did not really "join" the King Movement at all, nor did he put the *mana* of his land under it – he was merely calling its bluff.

Kingi had, in effect, "done a Teira". Teira had taken one step backwards into oblivion and left Governor Browne to do all the legwork, prove Teira's claim, and take the flak for any decision. Now Kingi had done precisely the same and challenged the King Movement to fight on *his* behalf. What should have been a Maori to Maori affair sorted out at a personal level between Teira and Kingi had been cunningly converted into a battle for sovereignty between the two races. Governor Browne and King Potatau are left standing there looking dazed and confused, holding the baby and asking "what just happened?"

Another speaker at this May 1860 meeting was Paora of Orakei, who was not having a bar of getting involved in Taranaki and had some harsh words for the King Party into the bargain:

> "I perceive that you are very eager to pick out the errors of the Governor, but I have not discovered his error. You say that you have not seen wrong on the part of Te Rangitake [Wiremu Kingi]. I have seen his wrong doing. Letters have reached you that convict him of wrong. Yet you say you have not seen it. I repeat I have seen it, and I believe there is not a chief in Waikato that is not convinced that Te Rangitake is wrong. I have seen Wi Tako's letter addressed to you all, and that letter set my mind at rest on the subject. You have all seen that letter, and its statements should settle the question. Addressing himself particularly to W. Thompson [Tamihana] he said, I have heard of your zeal in this work, and now I see it, what is it? You have nothing to say, the sharp edge of your sayings is this day broken off. I came expecting to hear the wisdom of Solomon, but I hear it not. The edge of your work is broken. Tamati has said he is father, that may apply to the land, but to nothing further. You speak of mana, what is the mana? Where is the mana? There is no such thing as putting mana on the land, and therefore he is wrong. I came to see the work you are doing, not to oppose you, but to see for myself. I thought it might be good, but it will not do for me. You have set up a king without authority, and this is the source of all our present troubles. (Signs of disapprobation.) Ah you would silence all who do not agree with your plans."[341]

"*You have set up a king without authority, and this is the source of all our present troubles*" – Paora has hit the nail squarely on the head.

The letter of Wi Tako's to which Paora refers contained the results of the investigation he was charged with performing on his way home from the Waikato, as mentioned previously. His somewhat gnomic report reads:

> "This is a messenger from me to Waikato that they may sit in light regarding this stupid work of Taranaki. I have arrived here, and have ascertained the cause of this evil... My friends, the evil comes from

[341] *The Maori King Movement in New Zealand*, Thomas Buddle, pp51-52.

> Wi Kingi. Taranaki have also committed an evil, which is greater than all the evils of the world. Let your thoughts be right to the words you agreed upon for me, which we have seen. My friends, the work for you is only the right. Do not look towards the stupid things of the world. My friends, listen to me all of you; the evil is from before, the right is since; the only work for you is the word from the Great Father in Heaven, which is, one end of the rope is above the other end is near the ground. That must be our enemy, let these words from you be quite true to me. My friends, listen. The root of this evil is the land alone. It is not for the King. Be not tempted by the evil spirit. From your true friend in the Saviour. From Wi Tako Ngatata,"[342]

The meeting was, as one would expect, conducted in the traditional Maori manner and more concerned with providing an opportunity for everyone to express their opinions and play devil's advocate than with making decisions. Interesting as this back and forth debate might be, what – if anything – did all these diverging opinions actually mean? To get clarity we need to step back and summarise the goals and achievements of the King Party as they deliberated on their response regarding Waitara.

At the time of the King Movement's Ngaruawahia meeting in May, 1860, the Maori King has been installed for two years and his "subjects" represented perhaps 10% of the Maori population[343] concentrated in the very small area of the Upper Waikato, Taupo and parts of Taranaki. The party's stated dual goals are to establish "law and order" and to stop land-sales among its members. While appointing a figurehead to rally around is sensible enough the choice of the misunderstood title of "King" is regrettable since it marks it out as a challenger for sovereignty of the country, something that can only lead to a showdown between the two races. There *is* no other choice – if it is not a showdown sparked by

[342] *Taranaki Herald*, 14 April, 1860, p2.

[343] Say 5,000 out of the estimated 56,000 total population.

Waitara it will be sparked by something else. The mere existence of the King Party is a war waiting to happen.

In the two years since Potatau's installation there is little evidence to suggest that the King Party has made significant progress in its goal of achieving an ill-defined "law and order". Yes, some issues such as addressing adultery and drink prohibition have been tackled but it is hardly ground breaking and certainly not worth starting a war for. If Grey and Browne's attempts to introduce law and order in the form of resident magistrates and systems of District Courts had not been stellar successes then the same could equally be said of the King Movement's efforts.

And what of the King Party's performance regarding land sales in general and Waitara in particular? If over a period of two years Waitara was the first instance in which the King Party were moved to get involved in land related issues it would seem to indicate that land-sales were not exactly a hot-button issue and one wonders what all the fuss was about.

As for the King Party's response to Waitara, from a modern, Western perspective we could ask questions such as – why did the King Party not get Kingi and Teira together to state their cases? Tamihana says he "wishes to understand the case"– but he has had over a year to do this so why hasn't he? Kingi is represented at the meeting by someone called Patene – why could Kingi himself not have been there? Why was Wi Tako assigned to report on the case only to have his evidence and opinion summarily dismissed? Why did the King Party not proactively consult with the Governor/Government on the issue? The King Party criticised the Governor for not consulting *them* but life is a two way street – you can hardly expect the sovereign power to ask its potential usurper for an opinion but you *would* expect a new movement trying to raise its profile and inspire potential new members to demonstrate its strength and purpose by flexing its muscles and showing some sort of initiative for the betterment of its people.

Why was it that the only voices against the war at Waitara were European ones? Why was a vast array of would-be European experts going through the fine print of Maori lore with a fine tooth comb, trawling up arcane objections, when no one in the King Party – or any Maori – so much as mentioned them? Where was the debate about what criteria the King Party should use to determine the rights and wrongs of the Kingi/Teira case? The only recorded attempt to quantify the rules by which a decision could be made was given by Kopara:

> "The question is, was the flag [the King's flag received by Kingi's tribe referred to earlier] first or the money first? If the land was paid for, before the flag reached it, Governor is right – if not, then the matter cannot rest where it is. If the mana and flag went before we must contend for our land."[344]

Kopara's criterion for support or non-support of Kingi is not based on principles of customary Maori land ownership, of whether Kingi does or does not have right of veto as chief, or the relative merits of Kingi's or Teira's claims. It is deathly silent on all the mysterious, hypothetical lores of "seigniorial right" which various European commentators on the war are writing 100 page pamphlets about and firing back and forth at each other with gay abandon. His "reasoning" is a simple matter of whether the King has "*mana*" over the land in question or not – if he *does* have *mana* over the land, then logic, reason or questions of "right" and "wrong" have nothing to do with it, which makes a mockery of any effort by either Europeans or Maori to make it so.

As to the outcome of the May 1860 Ngaruawahia meeting itself what could be realistically expected? With such a process there could be no formal decision and the meeting ended precisely as it began – many words had been spoken, positions may have shifted but ultimately there could be no decision that could be enforced by anything other than that old standby which in English has been called "moral suasion" and which in Maori is termed "*mana*".

---

[344] Words of Kopara (*The Maori King Movement in New Zealand*, Thomas Buddle, p58).

The simple truth is that this meeting was a waste of time, for a contingent of Waikato warriors had not only already left for Taranaki to join Kingi in his fight but had done so contrary to the King's express wishes:

> "We sent messengers to Tapihana and Epiha and Waitere [leading men in the contingent on its way to Waitara] to detain them, but they would not be detained."[345]

> "But Tapihana has made all fly, [i.e., a leader in the King party gone to Taranaki has disregarded all that has been said.]"[346]

While the big wheels had been wringing their hands the Waikato horse had already bolted for Waitara. There was thus no decision that could be made and 3,000 people had met for nothing.

The King Party had entered the contest, whether it wanted to or not, and by that action Waikato had just become fair game for war.

---

[345] Words of Karaka Tomo te Whakapo (*Ibid*, p37).

[346] Words of Hoani Kingi (*Ibid*, p48).

Chapter 2.3

The "First Waikato War"

"It was a sad thing that so fine a tribe, possessing magnificent land and everything necessary to grow civilized and wealthy, should immolate itself in this ridiculous quarrel about 600 acres of land." [347]

The first shots fired against the L-Pa on March 17, 1860, marked the start of what is conventionally referred to as "The Taranaki War"[348]. While that title is to some extent accurate in that it describes *where* the war took place it is very misleading. A more accurate label would be "The First *Waikato* War", which just happened to take place in Taranaki.

When those first shots were fired it marked the start of a conflict between the might of the British Empire and what was estimated to be a maximum of 300 members of Kingi's tribe. As such it could have – and should have – been a very short, very local "skirmish", insignificant to the point of being forgotten. If that had been the case there would have been no "New

[347] *New Zealand Revisited*, J. E. Gorst, p131.

[348] Sometimes referred to as the "The *First* Taranaki War".

Zealand Wars", no land confiscations and no lasting ill-will between the races.[349]

If there is one thing that history tells us it is that it is "intervention" from non-involved parties which turns trivial, localised "spats" into catastrophic, widespread "wars".

The "no-brainer" intervenor in "Kingi's" little war was the Ngati Ruanui tribe of South Taranaki, who for reasons best known to themselves became heavily involved in the Puketapu Feuds and could therefore be relied upon to support Kingi in this latest escalation. It was in fact the Ngati Ruanui, together with the Taranaki and Ngati Rauru, rather than Kingi himself, who dealt the first acts of Maori retaliation to the attack on the L-pa with a skirmish at Waireka on 28 March, 1860.

Although the addition of these south Taranaki tribes to Kingi's forces would no doubt prolong the Waitara conflict it would at least still have been confined to Taranaki. It is the next lot of intervenors who turned the "Taranaki War" from what could have been an isolated "Taranaki War" into the first chapter of "The Zealand Wars". This second lot of intervenors were the Waikatos[350] and the first contingent were those we have already mentioned who proceeded to Taranaki in defiance of the King's instructions.

Their first major engagement was at the battle at Puketakauere *Pa* on 27 June, 1860, in which an ill-planned – or more accurately *unplanned* – attack by Major Nelson commanding a force made up largely of the 40th Regiment failed to take the *pa* and was routed with great loss and

---

[349] In all probability at least one of these things would have happened at a later stage, for similar or other reasons, but "Waitara" would not be the go-to explanation for them

[350] For simplicity this book uses the term "Waikatos" to embrace the confederation of the actual "Waikato" tribes plus Ngati Maniapoto, Ngati Haua and Wanganui tribes.

merciless ferocity by the Maori defenders.[351] With this involvement Waikato and the King Party, whether they authorised this action or not, were now official enemies of the state. Perhaps it was of some small consolation to Governor Browne and the colonial Government that if they had failed to bring Maori under sovereign control then the Maori King had fared no better with his own people, who had once again proven themselves laws unto themselves, beholden to no-one, not even to their presumed sovereign King.

The Waikatos had now officially crossed the Rubicon. It would be difficult, if not impossible, to turn back, even if they wanted to – and time would show that they did not want to. While in 1860 the war was still confined to Taranaki the Waikatos/King Party had penned the writing on their own wall for a future battle in their home territory. One wonders if they have thought this through.

Unsurprisingly this major rout of British troops at Puketakauere was a massive propaganda coup which resulted in a flood of additional Waikato warriors streaming into Taranaki to share in the glory.

By the third quarter of 1860 it is clear that it is the Waikatos who are providing the lion's share of "Kingi's" force:

> "The strength of the enemy at the Waitara was variously computed; but I think it would be fair to estimate it at 1,600 men. In a despatch, Auckland, October 2nd, 1860, I see the governor says, 2,000. They were mostly fresh arrivals [the Waikatos], the flower of the Maori nation, who had come down to join in William King's quarrel, not as his allies, but as his masters, to take the war into their own hands, boasting that they would now soon bring it to an end, and would drive the Pakeha into the sea. They most thoroughly despised William King and his tribe, as also the Southerners [Ngati Ruanui], who certainly

---

351 According to Tamati Napora the number of Waikato who took part in this event "exclusive of the natives of Kawhia, was 140, and of that party none were killed" (*Narrative of the Late War in New Zealand*, Lieutenant-Colonel Carey, p39).

were a very inferior race, and were treated by them more as slaves than as friends. And from the arrival of these powerful allies to the end of the war, what between English bullets, and the abuse and extortion of the Waikatos, the Taranakis [the Ati Awa's and specifically Kingi's men] must have led an unhappy existence"[352]

By this estimate the Waikatos represented between 50 to 70% of the Maori combatants of the "Taranaki War", for which reason, as the title of this chapter suggests, it is probably more accurate to call it "The First Waikato War" that just happened to take place in Taranaki.

But if these Waikato warriors had come to Taranaki in search of glory they were to be sadly disappointed. The great victory of Puketakauere was the first and last occasion on which they were unequivocally successful. Waikato had had its fleeting moment in the sun and it was all downhill from there on.

Early in November, 1860, our old friend Robert Parris must have been surprised to receive the following letter:

> "To Mr Parris.
>
> Pukekohe: November 1, 1860.
>
> Friend, I heard your work: come to fight with me, that is very good. Come inland, and let us meet each other. Fish fight at sea! Come inland, and let us stand on our feet. Make haste, don't prolong it. That is all I have to say to you. Make haste!
>
> From Witini Taiporutu, Porohuru, and from all the Chiefs of the Ngatihaua and Waikato." [353]

With this chivalrous and gung-ho letter the Waikato chief Witini[354] threw down the collective gauntlet of the Waikato tribes, inviting the British

[352] *Narrative of the Late War in New Zealand*, Lieutenant-Colonel Carey, p122.

[353] *Ibid*, p123.

troops to a fight. If Major Nelson can be justly accused of bravura bordering on incompetence at Puketakauere, then Witini is about to outdo him in that regard at an old, abandoned *pa* at Mahoetahi. On 8 November Witini's cheerful challenge is met and this time the routing is of the Waikatos, Witini himself being killed in the process.

From here on the war changed to one of attrition as the latest British commander, General Pratt, got smart, stopped playing Maori at their own game and started playing by his own rules. His change in *modus operandi,* from the exciting but disastrous game of attacking useless *pa* with high loss of life to the exceedingly boring but relatively safe method of sapping up to them, totally perplexed Maori who were helpless and disillusioned in the face of Pratt's relentless advance.

By March, 1861 things were looking desperate for Maori in Taranaki. They could not escape the inexorable, slow march of Pratt's saps and the Waikato losses were brutally high:

> "The enemy's loss could not be ascertained, but we buried above 120 bodies on the field; and in our advance we found large vaults, where they had buried many more. The Waikato confessed to 400 killed in all, probably not half his loss. The wounded, known to be most

---

[354] More commonly written as "Weteni". Wetini was a "chief of the Ngatihaua tribe, inferior only to Wiremu Tamihana, whose relative and close friend he was". Tamihana tried and failed to prevent Wetini and "a considerable number of his tribe" from fighting at Taranaki. It is just another example of the lack of authority and accountability not just within the King Movement but within a particular tribe – evidently Tamihana's authority as "paramount chief" over his own tribe is no better than Kingi's over his. All in all it does not reflect well on the King Movement's progress towards its stated goal of achieving "law and order". Quotes are from *The Maori King*, J. E. Gorst, p148.

> numerous, were scattered all over the country, and were not likely to encourage the martial ardour of the more peaceable races."[355]

In March, 1861, it is a year since war began and all parties are getting tired of it. Things are at a stalemate and while Pratt's sap is progressing well the inevitable outcome *must* be a stalemate, with the slipping away of the enemy into the bush at his leisure and his hour of choosing. It is like fighting shadows and there is no end in sight. It seems as if there is an opportunity here to come together and talk.

---

[355] *Narrative of the Late War in New Zealand*, Lieutenant-Colonel Carey, p192. Figures for Maori casualties are notoriously unreliable and other sources give different numbers. But if taken at face value, and using Fenton's numbers for the estimated population of Waikato, 400 dead would mean over 10% of the male population over 14 were killed, with a much larger percentage wounded. If that is the case, it is a crushing blow to Waikato.

Chapter 2-4

The Armistice that wasn't.

This chapter describes the attempts made to end what is conventionally called the "Taranaki War". Often this topic is glossed over, leaving the misleading impression that the "Taranaki War" was one isolated war caused for one set of reasons while the subsequent "Waikato War" was a separate, isolated event caused for another set of reasons. This chapter progresses the argument that the Taranaki War is more accurately seen as the "First Waikato War" which just happened to be fought in Taranaki and caused by reasons that had little or nothing to do with the Waitara Purchase. It might be *even more* accurately seen as phase one of "*the* Waikato War", a single war which took place throughout the central North Island, including Taranaki, between 1860 and 1864, all for one reason and all ultimately attributable to one person.

How exactly does one stop a war? How hard can it be? Quite difficult it seems.

In Hone Heke's War in 1846 no-one "won" the war. No armistices were signed and no reparations were made. Although he caused no further trouble Heke remained undefeated, unpunished and unrepentant.

In the wars around Wellington in 1846-1847 no-one "won" the war. No armistices were signed and no reparations were made. Although he caused no further trouble Rangihaeata remained undefeated, unpunished and unrepentant.

What, then, might we expect of any attempt to "stop" the war in Taranaki? Can we expect the losing party to actually acknowledge they are the losing party, take their punishment like a good little European country and that all will then be sweetness and light? Based on history this seems a doubtful prediction.

With the wonderful wisdom of hindsight the process for negotiation of peace at Taranaki was doomed to failure from the outset.

It seems that the negotiations to end war in Taranaki were initiated unilaterally by Wiremu Tamihana under pressure from his own people and from Bishop Selwyn:

> "The chief consideration that constrained Tamihana to visit Taranaki, was the great loss which his tribe had suffered in war, in most instances for want of a prudent leader. It was his obvious interest to endeavour to stay that slaughter of his people, which threatened soon to destroy his own influence and importance. He determined to go, however, not as a belligerent, but as a peacemaker".[356]

> "At the time we were fighting at the Waitara your (plural) letters came to me, and they said, "William, go and make peace." There was no question in them about the king. Therefore I went and made peace.[357]

This touching theory of Tamihana as "peacemaker" is, however, contrary to his subsequent actions which, as we shall see, virtually guaranteed the

---

[356] *The Maori King*, J. E. Gorst, p158.

[357] Tamihana to Selwyn, meeting at Peria, 11 Oct 1862 (*Colonist*, 13 January, 1863, p3).

destruction not only of his own tribe but of every tribe in the central North Island.

It is difficult to know what Tamihana thought might be accomplished by negotiations at this point in the conflict.[358] When he arrived at Taranaki the military situation was if not a zero-all draw then at least a stalemate in which no side had a clear advantage over the other. While both sides might be heartily sick of the war neither of them was likely to give up everything they had fought and died for. As one newspaper put it:

> "...no prestige has as yet been won in the field which can enable the representative of her Majesty, or those acting in his name, to speak with that weight with which rebels ought to be addressed, who imagine that they have a right to treat for peace, whilst in reality they are only entitled to sue for pardon."[359]

Tamihana's negotiations were therefore doomed from the start.[360]

It is a rather tangled process to follow. The negotiations – if they can be called that took place over a period of months under conditions of considerable secrecy.[361] Newspaper accounts over the March-June period of 1861 faithfully report the raising and lowering of truce flags and

---

[358] There is a theory that Tamihana wanted "an appeal made to the Queen and Imperial Parliament" over the Waitara issue and that he would abide by their decision whatever it was. Based on his future actions in which he shows time and again that he will bow to no "man" but God that seems a highly unlikely outcome. Quote is from *The Maori King*, J. E. Gorst, p158

[359] *Southern Cross*, 19 March, 1861, p3. Selwyn should have appreciated this and let the Government decide when the time was right for peace making.

[360] Gorst notes that after the negotiations "...At Mokau, Tamihana's followers broke out into open complaints, and bitterly upbraided him with an ill-timed and useless interference in the war." *The Maori King*, J. E. Gorst, p166.

[361] "The real fault lies, and it is one heavy enough, in letting week after week pass away with no information, no word to the settlers as to their future prospects except what they darkly gather from this strange publication. No government has a right to tax the confidence of its subjects so severely. A few

the coming and going of various dignitaries but are unable to do anything other than speculate as to what might actually be happening.

It is clear that in March, 1861 Maori in no way see themselves as defeated and consequently expect that it is the Europeans who will have to concede to *their* terms rather than vice versa.

The tone of the first meeting with Tamihana confirms this view:

> "On Wednesday [13 March 1861], a flag of truce was hoisted by the rebels [Maori], in order to the proposal of terms of accommodation, and a meeting took place between Mr. Commissioner G. D. Hay, of the Native Department, and Wm. Thompson [Tamihana], who appears to be acting in this matter to some extent as a mediator between the contending parties. Thompson, who had been in communication with Te Rangitake [Wiremu Kingi], first proposed the following conditions of peace: "The Waikatos to return to their own country, Wm. King to Mataitawa, and the troops to Waitoki, and the land at Waitara to remain undisturbed until some final decision should be arrived at."
>
> A long discussion ensued upon this, William Thompson evidently wishing to assume that the only question at issue was the title to the land at Waitara, apparently forgetting that the Waikatos and other tribes had joined the rebels without a shadow of a pretext, whilst Mr. Hay pointed out that Thompson himself had been much to blame in the whole affair personally as the prime mover in the land league.
>
> Thompson reiterated his desire for peace, but by no means in the language of a penitent rebel: on the contrary, he complained that there was a desire to impose harsh terms, and so far from wishing to give material guarantees for future good conduct, expressed his intention of acting in the same manner should a similar case occur elsewhere in the purchase of land. He assumed his right of

---

days – perhaps a few hours – will dissipate the mist of Celtic diplomacy and shew us our deliverance." (*Taranaki Herald*, 6 April, 1861, p2).

interference, and declared that he would fight wherever land was sold by the wrong people.

Mr. Hay of course pointed out the absurdity of supposing that the Governor would be willing to make peace without having some guarantee that it would be kept by the Maories and that war would not break out again elsewhere in a few months. Thompson, unconvinced, then proposed that the troops and the Waikatos should remain where they were, and that he and Mr. Hay should proceed to Auckland, the former by land and the latter by sea, and should meet at Tuakau so as to be able, we presume, to discuss terms at headquarters.

The Commissioner, finding that Thompson was not likely to accede to any reasonable terms, retired; but subsequently again visited the native chief, who, after complaining that the Government was harsh and difficult to deal with, brought forward a third proposition – namely, to remain in peace at Taranaki till the Governor was communicated with and entreated to go down there. Mr. Hay gave him to understand that, in his opinion, it was not likely that his Excellency would do so, and the negotiations broke up; but subsequently, a letter was forwarded to Thompson recapitulating the terms which Government would be willing to grant, and requesting the natives' ultimatum by the following Friday morning.

We are not aware whether any further communication took place, but no terms were arrived at, as the guns had opened fire on the pa again, on Friday, when the "Victoria" left. We understand that his Excellency wished to have gone to Taranaki himself, on receipt of the above news, but it was not considered advisable for him to do so, as his presence, it is presumed, would be more likely to retard than advance the conclusion of a peace.

Mr McLean has consequently been sent down to Taranaki, in the "Victoria" and directed to communicate with Thompson and King;

> and, if there is any prospect of their at last agreeing to reasonable terms, the sloop will be sent back for the Governor..." [362]

An article in the *New Zealander* newspaper gives an excellent summary of the "peace making" process:

> "The great losses which his tribe had suffered, in many instances for want of a prudent leader, weighed strongly in Thompson's mind, and was perhaps the paramount consideration which prompted him to visit the scene of conflict, and endeavour to stay that destruction of his tribe which would soon destroy his own influence and importance. In the early part of the present year [1861] he was also urged to visit Waitara as a peace-maker: he did not doubt the injustice of the Governor to William King in the purchase of Teira's land; and although he readily agreed that it was right for King, if he considered himself wronged, to appeal to law, and not to arms, he maintained that the Governor's haste and rashness had forced on and commenced a war, leaving William King no option in the matter; still he felt that it was by no means certain that the Home [British] government would back up the proceedings of the Governor; he was aware that the Duke of Newcastle's [the current Colonial Secretary of State] absence in America had postponed the examination of the Waitara question; so that after all the war going on at Taranaki might be a useless waste of life and property. He therefore resolved to go down and propose to William King and the other fighting chiefs that all hostilities should be stopped, and an appeal made to the Queen and the Imperial Parliament. If they wished to have the title investigated by law, it should be so investigated, but if they upheld the Governor's policy, it would be time enough to fight then.[363] With these designs he left Waikato at the end of February, in direct opposition (it may be added) to the wishes of the Maori King, who throughout steadily and

---

[362] *Southern Cross*, 19 March, 1861, p3.

[363] Clearly an appeal to the "Queen and the Imperial Parliament" is a complete waste of time since Tamihana will not honour the outcome if the decision goes against him.

constantly opposed all going to Taranaki whatever, whether for peace or war.

William Thompson arrived at the Waitara on Monday the 11th March... The greater part of Tuesday was taken up in talking over those Waikato chiefs who had already taken part in the war, and who, when Thompson's pacific intentions were made known, cried and shouted against them. It was already afternoon before the desired unanimity among the Waikatos had been attained – a message was then sent to Rangitake [Wiremu Kingi] to desire a talk, which was at the request of that chief fixed for the following morning.

On Wednesday morning a meeting of Thompson's party, the fighting Waikatos and William King's tribe, took place. The proceedings were opened by Thompson, who declared the reasons which had led him to Waitara; he had been desirous to visit the fighting chiefs, and particularly Rangitake, and to inquire into the causes of the quarrel: he was quite satisfied that the cause of the quarrel was not Waikato's but Rangitake's.

> "No", said Rangitake [Kingi], interrupting him, "neither Waitara nor the quarrel is mine, they are yours."
>
> "No", retorted Thompson, "they are yours."
>
> "No, they are yours".
>
> "Why look at a man", continued Thompson, "his head is head, his hands are hands, and his legs, legs: you are the head, Waikato is the legs".
>
> "No, you are the head."
>
> "No, you"
>
> "Yes!" said William King - "I am the head, Waitara is mine, the quarrel is mine. There! I give Waitara to you."

This is an illuminating exchange indeed. While it is perhaps dangerous, arrogant and futile to try to decipher such an allegorical dialog in the present this seems to be saying some puzzling things. Could it really be possible that a full year after fighting began this is the first time that Kingi and Tamihana have met and discussed it? That seems so incredible as to be unbelievable but clearly, a year later and just as he has come to make peace, Tamihana is still confused as to the rights and wrongs of Kingi's case. Second, he seems to be saying that right or wrong it is not the King Movement's problem, which in turn confirms that Kingi has not passed the "*mana* of the land" to the King. The dialogue itself gives the final confirmation of this – that it is at this point – a year after the war started – that Kingi finally passes the "*mana* of the land" to the King Movement.

The *New Zealander* continues its story:

> "He [Kingi] further declared that his gift of the land [or the *mana* of it, to the King Movement] was free and unreserved, and that he claimed no further voice whatever in its disposal. Hapurona [Kingi's fighting chief], who since has made a separate peace with the Governor, and the various Waikato and Ngatimaniapoto Chiefs were successively challenged, and publicly announced their assent to Wm. King's gift, and their willingness that the unreserved disposal of the land should be yielded to William Thompson.
>
> He [Tamihana] then announced his award - "Waikato!" said he "back to Waikato! Ngatiawa! away to Mataitawa! Ngatiruanui! return to your homes! Let the soldiers be taken back to New Plymouth; Waitara shall be left under the protection of the law".
>
> A letter was sent the same evening to the General [Pratt] to propose a cessation of hostilities on both sides, and that the land question should be reserved for the decision of the great Runanga [of the King Movement].
>
> An interview took place on Thursday morning between Thompson and an officer of the Native Department; the former repeated his proposals and begged that the troops might be at once taken back to New Plymouth; he was told that the Governor alone had power to order such a step, and was invited if really desirous of making peace to proceed by ship to Auckland. "What", asked Thompson, "was the crime of Rauparaha? and what was the crime of Pomare? These men's crimes were mere trifles; I am a very bad man, far worse than either of

them: I am both a King maker and the head of this quarrel: I dare not go on board your ship, lest I should be treated as Rauparaha and Pomare were". He offered to go by land and meet the Governor at Tuakau, the nearest point of the Waikato river to Auckland.

...As it was found impossible to persuade the Chief to adventure himself into our power, it was at last agreed that his proposals should be sent by steamer to the Governor at Auckland. The General would not agree to a suspension of hostilities until an answer should be received; Thompson in vain urged the desirability of saving human life, the General replied that it would be a waste of time, that firing would re-commence on the following morning.

On Friday morning our white flag had disappeared, but that of the Maories, was, by Thompson's orders, kept flying. The soldiers entered the sap and commenced digging: no opposition was offered. They proceeded to fire upon the Maori pa. "Now", said Thompson to the fighting chiefs, "do what you please." The white flag was hauled down, and the war flag hoisted, firing continued on both sides during that day, Saturday and Sunday.

... On Monday, Mr. McLean the Native Secretary arrived, and had an interview with Thompson, he had not brought the Governor's consent to the troops being taken away from Waitara. Thompson was much annoyed, and asked what he had come for, he thought the Governor was very foolish, however, he would have no more to do with Waitara, he had ordered all the Maories to disperse, Waitara was left under the protection of the law and he should return to Waikato forthwith. Mr. McLean said that if the various tribes would cease hostilities and disperse, the Governor would treat with them separately: he would deal with William King and the Ngatiawa at Waitara; with the Ngatiruanui and Taranakis, at New Plymouth; and would meet Wm. Thompson at Mangere, a village a few miles from Auckland, to settle the affairs of Waikato. There were four matters to be disposed of; (1) the disputed land at Waitara (2) the murders (3) the property of settlers that had been destroyed or plundered (4), the Maori King.

> Thompson returned from Waitara, mortified and disappointed; he went down with intentions friendly to the English, desirous of distinction no doubt, but of the distinction of a peace-maker; his advances were rejected, he was accused of promoting war and rebellion, he was forced into the position of a belligerent though he had never fired a shot; and came back under a threat of war. After visiting several tribes on and near the Waikato to ascertain their sentiments about the surrender of the Maori King, he settled quietly down at Tamahere, hoisted a white flag, and waited for the Governor's next move."[364]

By 20 March, 1861, all Maori participants in the war had dispersed[365] and were waiting on the Governor to submit terms of surrender for their consideration. There was a temporary and tenuous peace in Taranaki which could be broken at any moment by any one or all of the participants.

As stated by McLean Browne's strategy was to treat with the three groups of participants – the Ati Awa[366], the Waikatos and the Ngati Ruanui – separately – which at first sight seems needlessly complex but on further reflection is not only fair but unavoidable.

---

[364] *New Zealander*, 3 August, 1861, p3.

[365] The Waikatos are reported to have left for home on this date (*Taranaki Herald*, 23 March, 1861, p3). Kingi's /Hapurona's Ati Awa warriors had "retired to some distance inland of Mataiwa... and that the Taranaki, Ngatiruanui and Wanganui tribes have left the district and dispersed" (*New Zealander*, 23 March, 1861, p2).

[366] Although the term "Ati Awa" is generally used in this context it is Wiremu Kingi's hapu, or possibly all four "Waitara" hapu, who are the nominal "enemy". The role of other "Ati Awa" factions such as the Puketapu and Ngamotu in the war is less clear. Similarly, although the term "Waikatos" is generally used, it was actually Tamihana's Ngati Haua tribe, and the Ngati Maniapoto tribes, who supplied the bulk of the "Waikato" fighting force in Taranaki.

It is fair because in Browne's view each of these three participants played different roles and behaved in different manners and therefore should be punished according to their respective "crimes". The Ati Awa were considered the nominal enemy, seen as fighting honourably for a cause and therefore were to be treated with relative leniency and respect. The Ngati Ruanui were seen as opportunists who had killed civilians and plundered mercilessly and who deserved the severest punishment. The Waikatos were also seen as interlopers in a cause that was not their own but who had at least behaved with some respect.

And it is unavoidable because more pragmatically there was no single authority that could represent all three groups.

Browne's terms for the Ati Awa (or possibly only the "Waitara" component thereof) were:

> "Hapurona and Ngatiawa,
>
> For twelve months you have been carrying arms against Her Majesty the Queen and the authority of the law; you have now laid down your arms and expressed your desire for peace; believing you to be sincere, I have come from Auckland for the purpose of stating the terms upon which it will be granted, and upon which Her Majesty's gracious pardon and protection will be extended to you.
>
> They are as follows:—
>
> 1. The investigation of the Title, and the survey of the land at Waitara to be continued and completed without interruption.
> 2. Every man to be permitted to state his claims without interference, and my decision or the decision of such persons as I shall appoint, to be conclusive.
> 3. All the land in possession of Her Majesty's forces belonging to those who have borne arms against Her Majesty to be disposed of by me as I may think fit.
> 4. All guns belonging to the Government to be returned.
> 5. All plunder taken from the settlers to be forthwith restored.

6. The Ngatiawa who have borne arms against the Government must submit to the Queen and to the authority of the law, and not resort to force for the redress of wrongs, real or imaginary.

7. As I did not use force for the acquisition of land, but for the vindication of the law, and for the protection of Her Majesty's native subjects in the exercise of their just rights, I shall divide the land which I have stated my intention to dispose of, amongst its former owners, but I shall reserve the sites of the blockhouses and redoubts and a small piece of land round each for the public use, and shall exercise the right of making roads through the Waitara district. In conformity with the declaration made on the 29th of November, 1859, the rights of those who may prove their title to any part of the piece of land at Waitara will be respected.

On your submission to these terms you will come under the protection of the law and enjoy your property, both lands and goods, without molestation." [367]

Our first question might be – why was this ultimatum not addressed to Kingi himself – surely as presumed "paramount chief" of Ati Awa he would be the man to sign it off? In fact, although in the literature the "Waitara insurgents" are commonly referred to by phrases such as "Kingi's forces", as if to suggest that Kingi himself was personally leading his men, Kingi was throughout this period generally nowhere to be seen and living in safety either in Ngati Maniapoto or Ngati Maru territory. In fact it was Wiremu Kingi's "fighting chief" – Hapurona ("Absalom") Pukerimu – who was the man on the spot doing Kingi's fighting for him in Taranaki, facing the bullets.

Browne's ultimatum was signed off by Hapurona in a document dated 8 April, 1861[368] but as was entirely predictable his signature, or indeed anyone's signature, meant absolutely nothing. Kingi himself did not

[367] "Copy of the terms offered by the Governor to the Waitara insurgents" (AJHR 1861, Session 1, E-01b, p4).

[368] *Ibid*, p5.

agree[369] and, as was traditional in a system which had no law and order beyond that obtainable by "*mana*" or "moral suasion", it was every man for himself. Browne no doubt realised this even as he was drafting his ultimatum but he could only try.

The terms in Browne's ultimatum for the Ngati Ruanui and Taranaki tribes were, as intimated, more draconian. Since these tribes are largely irrelevant to our story we will say only that, knowing the intractable nature of the Ngati Ruanui as he did, Browne must surely have known that in writing his ultimatum he was wasting his time, his breath and his ink. The Ngati Ruanui "response" to Browne's ultimatum was as inevitable as night follows day – namely silence.

To complete his trifecta of useless ultimatums Browne addressed the final – and most crucial one – to the "Waikatos". While the other two ultimatums focused on conditions to ending conflict in Taranaki this ultimatum was entirely different, tackling as it did the big picture issue on which the fate of the entire country rested – that of the King Party's contesting of British sovereignty. For this reason Browne's third ultimatum was addressed not to the "Waikatos" but to the "Natives assembled at Ngaruawahia"– in other words, specifically to the King Party[370].

In this letter Browne makes the issue of sovereignty crystal clear, claiming that with the creation of the King Movement:

> "An authority has been set up inconsistent with allegiance to the Queen, and in violation of the Treaty of Waitangi."[371]

---

369 There are various accounts of Kingi's involvement in this "peace making" process. As we have seen, Gorst has him personally involved and quotes an interesting dialogue with Kingi. Other accounts however mention Kingi as sending his daughter on his behalf, while others imply he is uninvolved and simply absent.

370 See Appendix 5 for the full text of Browne's terms.

371 AJHR, 1861, Session 1, E-01B, p11.

He lists what "submission to Her Majesty's sovereignty" requires, and demands both "submission without reserve" and restoration of or compensation for plunder taken during the Taranaki war. His ultimatum is extremely clear both in meaning and in the implied consequences that *must* arise should it not be complied with. With Waitara Browne has already shown he is not a man to be messed with and the meaning is clear – failure to comply *will* bring war.

The King Party duly responded to Browne's ultimatum not as one might expect with a single, unified response representing the collective will of the people but with at least *two* responses.[372] The response from the King's *runanga* – what one might have expected to be the "official" King Movement reply – was reasonable in tone and relatively short, calling for calm, communication and co-operation and with absolutely no undertones of hostility. It is a masterful work of diplomacy which cunningly makes precisely zero reference to Browne's ultimatum. But even if it does not really advance or clarify anything it is at least positive and encouraging in its calls for better communication on the part of *both* parties.

The second response to Browne's ultimatum is a solo effort from Tamihana himself[373] and is a letter of a very different colour. It is, as befits Tamihana's style, a much longer letter, complete with an elliptical song and copious Bible references. But as letters from a humbled, defeated man go, it is not one. Browne was expecting a simple yes or no answer, not an argument, a justification or a tirade. If it is not openly hostile it is implacably defiant, a letter of no give and take whatsoever – Tamihana is adamant he is 100% correct on every subject and that everything he or the King Party has done is right while everything Browne and the Government

---

[372] See Appendix 5.

[373] See Appendix 6. This letter is included to give the reader an insight into the unique mind of Tamihana and to demonstrate the completely different planes of communications and logic European and Maori were operating on. Given the two parties were essentially from other planets it makes one wonder why it took so long for war to break out.

have done is wrong. There is not a thing he would change and he knows the Bible, and the worlds, both Maori and European, better than anyone. He will not negotiate, not budge a millimetre. An irresistible force has met an immovable object.

Tamihana's letters are always interesting and very distinctive. His communication style is the complete opposite of Wiremu Kingi's, which if frustratingly sparse, is at least honest and to the point – Kingi will not give up Waitara for the simple reason that he chooses not to and for reasons of sentiment, something that anyone can relate to. Tamihana, on the other hand, gives us chapter and verse – literally – and in the process reveals his "logic" to be specious, flawed and contradictory.

Tamihana denies any obligation to the Treaty of Waitangi, something he must surely understand makes him an immediate enemy of the state. Unsurprisingly there had been much speculation and many disparate views – as much in the Maori world as the European one – as to how exactly this new "Maori Kingdom" might interact with and co-exist with the European world. The optimists have hypothesised a "Maori Kingdom" *within* the "European system". Tamihana's letter, however, removes any possibility of this rose-tinted possibility – he is adamant that he wants to create a *separate* Maori nationality and he will not entertain any compromise or combination that involves Europeans. Those dirty words "amalgamation" and "assimilation" are off the table and into the bin. The judge's decision is final and no correspondence will be entered into.

Since Tamihana personally, and his emissaries, have been scouring the entire country for new converts to the King Movement it is clear he is not thinking in terms of what might be called either a Maori "province" or even a small Maori "Kingdom" within the wider country of New Zealand – his goal seems to be a complete *nationwide* Maori Kingdom, or worst case a complete North Island Kingdom, in which the fate of Europeans is left unspoken and undefined. Tamihana must still have his King, even though the King who took two years to select has in the meantime inconsiderately died and been replaced by his son, someone of limited *mana* and who has no influence as a "Maori King". Indeed conspicuous by its absence throughout this critical period is *any* communication from or about this fabled must-have King, who seems to be missing in action but is none the less mysteriously the key to everything.

It seems that Tamihana is not just the kingmaker but the de-facto King, writing parallel letters that can only cause confusion and make a mockery of what should be the one and only, official response of the *runanga,* of Tamihana's presumed sovereign state. The Maori Kingdom seems to be his personal fiefdom and he is beholden to nothing and no one but God, and even then, to his own personal interpretation of God.

Browne and his representatives have had the decency to acknowledge and respect the Maori decision-making process which to them involves interminable meetings the outcome of which no one takes any notice of anyway. Tamihana on the other hand fails to acknowledge European protocol and castigates Browne personally for what he perceives to be his indecent haste in taking *only a year* to investigate the Waitara purchase.

A few months prior to writing this letter Tamihana went to Taranaki with the ostensible goal of stopping a few of his people getting killed. Now, it seems, he is happy to unilaterally commit the entire Maori race to destruction. He does not seem to understand that he is not holding the winning hand and that the price for his arrogance and intransigence is the potential death of his race.

While we can understand Tamihana's position and empathise with his passion and motives we can also sense that he is possibly not the best person to advance the Maori cause and that he is on the brink of singlehandedly and unilaterally martyring his people.

If Browne had received only the *runanga's* response to his ultimatum things might have turned out very differently. The *runanga's* response, vague and noncommittal as it is, is something Browne can work with but Tamihana's alternative response of unremitting hostility is definitely not. Tamihana is clearly at odds with the *runanga* and seems to have assumed the role not so much of King as of dictator. This is something Browne *cannot* work with.

Browne acknowledges his perception that Tamihana is the de-facto "Maori King" in his reports to his bosses back in England, in which he refers to Tamihana's letter rather than that of the *runanga's:*

> "Tamihana's reply must convince the most sceptical that the purchase of land at the Waitara was the excuse and not the cause of the war; that its real cause was a deep-rooted longing for separate nationality, which had been growing for years, and could never have been stifled by palliatives of any sort: and there is every reason to believe that it has spread far and wide throughout the South of this Island. All doubt, therefore, is now at an end; and it is evident that, if the Maoris will not submit, this part of the Colony must be abandoned by all who will not yield obedience to Maori Law, of which the aptest symbol is the tomahawk."[374]

Browne has tried his best but he is back at square one again, only worse. Waitara was a nothing affair involving 600 acres in Taranaki which would have been over long ago had it not become embroiled and conflated with what is clearly the major issue – the King Party and its pursuit of a separate sovereignty. Diplomacy has failed. The Waikato *runanga's* more optimistic and diplomatic response has been overruled by Tamihana's belligerent and immovable one and there can now be no other resolution than war, but this time directed solely towards the prime and clear offender – the Waikatos, or more specifically, the King Party.

With Tamihana throwing the gauntlet down Browne prepares for not just a continuation of the war but an escalation to subjugate Tamihana's would-be sovereignty. With Taranaki at least temporally under control he gathers his troops in Auckland for the dual purposes of offensive action against the Waikatos and defensive action in protecting that extremely vulnerable city against incursions from the Waikato Maori who are alarmingly close:

---

[374] "Copy of a despatch from His Excellency Governor Gore Browne to his Grace the Duke, 6th July, 1861" (AJHR 1862, E01, p21).

> "Immediately after the truce was made, in May, 1861, the Governor called on the natives by proclamation, to make submission and take the oath of allegiance. Very few did; and as the year wore on he made his intention known of invading Waikato, to compel submission and punish those tribes which had joined in the Taranaki disturbances. The Assembly met again in June, 1861. It was now winter, but by September (the New Zealand spring) it was understood operations would commence. General Cameron had arrived and had expressed his anxiety to find some employment for his soldiers. To the old colonists of the Northern Island the prospect was most gloomy, particularly to those in its southern portion. We were well aware of the preparations which the natives had made for war; we knew that we ourselves were entirely unprepared, almost without arms, untrained, unorganized, and scattered over large tracts, with our families and properties exposed to attack on every side. The Wellington members sought an interview with the Governor, and asked him if it was true that he intended to invade Waikato. He said it was, and that he had no doubt that the first shot fired there would be the signal for a general rising [by Maori] all over the island. We called his attention to our unprepared and unprotected state. He said we must build redoubts and defend ourselves, as the colonists at Taranaki had done. As that settlement had been swept as bare as the floor, we thought this a poor prospect, and told him so. He replied that "War is not made with rose-water."[375]

The *Daily Southern Cross's* take on the situation gives what one presumes to be a typical contemporary view of this "armistice that wasn't an armistice" and lays out what seems a predictable and pessimistic view of what must inevitably follow:

> "Much as we have always desired to see the natives recognise the necessity of submission, and thus save the country from the horrors of war, we were never sanguine on the subject; and, though we believe

[375] *The Waikato War, 1863-4,* John Featon, p11.

no formal refusal has been received by the Government, enough has transpired as to the intentions of the natives, and the line of conduct which they intend to adopt, to convince us that, whilst hoping for the best, we have not been wrong in apprehending the worst – that the natives will elect for what is unmistakeably a suicidal policy on their part.

A few days will prove that they have done this: that they have refused terms granted in a spirit of liberality almost Quixotic, and that they are determined to abide by the consequences of their refusal. For the present, however, we need not anticipate any overt acts of rebellion, beyond the hoisting of King's flags in various parts of the country. The natives, whilst braving the Queen's power, are aware of the advantages derivable from their not being the first to strike a blow; they acted on this principle at Taranaki, where, when insult and provocation had gone so far that it became necessary to resort to strong measures, they found Europeans ready to support them against those who, in self-defence, were forced to become aggressors.

The Waikatos choose to consider that, so long as they are not actually in arms against us, we ought to leave them to their own devices – that their country is tapu – that they may hoist what flag they like, so long as they are not fighting under it, with impunity. In short, they consider themselves an independent nation, lately at war with us; and they are willing to revert to the former state of things without any formal treaty of peace, because their common sense tells them that we have a right to demand some material guarantee that we shall not be subject to any such wanton attacks for the future. They feel that such a right must be recognised if they once enter into negotiations, whilst they are totally unable, with all their ingenuity, to raise any counter claim as a set-off. They sullenly refuse to treat, and, misled probably by false friends[376], imagine that they cannot be dealt with in another and more summary manner.

---

[376] Unspecified but almost certainly alluding to Bishop Selwyn, Octavius Hadfield, William Martin and their acolytes.

The natives, however, have learnt from their European supporters the art of defending rebellion with pretty plausible, but very impudent arguments. They actually urge, we are informed on reliable authority, that their King's flag is a symbol of an authority and of a law, of which we never would give them the benefit: that we neglected our duty in this respect, and that for their own self-protection they have been obliged to undertake the duty themselves.

The idea is evidently not Maori. It smacks of a document called Renata, and a locality called Te Aute; but it shows us what we have to expect in the struggle impending. Open savage warfare, and concealed European influence; murder, and justified on the ground that it is committed by men anxious for social improvement and frustrated in their aspirations after it by the Queen's Government. The natives, or rather those who put their ideas into shape, are very indignant that European law has not been introduced into their country, although they refused to receive it except in particular cases where it suited their purpose. They taunt the British Government with not having given them laws, and attempt thereby to justify their own conduct in rebelling; forgetting that it is their own fault that law and order are at present unknown in Waikato.

The British authorities in the Colony wisely abstained from attempting to enforce law till they knew that they had the power of enforcing it; and these clever rebels, white[377] and black, now presume on the unavoidable impunity which has hitherto followed disobedience, to tell us that we have neglected our duty, that we have not given them the protection of the law, that they are justified in setting up a rival government, and in hoisting a rival flag.

The day has passed for such arguments. The interesting race is becoming a very dangerous race, and their interesting – we will not say interested – supporters a very objectionable set of men. We hope that the Waikatos may soon be taught what it is to refuse the

---

[377] Another unsubtle dig at Selwyn and his cronies.

clemency of the Crown, and their European advocates what it is to interfere between the Crown and rebels."[378]

[378] *Daily Southern Cross*, 11 June 1861, p3

Chapter 2.5

When the Gods wish to punish us they answer our prayers.

We have now reached an "and the rest is history" moment. The stage is set, the fuse has been laid and lit and it is just a matter of following the spark as it wends its leisurely and inevitable way towards a very large barrel of gunpowder. Yes, there will be points at which the fuse could possibly have been stamped out by one or both parties but it has been a long time in the making and the momentum is just too great to be stopped.[379] We have followed the story long enough, and know the lead characters well enough, to predict what *must* happen next, so we will give only the barest of summaries of the ensuing proceedings:

---

[379] Readers who know a little about this era might be saying – hang on a minute – what about Grey's building of the Great South Road? What about Grey's oft-quoted hoary chestnut of "I will dig around him [the Maori King] until he falls"? What about the disputed schools/barracks at Te Kohekohe and Gorst's printing press? What about War parties and Peace parties? What about this, or that? These events are interesting but irrelevant. If Browne had not been replaced by Grey the invasion of the Waikato would have begun in the spring of 1861. The period of 1860 to 1864 is like a game of rugby between Waikato and the Crown. The first half was played in Taranaki and ended with a nil-all draw. At half time the contestants regrouped, regained their strength and reviewed their strategies. In July 1863 the game resumed, this time in Waikato itself.

- In April, 1861, hostilities in Taranaki "cease". It is however an "arming truce" in which both parties prepare for a continuation of war. The imminent approach of winter means that any action by either party will have to wait for spring.
- On July 27, 1861, Browne learns that his term as Governor has not been extended and that his successor will be Sir George Grey.
- In September, 1861 Grey arrives as Browne's replacement, handily provided with unprecedented funding never available to Browne.
- Grey halts Browne's plans to invade the Waikato and adopts the policy of simultaneously attempting to avoid further war by meeting King Party needs while preparing for war should that fail – a "hope for the best but plan for the worst" policy. While it is a somewhat self-defeating approach he would have been a fool to do otherwise – none of the three belligerents of the Taranaki War have agreed to the terms of surrender and the only other option is immediate war.
- Kingi refuses to have the situation at Waitara investigated:

> "The Waitara still remained in the occupation of our troops, and Wiremu Kingi was obstinate in his determination to reject all proposals for investigation into the title. It was in vain that his European friends, who had upheld his cause against the late Governor, represented that their advocacy had been based on the assumption that no opportunity had been given him of appealing to any impartial tribunal, and that, such an opportunity being now offered, his refusal to avail himself of it was shaming all who had supported him. Wiremu was stolidly indifferent to every remonstrance. "Waitara is in my hands. I will not give it up" was his ultimatum to Colonel Browne, and it was his ultimatum still. His reply to everyone who argued the question with him was, "If Governor Grey wants peace, let him give back Waitara to me."[380]

---

[380] *The Maori King*, J. E. Gorst, p286

- On 4 April, 1863, the colonist-owned Tataraimaka Block, taken by the Ngati Ruanui during the earlier Taranaki War and not yet returned, is occupied by British troops under instructions from Grey.

- In late April 1863 Grey finds "new evidence" he believes vindicates Kingi's claim to Waitara and lobbies the Government to abandon the Waitara purchase and return it to its former owners. The import and relevance of this "new evidence" are disputed by ex-Governor Browne and much debated among senior Government figures

- On 4 May 1863 Grey's "new evidence" becomes instantly moot when a party of soldiers from the Tataraimaka Camp is ambushed by the Ngati Ruanui and 8 men are killed.

- On 12 June, 1863, after two years of an armed truce during which both "sides" prepare for war, General Cameron begins the subjugation of the Waikato working from North to South. There are battles at Koheroa, Meremere, Rangiriri and Orakau.

- By April, 1864, the Waikato is subjugated and its population disperses, the majority into Ngati Maniapoto territory south of the Puniu River which will subsequently become known as the King Country.

- On 6 April, 1864 the Pai Marire movement gains instant infamy by slaughtering Captain Lloyd and 6 of his men at Oakura in Taranaki. The "HauHau Wars" have now officially begun and the movement spreads throughout central North Island to the East Coast.

- In April, 1864 the war shifts from Waikato to the Bay of Plenty for precisely the same reasons it spread from Taranaki to Waikato – because Bay of Plenty Maori have supplied both men and supplies to Waikato they have become the new target. Such has always been the fate of intervenors throughout history. There are battles at Gate Pa and Te Ranga.

- On 17 December, 1864 Governor Grey issues a proclamation calling for confiscation of large areas of Waikato and Ngati Haua land, that of the Ngati Maniapoto curiously escaping this fate.

- On 27 May, 1865 Tamihana formally "makes peace" during a meeting with General Cary at Tamahere. However like all such Maori "armistices" it means nothing since in 1865 – seven years after the installation of a King for the specific purpose of creating a Maori "sovereignty" – there is still no King party "government" structure or single authority who can sign unequivocally on its behalf. Tamihana's "submission" thus applies only to himself personally.

- From June, 1868 until February, 1869 Titokowaru and his followers wreak havoc in the south Taranaki district in what is known as "Titokowaru's War".

- In July, 1868 Te Kooti, a suspected Hauhau exiled to the Chatham Islands, returns to New Zealand with many followers, leading to massacres at Matawhero and Matata and generally causing mayhem in the eastern and central North Island until 1872.

Thus ended the ten-plus years of what is now collectively referred to as "The New Zealand Wars" although arguably the wars of Te Kooti and Titokowaru could be considered as "personal wars" along the lines of Heke's War rather than part of a more general war.

The terms Browne had tried and failed to achieve at the abortive "conclusion" of the Taranaki Wars were, as conditions of surrender go, very generous, with no punitive measures as such. While pledging submission "to the Queen and to the authority of the law" may have been a bitter pill for a "rebel" to swallow it was no more than what the great majority of Maori – the "Queenites" – were already very happily doing.

At the end of what is often referred to as the "Waikato War"[381] component of the "The New Zealand Wars" things are different. Unlike the early 1861 stalemate situation of Taranaki, in June 1864 there is now a clear winner and a clear loser. This time around there will be no negotiations and the winner will call whatever shots he wants. Throughout history – including

[381] Which although not taking place in "Waikato" includes the associated actions at Gate Pa and Te Ranga in the Bay of Plenty.

Maori history – punitive measures are always taken in this situation to hammer home the lesson that actions have consequences, a lesson which in the case of Maori – of all people – should not have been necessary because *utu* is exactly that – every action has a consequence and there are no freebies in life.

In the present we hear a lot about Maori *tikanga* and customary usage, as if they are unique to Maori. They are not – every country and every culture that has ever existed has its own "*tikanga*" and own customary usage.

We have already remarked that given that there are only a few principles which allow a culture to thrive, the various "*tikangas*" of the world must have a lot of commonalities. The universal, customary rule of reciprocity, called in Maori *utu*, is an example. Another example of "universal customary usage" is confiscation. Confiscation has always been the universal and time honoured punitive measure imposed on the losing party after war everywhere in the world. In Maori culture confiscation is no more and no less than the Maori principle of *take raupatu*. If Te Rauparaha – who evidence suggests was at least an honourable rogue as well as the world's foremost authority on *raupatu* – was alive today it is hard to imagine that his reaction to the post-war confiscations would not be a shrug and a "Well, what did you expect?"

Confiscation is, of course, a non-ideal, two-edged sword, since the long-term legacy of land confiscation is invariably a deep-seated hatred and resentment which only increases with time and which *must* erupt sometime in the future. On the other hand, as demonstrated by the non-armistice of Taranaki, *not* imposing sufficient punitive action almost guarantees an immediate flare-up of hostilities which results in a never-ending, festering war. There is no perfect answer and you are damned if you do and damned if you don't. You pay your money and you take your choice between two bad options – a guaranteed never-ending war, or cycles of guaranteed peace followed by guaranteed war.

PART 3

THE GASOLINE.

Chapter 3-1

Rewi pours on the gas

We have travelled the long path to the New Zealand Wars for a full forty years – from 1820 to 1860 – and we are now nearing the end of our story.

The intent of this chapter is two-fold. First it can be considered as a postscript which adds extra detail to our nominal story. It is not a long story and we will not cover it in great detail. Second, and perhaps more importantly, it reinforces a more generic point that applies to all history and indeed most things in life – that history is not about events but about *people*. Generally the only difference between one outcome in history and another outcome is the personality and characteristics of the individuals who made the decisions. Nowhere is this truer than in our story of the New Zealand Wars.

Many individuals appear on the European "side" of the story – Governors Grey and Browne, Donald McLean and a host of lesser civil servants and missionaries. Their side of the story is well documented both in contemporary records and in more recent biographies and histories. You can walk into a library and instantly access hundreds of pages on most of these people. Grey, Browne, McLean and all the rest were all good, intelligent and well-meaning people but in all probability – individuals being individuals – they would all make different decisions in response to the same situation. Whatever the result of history is it is not a conspiracy – it is simply the results of individuals doing the best they can.

We are not so fortunate in our knowledge of the Maori "side" of the story. The lives of most of the key players are almost a complete blank and 99.999% of what Maori said and thought is unrecorded. The .001% that survives comes as tiny snippets of observation and speculation from European sources. Is that ideal? Obviously not but it is the best we have.

The three key Maori personalities relevant to our story are two we have already met and discussed in some detail – Wiremu Kingi and Wiremu Tamihana – and the subject of this chapter – Rewi Maniapoto.

Before we describe Rewi's place in the story let us add some closing comments about Wiremu Tamihana.[382]

Tamihana has gone down in the history books as a peacemaker. The evidence, however, suggests this is an over-simplification.

Gorst says of Tamihana:

> "His policy has always been to make a passive resistance to our encroachments, to assert Maori independence by just and lawful acts, and to let our side, if there must be war, be clearly the aggressors..."[383]

Gorst must have been having an off-day when he wrote this. The "just and lawful acts" to which he refers were in fact rebellion against the sovereign state. While we may empathise with Tamihana's motives the

---

[382] Why single out Tamihana for detailed analysis rather than Grey, Browne and all the rest? Because while all the European players also had their quirks and shortfalls ultimately they all did the bidding of the Colonial Office, whose brief was consistent. Any personal quirks of the Governors were random noise superimposed on a never-changing baseline which was broadly specified by the Treaty of Waitangi and the humanitarian norms of the age. Tamihana, on the other hand, was the architect of a fundamental change in the organisation and operation of Maoridom and ultimately the creator of biggest of the "logs" of war – the King Movement – without which the New Zealand Wars would not have happened, at least not at that time in that way.

[383] *The Maori King*, J.E. Gorst, p161.

consequences of his actions, and their outcomes, were most definitely not "lawful".

Gorst raises the concept of "passive resistance", a specious misnomer if ever there was one. There is no such thing as "passive resistance" – any act for which the only possible means of remediation requires the use of violence is not passive.

Not only is this so-called "passive resistance" not passive it is not clever and it is not noble. It is, in fact, the opposite of noble – a childish, manipulative tactic such as we might see in a child who commits crimes with impunity knowing they cannot be charged under the law. Gorst admits as much when he says that the goal is not to prevent war *per se* but to make sure that the other side is seen to be the guilty party – as we have seen with Kingi at Waitara it is all about creating moral high-grounds. And interestingly it is a tactic that would not be possible without European law, prior to which the response to "passive resistance" would have been a swift cleaving of skulls with a *mere*.

If Tamihana scores a ten out of ten for passion, integrity vision and intent he must score a zero on execution and outcome. This, I know, sounds an unreasonably harsh, even brutal, assessment of an unarguably great man whose only intent was for good and whose goals we can easily empathise with. Yet, regrettably, historical figures must ultimately be judged by their outcomes rather than by their intentions and Tamihana must be judged by what he caused to happen.

In virtually single-handedly converting the prosperous and generally content state of Waikato Maoridom[384] which existed prior to the introduction of his pet "King making" project in 1858, to the desolation, destruction and despair that existed in 1864 because of it, he proved himself a master of kicking a massive own goal. He is the classic hero in a Greek tragedy, a "great man" brought low by his own flaws, but

---

[384] Of course this is a general statement and of course things were not perfect but there was nothing that could not have been remedied with time, patience and a more intelligent approach.

regrettably he has gone one step further – he brought his entire people low by his flaws.

In insisting on a King Movement Tamihana was like Doctor Frankenstein[385] – he created a monster beyond his control. He did this against the wishes and advice of the great majority of his countrymen and in the process, far from creating unity, created the complete opposite – a division of the Maori people into Kingites and Queenites. Harsh as it may sound the brutal reality is that the supposed "unity" within the Kingites was an illusion – the King Movement was not a movement but a collection of independent entities who occasionally met in the same place.

As the saying goes, a little knowledge is a dangerous thing, and that is precisely what Tamihana had. He knew of the existence of "kings" but failed to understand either their function or that in 1860 they were obsolete. And while there was an attempt to create a "Government" in the form of the King's *runanga* at Ngaruawahia[386] it does not seem to have been understood that such an institution could not possibly work in a traditional Maori, non-sovereign environment[387].

Tamihana stood by claiming to be a peaceful man and watched while his creation ran amok. While he was thinking peaceful thoughts at his home in Peria, ploughing his fields, wringing his hands and praying as he watched the dead and wounded bodies of his people returning from the war in Taranaki, it was his own tribe who had to prod him into making it stop. He missed so many opportunities to make peace and, even after

---

385 The Sorcerer's Apprentice would be an equally good analogy.

386 See for instance *Daily Southern Cross*, 6 August, 1858, p3 for the selection of representatives to form a "council" at Ngaruawahia, during the King Party meeting of 8 June, 1858 at Rangiaowhia.

387 As Gorst puts it – "It is not the custom at Maori meetings to pass definite resolutions; indeed, it would be useless to do so, as the majority have no means of forcing the minority to conform to their decision. The only use of these gatherings is to make public opinion heard, so that each man, in determining for himself what he will do, may know what chance there is of being supported therein by comrades." (*The Maori King*, J. E. Gorst, p143).

committing his people to their destruction, was defiant, unrepentant, and insistent on the absolute correctness of his decisions until his dying breath.[388]

In providing an unprecedentedly large forum for militant individuals to spread their views, and unprecedentedly large numbers to respond violently to them, the King Movement created an environment tailor-made for the eruption of chaos and anarchy. Although Tamihana's "peaceful" policy of "passive resistance" was in itself sufficient to lead to war it is these fire-brands who accelerated that process and fanned the flames to uncontrollable, bon-fire like proportions.

That said, none of the above precludes him from being considered one of the finest people New Zealand has ever seen – it is possible to simultaneously celebrate the intent while ruing the result. Ultimately the parable alluded to by the epigraph of Chapter 2-1 applies - "when you seek to change your condition, be sure that you can better it".

Let us now leave Tamihana and turn to the "fire-brands", the appliers of the gasoline to the smouldering embers kindly created by Tamihana. A small handful of individuals stand out as minor "fire-brands" within their respective tribes – such as Wetini, the Ngati Haua fire-brand who met his fate at Mahoetahi, and Te Tapihana who led his Ngati Hakairo kinsmen of Kawhia to fight at Taranaki.

There is one name, however, that appears again and again in the history books as being the cheer-leader for the militant faction of the King Party

---

[388] The following excerpt may or may not indicate that Tamihana did have his moments of humility and the ability to learn from his mistakes – if so his future actions indicate it was a passing stage he was going through – "We learn on unexceptionable authority that Wiremu Tamihana Tarapipipi, the principal chief of the Ngatihaua, who is generally regarded by the natives as the author and chief promoter of the movement, has detached himself therefrom. He admits that it has proved a failure – that kingism is not reconcilable with Maorism – that real prosperity will only be found under the Queen's rule – and he declines to assist in or sanction the installation of a new king." (*Wellington Independent*, 21 September, 1860, p3).

- Rewi Maniapoto - the man to whom the metaphor "gasoline" in the title of this book applies. Gasoline is an accelerant, meaning it does not start fires it simply makes them burn faster and stronger. Tamihana's poorly executed dream of a King Movement started the fire - Rewi's actions simply made that foregone conclusion happen sooner and faster.

Like Kingi and Tamihana not much is known of Rewi's early life. As his name suggests he was a member of the Ngati Maniapoto tribe[389] and was descended directly from the ancestor after which that tribe is named. Although there are different theories as to his date of birth it is said that at the age of twelve he accompanied his father as part of the "Waikato" force who slaughtered the Ati Awa *pa* of Pukerangiora in 1832, which would put his birth date at 1820[390] and thus a generation younger than both Wiremu Kingi and Wiremu Tamihana.

In his early twenties he was exposed to all three of the competing Missionary denominations represented in the vicinity of his home at Kihikihi, a little south of what is now Hamilton. He was educated at the Wesleyan mission at Te Kopua and was baptised, replacing his birth name of *Manga* by the baptismal name of Rewi ("Levi"), by which he is better known to history.

Although there are few records of his activity it is clear that by the 1850s he is - unsurprisingly given his esteemed descent - *the* big wheel in the Ngati Maniapoto tribe and *a* big wheel in the King Movement. His name appears spasmodically in the few well-known speeches that record the gestation of the King Movement and in 1860 he is recorded as being "head of council" of the Ngati Maniapoto tribal *runanga* [391] as well as the Ngati Maniapoto representative on the King Movement *runanga*.

---

[389] Gorst describes the Ngati Maniapoto as "the largest and most powerful in New Zealand, [and] is also the most inveterate in hostility to the white race" (*The Maori King*, J. E. Gorst, p24).

[390] *The New Zealand Wars... - Vol 1*, James Cowan, p194.

[391] *Ibid*, p184.

While he was no doubt known in Government official circles his name, status and importance in the King Movement were not yet well known to the general European public. It was only during the latter part of the Taranaki War that his name began to appear in the European press, and even then as a mysterious name without a face:[392]

> "January 23 – Since my last, nothing of great importance occurred till this morning, when the rebels, headed by Rewi, Epiha, Tapurona, and others, supported by a reserve force of about 300, had the courage to attack No. 8 redoubt, at Kairau, there being at the time about 350 of the 10th Regiment in the redoubt." [393]
>
> "Wi Te One, we are told, narrowly escaped being shot, after his return to his friends. He urged the people of his tribe to retire from the unequal contest they were engaged in; on hearing which, Rewi proposed he should be shot, and was only prevented from doing so himself by the voice of the tribes."[394]
>
> "Moreover, while it was rumoured that Wiremu Kingi was himself desirous of a compromise, 'it is certain that previous to the late defeat the Waikato Chief Rewi, Potatau's chief Minister, and who is now down here (Taranaki) with his followers, would not hear of it, and told Kingi that if he attempted to bring it about he would tomahawk him.' " [395]
>
> "Sir – A letter received last week per "White Swan" states that the Ngatiawa natives at Otaki had been informed by a letter from

---

[392] It is clear from contemporary newspaper reports that there was much confusion about who Rewi actually was – while the name "Rewi" seems to be recognised as "prime minister of the Maori King cabinet " (*Taranaki Herald*, 26 May 1860, p2) it is also used interchangeably with a number of other people (such as Rewi Raureti and "Rewi" Tukorehu, the later evidently being a mis-hearing of the name of Peehi/Rewa Tukorehu)

[393] *Nelson Examiner*, 30 January, 1861, p3.

[394] *Nelson Examiner*, 9 February, 1861, p6.

[395] *New Zealander*, 10 April, 1861, p3.

> Wiremu Kingi that after the fight at Puketakauere a Waikato chief named Rewi proposed to attack the town [New Plymouth] immediately; but Wirimu Kingi positively refused saying that he had no intention of carrying on a general war with the English, but that he only wished to defend himself on his own land, and upon this Rewi left W.Kingi and joined the Ngatiruanui."[396]

> "It is stated in late Auckland papers that the rebel Kingi has expressed a desire to return to the status quo ante with the government. It is also rumoured that the rebel tribe of Taranaki have intimated a similar desire. Rewi, the Waikato chief, opposes Kingi, and has threatened him with violence should he think of peace without his sanction"[397]

The only thing we can glean from these few snippets is that whoever this man "Rewi" actually is his actions have a recurring theme of violence, or at least belligerence.

It was not until after the war that Rewi's strategic role and importance became fleshed out. Gorst's classic work *The Maori King*, published in 1864 was one of the first to articulate his influence within the King Movement and how he was the militant yin to Tamihana's supposedly pacifist yang:

> "Wiremu Tamihana, the chief of this tribe, though an uncompromising supporter of Maori nationality, has always laboured to keep peace between his race and ours; and since he succeeded in stopping the Taranaki war there has been a constant

---

[396] Letter from "A Looker On", dated 27th August, 1860 (*Daily Southern Cross*, 28 August, 1860, p4.) This letter is illuminating in showing Kingi's desire to separate his personal, limited struggle regarding Waitara from the King Movement, from whom he has reluctantly asked for assistance but simultaneously actually detests.

[397] *Taranaki Herald*, 10 November, 1860, p2. Once again the dominant message is that Kingi is fighting the King Movement as much as "The Europeans" – the King Movement has taken over his fight and turned it into something Kingi never wanted or endorsed.

feud between himself and Rewi, the chief of Ngatimaniapoto – the former striving to prevent, the latter to promote, a fresh struggle."[398]

"Still, much passive sympathy [for Wiremu Kingi] had been expressed, and many had shown great eagerness to pick a quarrel as soon as possible with the Pakeha, and have a trial of strength. This party had a strong though secret supporter in Rewi Maniapoto, whose intrigues were so successful, that, at length, a band of volunteers from Waikato went down to take part in the Taranaki war. Epiha, a Waikato of Kihikihi, was the leader. Rewi persuaded him that Potatau and the chiefs of Ngaruawahia wished some of them to go. The untruth was eagerly received by Epiha, who longed to take part in a war in which he hoped to gain personal distinction. Before, however, actually setting off, he wrote a letter to Potatau, saying that if Potatau disapproved, though he should be already on the way to Taranaki, he would return. It is said that, in fact, an imperative order was despatched by the Ngaruawahia [Maori King's] Council to recall the too zealous chief; but Epiha always denied having received any such order, and it is more than probable that Rewi intercepted the letter."[399]

"But though most of the Maori warriors were thus animated by pure love of mischief, and had no definite political object in fighting for Wiremu Kingi, it was not so with Rewi Maniapoto, who having seen the war mania fairly progressing in Waikato, threw off all disguise, and went down in person to Taranaki, to pursue his design of involving the whole Maori people in a contest for supremacy with their European rivals."[400]

---

[398] *The Maori King*, J. E. Gorst, p26.

[399] *Ibid* p144.

[400] *Ibid*, p146.

Gorst also fills in some gaps as to Rewi's personal contribution to the Taranaki War as we see in these comments, castigating Rewi for his perceived failure to support Wetini in his ill-advised battle at Mahoetahi:

> "The greatest indignation was felt and expressed by the Ngatihaua against Rewi and his men, to whose failure to support them they attributed the disaster [the Maori defeat at Mahoetahi]. Rewi, on his part, says that Wetini was a rash fool, who would not listen to advice; that he sent him down messenger after messenger urging him to retire before it was too late; that his last messenger actually followed too far and was caught in the snare with the others and killed (being one of the very few Ngatimaniapoto who fell in the war); and that he could not have done more for Wetini without injury to the common cause. All this is quite true, but the loss of Wetini while Rewi sat inactive has ever since rankled deeply in the minds of the Ngatihaua, and increased the hereditary hatred between the two tribes."[401]

While we are on the subject of Mahoetahi, and although not directly related to Rewi, we can add to the rapidly growing pile of observations revealing the uneasy marriage of convenience between Wiremu Kingi and his "saviour", the King Movement:

> "The Waikatos are still in a state of uncertainty as to what to do. War has not proved the pleasant occupation which they anticipated, and peace they are ashamed to ask for. A feeling of animosity has naturally been awakened in their breasts by the conduct of the chief [Kingi, who did not help the Waikatos when they were attacked at Mahoetahi] whom they went down to assist, and who stood aloof whilst they were being cut to pieces. William King is, we dare say, at present more in fear of the Waikato than are any settlers in the country."[402]

After the "peace making" at Taranaki this strange relationship continued:

---

[401] *Ibid*, p155.

[402] *Nelson Examiner*, 11 December, 1860, p3.

> "The Waikatos followed him [Tamihana] sulkily; Rewi stayed behind to hatch mischief if he could, and succeeded at last in carrying off Wiremu Kingi, who might, he feared, patch up his quarrel with the Governor, to a sort of honourable captivity at Kihikihi." [403]

Rewi remained determined not to entertain overtures of peace with the new Governor, Sir George Grey:

> "Wi Kingi, the hero of Taranaki, was in Rewi's custody at Kihikihi. The people of that village were gaily attired in military caps and coats, and carried rifles and accoutrements taken at Taranaki. Rewi and all his myrmidons refused even to be present at Ngaruawahia to discuss the propriety of sending a deputation to Sir George Grey." [404]

During the nominal "peace" between July, 1861, and early 1863, Rewi's name largely disappeared from the public eye. He was hard at work, however, behind the scenes, scuttling any plans that might result in peace:

> "Rewi denied that the absolute disposal of Waitara was in Tamihana's hands; whatever the latter proposed would be considered by himself [Rewi] and Wiremu Kingi, and if it did not appear good to them, they should keep Waitara in spite of it. The best way Rewi could see of settling the dispute, was by the English Government confessing their error, and restoring Waitara to the lawful owners.
>
> Wiremu Tamihana himself was very reluctant to stir in the matter at all; he had, he said, little hope of getting his proposals adopted by the rest, and when there were so many grounds of quarrel unsettled".[405]

Rewi, it seems, had taken the rudder of the King Movement from Tamihana and was calling the shots. Tamihana himself seemed to be licking his wounds and wondering what went wrong with his precious

---

[403] *The Maori King*, J. E. Gorst, p165.

[404] *Ibid*, p205.

[405] *Ibid*, p287.

creation. He had lost control – if he ever had it – and was trying desperately to dig himself out of a hole of his own creation. It is difficult not to feel a little sorry for him. He was a good, if stubborn, man trying to implement his vision of "the right thing" against hopeless odds.

In October, 1862, following exhortations by Bishop Selwyn at yet another great meeting at his home of Peria, Tamihana:

> "...rode over with his followers to Kihikihi, and publicly demanded from Rewi and Wiremu Kingi, that an investigation should be made into the title to Waitara in the manner which the Government had proposed. Wiremu Kingi refused. A stormy discussion ensued, in which Rewi and all the Ngatimaniapoto supported Wiremu Kingi's refusal; and ultimately their opinions gained the day. Tamihana, thus baffled in his first attempt, next demanded that Tataraimaka should be given up to the owners [the Europeans]. This demand was, however, as obstinately opposed as the former one. The resolution of the Ngatimaniapoto was immoveable. Wiremu Tamihana could affect nothing without an open quarrel. Such a breaking up of the league would sacrifice Maori independence, which Tamihana, in his love of his country and fear of Sir George Grey, was not prepared to do."[406]

Rewi's next notable achievement, sufficiently audacious to hit the local newspapers, involved his removal of Resident Magistrate John Gorst's printing press from his base at Otawhao:

> "The seizure of the printing press at Te Awamutu on the 24th ult. [24 March, 1863], by Rewi Maniapoto and eighty armed men, has created a profound sensation and great uneasiness, as we learn, amongst the more thoughtful of the Waikatos; we are enabled to state, on good authority, that steps were taken by the King's party to recover the property immediately after the outrage was made known. Te Paea, known as Princess Sophia, waited on Rewi at his settlement, Whakatereparera, and Matutarera, the [second] Maori

---

[406] *Ibid*, p321.

> King, followed his sister to the same place, and demanded the immediate restoration of all that had been taken from Mr. Gorst's establishment. The printing materials and the other articles taken by Rewi and his followers, it was understood, were to have been returned to the Civil Commissioner on the 31st ultimo. It appears that the daring act perpetrated by these people had for its avowed object the driving away of Mr. Gorst, whose industrial establishment and opposition journal, the Pihoihoi, are looked upon by the extreme king party with a very jealous eye, and that Rewi's myrmidons, before they broke into the printing office, went through the formality of prayer, their guns in their right hands, one knee bent.[407]

Clearly at this point Rewi was a loose-cannon and a liability and source of embarrassment to the horrified, more well-meaning King Movement members:

> "Te Paea[408] sat in our tent, near the house where the discussion was going on. She said it was neither the Pihoihoi, nor the words of the Ngaruawahia chiefs, that had caused Rewi's acts; it was Tataraimaka. Rewi had done his best to prevent peace being made in 1861, and had been trying ever since to renew the Taranaki war; he was now doing his best to provoke a war in Waikato. She said that Rewi insulted Tamihana, when he went to Kihikihi to expostulate: she should go too; but it was unlikely Rewi would listen to her, after mocking at so good a man. Finally, having worked herself into a frantic state, she rushed, tears running down her cheeks, into the adjoining house, and addressed the meeting in a very loud voice, abusing their acts and designs for about an hour."[409]

---

[407] *New Zealander*, 2 April, 1863, p5.

[408] Princess Te Paea ("Sophia"), daughter of the first Maori King and sister to the second, considered by many to be a worthier successor to the throne than her brother Matutaera ("Methuselah").

[409] *The Maori King*, J.E. Gorst, p353.

The magnitude of the tragedy that the King Movement became is now becoming painfully apparent. So many of its members were good, well-intentioned people who could have, in the right conditions, achieved both peace and great things for their race and their future. That it could be subverted and thwarted by a few uncontrollable individuals was a tragedy.

Things were now beginning to move quickly and it was only three weeks later before Rewi truly surpassed himself.

During the "Taranaki War" the European-owned Tataraimaka Block, south of New Plymouth in the territory of the Taranaki tribe, had been retaken by that tribe to be held "by right of conquest" as a bargaining chip to be used against the return of Waitara. On 4 April, 1863, in a bold move on Governor Grey's orders, this block was entered by 100 cavalry and 200 infantry and reclaimed as a European possession. On the local Taranaki tribe asking for advice from Ngaruawahia as to what their response should be they received on 15 April Rewi's short but memorable and unsubtle reply:

> "Me ki ki tona taringa, me patu te pakeha
>
> (Whisper in his ear, kill the pakeha)" [410]

Rewi's wish was evidently the Taranaki tribe's command for just a few weeks later eight soldiers were ambushed and murdered at Oakura en-route from the Tataraimaka Block to New Plymouth.[411] If Waitara can be said to be the spark that raised the curtain on the short, first act of the New Zealand Wars, generally called the "Taranaki War", then Oakura is the spark that raised the curtain on the much longer second and final act that embraced The Waikato War, the HauHau Wars and Titokowaru's and Te Kooti's wars.

The tragic loss of life aside, Oakura had profound political and psychological effects for both parties which had both of them racing for

---

[410] *Sir George Grey*, J. Rutherford, p482.

[411] The intended target, it seems, was Governor Grey himself, who was in the habit of riding along this route.

their hammers to drive in the last nails in the coffin of peace. In times of tension the rumour mills go into overdrive – speculation and gossip are flying in all directions, there are enemies under every bed and sudden death behind every bush.

Prior to the attack at Oakura European authorities had had warnings from friendly Maori of an impending attack but chose to ignore them. It was not a mistake they would make again. After Oakura the constant rumours of an attack on Auckland could no longer be ignored and it would be both actual and political suicide to do otherwise. After two years of trying to reconcile the irreconcilable using words it was time to try bullets. The age-old philosophy of "the best form of defence is offense" was now a regrettable but inevitable certainty.

For the King Party the effect of Oakura was no less dramatic. The long-term, fine balancing act of the ever-strained and un-easy tug of war between the more peaceable faction represented by Tamihana and the belligerent faction headed by Rewi, now reached breaking point resulting in a complete schism. There was no longer a singular King Movement but a peace movement and a war movement, which, since a peace movement can by definition have no control over a war movement, means the King Party was essentially a war party.

Both the European and Maori "war party" sentiments were now in complete alignment – there were no more decisions to be made, no more meetings to be had – there *would* be war.

Decisions are always the hardest part. Once they are made there is a feeling of release, relief and blinding clarity. A great weight is lifted and replaced by a deep sense of purpose and righteousness. It must have been liberating for both sides.

Rewi had for months been angling to take the initiative and make a pre-emptive strike at the crucial point of Te Ia, the strategic bend in the Waikato River that marks the northern boundary between the Waikato to the south and European settlement to the North and to which point Grey had constructed a road terminated in a military outpost called the Queen's Redoubt at Pokeno:

"A great discussion has been going on at Kihikihi, between Rewi and his followers; together with Reihana on the one side, and Te Paea, Potatau and Patara, of Ngaruawahia, on the other. Rewi's side are urgent for an immediate descent upon the Ia (with a view, as I am told, not of attacking the troops, but of making a raid against the settlers).[412]

It was only a matter of who struck first and since – as we have seen time after time – in the Maori world it was always about keeping the moral high ground, it would not be Maori.

Thus inevitably it was the European "side" which struck first and on 12 July, 1863, two years after the failure to come to terms at the "end" of the Taranaki War, that war was officially resumed when British troops waded across the Mangatawhiri stream and began its slow descent up the Waikato River under the command of General Duncan Cameron.

We need not follow Cameron's path south or recount Rewi's involvement in it, important though these may be in other contexts. Rewi's work was done before the first boot of Cameron's troops disturbed the stillness of the Mangatawhiri, if not by starting the war precisely then by guaranteeing it and greatly accelerating it. He was the gasoline that would keep the war alive until the bitter end when, as fate would have it, he also played a pivotal role at the battle of Orakau culminating in his immortal words of "*ake, ake, ake*".[413]

---

[412] Letter of Rev. Arthur Purchas to Native Minister, dated 25 April, 1863 (AJHR, 1863, E3, p31). The "Ia" refers to "Te Ia", the point where the Waikato makes its turn west to its outlet and which could be regarded as the northern demarcation point between Kingite Maori and Greater Auckland. Gorst says of it: "A pretty wooded bluff overhanging the Waikato, at a place called Te Ia, just below the junction of the Mangatawhiri, was at the same time stripped of its trees, and an ugly-looking stockade perched upon the top" (*The Maori King*, J. E. Gorst, p12)

[413] The stirring, defiant final words of a rebuttal given by the Orakau occupants to an offer of surrender by its besiegers, often translated as "For

In this ironical way fate has been very kind to Rewi. Thanks to those few hypothesised words at Orakau not only is Rewi one of the very few names in New Zealand history remembered to this day, but perversely he is remembered as the *hero* of the New Zealand Wars rather that its prime mover and the author of so much misery and dissent in the present.

History is brutal – it gives no points for trying, and intelligence and good intentions count for nothing. The name of Wiremu Tamihana may take its honourable place in weighty, unread tomes on dusty shelves but Rewi's is immortalised on the screen, in novels, in received myths and implanted in the easily manipulated hearts and minds of a captive audience of school children. His story is a nation-builder's dream. History just loves a hero and a good, endlessly quotable catchphrase.

---

ever and ever and ever". Apocryphally said to have been Rewi's response at least two others have also been credited with uttering these immortal words.

Chapter 3-2

The players leave the stage.

We have already observed that history is not about events but about individuals, normal people, with their many quirks and unique personalities. And invariably, if you truly take the time to dig a little deeper and put yourself in their shoes and in their time, the terms "hero" and "villain" start to become absurd. On average we are all average. When we look at these characters and the literally thankless roles they played it is hard to suppress a feeling of "there but for the grace of God go I" and shudder at the decisions we might have made in their place and the havoc we might have wreaked. The very "worst" of the actors of the past is a better person than most of us.

Anyone brave enough to trawl through the thousands upon thousands of assorted documents that record New Zealand's history may well find thoughts and deeds that time has subsequently proven to be "wrong". But they will search in vain for a solitary statement that implies anything but the absolute best of intent and the peak of morality. The reader's most likely response to these documents will be a sense of awe at the intelligence, humanity, literacy, morality, articulateness, ability to reason, caution, wisdom, concern and sheer breadth of knowledge that distinguished both European civil servants and Maori of that time. We can only lament the loss of this level of ability in the present.

If we have reached an imperfect place in the present it is certainly not for want of trying in the past. To be honest the chances are that if the development of New Zealand had been given to a dream team of King Solomon, Nelson Mandela, Mother Theresa, Ghandi, Martin Luther King and Jesus Christ it is doubtful if the result would be any better, and very probably much worse. Although it runs against the current political flow the idea that the key to reaching a less imperfect place in the future is to dissect with righteous hindsight the supposedly "villainous" acts of the past is the definition of stupidity. It is about as relevant and intelligent as the post-match critique of the big game by someone who has never set foot on a rugby field.

As Shakespeare has wisely and famously told us:

> "All the world's a stage,
> And all the men and women merely players;
> They have their exits and their entrances;
> And one man in his time plays many parts..."

In our story we have seen many men enter the stage and play greater or lesser parts. Some are bit actors who have wandered on stage, lobbed a grenade, and wandered off again. Others have played long and demanding parts. Few of their names are now remembered, let alone revered, which is a shame because they defined what New Zealand is and who we are. The evolution of New Zealand was their big role after which all of them shuffled off-stage to obscurity at best or infamy at worst. It seems only fitting to acknowledge our debt to them by summarising their short journey from the stage to their final exit to the great Green Room in the sky.

Te Teira Manuka.

Te Teira definitely falls into the "grenade lobber" category, striding on-stage a mystery, creating havoc across the central North Island, and disappearing into the obscurity from whence he came – although in his defence he was probably as mystified as anyone as to the disproportionate consequences of his actions. After his brief cameo role in March, 1859, for the next 15 years he kept a very low profile, his name appearing only sporadically in matters such as land depositions. He reappeared in the public eye only once, fleetingly but perceptively during the great meeting between Premier Sir George Grey and Rewi at Waitara in 1878:

> "A noteworthy man here is Te Teira, the chief who first offered for sale the Waitara block, and persisted that he had a right to sell it in opposition to William King. This morning I went to see Te Teira at his pah near the mouth of the river. I found him sitting amongst his people, a quiet, self-possessed intelligent man, with a European cast of countenance. He was quite ready to answer any question put.
>
> I said to him:
>
> "Looking at all that has taken place since the original dispute about Waitara, which brought about the war, who do you say now was right – you or William King? Teira replied: Both William King and myself were bad men. I was wrong because I sold my land to the Europeans; King was wrong because he resisted all selling at the first. The setting up of the Maori King had nothing to do with the dispute which arose about Waitara. The questions there involved were of old Maori custom. At first I wanted to sell this place where we are, and I had a right to sell that, but William King was against it, and opposed me selling what I believed I had a right to sell; and then I went over my boundary and offered to sell to the Government land that belonged to William King as well as myself. This piece here, running up to where the hotel now stands, belonged to me. This piece where the railway is now, and the goods shed, and the wharf belonged to both William King and myself. I ought not to have offered to sell that. I have nothing to say in this meeting. I am a man who is dead (meaning that he had committed wrong). But Waitara, which I offered to sell, was not the entire cause of the war. There was the raising up of the King, which I had nothing to do with. If there had been nothing else but the land quarrel at Waitara there would not have been much fighting, and there would have been no war with the Europeans. I have been grieved that the dispute which arose here was followed by a war with the

> Europeans extending over the Island. I was grieved on account of the destruction of the people.
>
> You ask me if I think the Waitara war might have been averted by a better knowledge of our laws and customs amongst the Europeans, and I answer that I think it might. I believe if Sir George Grey had been here instead of Governor Browne, there would have been no war so far as Waitara was concerned. Sir George Grey would have looked into the Maori custom of land owning, and seen the right and the wrong. During the war we were with the Europeans. We did not know that a party of Waikatos had come down to assist William King till after the battle of Mahoetahi. A European was there who knew Wetine, and recognised his body, and told us that he was amongst the slain. I should like to see the object of this meeting fulfilled, and the Europeans and Maoris living in peace together. Can that object be obtained?" [414]

This is what history is all about. In this random, off-guard and candid exchange Teira emerges from the page transformed from a cardboard cut-out of "Teira did this, Teira did that" to an actual, three-dimensional, human-being with a brain and a heart. Although we might suspect this dialogue has been anglicised to some extent the interviewer obviously likes Teira and it is difficult for us not to do the same. Teira seems deeply human, if not racked with guilt for the part he played, and deeply affected by what came to pass and which he could not have foreseen. He seems fair

---

[414] *Taranaki Herald*, 25 June, 1878, p2. This report was subsequently corrected by Teira in this message published in the 27 June edition of the same paper – "We have heard to-day what is stated in the newspaper – it says if Grey had been here at the beginning there would have been no evil ; it says also I took Wiremu Kingi's land. Not so – it was confiscated. I had nothing to do with it. Mine alone is what I gave to the white man – to Brown (Governor Browne). From Te Teira".

and happy to admit his own failings, a winning combination which we could wish was more common. [415]

Even in death it seems Teira was fated to be as inextricably linked to that of Wiremu Kingi's as he was in life:

> "It is a strange coincidence that Te Teira, the opponent of Wiremu Kingi re the sale of the Waitara, which caused the war, should be taken ill the same week as the latter died and was buried. Teira is not expected to live, and his friends are gathered around him prepared for the worst, which is fully expected.[416]

Teira finally died on 16 September, 1882, receiving the scantiest of obituaries:

> "The chief Te Teira, of Manukau, died at Waitara on Saturday, aged 70 years. Te Teira was the chief who sold to the Government the land which was the cause of the war commencing with the natives in 1860."[417]

Wiremu Kingi.

It is a great shame we know so little about this man. He remains an enigma wrapped in a riddle, known only to posterity by a small handful of fragmentary and contradictory evidence and some photos that may well be of someone else. The few snippets we have suggest an intelligent and worldly man, receptive and even encouraging to European settlement prior to his father's death, morphing to an intransigent, irascible man of

---

[415] This interpretation is confirmed by the only surviving photo of Te Teira, which regrettably I have been unable to obtain permission to use in this book alongside that of Wiremu Kingi. I would highly recommend readers seek out this photo on-line for it tells us more about Te Teira than a thousand words ever could.

[416] *Hawera and Normanby Star,* 25 January, 1882, p1.

[417] *Daily Telegraph*, 18 September, 1882, p3.

few words after it. At times he seems to have been as much at odds with his own people as to Europeans.

Like Teira, Wiremu Kingi kept a low profile after the war, both of them finding that fifteen minutes of fame was not all it was cracked up to be and more than sufficient for any lifetime.

After the war Kingi lived quietly in seclusion for twelve years in the Ngati Maru territory to the east of his ancestral home of Waitara. In 1872 he emerged briefly into society – apparently after much cajoling by Robert Parris – passing through New Plymouth en-route to his next point of seclusion at Parihaka:

> "...In our last Saturday's issue we recorded the event of William King quitting his seclusion at Ngatimaru, that he was then at the Waitara, and would be in town in the course of a few days...
>
> William King walked with eyes cast down upon the ground, never once looking up at the number of persons who lined the footpath to see him. He was dressed in his native costume, and wore a black skull cap, from beneath which his locks of grey hair were visible... William King was seated amongst his people, with his daughter behind him. The old man seemed very quiet and thoughtful Hapurona (who is William King's chief man) was seated near the Waikato party...
>
> Mr McLean [said]: I have little to say to you, William King, and to your people. In past times your father, Reretawhangawhanga, welcomed the Europeans to the shores of Kapiti. After their arrival they received at one time good treatment, at another time bad treatment; but this was in days gone by, and there is no necessity, for our alluding now to those past occurrences. There are but few of your relatives left to welcome you back; the trees of the forest remain the same, but they cannot greet you. You see now here the Europeans whom your forefathers welcomed occupying the land, and, after many years of separation, they all unite in according you a welcome back on your return from the forest to the sea shore. Come and tread the paths traversed by the footsteps of your ancestors; come over the ground where the dead have fallen, that revenge for the past may be stamped out (i.e., in allusion to a Maori custom ratifying peace.) The warfare

with you has been in open daylight, and you need not fear that the Europeans have any hostile or evil intentions against you. No: come and go as you think proper; the sun is shining, and under its influence let the angry feelings and misunderstandings which have estranged you from us for so many years be dispelled; let us in future meet each other with smiles and not with frowns or disguised feelings of enmity; and here, in this marae, let us have our talk – be it smooth or be it rough – to-day and to-morrow, or as long as you choose, to discuss matters. Welcome to you, William King, and your people.

Wi Kingi here said to his people, Manawanui (be forbearing)

Hapurona [said]: Salutations Mr McLean... Listen, my talk to you is about him (W. Kingi). There he is before you and Mr Parris. (Here he quoted an ancient Waiata on the subject of the reconciliation of two tribes after fighting). We have come forth to be saved; you have spoken clearly unto us, Mr McLean. My work was to bring him into your presence; behold him – you did not ask for him to come, but we thought over it and determined upon coming to meet you. I have no evil words to speak; I only wish to act rightly; I did not wait to tangi with our relations, so anxious was I for you to see him (Wi Kingi); behold him, he is there with his wife and child. I concur with what you have said, namely, that we should come and tread in the footprints of our ancestors. It is also correct that you did not fight in an underhand manner. There is nothing to say but that he has come to lie down in the presence of yourself and Mr Parris.

At an interview which took place yesterday between Mr McLean and William King and Hapurona, the two chiefs stated that they had nothing to ask for and nothing to conceal. The fact of their voluntarily coming out of their seclusion and placing themselves in the hands of the Europeans was the best evidence they could give of their peaceful intentions, and of their determination to live on friendly terms with the pakeha, and to induce other natives to follow their example.

...During the whole of yesterday the Native Office was the scene of attraction, and in the afternoon especially, large numbers of persons were there endeavouring to get a sight of William King, who in no way hid himself. It was amusing to see the curiosity of the children, who were allowed to come into the room in the Native Office where William King was sitting, and to shake hands with him. The old chief seemed to enjoy the levee, for as each batch of children came in, he laughed with delight as he took their tiny little hands in his and kindly shook them. The natives will remain here till Sunday or Monday next, when they will take their departure in the direction of Parihaka.[418]

Once again, this single, seemingly throwaway sentence recording Kingi's simple delight in the presence of children, tells a tale a thousand times more powerful, and brings to life a human-being very different from, the gruff, dour, intransigent man we see in most history books. Kingi's dignified seclusion continued until his death on 13 January, 1882:

> "..."Wiremu Kingi", says a New Plymouth telegram to-day, "is being borne to Parihaka on a stretcher, accompanied by the remnant of his tribe, to end his days there. Only twenty years have elapsed since this chief was the absorbing topic in the Legislature and the Press. Commissioners waited upon him, long dispatches to the Imperial Government were filled with his sayings and doings, and an army was summoned to oppose his crusade against the Pakeha: and now only thirty adherents remain to awaken in the minds of old colonists recollections of the past. The melancholy pilgrimage of the old chief and the few survivors of his tribe in search of a resting place might be taken as typifying the decline of the native race. With startling rapidity these people are fading away before advancing civilisation. What war began with Wi Kingi, land sales, frontier grog stores and blankets are completing with a great majority of the tribes throughout these islands, and another twenty years may see changes with respect to the whole Maori people in comparison with which Wiremu Kingi's decline is only a faint prototype." [419]

---

[418] *Wellington Independent*, 26 February, 1872, p2 (greatly edited for brevity).

[419] *Auckland Star*, 13 September, 1880, p2.

"The old chief Wiremu Kingi is dead and buried, and the neighboring tribes are engaged in a prolonged tangi. Chief of the Land League, Wi Kingi, through his opposition to the sale of Waitara by Te Teira, was the approximate cause[420] of the first Taranaki war. He was upwards of 90 years old when he died, and had great influence over his tribe to the last, although of late years he has abstained from any active interference in the policy of the Natives. He resided for some years at Parihaka, from whence he removed in 1875 to a settlement up the Waitara river. In 1878 he left the latter place and took up his residence some five miles from the Waitara township, where he lived a very retired life. His former opponent, Te Teira, is now lying sick unto death, and one month may see the death of both these men of notoriety in the history of Taranaki." [421]

"After the peace the old chief led a secluded life for twelve years in the inland native district of Ngatimaru. On the 22nd February 1872, he came to New Plymouth to see the late Sir Donald McLean, and on his arrival in New Plymouth he was welcomed in a friendly manner by the Europeans. He then went to Parihaka on a visit to Te Whiti, where he remained about five years. He afterwards went to reside at Manutangihia, inland of Taurangi, but about two years ago he removed to Kaingaru, a native settlement about two miles inland of the junction of the Waitara and Manganui rivers, where he died on Friday last. He leaves a son and daughter, named respectively Edward and Georgiana. He used to be represented in his younger days as being a man of great craft and subtlety, and to him may be fairly attributed the difficulties and troubles this district has had to contend with. He never would make free with the Europeans, or intimately associate with them. He had commercial relations with the pakeha, like other natives; but he always lived a purely native life, and was a strong

---

[420] "approximate cause" – an interesting and not inappropriate way of putting the Waitara affair in true context within the very "long road" to war recorded in this book.

[421] *New Zealand Times*, 30 January, 1882, p3.

opponent to selling land to Europeans. His power as a Maori chief, however, became impaired by the civilisation of his followers and their emancipation from barbarous customs; and, seeing his weakness as a chief as he grew older, he has preferred the seclusion of the bush to the active life of the pakeha. In the death of Wi Kingi another historical personage connected with the history of New Zealand will have made his exit from a stage on which he has on more than one occasion played no unimportant part.[422]

Rewi Maniapoto

Throughout history nothing and no-one has tugged at the heartstrings of posterity with such irresistible force as a rebel fighting for a cause, the little guy sticking it to the establishment, generally for something called "freedom". Somewhere in this pantheon of rebels – between Spartacus and Luke Skywalker – is Rewi Maniapoto.

Rewi was lucky. At the end of the wars he was still relatively young, perhaps in his early fifties, and unlike Tamihana who died a bitter man in the middle of the wars, Rewi had the luxury of many decades of life ahead of him to mellow, mature, reflect and philosophise on the ways of life.

With all the perversity of human nature, with the war over Rewi gradually transitioned over a period of decades from a villain to a hero in the eyes of those he rebelled against. It did not hurt that thanks to the fabled battle of Orakau he was not only a classic "rebel with a noble cause" but a bona-fide military hero. Ironically he became a folk hero and symbol not of the independent Maori nationality for which he fought, but, as sometimes happens, he was appropriated by and incorporated into the emerging folk-lore that would become the "European New Zealand" nationality and identity.

In a young country in need of legends Rewi's romantically re-imagined role in the battle of Orakau became a thing of legend and it could be said with justification that Rewi was New Zealand's first true celebrity, feted

---

422 *Taranaki Herald*, 19 January, 1882, p2.

wherever he went and immortalised in turgid poems and painted memorial plates.

Thirty years after Orakau, and long enough for the rashness of his relative youth to be at least somewhat tempered by the mellowness that comes with age, Rewi – unlike some of his former comrades such as King Tawhiao – came to accept, if with mixed feelings, changes in the Maori way of life and the need to meet European co-existence halfway. If Tamihana was a dogmatic philosopher Rewi was a realist who saw that the best way forward for Maori as a people was negotiation and give and take, rather than the intransigent, all-or-nothing stance taken by King Tawhiao.

Rewi played a key role in the decades long process which historian Michael Belgrave aptly terms "dancing with the King"[423] – the tortuous, diplomatic minuet played out over a number of decades between a revolving door of changing partners representing the Maori King and the New Zealand government in an attempt to open up the area known as the "King Country". Rewi's regret for his past actions is evident in the records of this process, for instance in this excerpt from the Waitara meeting of June 1878:

> He [Rewi] explained to them that Karaitiana [Takamoana] was one of the leading chiefs of Hawke's Bay – that, when the King movement first began in the Waikato, Karaitiana came with some of his people to Ngaruawahia and spoke thus to the Waikatos: "Now you have a King in the island for the Native race. My idea is we cannot have a King, because all the chiefs in New Zealand have signed the treaty of Waitangi, whereby they pledged themselves to come under the Queen, and to obey her laws. We cannot have a King with a few people; we must have a King with a large number of people to govern. We are only a few among so many Europeans. It will only create ill-feeling between the two races if you attempt to set up a King." The answer

[423] The opening up of the King Country is a fascinating story in its own right and Belgrave's book of the same name is highly recommended.

Karaitiana received from the Waikato chiefs was: "Slaves are not allowed to talk to us, or to guide us." Karaitiana said: "Right; you take your own course, and die in following it. I will take my course, and die in maintaining the laws of the Government. Rewi, you will find my words come true. We shall see each other when my words come to be fulfilled." Rewi said to his chiefs: "The words of Karaitiana have come true; Aye lost all our land and the people."[424]

Nowhere is Rewi's change of heart better demonstrated than in the weeks before his death.

On 20 February, 1894, his old nemesis Sir George Grey, now equally aged, long retired from political life and living in Parnell, received this message:

"Kihikihi, 19th February, 1894. To Sir George Grey. My friend, – I greet you because of our long mutual affection for each other. We have now both of us reached the limits of the days of our forefathers. Let this suffice by way of greeting, and let me touch upon another subject, and mention, that as your body and mine appear to be equally affected by age during those days of our unbroken unity of feeling, even until this very day, my most earnest request is that your name and mine be recorded on the Same memorial stone. Enough!

From your affectionate friend, Rewi Maniapoto."[425]

In response Sir George set off immediately to Kihkihi on the next available train:

"Sir Geo. Grey has just returned from Kihikihi, after his interview with Rewi. Sir George is on his way to Rotorua by today's train. He tells us Rewi was delighted to see him. Rewi is very feeble now, and amongst other things, seemed to be much taken up with the idea that when he was gone the Europeans might think badly of him for having fought against them formerly. Sir Geo. set his mind at rest on that point, and said it was well known that Rewi fought only after having

---

[424] AJHR, 1878 Session 1, G-03, p44.

[425] *Taranaki Herald*, 2 March, 1894, p2.

> tried his best to dissuade his countrymen from so doing. Rewi was pleased at his old friend taking the trouble to come all the way up to see him at his advanced age."[426]

While we can see that under the circumstances Grey could have hardly answered Rewi's concerns for his posterity any differently, his diplomatic reply was the complete opposite of the truth.

On June 22, 1894, the newspapers of the nation were united in a headline which in its brevity summed up his celebrity:

"Death of Rewi".

Amongst the many hagiographic obituaries reflecting Rewi's newly acquired hero status by those who knew nothing about him is this somewhat enigmatic and less forgiving one from those who did – which is a good deal nearer the historical truth for a man who practically single-handedly caused the destruction of his people:

> "By the death of Rewi is removed another of the grand old chiefs of the olden time, of whom now scarcely any remain. From what I hear, the old soldiers have been too dilatory with their address of sympathy with the aged chief, and he has gone into the land of spirits taking the will for the deed."[427]

Sir George Grey.

When Grey returned to New Zealand to replace Thomas Gore Browne in 1861 his glory days were behind him. In the few short years since his previous and successful New Zealand governorship the role and power of the Governor had been greatly reduced, he had been recalled in bad grace from his previous role of Governor of Cape Colony and his marriage had acrimoniously and scandalously imploded. He would never be the same

[426] *Auckland Star*, 22 February, 1894, p12.

[427] *New Zealand Herald,* 23 June, 1894, p1. The nowadays rarely heard expression "taking the will for the deed" loosely means "giving a person credit for his good intentions even though he did not act on or achieve them".

again and it is not infrequently considered that his second governorship destroyed much of the kudos he obtained in his first. This seems somewhat unfair for New Zealand in 1860 was a far more difficult, complicated and untameable animal than it was in 1850. Only in a fantasy world could any mere mortal prevail with 100% success against such odds.

In 1868 Grey was recalled as Governor for his unwillingness to march to the drum of his bosses back in Britain. After a stint back in Britain he returned to New Zealand and gradually returned to political life in its new responsible and representative form, rising to the rank of Premier between 1877 and 1879 and remaining in politics until 1894.

In an uncanny parallel to that of Kingi and Teira, Grey's and Rewi's lives also seem to have been cosmically joined at the hip, for within a few weeks of visiting Rewi on his deathbed Grey seems to have abruptly reconciled himself to a similar fate:

> "Sir George Grey has slipped off almost unnoticed. The other day he was here in Napier, having come overland after paying a visit to his old acquaintance Rewi, and now he is gone. There was never a word about his purpose to visit the Home Country, for the very good reason that he seems to have had no such purpose. Happening to go down to Wellington he found the Gothic about to sail, and was tempted to step aboard. Even after taking his passage in the big ship he was still undecided. But he is off, to return soon, let us hope, with renewed vigour. Sir George has often of late talked of going Home."[428]

After an ill-conceived and disastrous attempt at reconnecting with his long estranged wife Sir George Grey died on 19 September 1898 and was buried in St Paul's Cathedral in London.

---

[428] *Daily Telegraph*, 10 March, 1894, p2.

Wiremu Tamihana.

In September 1863, at the height of what is generally known as "The Waikato War", Wiremu Tamihana sent his *mere* to General Cameron, signalling his recognition that the war in Waikato was lost, a mere three months after it started in July. Nice gesture as that may have been it meant nothing since Tamihana had long lost any say in, or control of, the war, and Rewi and his ilk would fight on no matter what Tamihana did or said.

After the Waikato phase of the New Zealand Wars "ended" Tamihana returned to his home in Peria, it is said, a broken man, leaving – as if we could not have guessed – the traditional "peace" in which no armistice had been signed, no terms had been made and no-one had agreed to anything.

Tamihana was eventually persuaded by European friends – with great reluctance and against the wishes of many of his people – to formally agree to peace and on 27 May, 1865, he laid his *taiaha* at the feet of Brigadier-General George Jackson Cary at Tamahere as a symbolic sign of submission.

This, however, meant nothing but a change in tactic, for in 1865 and 1866 Tamihana wrote two petitions to Parliament exonerating his past actions, railing against perceived injustices and asking for the return of the confiscated Waikato land. While he may well have been a broken man he had lost not an iota of his defiance and still declared himself without fault and answerable only to God.

Around the new year of 1867 messages such as this began appearing in the newspapers:

> "Intelligence reached town yesterday that William Thompson, the renowned Maori leader, died on the way between Cambridge and Matamata. He expired on the 28th December[429], while being

[429] Various dates between 26 December 1866 and 8 January 1867 are given.

> conveyed across the Maungakawa ranges. We believe that Thompson wrote to Mr. Firth, stating that he would die on the 28th; and accordingly, at half-past four o'clock on that day he expired. Up to the hour of his death Thompson used his influence in favour of the peaceable settlement of the country by leasing land to Europeans."[430]

History is a fickle and selective scribe. Tamihana's biggest mistake was possibly not to utter a pithy catch-phrase such as "*ake, ake, ake*" around which his legend could be constructed, and unlike the outpouring of grief that would later be given to Rewi on his death, the response to Tamihana's death was sadly muted and somewhat equivocal. This euro-centric assessment of his life is probably not atypical:

> "Like all his race, Thompson was a man with almost unlimited confidence in himself and his people. He acknowledged the superiority of his European neighbours, but he thought that, with a very few advantages, his own people could equal them. These advantages were wanting to them, because there was no power in the country to compel obedience to anything...
>
> He wanted one thing, and he was working along with men who wanted another. His objects were above the level of his own people's comprehension, and those of his associates were exactly on that level – hence he was invariably an unsuccessful man, and was dragged along in the wake of men far inferior to himself. Thompson's own feeling latterly was, we believe, that his career had been a failure, and it dawned upon him at last that he had over-rated the power of the Maori race to raise itself to civilization...
>
> Thompson was an educated native, and the representative of the better aspirations of young New Zealand; but when he engaged in the King movement he became connected with men who were

---

[430] *Daily Southern Cross*, 1 January, 1867, p4.

uneducated and savage, and who equally fairly represented old New Zealand. From that moment Thompson was in a false position."[431]

Unlike Rewi, Tamihana did not live long enough for the softening effects of time to work their magic and which might have made him less of a dogmatist and more of politician who could have achieved his goals through compromise. Regrettably we will never know.

In 1865, just months after the "end" of the war in Waikato and in an almost inconceivable *volte-face* against the goals of the King Movement he had single-handedly created, Tamihana began leasing portions of his own land at Matamata to his European friend Josiah Firth. These lands were subsequently granted freehold title under the Native Land Court process and sold to Firth, much to the chagrin of Tamihana's own sons, and lost to Maori forever.

Thomas Gore Browne.

If Teira and Kingi, and Grey and Rewi, were cosmically linked then surely the same can be said of Thomas Gore Browne and Wiremu Tamihana.

Like Tamihana, Browne resolutely stood by his decision regarding Waitara and defended it unwaveringly until his death. They were both infuriatingly stubborn men of high principle who would rather take the honest way straight through a problem rather than hedge dis-honestly around the edges. In this respect they were the polar opposites of the practical and politically minded pairing of Rewi and Grey. It is perhaps an unlucky twist of fate that these two identical personalities should meet in the same place and time but on opposite sides, but such is the lottery that is history.

It is clear that when Browne left New Zealand in 1861 to take up Governorship of Tasmania he did so to the great regret of at least the European component of the population, an achievement that was surely both a first and last in the annals of departing New Zealand governors. Six

---

431 *Nelson Examiner*, 8 January, 1867, p2 (edited for brevity).

years after his departure the good citizens of New Zealand were still waxing eloquently and nostalgically about him:

> "Sir George Grey has exceeded his time by nearly a year, and might continue to do so as long as he could keep up "a native difficulty" were it not for the change of Ministry. We shall be anxious to hear the name of his successor, but greatly fear that Gore Browne will not be the man. Never did this colony make so grave a mistake as in parting with Governor Browne."[432]

Even in his distant absence his name popped up frequently, if briefly, in the local newspapers, more often than not used as a measure of virtue against which to compare Sir George Grey's many perceived or real faults. If his name is now long forgotten Browne was, then, at that time, the high-water mark against which all New Zealand governors would be judged and inevitably found wanting.

Thomas Gore Browne's governorship of Tasmania ended in 1868, and the following year he was knighted and the family returned briefly to England. Browne then became Governor of Bermuda for a year and retired in 1871. All of his post-New Zealand activities were recorded in great detail in the New Zealand press and followed with interest by his many appreciative fans. In their extreme enthusiasm to keep Browne's name alive the New Zealand press even managed to incorrectly report the death not only of his youngest daughter in 1869 but of Thomas Gore Browne himself in 1871.

Sixteen years later the newspapers eventually got it right, announcing his death on 17 April, 1887, at the age of 80. His wife Harriet died 19 years later at the age of 77.

In eighteen years of gubernatorial service in such far-flung and disparate places as St Helena, Tasmania, Bermuda and New Zealand Thomas Gore Browne's resume is brief and undramatic, the record of a stolid journeyman rather than a maverick, rising star such as Grey. Surely of all his posts his five years in New Zealand must have been his most

---

[432] *Hawkes Bay Herald*, 14 September, 1867, p3.

challenging by far, inheriting as he did a country on the verge of civil war and having to make some very tough calls, the only possible consequence of which was war. If he is remembered for anything in his five years in New Zealand it is for the Waitara Purchase and for this he has generally escaped the vilification that is routinely and enthusiastically lavished on Grey.

Today Thomas Gore Browne's name is unknown to all but a tiny fraction of New Zealanders. Since in history it is only the bad and wrong deeds of man that are recorded his obscurity is probably the highest compliment that he can be paid.

Appendix 1

Commissioner Spain's draft report to Governor Fitzroy regarding the outcome of the Taranaki land investigation[433]

"SIR - I avail myself of the opportunity afforded by the Auckland overland mail, which leaves this place on Saturday next, of informing your Excellency of the result of my proceedings in investigating the New Zealand Company's claim to land in this district, and I have the honor to enclose a copy of the minutes of my court, which will put you in possession of my decision, which is to recommend a Crown grant to the Company of a block of (60,000) sixty thousand acres of land, commencing on the north side of the Sugar Loaf Islands, and extending to a place called Taniwa, including native reserves, and with certain exceptions, which you will find particularly explained in my judgment. This will include all the

---

[433] Copy of a Despatch from Commissioner Spain to Governor Fitzroy, Dated 12th June, 1844. (AJHR 1860, E2-No.7, pp6-9).

Spain's final report on the Taranaki Deed, too long to be inserted here, can be found in BPP 8 April, 1846, *New Zealand, Copies of Despatches from the Governor of New Zealand, enclosing or having reference to Reports and Awards made by Mr Spain, Commissioner of Land Claims, upon the Titles of the New Zealand Company*, pp 49-64.

land that the said Company have already sold, or offered for sale, in this district.

I shall prepare my official report when I have finished my inquiries into all the Company's claims, which will, I think, be the most convenient course, as affording your Excellency the opportunity of having the whole subject of their purchases before you at the same time; but well knowing your great anxiety to have these all-important land questions brought to a speedy settlement, I lose not a moment in putting you in possession of the fact, that this case has been completed, so as to enable me to make my final report upon it

Great misapprehension has existed as to the purchase of this place, as it was generally believed to be the Taranaki district, which was formerly occupied by branches of the Ngatiawa tribe, who, being driven away by the Waikatos, about nine or ten years ago, went to reside at Waikanae, Port Nicholson, and other places to the south, where the majority of them have remained ever since. But it now turns out that the Taranaki district commences on the south side of the Sugar Loaves, and extends towards Waimate, where the great majority of those Natives formerly resided, and were called the Taranaki tribes, and that it is outside the block of land which I have awarded to the Company.

The agents of the Company claimed a very large tract of land in this district under three purchase deeds, the first from the Ngatiawa, in Queen Charlotte's Sound ; the second, from the resident Natives of this place, Ngamotu ; and the third, from the Taranaki tribe. Colonel Wakefield offered no Maori evidence in support of the Taranaki deed, but informed me that it was not the intention of the Company to claim any block of land under it. This narrowed my inquiry to the block of (60,000) sixty thousand acres, under the deed from the resident natives of this place, also branches of the Ngatiawa tribe.

I have, in my first report to the late acting Governor (which I had the honour to lay before your Excellency on your arrival in this colony), most particularly referred to the way in which these alleged purchases of the Company, which I had investigated, had been conducted ; namely, by getting the signatures of some leading chiefs, and inserting in the deeds boundaries comprising millions of acres, upon the surface of which thousands of natives were living, without having consulted those resident natives who were the actual cultivators of the soil.

I then stated, that although a tribe might have marched through a country, conquering all the natives occupying the ground over which they passed, yet if they failed to retain the lands so conquered in their possession, and allowed the former owners still to occupy it, or to return immediately afterwards, and cultivate it without interruption for a period of years, in that case the consent of the conquerors to a sale to the Europeans, without that of such resident natives, could not be admitted by me as a valid purchase. And I know of no rule laid down as binding upon or generally adopted by the nations of Europe, in colonizing a new country, peopled by aboriginal inhabitants, which would justify the taking of land from the actual occupiers and cultivators of the soil, without their consent. On the contrary, I had the honour to quote, in my last despatch, the very opposite doctrine, as laid down by De Vattel.

I had also occasion to express, in my report, a very strong opinion that these purchases had been conducted with great carelessness, and that the consent of a certain number only of natives had been obtained ; that the great object of the parties seemed to be to insert in their deeds the names of places, so as to comprise degrees of latitude and longitude, instead of ascertaining who were the resident natives upon this immense territory, and endeavouring to obtain their consent to its sale ; and I also remarked upon the imperfect way in which the transactions had been explained to the natives.

This purchase is, I am happy to say, free from these objections. Colonel Wakefield had previously effected a partial purchase of Port Nicholson, and had got another deed executed by the Ngatiawa, resident in Queen Charlotte's Sound, purporting to convey this district.

Puni, one of the principal chiefs of Port Nicholson, who joined in and has ever since admitted the sale of that place to Colonel Wakefield, and who had formerly resided at this place, recommended Colonel Wakefield to purchase it. Here, then, it appears that the Port Nicholson natives who had formerly resided here, and the Ngatiawa, in Queen Charlotte's Sound, had ample notice of the intended purchase.

Subsequently, Richard Barret, who had been many years in New Zealand, having a native wife and family, speaking their language, and understanding their customs, was landed here, and remained on shore, living with the resident natives for a period of between two and three months, negotiating for the purchase, and explaining to them the boundaries of the land he was desirous of acquiring for Colonel Wakefield; and the bargain was not concluded until the natives had seen the goods offered in payment brought by the "Guide" brig. They then consented to accept the payment, had the trade landed, and forty men, besides women and children (including, I believe, the greater part of the residents), signed the deed, and took away the goods.

During Barrett's residence here, before he effected his object, there was ample time for any of the Ngatiawa of Port Nicholson and the other places to have opposed the sale; but none appeared to dispute the right of the resident natives.

About ten years ago, a battle was fought between the Waikato and the Ngatiawa residing in this district, at a place called Pukerangiora, when the former completely conquered the latter, taking a great many prisoners with them to Waikato, whom they made slaves.

The majority of those that escaped, fearing a further attack from the Waikato, migrated to Waikanae, Port Nicholson, and other places to the south, took possession and cultivated the land there, and in the case of Port Nicholson, I have already admitted their title, by reason of their occupation of the soil for a period of nine or ten years, as against Rauparaha and others, who pretended to claim that district by right of conquest.

The natives of whom Barrett made the purchase in question, appear to have been permitted by the Waikato to occupy this district between the Sugar Loaves and Taniwa, without interruption, from the time of the taking of Pukerangiora, until the purchase ; but they appear to have lived opposite the Sugar Loaves for the purpose of being ready to escape in the case of a further attack ; and it seems to me, that fear of the Waikato, coupled with a desire to have Europeans to reside amongst them to protect them from their enemies, was one of the principal causes that induced them to consent to the sale of the district.

It appears to me that the Ngatiawa, who left this district after the fight, sought for and obtained another location, where they lived and cultivated the soil, and from fear of their enemies did not return, cannot now show any equitable claim to the land they thus abandoned ; and having admitted their title at Port Nicholson, by reason of their occupation and cultivation of the land there, from the time of their arrival there from this place up to the time of my decision, I could not, with the slightest regard for consistency in my awards, for one moment entertain any claim of theirs to this district. Had they returned before the sale, and, with the consent of their countrymen again cultivated the soil, I should have held that they were necessary parties to the sale.

It appears, however, that some of this tribe, after the arrival of the Europeans, and the formation of the settlement, and when they thought themselves in consequence safe from their enemies, did return here and commenced cultivating land within the limits of the block previously alienated to the New Zealand Company. But I cannot, for the reasons before stated, admit their title; and if I did, I should be also obliged to admit that of all the others who might at any time think proper to return and claim payment.

From my first arrival at Wellington, the chiefs Moturoa, Wairarapa, and others, who disputed the sale of that place to the Company, constantly told me that they should remain there until they got payment, and then come here and claim payment also for this place.

I invariably discouraged them from taking a step which appeared to me so unfair and unjust, and I was much pleased to find that not one of them appeared here to assert any claim, although they had full notice of the intention of my visit to this place, and some of their people and Wairarapa's son travelled with me the whole journey.

If, however, the claims of those who had returned since the purchase had been once admitted, no doubt all the others would immediately have claimed payment, and my inquiry would have been almost interminable.

I have not seen any block of land claimed by the Company which can be spared from the aborigines with so little interference with, or injury to their interests, as the one in question.

By the enclosed return from the resident agent of the New Zealand Company, your Excellency will observe, that the natives have only 120 acres in cultivation (and many of these commenced upon long after the sale) in the whole block of 60,000 ; yet I have, in order to avoid as far as possible the cause of any misunderstanding between the two races, carefully reserved all these cultivations, their pahs and burial-grounds, in addition to the 6,000 acres, to which they are entitled as native reserves ; so that ample provision has been made for them in the reservation of land, more than sufficient for their wants.

The original block claimed by the Company was two miles more in length, and two more in breadth, than the one shown in the accompanying plan, which I have obtained for your Excellency for reference, as occasion may require, and was thus reduced after my arrival here, leaving another immense block of the very best and most available land immediately adjoining that of the Company, for the natives. I have had two plans of the block made, and signed by myself, Mr. Clarke, and Colonel Wakefield, taking one to attach to my report, and leaving the other with the resident agent, so as avoid the possibility of misunderstanding about boundaries hereafter. This map will show you where the native reserves in the suburban sections have been chosen, but none have been made for them in the rural sections (although 159 out of 500 sections have been already selected by the Company's purchasers), owing to the absence of any authorized agent to select for the natives. As this might very probably inflict an injustice upon the natives in depriving them of their one choice in ten, I have written to the resident agent upon the subject, of which letter I enclose a copy.

I should recommend the trustees of native reserves to appoint an agent here, to make these selections as soon as possible, as it must tend to convince the natives that their condition is really improved by the sale. Your Excellency will see by the minutes of my proceedings that, after Colonel Wakefield had closed his case, I gave Mr. Clarke every opportunity of bringing forward whatever evidence he thought necessary on the part of the natives, and adjourned the Court to the day he mentioned, to give him time to be prepared. He, however, called only one witness, who, having at first prevaricated, at length admitted that he had been taken prisoner by the Waikato, and was only released from slavery in consequence of the introduction of Christianity amongst that tribe, which taught them to abandon the practice, and that he had returned to this place since the sale to Barret.

Mr. Clarke then declined calling any more witnesses; and I adjourned my court until Saturday, to give me time to consider the evidence, and determine upon my award.

I had no claim brought forward on the part of the Waikato; but this may be accounted for by the contents of a letter from the late Governor, Captain Hobson, to Captain King, the original of which is in my possession, and an extract from which I now enclose; nor was there any evidence offered to shew that that tribe had ever cultivated any land within the Company's block.

Previous to entering upon the case, and several times after its commencement, I inquired of Mr. Clarke whether he considered it would be expedient to offer any further payment to the claimants ; but he informed me that this could not be done with safety, and that he had not the slightest chance of getting the natives to accept a compensation ; that if they received any further payment, the Waikato would immediately come down upon them and take it away; which would in all probability lead to a fight between them. I also heard from several sources, that the Waikato, looking on these natives as slaves, were continually threatening to come here and take them back into a state of slavery.

If it had appeared expedient I might, as a matter of policy only, but certainly not according to the evidence as a matter of right, have recommended that some payment should have been made to the natives, as an act of grace on the part of the Company, calculated to assist in procuring a good understanding between the two races ; but under the circumstances, and with consequences pointed out to me as almost certain to follow, I felt it would have been unwise, and justly censurable to have pursued such a course. If the offer of any money had been made, even by way of gratuity, I am satisfied that with the evident spirit manifested by all the aborigines I had seen since my arrival, it would have been refused; and construed into an admission that they had not sold any part of the land, besides making them still more determined to withhold the land from the Europeans.

If on the contrary, it had been accepted by those present, we should have had immediately hundreds of other claimants from among the members of the same tribes, whom I have before described as now residing at Port Nicholson, Waikanae, and the other places; together with the strong probability of an attack from the Waikato.

Under these circumstances, it appeared to me to be a case where my duty pointed out the necessity of deciding whether there had been a purchase or not; and, as I found considerable anxiety manifested alike by the European and Maori population to learn the result of my investigation, and feeling that any further delay would not only prove injurious to both places, but was calculated to keep alive and prolong feelings of animosity between them, I delivered my judgment in the presence of a considerable number of natives, as well as Europeans; but wherein I have most carefully explained, that the same is subject to confirmation by your Excellency, and cannot be carried into effect without your approval.

I was the more anxious to do this, from a feeling that the decision being against the Maories, it was much better that at the time it was first made known to them, some officer of the Government should be on the spot to explain fully to both races, the reservations of the pahs, cultivations, and burying-grounds, as well as one-tenth of the block, for the benefit of the aborigines; and it also afforded me the opportunity of offering a few words of wholesome advice, to both Europeans and natives.

It further occurred to me, that it would be more expedient that any disappointment experienced by the natives at the first decision against them should be visited upon me as the officer appointed for this special duty, rather than expose your Excellency to the chance of sharing it; which would in all probability have been the case, had my decision been first made known to them, after it had been submitted to your Excellency for approval.

It is remarkable, that out of the millions of acres claimed by the New Zealand Company, this is the first case where I have been able to award even so small a block as (60,000) sixty thousand acres ; and even here something else remains to be done to perfect the transaction. It appears that, pending the negotiation the natives pressed Barrett for some double-barrelled guns, but finding that there were none on board the vessel, they at length accepted the payment offered, without them, and signed the deed; Barrett, however, still promised them at some future period he would procure them a case of double-barrelled guns.

Now, for the reasons before alleged, if I had given them (25) twenty-five guns (the number contained in a case), it would have exposed them to the risk of the Waikato coming down and taking them away, and probably using them against their lives ; while, if I had given them the value in money, the same difficulty and confusion would have arisen in the distribution of so small a sum, besides opening a door, as I have before explained, to claimants beyond number.

Under these circumstances, I called upon the principal agent of the Company to place at my disposal such a sum of money as I might value the guns at, to be disposed of as your Excellency may decide for the benefit of the natives; with which request he immediately complied, as will appear by his letter a copy of which is herewith enclosed.

The natives of this place are scattered over a large tract of country, whence great difficulty arises in cases of sickness amongst them, in administering medical relief; again, medical men complain that in many instances the medicines they prescribe have not the usual fair chance of success, for want of the patients being kept properly warm and sheltered from the weather, when under their influence.

I have the honour to recommend that the (£200) two hundred pounds (the sum at which I have valued the guns) should be laid out in building a Maori hospital upon the native town reserves (half an acre), and I have reason to believe that sum would be sufficient to build a male and female ward, a receiving-room with a bath, and a kitchen, which might also be used as the residence of the Maori nurse appointed to take care of the hospital.

This would afford the opportunity to the white population who are disposed to assist the natives in times of sickness, to direct their charitable efforts to a concentrated point where an arranged plan would be mere likely to be generally useful than single acts of assistance rendered in individual cases. It would also be much more convenient to the medical men, and enable them to devote more time to these patients; and, lastly, it would in my opinion effect a great moral improvement in the condition of the natives, by teaching them some of our civilized habits, and how much cleanliness contributes to restore them to health; as well as convincing them that the reserves are really intended for their benefit; and that one of the objects, at least of many of the Europeans coming to reside amongst them, is substantially to improve their condition.

I have mentioned my plan to the different ministers of religion here, to the police magistrate and the resident agent, and they all approve of my suggestion. I have taken every pains to impress upon the principal as well as the resident agent of the New Zealand Company, the absolute necessity of not giving out to the Europeans at present, any spots of land within the block the natives object to part with, but to put them upon those places which are not disputed, and that no force must be used in taking possession of land, nor will any act of violence or aggression towards them be for one moment permitted, and they have both promised to attend to my suggestions.

I have, &c, William Spain

[to] His Excellency the Governor [Robert Fitzroy]"

Appendix 2

Wiremu Kingi's response to Spain's Taranaki judgement

"Wiremu Kingi Whiti and other Ngatiawa Chiefs to Governor Fitzroy.

Taranaki, June 8th, 1844.

Friend Governor: – Salutations! Great is our love to you; this is our speech to you. Listen to us respecting this land, respecting Waitara. Our hearts are dark by reason of Mr. Spain's words. Indeed the Europeans are wrong in striving for this land which was never sold by its owners, the men of Ngatiawa.

Now, when the Ngatiawa tribe went to Kapiti they left some men behind on our lands, who were surprised by the Waikatos, and some of them led away captive, who having arrived at Waikato were afterwards returned by the Waikatos to Waitara to dwell there. Others came back from Kapiti. We love the land of our ancestors; we did not receive any of the goods of Colonel Wakefield; it was wrong to buy the land which belonged to other men. There are many chiefs to whom this land belongs who are now at Waikanae and Arapaoa. It was love for the land of our forefathers that brought us back to those lands. Friend Governor our thoughts are that those lands were never settled by the Waikatos; and when we embraced Christianity, we learnt the rules of the Gospel and to dwell in peace.

This also is the determination of our people; Waitara shall not be given up; the men to whom it belongs will hold it for themselves. There was not a single man of the Ngatiawa tribe who received the payment of Colonel Wakefield. These are the only men who took the payment – the men of Ngamotu and Puketapu, and they had no right in Waitara. The Ngatiawa are constantly returning to their land, on account of their attachment to the land of their birth – the land which we have cultivated and which our ancestors marked out and delivered to us.

Friend Governor, do you not love your land – England – the land of your fathers, as we also love our land at Waitara. Friend, let your thoughts be good towards us. We desire not to strive with the Europeans, but, at the same time, we do not wish to have our land settled by them; rather let them be returned to the places which have been paid for by them, lest a root of quarrel remain between us and the Europeans. Friend Governor, be kind to the natives. The places which have been justly purchased by the Europeans, let them have them, that your judgment may be just.

This is not from us only, but from all the Ngatiawa, though the greater part are absent.

From Hakopa, Tipene, Te Wataraui, Tutarahaina, Paturoi, Te Wareraka, Tamete Tiraurau, Hirini Mangonui.

By us, by all the men at Waikanae and Warekauri

Written by me, Wiremu Kingi Whiti."[434]

---

[434] Quoted from *The History of Taranaki*, Benjamin Wells, p111-112.

Appendix 3

Te Teira's account of meeting of 8 May, 1858 with Gore Browne.

Four years after the meeting Te Teira gave this account of the meeting, speaking of himself in the third person:

> "... in the year 1858, Te Teira began to speak about Waitara, that it might be sold to the pakeha. In December [of that year], Katatore was killed, and the war [of William King] with Ihaia was begun, and he went to Otihoi. When Governor Browne arrived, Mr. M'Lean and Mr. Parris went to Waitara to speak to us about the coming of the Governor to Taranaki. Mr. M'Lean said if a gun fires it will be for the arrival of the Governor, and do you and William King then come [to town]. At twelve o'clock, the gun fired, and in the morning Te Teira proposed to go at once, but he said, you go now, and I will come in the evening.
>
> They slept that night at Te Kawau, the pah of Te Waka [in town], and in the morning [8th March, 1860], went to the house of Mr. Parris. Mr. M'Lean asked William King concerning his agreement with Governor Grey about Waitara when they talked together [at Waikanae], but William King did not approve of those words of his, Mr. M'Lean's [that he had agreed to give one side of Waitara].
>
> Afterwards, Governor Browne came [to the field] beside Mr. Parris's house - was welcomed by the people there. Then Teira stood up and said, "Listen, O Governor, Mr. Richmond, and Mr. M'Lean. There is no man, not even a minister, equal to Mr. Parris in courage in carrying words among the Maoris during war [in efforts to make peace]. Now, I say I give up Waitara to Mr. Parris, for him to give to you, O Governor, and to Mr. Richmond, and Mr. M'Lean - he will give it to you all.

"Te Teira said, "I will give to you, O Governor, my peace [sic] of land at Waitara. Hearken, all the tribes [Apataki], if you interfere with me, I will return it to its proper boundaries [will make the piece larger]. Listen to me the tribe [the Ngatiawa], if you spring forward [to dispute my claim] I will return it to its proper boundaries.

Te Teira proclaimed the boundaries to be, commencing at the Taumata (a tree in the Waitara river), thence straight to Poutona, thence straight to Mataiwhetu, thence to Pukekohe, thence straight to Tokanga [stream] ; thence it runs to Opatito, to Maungakahia, thence to the water, which is called Maungahinau, thence in a southerly direction over [the hill] Pukeruru to Te Kohia, till it reaches the Devon-line between the Ngapara and the Kohia streams, thence straight towards the beach over the land at Whatiwhati, through Okihi and Wahamoko streams to Taukaponga, Painanga, and Onatiki ; thence to the beach to the house of Tamakete, along the beach to Waitara, till it reaches Otupaia; thence in the River Waitara to the Taumata [tree].

The Governor answered, "Is it your own?" He said, "Yes, my own."

Then Governor Browne consented, and Te Teira gave him his kaitaka [mat] into his own hands. Governor Browne asked, "Who are your friends?" Teira answered, "They are gone to Otihoi, engaged in the quarrel between Ihaia and William King, namely, Hemi, Paranihi, and Rawiri. We only are here, myself, Retimana Taikehu, Rawiri Rauponga, and Tamati Tarepa. These are all of us."[435]

---

[435] *Taranaki Herald*, 15 August, 1863, p2.

Appendix 4

Governor Browne's terms of surrender submitted to the King Party at the "conclusion" of the Taranaki War.

"COPY OF A DECLARATION BY THE GOVERNOR TO THE NATIVES ASSEMBLED AT NGARUAWAHIA

THOMAS GORE BROWNE, GOVERNOR.

In order to avoid misapprehension, the Governor directs the attention of the Chiefs and people, assembled at Ngaruawahia, to the present condition of affairs in New Zealand, and states distinctly the course necessary to be taken in order to avert the calamities that threaten the country. In the year 1858 a portion of the Maori people, resident in Waikato, pretended to set up a Maori King, and Potatau was chosen for the office. He was installed at Rangiaowhia in the month of June in that year. On Potatau's death, in 1860, Matutaera his son was nominated his successor. Diversity of opinion existed from the commencement as to what would result from this movement. Some were led to believe that its supporters desired only the establishment of order, and a governing authority amongst themselves; while others viewed with apprehension a confederacy which they deemed fraught with danger to the peace of the Colony. The Governor at first inclined towards the more favorable view of the movement, but soon felt misgivings, which have been justified by the event.

The Governor however has not interfered to put down the Maori King by force. He has been unwilling to relinquish the hope that the Maoris themselves, seeing the danger of the course they were pursuing, and that the institution of an independent authority must prove inefficient for all purposes of good, would of their own accord, abandon that course. The Governor can now only look with sorrow and displeasure on what has been done in the name, and by the adherents, of the Native King :

1. An authority has been set up inconsistent with allegiance to the Queen, and in violation of the Treaty of Waitangi.

2. A large number of the adherents of the Native King have interfered between the Governor and other Native tribes in matters with which they had no concern; have levied war against the Queen, fought against her troops, and burnt and destroyed the property of her peaceful subjects.

3. Other adherents of the King have assisted, encouraged, and harboured the men who have committed these outrages.

4. A war party of several hundred men some time since assembled, and advanced to within forty miles of Auckland, for the purpose of interfering with the due course of the administration of Justice.

5. Her Majesty's Mail has been stopped; jurisdiction has been usurped over Her Majesty's European subjects; and other offences have been committed to the subversion of Her Majesty's sovereignty, and of the authority of Law.

At this very time the adherents of the Native King, are using the most strenuous efforts to possess themselves of arms and ammunition for the purpose of effecting their objects by intimidation and violence.

The Governor cannot permit the present state of things to continue. No option now rests with him; he has been commanded by Her Majesty the Queen to suppress unlawful combinations, and to maintain Her Majesty's sovereignty in New Zealand.

Submission to Her Majesty's Sovereignty requires -

1. That every man yield implicit obedience to what the Law (which is the same for all) prescribes for the public welfare. But while the law exacts what is essential for this object, it confers great benefits and guarantees freedom and security to the weak as well as to the strong.

2. That rights be sought and protected through the Law, and not by a man's own will and strength. No man in the Queen's dominions is permitted to enforce rights, or redress wrongs, by force: he must appeal to the law.

3. That men do not enter into combinations for the purpose of preventing other men from acting, or from dealing with their own property, as they think fit. This is against the law.

4. That every man, European or Native, under the Queen's Sovereignty, submit to have roads and bridges made on his land, wherever the public convenience r. quires them. But land can only be taken for these purposes under lawful authority, and on payment of reasonable compensation.

On the other hand Her Majesty's Sovereignty, secures "to the Chiefs and Tribes of New Zealand, and to the respective families and individuals thereof, the full, exclusive, and undisturbed possession of their lands and estates, forests, fisheries and other properties, which they may collectively or individually possess, so long as it is their wish and desire to retain the same in their possession." This is the Maori's safeguard for their lands, and it has never been violated. The Governor has been falsely accused of desiring to introduce a new system in dealing with Native Lands. This he has never attempted, nor has he the power to do so. The Queen's promise in the Treaty of Waitangi cannot be set aside by the Governor. By that Treaty, the Queen's name has become a protecting shade for the Maoris' land, and will remain such, so long as the Maoris yield allegiance to Her Majesty and live under Her Sovereignty, but no longer. Whenever the Maoris forfeit this protection, by setting aside the authority of the Queen and the Law, the land will remain their own so long only as they are strong enough to keep it:- might and not right will become their sole Title to possession.

The Governor sincerely hopes that a correct appreciation of the real interests of the Maori race will induce the adherents of the Native King to conform to Her Majesty's declared wishes, and to abandon the baneful and dangerous course they are pursuing.

Her Majesty has an earnest solicitude for the welfare of her Native people, and it will be the duty of the Governor to give the fullest effect to measures calculated to secure that end.

The Maoris cannot be more anxious than the Queen and her Governor for the complete establishment of law and order amongst the Maori people, and that the institutions of the Government should be, as far as practicable, in accordance with their interests and wishes; but the Maoris must not forget that these objects are unattainable without their own cordial co-operation.

The Governor last year convened a meeting of Chiefs to consult with him upon Native Affairs and has declared his intention again to assemble Chiefs from all parts of these Islands, for the same purpose. Her Majesty has been pleased to approve of these proceedings.

It is the Governor's wish that the coming Conference should devise measures for the introduction of law and order, and the establishment of useful institutions in Native districts, and it will be his earnest, desire to give effect to any measures approved by the Conference, which appear likely to promote the welfare of the Native People, and to bring all Her Majesty's subjects in these Islands, both European and Maori, under one law, upon terms of equality. The Governor earnestly hopes that the Chiefs and people, who are adherents of the Maori King, will abandon their present perilous position: they will then receive the same invitation as the other Natives in New Zealand to choose some of their most respected and influential Chiefs to represent them in the approaching Conference, and to afford assistance in its deliberations.

The Governor now states specifically what his demands are:

1. From all, - Submission without reserve to the Queen's Sovereignty, and the authority of the law.

2. From those who are in possession of plunder, taken from Her Majesty's European or Native subjects, - Restoration of that plunder.

3. From those who have destroyed or made away with property belonging to Her Majesty's subjects, European or Native, - Compensation for the losses sustained.

Compliance with these demands will satisfy the Queen and Her Governor, no other demand will be made on Waikato, - the past will be forgiven, and for the future the well conducted will be protected, offenders punished, and the rights and privileges of all maintained by the Queen and her Laws.

Government House, Auckland, 21st May, 1861." [436]

[436] AJHR, 1861, Session 1, E-01B, p11-12.

Appendix 5

The Ngaruawahia runanga's reply to Browne's conditions of surrender.

"Friend, the Governor,-

Salutations to you. This is a word to you from the Maori Runanga. Hearken! This is our thought to you. Tell us of the death for this Island first, and let the fighting be afterwards. Let not the proceeding be like that in the case of Taranaki, which we and you worked at in the dark: who did not understand what was the good of that quarrel. Let you and me deliberate carefully this time. These are our thoughts at the present time. We hear talk, the report of which is going about Waikato, and comes from where you are : that the General insists upon (urges) a war with Waikato : If this report is correct, write to us ; let the talk come first, and do you carefully weigh the matter (turn the matter over in your mind.) Let this be the result of reflection, even the withdrawal of the troops, who we hear are clearing the roads. If a stockade is made for the soldiers at Te la (Mangatawhiri), and at other places, our opinion is this:—Be not in haste to begin hostilities; let us duly remember the words of St. James, "Slow to wrath, swift to hear." This, 0 Governor, is what we think ; do you look to these things, even fighting with words against the error or offences .of the Maoris, and let it (the offence) be clearly laid down, that the eyes of the great and of the small may clearly perceive it, ere you be swift to wrath. This is our intention. We are not going to rise up to fight; rather will we wait until the eyes have seen, the ears heard, and understanding has entered into the heart ; then shall we see what is the good of fighting, and whether there be a just cause for the chastisement inflicted upon evil men, that is, upon us Maoris. . But now, oh Friend! restrain your angry feelings against all parts of New Zealand. Let our warfare be that of the lips alone. If such be the course pursued by us it will be a long path, our days will be many while engaged in fighting that battle. Let it not be transferred to the battle (fought) with hands. That is a bad road, a short path: our days will not be many while engaged with the edge of the sword. But do you, the first born of God's sons, consider these things. Let not you and me be committed to the short path; let us take the circuitous one; though circuitous, its windings are upon firm land. PROVERB. 'Not by the direct path, that means, traveller's fare, short commons. Let us take the circuitous route, that means abundance, or the portion of the stayer at home.' No more, oh friend. .It is for you to interpret the meaning of these proverbs. There are more to come. Enough. From the Runanga Maori."[437]

---

437 "Translation of a letter to his Excellency the Governor from the Runanga assembled at Ngaruawahia, June 7, 1861" (AJHR 1861, Session 1, E-01b, pp17-18).

Appendix 6

Wiremu Tamihana's reply to Browne's conditions of surrender.

"TRANSLATION OF THE REPLY OF WIREMU TAMEHANA TE WAHAROA TO THE DECLARATION ADDRESSED BY HIS EXCELLENCY THE GOVERNOR TO THE NATIVES ASSEMBLED AT NGARUAWAHIA.

The thought of the Maori with reference to these causes of jealousy which are agitated in this Island: Alas! Alas! Well, go on, O mocker, O writer hither!

A SONG.

Ere a threat to strike fell from the lips,
The paddles of Kehu in the south are plashing;
The heart misgives by reason of the rumour;
I hastened through to To Wake Wake,
I was not mindful of the shade of Nga motu;
Thy person was with thy friend, thy feet were given to me,
That it might be supposed that thou regardest me;
The barrier of Kirikiri now divides us,
The dizzy height of Hikurangi.
I must plunge unwittingly into the place of departed spirits,
Barely holding on at Morianuku.
With the loved one, fruit of mutual embrace.

My song refers to those who are double-hearted, whose lips are given to this side and the heart to the other side. That is it. Hearken! This is my thought with reference to the currents of the inland streams which flow into their deep channels from their sources, with the mouth open until they reach the point where they terminate. I thought that the currents of every river flowed together into the mouth of "Te Parata" where no distinction is made, nor is it said, you are salt water, and that is fresh water; remain you away, - from a preference for the salt water only. Nay, but it is for them all. In like manner as the currents from the various islands flow into the mouth of "Te Parata," so also all the kingdoms of the different nations rest upon God, as the waters rest in the mouth of "Te Parata."

When this work is arrived at we are rebuked. Now, when I worship God I am not rebuked. This great name of God which is spoken of to me, why is this free to me, while of this name of King it is said, It is not right (to mention it); it is a sacred thing. Enough, O friends, it is founded only upon the relation subsisting between the master and his slave. Although the word of the slave may be right, the Chief will not admit it to be right. This is it, O friends. Look you at Deuteronomy 17c, 15v. If all the kings of the different islands (countries) were from Rome only, from thence also might come one for here; but is not the Queen a native of England, Nicholas of Russia, Buonaparte of France, and Pomare of Tahiti, - each from his own people? Then why am I or these tribes rebuked by you and told that we and you must unite together under the Queen? How was it that the Americans were permitted to separate themselves; why are they not brought under the protecting shade (sovereignty) of the Queen? —for that people are of the same race as the English. Whereas, I, of this island, am of a different race, not nearly connected. My only connection with you is through Christ: Ephesians 2 c, 13v. Were all the different islands (countries) under one sovereignty - that of the Queen - it would be quite right; no one would differ: all this island would also be united with the rest. Instead of which each nation is separate, and I also, standing here in my own thought, which is this, that I must have a King for myself.

Friends, do not be offended: leave me to make known my thoughts with respect to this great matter which has furnished us with a cause of dispute. Is it on account of the Treaty of Waitangi that you are angry with us? Was it then that we were taken possession of by you? If so, it is wrong. Look; there are two stores of goods (or shops). The goods in one store are sold. Those of the other are not sold. Now do you consider that because the goods of one store are sold, that the goods of the other all went also? I say that they did not go. So, with the consent of one Chief, that which belonged to another did not go by such consent being given.

It is a similar case to that of the two stores. What harm is there in this name that you are angry about? The great thing has been given to us, even the sacred things of God. We accepted those sacred things; Baptism, the Lord's Supper, and Marriage. I say, O my friends, that the things of God are for us all. God did not make night and day for you only. No; summer and winter are for all, the rain and wind, food and life, are for us all. Were those things indeed made for you only? I had supposed that they were for all. If some were dogs, and others were men, it would be right to be angry with the dogs and wrong to be so with the men.

My friends, do you grudge us a King, as if it were a name greater than that of God? If it were that God did not permit it, then it would be right (to object), and it would be given up, but it is not He who forbids: and while it is only our fellow-men who are angry it will not be relinquished. If the anger is, lest the laws should be different, it is well: let me be judged by the great Judge, that is, by God, by Him in whom all the works that we are employed in have their origin. And now, O friends, leave this King to stand upon his own place, and let it rest with our Maker as to whether he shall stand or fall. This is sufficient of this portion of my words, and, although they may be wrong, yet they are openly declared. Those words of mine are ended: –

I will now commence upon another subject among the many which we talk about. At the commencement of this war at Taranaki, I meditated upon the haste of the Governor to be angry (to commence hostilities). There was no delay; no time given: he did not say to the Maoris, Friends, I intend to fight at Taranaki. No, there was nothing said, not a word. That was why my thoughts dwelt upon what is said Peter, 2c, 14v. I thought that he would have remembered that word, "to praise those that do well," and "condemn those that do evil." Come now, O friends, of the Pakeha and also of the Maori side. Look at the evil of Te Rangitake, or at his good (conduct). Wherein was Te Rangitake evil? Was it in holding his land that he was evil, or in what? It is for you to look. Was it in casting away the surveyor's chain? Where was the offence? Look! Is a man put to death before his offence is proved, or has the law been abandoned by which it is said, (Condemn) not from the word of one witness, but by the words of two or three witnesses shall the right or wrong be ascertained? Did the Governor send word that the men who lived near should assemble to point out the lands of Wiremu Kingi and Te Teira, by which you might know that Te Rangitake was in the wrong and Te Teira in the right, and then, when the wrong of one should have been seen, punishment should have been inflicted upon the wrong doer, and the well doer have been spared? That is my thought.

Do you consider that this was a just war? Is it good in your opinion to give vent quickly to anger? (to hasten to go to war). Yes; but, according to me, hasty anger is wrong. Paul says that, "Charity suffereth long and is kind; is not easily provoked; thinketh no evil; suffereth wrong".

Friends - Wherein is our friend the Governor right, whom you believe in? Te Rangitake, the man of calm thought, is misjudged by you; and the Governor, who hasted to anger, is supported and praised by you. Hence my thoughts are perplexed in my heart, for hasty wrath has been condemned by James, who hath said - "Be slow to wrath, swift to hear." As it is, the precept in Proverbs, xvi. c, 32 v., has not been carried out.

Friends, - Let *me*, let *me*, who am a child, get angry hastily. The proverb is, "A child, who breaks calabashes", or "who cries for food" which is another proverb for a child; but for you to adopt that hasty mode of proceeding is, I think, wrong. Rather is it for you to do things deliberately, as you have an example to go by. The Word of God is your compass to guide you - the laws of God. That compass is the Ten Commandments. The compass is for directing the thoughts to consider the orphan and the poor. The compass is, carefully considering before inflicting punishment. Enough upon that.

With reference to the going of the Waikatos to Taranaki, for which we are reproached by the Pakehas. Hearken, and I will tell you. It was Potatau who fetched Wiremu Kingi from Kapiti. He was brought back to Waitara, to his place: that was how the Ngatiawa returned to Taranaki. I look therefore at this word of yours, saying that it was wrong of the Waikatos to go to Taranaki. In my opinion, it was right for Waikato to go to Taranaki. Come now, think calmly: Rauakitua, Tautara, and Ngatata were blood relations of the Waikatos. It was not a gratuitous interference on the part of Waikato. They were fetched. They were written for by Wiremu Kingi and Hapurona by letter. And that was why Te Wetini Taiporutu went to that war. But I think that the man who condemns should possess judgment: he should look at the going of Waikato, (to join in the quarrel) and at the going of the Governor.

These were the grounds for Waikato's going:- The bringing back (of William King) by Potatau, out of friendship to Wiremu. In the second place, because of their relations, Rauakitua, Tautara, and Ngatata. The third, they were written for. The fourth, Potatau's word, that land-selling should be made to cease. These were all the grounds of Waikato's interference. If the Governor had considered carefully, Waikato also would have considered carefully; but the Governor acted foolishly, and that was why the Waikatos went to help Wiremu Kingi. For Wiremu Kingi was a man who had not been tried, so that his fault might be seen in justification of inflicting severe punishment. You mock us; saying that this island is one, and the men in it are one (united). I look at the Pakehas, who madly rushed to fight with Wi Kingi. Had he been tried - his offence proved - and he had then been contumacious to the law, their interference would have been right, as his conduct would have been a trampling on the law. As it is, that side (the Pakeha) has also done wrong. According to your word, that side is right: according to mine also, this side is right, but I think that side is wrong. Enough of these words. Here are others.

About the word relative to the murdering, my opinion is decidedly that it was not murder. Look Ihaia murdered Te Whaitere (Katatore). He caused him to drink spirits, that the senses of Te Whaitere might leave him. He was waylaid, and died by Ihaia. That was a foul murder. You looked on, and made friends with Ihaia. That which we regard as a murder you have made naught of; and this, which is not a murder, you call one. This, I think, is wrong: for the Governor did not say to Wiremu Kingi and the Ngatiruanui, O friends, do not kill those who are unarmed. Nor did he direct that the settlers living in the town should be removed to Auckland, where there was no fighting, and there stay. For he knew that he had determined to make war at Taranaki, and he should, therefore, have told his unarmed people to remove out of the way. He did not do this. Had he even said to the Ngatiruanui, Friends, do not kill the settlers, it would, to some extent, have been a little clearer. Enough on the subject of the murders.

This portion is about the property (plunder). With reference to the property, of which you say; that we are to restore what remains. That also I do not consider right. Hearken to what I propose with respect to that. The Governor was the cause of that. War was made on Wiremu Kingi, and he fled from his Pa. The Pa was burnt with fire; the place of worship was burnt; and a box containing Testaments: all was consumed in the fire; goods, clothes, blankets, shirts, trowsers, gowns, all were consumed. The cattle were eaten by the soldiers, and the horses, one hundred in number, were sold by auction by the soldiers. It was this that disquieted the heart of Wiremu Kingi - his church being burnt with fire. Had the Governor given word not to burn his church, and to leave his goods and animals alone, he would have thought also to spare the property of the Pakeha. This was the cause of the Pakeha's property being lost (destroyed). When Wiremu Kingi was reduced to nakedness through the work of the Governor, he said that the Governor was the cause of all these doings. He first commenced that road, and he (Wiremu Kingi) merely followed upon it. Friends, look you to this; one hundred horses were sold by auction; property and food consumed; houses burnt with fire; and the cattle eaten by the soldiers. Whose work was that? The Governor's own, for he commenced the work of confusion spoken of in this declaration. This is all I have to say to you at the present time. Hereafter I will send you some more of my talk, that is, when I receive an answer to this. Enough.
From your loving Friend, Wi Tamehana Te Waharoa.[438]

[438] AJHR 1861, Session 1, E-01b, pp15-17.

Selected bibliography

(Secondary Sources)

TITLE	AUTHOR	PUB'D
Histories, Power and Loss.	Sharp and McHugh, editors	2015, Bridget Williams Books
Taua: Musket Wars, Land Wars or Tikanga?	Ballara, Angela	2003, Penguin Books
Guns and Utu	Wright, Mathew	2011, Penguin Books
The Stirring Times of Te Rauparaha	Travers, W.T.L	1906, Whitcombe and Tombs
The making of Wellington	Hamer and McIntyre, editors	1990, Victoria University Press
History and traditions of the Maoris of the West coast, North Island of New Zealand prior to 1840.	Smith, S.P	1910, Polynesian Society
The early Journals of Henry Williams	Williams, Henry, edited Lawrence Rogers	1961, Pegasus Press
Dictionary of New Zealand Biography - Vol 1	Various	1993, Bridget Williams Books.
The History of Taranaki	Wells, Benjamin	1878, Edmondson & Avery
New Zealand...	Pollack, Joel	1838, Richard Bentley
The Old Whaling Days	McNab, Robert	1913, Whitcombe and Tombs
The Interpreter	Caughey, Angela	1998, David Bateman
Tales of old North Taranaki	Moorhead, Murray	1991, New Zealand Founders
The Coming of the Maori	Buck, Peter	1949, Whitcombe and Tombs

An Encyclopaedia of New Zealand	McLintock, A.H., Editor	1966, R. E. Owen
The Story of New Zealand	Thomson, Arthur	1859, John Murray
The Authentic and Genuine History of the Signing of the Treaty of Waitangi	Colenso, William	1899, George Didsbury
The Advance of the Missionaries	Fancourt, H.C.	1939, Reed
The Quest for Origins	Howe, Kerry	2008, Penguin Books
Samuel Ironside in New Zealand	Chambers, W.A.	1982, Ray Richards
Te Ika a Maui	Taylor, Richard	1855, Wertheim and MacIntosh
The New Zealand Wars: a History of the Maori Campaigns and the Pioneering Period - Vols 1&2	Cowan, James	1923, Govt. Printer
The Wounded Lion	Lethbridge, Chris.	1993, Caxton Press
The War in Taranaki	Grayling, William	1862, G.W.Woon
The Maori King	Gorst, John	1864, MacMillan & Co.
The War in New Zealand	Fox, William	1866, Smith, Elder& Co.
The Waikato War	Featon, John	1879, John Henry Field
Narrative of the late war in New Zealand	Carey, Robert	1863, Richard Bentley
The Maori King Movement in New Zealand	Buddle, Thomas	1860, the "New Zealander"
The Richardson-Atkinson Papers	Scholefield, Guy, Editor	1960, R.E Owen
Dancing with the King	Belgrave, Michael	2017, Auckland University Press
Fitzroy: Governor in crisis	Moon, Paul	2000, David Ling
Crown Colony Government	McClintock, A.H.	1958, Government

in New Zealand		Printer
A Sort of Conscience: The Wakefields	Temple, Philip	June 2002, Auckland University Press
Fatal Success	Burns, Patricia	Jan 1989, Heinemann Reed
Adventure in New Zealand – Vols 1&2	Wakefield, E.J.	1845
Early Victorian New Zealand	Miller, John	1958, Oxford University Press
He whenua te utu (The Payment will be land)	Parsonson, Ann	1978, University of Canterbury, Phd Thesis
Early History of New Zealand	Sherrin and Wallace	1890, H.Brett
Travels in New Zealand	Dieffenbach, Ernst	1843, John Murray
Sir George Grey	Rutherford, James	1961, Cassell
To be a hero	Bohan, Edmund	1998, Harper Collins
Our Maoris	Martin, Lady	1888, SPCK
The Origins of the Maori Wars	Sinclair, Keith	1961, Auckland University Press
War and Politics in New Zealand 1855-1870.	Dalton, B.J.	1967, Sydney University Press
Chiefs of Industry	Petrie, Hazel	2006, Auckland University Press
New Zealand Revisited	Gorst, John	1908, Sir Isaac Pitman & Sons
Economics of the New Zealand Maori	Firth, Raymond	1929, Govt. Print
Maori Warfare	Vayda, A.P	1960, A.H & A.W. Reed
Te Manihera	Garrett, Helen	1991, Reed Books
Those days, those men	Gordon, Mona	1950, Bascands
The best man who ever served the Crown?	Fargher, Ray	2007, Victoria University Press

Selected contemporary commentaries regarding the Waitara Purchase.

NO.	TITLE	AUTHOR	PUBLISHED
1	Further Papers relative to the Taranaki Question.	Various	(AJHR, 1861, Session 1, E-02). This document collects together Documents 2, 3, 4 and 5 below and thus provides a good summary of arguments for and against.
2	The Taranaki Question.	Sir William Martin	1860, Hocken Library (can be found in pp1-39 of Document 1)
3	Notes by the Governor on Sir William Martin's pamphlet entitled "The Taranaki Question".	Francis Dillon Bell, Thomas Gore Browne	1860. (can be found in pp39-67 of Document 1)
4	Remarks upon a pamphlet entitled "The Taranaki Question", by Sir William Martin, DCL, Late Chief Justice of New Zealand.	James Busby	1860. (can be found in pp67-72 of Document 1)
5	Memorandum by Mr Richmond in reply to a pamphlet by Sir. W. Martin.	C. W. Richmond	1861 (can be found in pp72-100 of Document 1)
6	Minutes of Proceedings of the Kohimarama Conference of Native Chiefs.		1860 AJHR 1860, Session I, E-09

7	The case of the war in New Zealand.	E. Harold Browne	1860, Bell & Daldy
8	The Land Question of Taranaki.	F. A. Carrington	1860, Taranaki News
9	One of England's Little Wars.	Octavius Hadfield	1860, Williams & Norgate
10	The Second Year of One of England's Little Wars.	Octavius Hadfield	1861, Williams & Norgate
11	Justice to New Zealand, Honour to England.	Montague Hawtrey	1861, Gilbert & Rivington
12	The New Zealand War of 1860; An inquiry into its origin and justice.		1861, "Copied, with additions, from the "Colonial Intelligencer;" the organ of the Aborigines' Protection Society".
13	New Zealand and the War.	William Swainson	1862, Smith, Elder & Co.
14	Advising start of War (Despatch from Governor T. Gore Browne, C.B., to his Grace the Duke of Newcastle, March 22, 1860)	Thomas Gore Browne,	1860 (BPP 1861, March 1861, Papers Related to the Recent Disturbances in New Zealand, pp17 -22).
15	On Seigniorial Rights (Despatch from Governor T. Gore Browne, C.B., to his Grace the Duke of Newcastle, Dec 4, 1860).	Thomas Gore Browne	1860 (BPP 1861, March 1861, Papers Related to the Recent Disturbances in New Zealand, pp169-255)
16	Memorandum on Bishop Selwyn's protest.	C. W. Richmond, et al.	1860 (AJHR 1860 Session 1, E-01b, pp1-7)
17	Opinions on Native Affairs.	Bishop Selwyn, William Martin,	1860 (AJHR 1860 Session 1, E-01, pp 22-32). This is not about Waitara *per se* but

		William Swainson	on the general principles of land purchase/usage.)
18	Petition for Governor Browne's recall by natives at Otaki, etc.	Various	1860 (AJHR 1860 Session 1, E-01a, pp1-17)
19	Various communications regarding the lead up to the purchase.	Various	1860 (AJHR 1860 Session 1, E-03, pp1-56)
20	Parris to McLean re the lead up to the purchase.	Parris	1860 (AJHR 1860, Session 1, E-04, pp1-32)
21	McLean versus Hadfield debate.		1860 (AJHR 1860, Session 1, E-04, pp1-32)
22	Letter from Wiremu Tamihana to Gore Browne.	Wiremu Tamihana	1861 (AJHR 1861, Session 1, E-01c, pp1-5)
23	Notes by Charles Heaphy.	Charles Heaphy	1861 (AJHR 1861, Session 1, E-03, pp10-13)
24	Related to Hadfield's opinion of the existence of a "Land League".	Various	1861 (AJHR 1861, Session 1, E-03f, pp1-16)
25	Letter to the Right Honourable the Lord Lyttelton on the relations of Great Britain with the Colonists and Aborigines of New Zealand	Crosbie Ward	1863 Discussion of the "war" as at 1863 including discussion on the "Moral responsibility for the War", detailing the Waitara purchase, pp30-46.

Index

Made in the USA
Las Vegas, NV
14 February 2025

18169692R00252